BIBLICA ET ORIENTALIA

(SACRA SCRIPTURA ANTIQUITATIBUS ORIENTALIBUS ILLUSTRATA)

49

biblica et orientalia - 49

PETER DUBOVSKÝ, SJ

HEZEKIAH AND THE ASSYRIAN SPIES

Reconstruction of the Neo-Assyrian Intelligence Services and its Significance for 2 Kings 18-19

EDITRICE PONTIFICIO ISTITUTO BIBLICO – ROMA 2006

ISBN 88-7653-352-4

Editrice Pontificio Istituto Biblico
Piazza della Pilotta, 35 - 00187 Roma, Italia

To my friends from Zipoli House

Acknowledgements

This monograph is a revised form of a Th.D. dissertation submitted to the Harvard Divinity School, Cambridge, in 2005. The present stage of this study would have never been attained were it not for the support provided by many people. Above all I owe my heartfelt thanks to my thesis director, Prof. Peter Machinist. His human and professional qualities have left traces not only on every page of this monograph, but also in the way I carry out my work as a scholar and teacher. I am also grateful to L. Stager and P.-A. Beaulieu, the readers of my thesis, who provided me with innumerable pieces of advice and fostered my love for Akkadian and archaeology.

My special thanks go to J. A. Blakely, E. D. Oren, P. Bikai, and A. Gilboa, who allowed me to consult their pottery collections, not yet published, and to experts in various fields who generously helped me to find my way through the labyrinths of intelligence studies, archaeological resources, ArcGIS software and geographical databases. This project was completed not only in the isolation of libraries but also in archaeological excursions in the Middle East facilitated by J. Rindoš and J. Bartkovjak. I also wish to express my appreciation to C. Llanos, J. O'Malley, M. Francisco, C. Frechette, W. Clark, E. McGarry, and J. Keenan, who read and commented on an earlier version of this manuscript.

I have received a lot of support, both moral and material, from the Weston Jesuit Community, the Maryland and Slovak provinces of the Society of Jesus, Brian Manning, my family, and the Slovak community in Boston. I fondly cherish the memory of my deceased cousin K. Bokorová, who encouraged me each time I felt lost in the desert of doctoral study.

Finally, I am especially indebted to S. Pisano, Rector of the Pontifical Biblical Institute, who generously supported the publication project, and to A. Gianto, who accepted this manuscript for publication in the *Biblica et Orientalia* monograph series.

Peter Dubovský, SJ
October 2006

Table of Contents

Abbreviations

AAA	*Annals of Archaeology and Anthropology*
ABL	Assyrian and Babylonian letters in Harper, R. F. *Assyrian and Babylonian Letters Belonging to the Kouyunjik Collections of the British Museum,* 14 vols. Chicago: University Press, 1892–1914.
ABD	*Anchor Bible Dictionary*
Aharoni	Aharoni, M. "Excavations at Ramat Rahel." *BA* 24 (1961): 96–118.
AJA	*American Journal of Archaeology*
AJBA	*Australian Journal of Biblical Archaeology*
AfO	*Archiv für Orientforschung*
AOAT 253	Römer, W. H., T. E. Balke, M. Dietrich, and O. Loretz. *Dubsar Anta-Men; Studien zur Altorientalistik: Festschrift für Willem H. Ph. Römer zur Vollendung seines 70. Lebensjahres, mit Beiträgen von Freunden, Schülern und Kollegen,* Alter Orient und Altes Testament, Bd. 253. Münster: Ugarit-Verlag, 1998.
AOAT 6	Parpola, S., C. H. W. Johns, and K. L. Tallqvist. *Neo-Assyrian Toponyms*, Alter Orient und Altes Testament, Bd. 6. Kevelaer: Butzon & Bercker, 1970.
APW	Assyrian Palace Ware
AS	*Anatolian Studies*
Ashdod I	Dothan, M. and D. N. Freedman. "Ashdod I: The First Season of Excavations 1962." *Atiqot* 7 (1967).
Ashdod II-III	Dothan, M. "Ashdod II-III: The Second and Third Seasons of Excavations 1963, 1965." *Atiqot* 9–10 (1971).
BA	*Biblical Archaeologist*
BagM	*Baghdader Mitteilungen*
BAR	*Biblical Archaeology Review*
BASOR	*Bulletin of the American School of Oriental Research*
BiOr	*Bibliotheca Orientalis*
BM	British Museum
Borger	Borger, R. *Die Inschriften Asarhaddons, Königs von Assyrien*. Graz: Selbstverlage des Herausgebers, 1956.
Brook	McLean, N., A. E. Brooke, and H. J. Thackeray, eds. *The Later Historical Books: I and II Kings*, The Old Testament in Greek: According to the Text of Codex

	Vaticanus; Supplemented from Other Uncial Manuscripts, with a Critical Apparatus Containing the Variants of the Chief Ancient Authorities for the Text of the Septuagint, Vol. 2/2. Cambridge: University Press, 1906.
BS	*Bibliotheca sacra*
CAD	*Chicago Assyrian Dictionary*
Counterint.	Counterintelligence
CTN 5	Saggs, H. W. F. *Cuneiform Texts from Nimrud*. Vol. 5. London: British School of Archaeology in Iraq, 2001.
Dor IB	Stern, E., and J. Berg. *Excavations at Dor: Final Report*. Vol. IB. Jerusalem: The Institute of Archaeology the Hebrew University of Jerusalem, 1995.
DtrH	Deuteronomistic History/Historian
E	Elohist source
EI	*Eretz-Israel*
EM VII	אנציקלופדיה מקראית VII (Jerusalem: Mosad Bialik, 1976)
En-Gedi	Mazar, B., T. K. Dothan, and E. Dunayevsky. "En Gedi: The First and Second Seasons of Excavations 1961–1962." *Atiqot* 5 (1966).
Fritz	Fritz, V. "Kinneret: Excavations at Tell El-'Oreimeh (Tel Kinrot) 1982-1985 Seasons." *TA* 20 (1993): 187–224.
Gerar	Petrie, F. *Gerar*. London: British School of Archaeology in Egypt, 1928.
Gezer I	Dever, W. G., H. D. Lance, and G. E. Wright. *Gezer I: Preliminary Report of the 1964–66 Seasons*. Jerusalem: Hebrew Union College, 1970.
Gezer III	Gitin, S. *Gezer III: A Ceramic Typology of the Late Iron II, Persian and Hellenistic Periods at Tell Gezer*. Jerusalem: Hebrew Union College, 1990.
Gitin	Gitin, S. "Tel Miqne-Ekron in the 7th Century B.C.E.: The Impact of Economic Innovation and Foreign Cultural Influences on a Neo-Assyrian Vassal City-State." In *Recent Excavations in Israel: A View to the West*, edited by S. Gitin, 61–79. Dubuque, Iowa: Kendall/Hunt, 1995.
Had. Arch.	*Hadashot Archeologiyot*

HALOT	Köhler, L., W. Baumgartner, J. J. Stamm, and M. E. J. Richardson. *The Hebrew and Aramaic Lexicon of the Old Testament*. Study edition. Leiden and Boston: Brill, 2001.
Hazor I	Yadin, Y., et. al. *Hazor I: An Account of the First Season of Excavations, 1955*. Jerusalem: Magnes Press, 1958.
Hazor II	Yadin, Y., et. al. *Hazor II: An Account of the First Season of Excavations, 1956*. Jerusalem: Magnes Press, 1960.
Horvat Qitmit	Beit-Arieh, I., P. Beck, and L. Freud. *Horvat Qitmit: An Edomite Shrine in the Biblical Negev*, Monograph Series of the Institute of Archaeology, No. 11. Tel Aviv: Institute of Archaeology of Tel Aviv University, 1995.
IEJ	*Israel Exploration Journal*
Int.	Intelligence
J	Yahwist source
JANES	*Journal of the Ancient Near Eastern Society of Columbia University*
JBL	*Journal of Biblical Literature*
JCS	*Journal of Cuneiform Studies*
JNES	*Journal of Near Eastern Studies*
Keisan	Humbert, J. B., and J. Briend. *Tell Keisan (1971–1976): Une Cité Phénicienne en Galilée*. Paris: Gabalda, 1980.
Kinneret	Fritz, V. *Kinneret: Ergebnisse der Ausgrabungen auf dem Tell El-'Oreme am See Gennesaret 1982-1985*. Wiesbaden: Otto Harrassowitz, 1990.
Lachish III	Tufnell, O. *Lachish III: The Iron Age*. London and Oxford, 1953.
Luckenbill	Luckenbill, D. D. *The Annals of Sennacherib*. Chicago: The University of Chicago Press, 1924.
MB	Merodach-Baladan II
MDOG	*Mitteilungen des Deutschen Orient-Gesellschaft*
Megiddo I	Lamon, R. S., G. M. Shipton, and G. Loud. *Megiddo I: Seasons 1925–34*. Chicago: University of Chicago Press, 1939.
Megiddo Tombs	Guy, P. L. O. and R. M. Engberg. *Megiddo Tombs*. Chicago: The University of Chicago Press, 1938.
MT	Masoretic Text
NA	Neo-Assyrian

NAB	New American Bible
ND	Nimrud Letter
NEAEHL	*The New Encyclopedia of Archaeological Excavations in the Holy Land*
Or	*Orientalia*
OrA	*Oriens Antiquus*
P	Priestly source
p.	person
PEQ	*Palestine Exploration Quarterly*
Piepkorn	Piepkorn, A. C. *Historical Prism Inscriptions of Ashurbanipal*. Chicago: University of Chicago Press, 1933.
pl.	plural
Prism	Gadd, C. J. "Inscribed Prism of Sargon II from Nimrud." *Iraq* 16 (1954): 173–201.
Prosopography	Parpola, S., R. M. Whiting, and K. Radner. *The Prosopography of the Neo-Assyrian Empire*. 3 vols. Helsinki: Neo-Assyrian Text Corpus Project University of Helsinki, 1998–2002.
Prunk	*Grosse Prunkinschrift* in Fuchs, A. *Die Inschriften Sargons II. aus Khorsabad*. 1. Aufl. Göttingen: Cuvillier, 1994, 189–248.
PsW	Psychological warfare
Psyops	Psychological operations
Qasile II	Mazar, A. *Excavations at Tell Qasile*. Jerusalem: Institute of Archaeology Hebrew University of Jerusalem, 1980.
Qiri	Ben-Tor, A., and Y. Portugali. *Tell Qiri, a Village in the Jezreel Valley: Report of the Archaeological Excavations 1975–1977; Archaeological Investigations in the Valley of Jezreel, the Yoqne'am Regional Project*, Qedem, no. 24. Jerusalem: Institute of Archaeology Hebrew University of Jerusalem, 1987.
RA	*Revue d'assyriologie et d'archéologie orientale*
Ramat Rahel	Aharoni, M. *Excavations at Ramat Rahel: Seasons 1959 and 1960*. Roma: Centro di Studi Semitici, 1962.
RB	*Revue Biblique*
RIMA 3	Grayson, A. K. *Assyrian Rulers of the Early First Millennium BC II, (858-745 BC)*. Vol. 3, Royal

	Inscriptions of Mesopotamia. Assyrian Periods. Toronto and London: University of Toronto Press, 1996.
S II Ann	*Annalen* in Fuchs, A. *Die Inschriften Sargons II. aus Khorsabad.* 1. Aufl. Göttingen: Cuvillier, 1994, 86–189.
S II	Sargon II
S1-5	*Türschwellen I-V* in Fuchs, A. *Die Inschriften Sargons II. aus Khorsabad.* 1. Aufl. Göttingen: Cuvillier, 1994, 249–75.
SAA	State Archives of Assyria
SAAB	*State Archives of Assyria Bulletin*
SAAS	State Archives of Assyria Studies
Samaria III	Crowfoot, J. W., G. M. H. Crowfoot, and K. M. Kenyon. *Samaria-Sebaste III: The Objects*. London: Palestine Exploration Fund, 1957.
SANTAG 5	Black, J. A., A. George, and J. N. Postgate. *A Concise Dictionary of Akkadian*. 2nd ed., SANTAG 5. Wiesbaden: Harrassowitz, 2000.
Senn A1	Sennacherib's First Campaign in Luckenbill, 48–55, 94–98.
Senn Ann	Sennacherib's Annals in Luckenbill, 23–47.
Senn B1	Bellino Cylinder in Luckenbill, 55–60, 99–102.
Senn C1	Rassam Cylinder in Luckenbill, 60–61, 102.
Senn F1	Bull Inscription in Luckenbill, 66–76.
Senn F2	Bull Inscription in Luckenbill, 76–78.
Senn H3	Bavian Inscription in Luckenbill, 78–85.
Senn H5	Nebi Yunus Inscription in Luckenbill, 85–93.
Stern	Stern, E., and A. Mazar. *Archaeology of the Land of the Bible: The Assyrian, Babylonian, and Persian Periods, 732–332 BCE.* 1st ed. New York: Doubleday, 2001.
Stier	*Die Inschrift auf den Stierkolossen* in Fuchs, A. *Die Inschriften Sargons II. aus Khorsabad.* 1. Aufl. Göttingen: Cuvillier, 1994, 61-74.
Streck	Streck, M. *Assurbanipal und die letzten Assyrischen Könige bis zum Untergange Niniveh's*. Leipzig: J. C. Hinrichs, 1916.
TA	*Tel Aviv*
Tel 'Ira	Beit-Arieh, I. *Tel 'Ira: A Stronghold in the Biblical Negev*. Tel Aviv, Israel: Emery and Claire Yass

	Publications in Archaeology Institute of Archaeology Tel Aviv University, 1999.
Tell el-Far'ah 1	Chambon, A., and J. Mallet. *Tell el-Far'ah 1*. Paris: Editions Recherche sur les civilisations, 1984.
Tell el-Kheleifeh	Pratico, G. D., and R. A. diVito. *Nelson Glueck's 1938–1940 Excavations at Tell el-Kheleifeh: A Reappraisal*, ASOR Archaeological Reports, No. 3. Atlanta, Ga.: Scholars Press, 1993.
TN II	McCown, C. C., J. Wampler, and W. F. Badè. *Tell en-Nasbeh II*. Berkeley, Calif.: The Palestine Institute of Pacific School of Religion and The ASOR, 1947.
TP III	Tiglath-pileser III
TP III Ann	Tiglath-pileser's Annals in Tadmor, H. *The Inscriptions of Tiglath-Pileser III, King of Assyria: Critical Edition, with Introductions, Translations and Commentary*. Jerusalem: The Israel Academy of Sciences and Humanities, 1994, 40–89.
TP III Summ	Tiglath-pileser's Summary Inscriptions in Tadmor, H. *The Inscriptions of Tiglath-Pileser III, King of Assyria: Critical Edition, with Introductions, Translations and Commentary*. Jerusalem: The Israel Academy of Sciences and Humanities, 1994, 122–204.
TP III RR	Tiglath-pileser's Mila Rock Relief in Tadmor, H. *The Inscriptions of Tiglath-Pileser III, King of Assyria: Critical Edition, with Introductions, Translations and Commentary*. Jerusalem: The Israel Academy of Sciences and Humanities, 1994, 112–16.
tr.	translation
Waterman	Waterman, L., and R. F. Harper. *Royal Correspondence of the Assyrian Empire*, 3 vols., *University of Michigan Studies*. Ann Arbor: University of Michigan press, 1930.
ZAW	*Zeitschrift für die alttestamentliche Wissenschaft*
ZDPV	*Zeitschrift des deutschen Palästina-Vereins*
Zyl	*Inschrift auf den Tonzylindern* in Fuchs, A. *Die Inschriften Sargons II. aus Khorsabad*. 1. Aufl. Göttingen: Cuvillier, 1994, 31–44.

1

Introduction

Neo-Assyrian (NA) royal campaigns during the ninth and first half of the eighth centuries B.C.E. appear to have been, as many scholars have argued, mainly raid-oriented invasions undertaken with the goals of collecting booty and acquiring cheap manual labor. Scholars also generally agree that Tiglath-pileser III transformed Neo-Assyrian foreign policy[1] with his "down-the-line approach."[2] S. Parpola summarizes this new strategy as follows:

> The strategy introduced by Tiglath-pileser III aimed at expanding the core area by systematically reducing semi-independent vassal countries to Assyrian provinces directly controlled by the central government. The reducing of a country to a province was carried out according to a standardized procedure involving … massive deportation; the installation of an Assyrian governor; the construction of Assyrian garrisons and forts.[3]

The constant threat of rebellion in annexed kingdoms and states, which were always ready to shake off the Assyrian yoke, required the founding of an efficient intelligence network able to keep the royal court posted about the situation in the periphery of the Neo-Assyrian Empire.

---

[1] H. Tadmor called Tiglath-Pileser III's reign a "watershed" in the history of the ancient Near East; see H. Tadmor, *The Inscriptions of Tiglath-Pileser III, King of Assyria: Critical Edition, with Introductions, Translations and Commentary* (Jerusalem: The Israel Academy of Sciences and Humanities, 1994), 9. However, some scholars have contested this claim; see P. Garelli, "Le Dynamisme Assyrien," in *Assyria 1995: Proceedings of the 10th Anniversary Symposium of the Neo-Assyrian Text Corpus Project Helsinki, September 7-11, 1995*, ed. S. Parpola and R. M. Whiting (Helsinki: The Neo-Assyrian Text Corpus Project, 1997).

[2] R. E. Tappy, *The Archaeology of Israelite Samaria*, vol. 2 (Atlanta, Ga.: Scholars Press, 1992), 530.

[3] S. Parpola, "Assyria's Expansion in the 8th and 7th Centuries and Its Long-Term Repercussion in the West," in *Symbiosis, Symbolism, and the Power of the Past*, ed. W. G. Dever and S. Gitin (Winona Lake, Ind.: Eisenbrauns, 2003), 100.

Failure to detect warning signs would delay Neo-Assyrian punitive intervention, potentially giving a local king sufficient latitude to reconsolidate his kingdom and to organize an alliance strong enough to detach an entire territory from the Neo-Assyrian Empire. For this reason, the Assyrians developed an elaborate system of gathering, processing, verifying, transmitting, and storing information necessary for the control of their vassals and provinces.

Three groups of scholars have already mentioned or even partly described the Neo-Assyrian intelligence services and operations. The first group has been historians and intelligence officials who have presented a broad review of the history of intelligence services.[4] Most of them have mentioned the importance of the Neo-Assyrian intelligence services, and F. Dvornik even claimed that the Persian intelligence network, as described in the Greek sources, was only a later development of the Neo-Assyrian intelligence network.[5] Some of these scholars were well trained in history, while others possessed long years of experience as intelligence officials in different capacities. Nevertheless, they faced an insurmountable problem. Since most of the Assyrian letters do not contain dates, are preserved in fragmentary form, and contain many unidentified geographical and personal names, these documents are practically inaccessible to non-Assyrologists.

The second group of scholars to treat the Neo-Assyrian intelligence services consists of those trained in Assyriology who have described the Neo-Assyrian intelligence services as part of their treatment of various aspects of the Neo-Assyrian Empire.[6] The first major study of this sort was done by R. Follet, who analyzed Neo-Assyrian letters and suggested that

---

[4] See, for example, J. P. Callot, *L'Espionnage à travers les âges* (Paris: Stock, 1977), 37–46, J. Piekalkiewicz, *World History of Espionage: Agents, Systems, Operations* (Washington, D.C.: National Intelligence Book Center, 1998), 36-92.

[5] F. Dvornik, *Origins of Intelligence Services: The Ancient Near East, Persia, Greece, Rome, Byzantium, the Arab Muslim Empires, the Mongol Empire, China, Muscovy* (New Brunswick, N.J.: Rutgers University Press, 1974), 27.

[6] See, for example, I. Eph'al, "On Warfare and Military Control in the Ancient Near Eastern Empires: A Research Outline," in *History, Historiography, and Interpretation: Studies in Biblical and Cuneiform Literatures*, ed. H. Tadmor and M. Weinfeld (Jerusalem: Magnes Press, 1984), W. Mayer, *Politik und Kriegskunst der Assyrer* (Münster: Ugarit-Verlag, 1995), 431–33, 470; B. J. Parker, *The Mechanics of Empire: The Northern Frontier of Assyria as a Case Study in Imperial Dynamics* (Helsinki: Helsinki University Press, 2001), 16, 92, 221–24; and H. W. F. Saggs, "Assyrian Warfare in the Sargonid Period," *Iraq* 25 (1963).

there was a *Deuxième Bureau* run by a crown prince.[7] Later, A. L. Oppenheim proposed that the Neo-Assyrian intelligence network constituted the "eyes and the ears of the king," by means of which he was informed about everything that happened in his kingdom.[8] Then, F. Malbran-Labat showed the role of scouts in the Assyrian army,[9] and S. Parpola suggested a connection between intelligence gathering and Neo-Assyrian treaties.[10] A major step forward in this research was Y. J. Kim's dissertation on the role of communication in the Near Eastern Empires. He proved that a sophisticated imperial communication system linked the royal court and provincial officials. Moreover, he described how written, oral, and signal communications were used for transmitting messages. The most efficient form of communication was written messages, delivered by means of an imperial express system. Finally, he demonstrated that each local official typically held several responsibilities, and he divided the objectives of imperial communication into five categories: political, administrative, economic, diplomatic, and military.[11]

The last group of scholars who have studied Neo-Assyrian intelligence are biblical scholars, some of them also trained as Assyrologists, for whom the Neo-Assyrian intelligence services represent a piece of the mosaic forming the historical background of eighth- and seventh-c. B.C.E. biblical events.[12]

The particular focus of this study marks it primarily as a contribution to biblical scholarship, but it also contributes to the study of the history of intelligence services in general, as well as to the study of the role of intelligence in the Neo-Assyrian Empire. I will investigate the Neo-Assyrian intelligence services with the goal of illuminating and contextualizing the biblical narrative of Sennacherib's invasion of Judah. The biblical account of this invasion has reached us in the form of two

---

[7] R. Follet, " 'Deuxième Bureau' et Information diplomatique dans l'Assyrie des Sargonides; Quelqe Notes," *Rivista degli Studi Orientali* 32 (1957).

[8] A. L. Oppenheim, ""The Eyes of the Lord"," *JAOS* 88 (1968).

[9] F. Malbran-Labat, *L'Armée et l'organisation militaire de l'Assyrie: d'après les lettres des Sargonides trouvées à Ninive* (Paris: Libraire Droz, 1982), 41–57.

[10] S. Parpola, "A Letter from Šamaš-šumu-ukin to Esarhaddon," *Iraq* 34 (1972).

[11] Y. J. Kim, "The Role of Communication in the Near Eastern Empires of the First Millenium BC" (Ph.D. diss., Hebrew University, 1999).

[12] W. R. Gallagher, "Assyrian Deportation Propaganda," *SAAB* 8 (1994); and idem, *Sennacherib's Campaign to Judah: New Studies* (Leiden and Boston: Brill, 1999).

parallel narratives (2 Kgs 18–20 and Is 36–39) and the Chronicler's account (2 Chr 29–32). I will focus mainly on 2 Kgs 18–20. The other biblical texts will be used as points of comparison and supplementary sources. According to 2 Kgs 18–20, the Assyrians had at their disposal a great deal of information regarding Judahite customs, military resources, domestic politics, and geography, as well as key information about Egypt and the whereabouts of the Egyptian troops. However, several scholars have argued that these biblical passages in their present form are compilations of multiple literary genres and different sources, and that they include additions dating from the exilic and Persian periods.[13]

As for the literary genres, B. O. Long has summarized the results of several literary analyses of chapters 2 Kgs 18–20 and demonstrated that these passages contain different literary genres, styles, and formulas: the edifying legend (18:19–32a), the disputation (18:19–25, 29b–35; 19:10b–3), the prayer of petition (19:15–9), the prophecy of salvation (19:3–4), the prophecy of punishment (19:21–8), the prophetic announcement of a sign (19:21–31), the prophetic oracle (19:20b–34), the invasion report (18:9–12, 13–6), the report of military defeat (19:35–6), the regnal resumé (18:1–6), the succession formula (19:37), the propaganda speech, and the letter-address.[14]

As for the principal textual witnesses, after more than one hundred years of critical scholarship scholars have reached a broad agreement, though not a strict consensus.[15] M. Cogan summarized the areas of agreement. The account is composed of two sources: A, a chronicle (18:13b–16, a factual source or a source factual in appearance); and B, a prophetic narration (18:17–19:37, a discursive source). Source B is divided into two strands: B^1 (18:17–19:9a.36) and B^2 (19:9b–35).[16] According to M.

---

[13] For a review of the bibliography on this topic, see L. L. Grabbe, *"Like a Bird in a Cage": The Invasion of Sennacherib in 701 BCE* (London and New York: Sheffield Academic Press, 2003), 2–35.

[14] B. O. Long, *2 Kings* (Grand Rapids, Mich.: Eerdmans, 1991), 193–246. For the propaganda speech and letter-address, see P. Machinist, "The *Rab Šāqēh* at the Wall of Jerusalem: Israelite Identity in the Face of the Assyrian 'Other,' " *Hebrew Studies* 41 (2000); and E. Ben-Zvi, "Who Wrote the Speech of Rabshakeh and When?," *JBL* 109 (1990).

[15] Machinist, "The *Rab Šāqēh*," 154.

[16] However, there is no agreement among scholars about the exact assignment of verses to strata B^1 and B^2.

Cogan and H. Tadmor, B^1 describes an Assyrian embassy at the wall of Jerusalem, Rab-shaqeh's speeches, and Hezekiah's response. In this source, the prophet Isaiah delivers a short oracle, and the story finishes when Sennacherib withdraws because of the rumor he heard (19:9a, 36). In source B^2, Rab-shaqeh does not appear. The king's message is transmitted through a letter and delivered by messengers. The emphasis is on Hezekiah's defense of the Lord's fame. King Hezekiah appears before God without any intermediary, and Isaiah delivers a short oracle, which is expanded in vv. 22–32. In source B^2, the story concludes with the miraculous salvation of the city: the Assyrian camp is decimated by an angel (19:35).[17]

Aware of the multiplicity of problems connected with the historical and textual interpretation of these biblical texts, I will first investigate what kind of intelligence the biblical redactors attributed to the Assyrians, how Neo-Assyrian intelligence services practiced, according to the biblical redactors, psychological warfare in this campaign, and what kind of information such psychological warfare (PsW) presupposed. Keeping these results in mind, I will then turn to the Neo-Assyrian documents. In particular, I will ask: What sort of information were the Assyrians interested in? How did they gather information? And, how were their intelligence services practically involved in warfare? Finally, I will compare these results with the conclusions drawn from my analysis of chapters 2 Kgs 18–20. Thus, the main goal of this study will not be to resolve the old problems connected with these biblical texts, but rather to contextualize the biblical sources in the sense of investigating to what degree they reflect the reality of the Neo-Assyrian intelligence services.

Since the central part of this study is a reconstruction of the Neo-Assyrian intelligence services and operations, I must say a few words about sources and about the different types of intelligence studied in this study.

First, the sources. A reconstruction of intelligence operations in any historical era must meet two basic conditions: first, historians must have access to actual intelligence archives; and second, they must possess sufficient information about the political and cultural events of a given country to place the archives and the reports they contain in the appropriate context. Thus, the reconstruction of Neo-Assyrian intelligence will require

[17] M. Cogan and H. Tadmor, *II Kings: A New Translation*, 1st ed. (Garden City, N.Y.: Doubleday, 1988), 242–44.

two kinds of resources: first, intelligence dispatches exchanged between units operating on the ground; and second, textual, archaeological, and geographical resources ample enough for understanding the political and cultural contexts in which the intelligence units operated.

The Neo-Assyrian letters, dated between 745 and 645 B.C.E.—thus, between the reigns of Tiglath-pileser III and Ashurbanipal—allow modern scholars to access intelligence files ample enough to permit a reconstruction of the intelligence operations of the Neo-Assyrian Empire. Moreover, numerous excavations conducted in Iraq, Turkey, and Syria-Palestine, as well as abundant textual materials, provide the geographical, political, and religious realia necessary for rounding out the laconic language of those intelligence dispatches.

Thus, the main textual sources for the reconstruction of Neo-Assyrian intelligence operations are the archival cuneiform texts unearthed in Nineveh and Nimrud[18] and published in the State Archives of Assyria series (SAA). Other major sources of textual material include the Neo-Assyrian annals, chronicles, eponym lists, and inscriptions.

The sheer quantity of the Neo-Assyrian tablets and inscriptions utilized in this study will not allow me to present the full Akkadian and English texts for each tablet and inscription cited. For practical reasons, I will present the Akkadian text only when I am particularly interested in some grammatical point or when scholars are divided regarding the translation or reconstruction of the text; otherwise, I will follow the English translation of the SAA series, not reproducing the Akkadian transliteration on which that translation is based. The designation of the tablets in this study follows the numbering in the SAA edition: the Roman numeral indicates the volume, and the Arabic numeral indicates the number of the tablet in that volume. As for the transliteration of the Akkadian texts, I will follow the SAA system. Occasionally, when I quote Akkadian texts that are not published in the SAA, such as royal inscriptions or some Nimrud letters (ND), I will preserve the transliteration of the original editions.

---

[18] Since A. N. Layard's first visit to Nineveh in 1845, excavations have recovered about 6,000 tablets containing various administrative, military, and personal documents; about 1,500 tablets are relevant to the purpose of this study.

In addition to the textual sources, I will also refer to archaeological sources. Most of the archeological data used in this study has already been published. However, some of the geographical areas alluded to in the archives, especially those within the boundaries of the ancient Urartian kingdom, have not previously been surveyed. I will therefore refer to a survey of some regions in Eastern Turkey, within the triangle formed by the modern cities Diyarbakır, Elaziğ, and Bingöl, conducted by Mr. M. Himmet, Mr. J. Bartkovjak, and myself. This preliminary survey took place between 13 May and 10 June 2004. Our survey focused on those Urartian sites that were either previously unidentified or poorly described in the scholarly literature. We looked for material remains (especially pottery) and architectural features. We also surveyed the tributaries of the Tigris for the purposes of clarifying the logging crisis (see 3.1.1.3). Mr. M. Himmet facilitated contacts with the local inhabitants and Mr. J. Bartkovjak served as photographer. It is the intention of the present writer to publish the results of this survey separately.

Second, definitions and divisions of intelligence. Because intelligence services, by their very nature, must be extremely flexible in order to respond to the needs of changing situations and environments, the theoretical models describing intelligence services must be flexible as well. So far only a few models, containing some very general theories and definitions, have been presented in the scholarly literature.[19] Most modern scholars prefer a case-study approach rather than speculative discussions, since this approach better reflects how a given intelligence service responded to a concrete situation.[20] For this reason, my reconstruction of

---

[19] The models of intelligence adopted for this study are based on the following studies: A. Codevilla, *Informing Statecraft: Intelligence for a New Century* (New York: Free Press, 1992); M. I. Handel, "Intelligence and the Problem of Strategic Surprise," in *Paradoxes of Strategic Intelligence: Essays in Honor of Michael I. Handel*, ed. R. K. Betts and T. G. Mahnken (London: Frank Cass, 2003); S. Kent, *Strategic Intelligence for American World Policy* (Princeton: Princeton University Press, 1949); M. M. Lowenthal, *Intelligence: From Secrets to Policy*, 2nd ed. (Washington, D.C.: CQ Press, 2003); and A. N. Shulsky and G. J. Schmitt, *Silent Warfare: Understanding the World of Intelligence*, 3rd ed. (Washington: Brassey's, 2002).

[20] See, for example, Y. Caroz, *The Arab Secret Services* (London: Corgi, 1978); D. R. Clarridge and D. Diehl, *A Spy for All Seasons: My Life in the CIA* (New York: Scribner, 1997); J. Frolík, *Špión vypovídá*, 1. vyd. ed. (Köln: Index, 1979); E. R. May, *Strange Victory: Hitler's Conquest of France*, 1st ed. (New York: Hill and Wang, 2000); and K. Pacner, *Československo ve zvláštních službách: Pohledy do historie Československých výzvedných služeb 1914 - 1989*, 3 vols. (Prague: Themis, 2002).

Neo-Assyrian intelligence services will be presented as a collection of case studies illustrating the Assyrians' priorities, their ways of gathering necessary information, and the types of agents used for gathering and processing intelligence. Nevertheless, this case-study approach presumes some basic definitions and models according to which I will classify intelligence operations. The term "intelligence" may be understood in three ways, according to A. N. Shulsky and G. J. Schmitt: as information, as an activity, and as an organization.

> Intelligence refers to information relevant to a government's formulation and implementation of policy to further its national security interests and to deal with threats from actual or potential adversaries. As an activity, intelligence involves the collection and analysis of intelligence information ...Finally, the term "intelligence" also refers to an organization that carries out these activities.[21]

The primary task of intelligence is the collection and analysis of pertinent information. Modern intelligence manuals divide these activities into several categories: military and political intelligence, domestic and international intelligence, strategic and tactical intelligence, legal and illegal intelligence, HUMINT (human intelligence) and TECHINT (technical intelligence such as photographic, imagery, and communications intelligence), etc. Neo-Assyrian intelligence, on the basis of our extant sources, was exclusively HUMINT.

Moreover, intelligence activities have never been limited only to gathering and analyzing data. Intelligence has often been directly involved in military and political operations ("silent warfare"). The best-known forms of active involvement by intelligence services are deception, counterintelligence, psychological warfare, and covert action. I will argue that both biblical and Neo-Assyrian sources indicate that the Assyrians knew and used techniques of psychological warfare (PsW).

Finally, Y. J. Kim's study has proved that there is no evidence for any separate organization dedicated exclusively to collecting and processing intelligence, which means there was no equivalent of the modern CIA,

---

[21] Shulsky and Schmitt, *Silent Warfare: Understanding the World of Intelligence*, 1.

KGB, etc. The same officials performed the duties of intelligence agents, soldiers, tribute collectors, and supervisors of construction and agricultural activities. Because the officials of the Neo-Assyrian intelligence network were required to report on everything they heard and saw, they gathered information on a wide range of subjects, from simple administrative matters through information on secret negotiations and covert actions. Consequently, most of the extant Neo-Assyrian intelligence reports would correspond to basic news briefings. Thus, it is impossible to draw a strict line dividing intelligence reports from military briefings and simple administrative reports.

2

Neo-Assyrian intelligence during Sennacherib's campaign against Judah

In this chapter, I focus on 2 Kgs 18–20 insofar as these chapters relate to Neo-Assyrian intelligence. In practical terms, I investigate how the biblical authors perceived Neo-Assyrian intelligence.[22] The biblical redactors presented the Assyrians as skillful masters of psychological warfare. Thus, the first and largest part of my analysis of the biblical texts is an attempt to reconstruct Neo-Assyrian PsW. I analyze it in terms of its media, its techniques, and the agents employed to conduct it, as well as its effect on the audiences to which it was directed.

Neo-Assyrian PsW could not be conducted without accurate information. Thus, in the second part of my analysis of the biblical texts, I focus on information that the Assyrians directly used in their PsW. I also reconstruct the types of intelligence they had to have at their disposal in order to lead their campaign against Judah. Unfortunately, the biblical texts provide almost no data regarding the intelligence structures by means of which the Assyrians gathered the information they needed.

2.1 Sennacherib's psychological warfare according to the biblical sources

Intelligence services can be involved in a military campaign on different levels. The best-known form of involvement is psychological warfare. The definition of psychological warfare has been exhaustively discussed by several modern scholars.[23] The following quotation captures well its most important goals:

---

[22] The reconstruction of Neo-Assyrian intelligence on the basis of these passages will not be per se a proof that these passages should be taken at face value. The historicity of these biblical passages will be evaluated in chapter 5.

[23] See, for example, F. R. Barnett and C. Lord, *Political Warfare and Psychological Operations: Rethinking the US Approach* (Washington, D.C.: National Defense University

> [PsW] can be used to demoralize, disorient, and confuse hostile groups. Against such groups, Psyops [psychological operations] are employed as an offensive weapon to enhance the overall effectiveness of military operations. They can be also used, however, to unite, inform, and bolster the morale of non-hostile groups. When targeting neutral or friendly groups, they are used to support military objectives by developing cooperative attitudes and behavior in the targeted group.[24]

Though one would search in vain for terms such as psychological, informational, or political warfare; diplomatic pressure; and psychological operations in the pages of the Bible, the biblical redactors were aware of the realities these terms represent. Not only were the Israelites the target of psychological warfare, they were also skillful practitioners (2 Kgs 10). Gideon, for example, ordered his soldiers to light torches and scream in order to incite panic in the enemy's camp (Judg 7). However, the best example of Psyops is the psychological pressure that the Assyrians exerted upon the Jerusalemites during the reign of Hezekiah.

2.1.1 Media, audience, and types of Neo-Assyrian Psyops

It is possible to identify four cases of Psyops in 2 Kgs 18–20. The first case of Neo-Assyrian PsW is described in 2 Kgs 18:13–6.[25] Sennacherib invaded Judah and captured all its fortified cities (18:13). After news of the destruction had reached Hezekiah, he opted to seek terms of peace. The psychological impact of reports of the advance of the victorious

---

Press in cooperation with National Strategy Information Center, 1989), P. Baroni, *La Guerra Psicologica* (Rome: Ciarrapico Editore, 1986), F. Géré, *La Guerre psychologique* (Paris: Economica, 1997), B. Glad, *Psychological Dimensions of War* (Newbury Park, Calif.: Sage Publications, 1990), V. Krysko, *Sekrety psikhologicheskoj vojny: Celi, zadachi, metody, formy, opyt, kommandos* (Minsk: Kharvest, 1999); P. M. A. Linebarger, *Psychological Warfare*, 1st ed. (Washington, D.C.: Infantry Journal Press, 1948), W. E. Odom, "Psychological Operations and Political Warfare in Long-Term Strategic Planning," in *Psychological Operations and Political Warfare in Long-Term Strategic Planning*, ed. J. Radványi (New York: Praeger, 1990), R. W. Rieber, *The Psychology of War and Peace: The Image of the Enemy* (New York: Plenum Press, 1991), and S. Rogerson, *Propaganda in the Next War*, ed. L. Hart, *The Next War Series* (London: Geffrey Bles, 1939).

[24] A. H. Paddock, "U.S. Military Psychological Operations: Past, Present, and Future," in *Psychological Operations and Political Warfare in Long-Term Strategic Planning*, ed. J. Radványi (New York: Praeger, 1990), 10.

[25] This story is missing in Isaiah's version.

Assyrian army, the destruction of the Judahite cities unable to resist Assyrian siegecraft, and the siege of Lachish compelled Hezekiah to surrender and accept Sennacherib's terms of peace. The second case of Psyops consisted of diplomatic pressure exerted on the Judahite royal courtiers (18:17–27), which most likely took place on an open field in the vicinity of Jerusalem.[26] Both the Assyrians and Judahites were represented by their top officials, who conveyed the will of their lords. A short dialogue[27] between both parties followed after Rab-shaqeh had communicated Sennacherib's message. While the Judahites tried to undermine the Assyrian arguments, the Assyrians bolstered their arguments and counterattacked. The third case of Neo-Assyrian Psyops is described in the famous speech of Rab-shaqeh at the walls of Jerusalem (18:28-35). The speech is presented by the biblical narrator as public propaganda intended to influence directly a large audience, the inhabitants of Jerusalem. The last case of Psyops is the speech of the messengers who delivered the letters[28] of the Assyrian king to Hezekiah (19:9b–13).

The four cases of Psyops described in 2 Kgs 18–20 used a broad variety of the media, techniques, and strategies accessible at that time. The Assyrians transmitted their message to the Jerusalemites by means of written and oral media: a written letter delivered by Assyrian royal messengers, the oral reproduction of the king's message by top Assyrian officials or by messengers carrying the royal letters, and a speech delivered by a high-ranking Assyrian official delivered at the city walls. News of the destruction of the Judahite cities was spread in a manner that is not specified.

---

[26] D. Bahat, "The Fuller's Field and the 'Conduit of the Upper Pool'," *EI* 20 (1989), and T. R. Hobbs, *2 Kings* (Waco, Texas: Word Books, 1985), 260–2.

[27] The change of the subject and objects of the address in verses 18:22–24 indicates that this dialogue took place during the negotiations. In the first and the last verses of the speech (18:20–21 and 18:25) the subject of the dialogue is the Assyrian king (1st p. sing.), and Hezekiah is the partner of the dialogue (2nd p. sing.). In verses 18:22–4 the partners of the dialogue are no longer Hezekiah and the Assyrian king (both in 3rd p. sing.) but the Judahite and Assyrian representatives (2nd p. pl. and 1st p. pl.). This shift may represent the intention of the final compiler to present not only the message of the Assyrian king but also the Jerusalemite courtiers' attempt to undermine the force of Assyrian argumentation by pointing out its shortcomings.

[28] The MT has in 19:14 the plural form, whereas G^L has the singular.

In all four cases, the Assyrians' psychological pressure was reinforced by the fact that their army was operating in Hezekiah's backyard. The Assyrian army was the muscle that enforced the Assyrian will. Thus, by accumulating the forces necessary for an actual war, the Assyrians tried to compel the Jerusalemites to surrender. On the one hand, such preparations increase the likelihood that combat will occur. On the other hand, however paradoxical it might seem, preparation for war can function as a deterrent.[29] Thus, by massing troops for an attack on Jerusalem, the Assyrians increased the psychological pressure exerted upon Jerusalemites in the hope that the threat of war would prevent any actual war.

Only in the first case (18:13–16) did Assyrian Psyops succeed, when Hezekiah paid tribute to save his life. In the rest of the cases, the biblical narrator claims that despite the devastating effects of Assyrian psychological pressure on the Judahites—the courtiers and the king tore their clothes and covered themselves with sackcloth (19:1–2), the king poured out his distress in the temple, and sought help from the prophet Isaiah (19:1–7, 14–34)—they maintained their resistance.

2.1.2 Techniques of Neo-Assyrian psychological warfare

The Assyrians were credited by the biblical redactors with having mastered the most important techniques of PsW: using quotation and verbal imagery in an attempt to discredit the ruler, creating the impression of the attacker's omniscience, fostering cognitive dissonance, delivering exhortations and promises, and adapting their speech to suit the target audience.

2.1.2.1 Direct speech

The rhetorical device of quotation shared by the first two speeches seems to be one of the most important psychological weapons with which the biblical narrator credited Assyrian propagandists. Taking advantage of the suggestive power of this rhetorical device, Rab-shaqeh[30] introduced

---

[29] D. Bakan, "Some Philosophical Propadeutics toward a Psychology of War," in *The Psychology of War and Peace: The Image of the Enemy*, ed. R. W. Rieber (New York: Plenum Press, 1991), 53.

[30] The biblical sources take the title of the Assyrian official Rab-shaqeh (LÚ. GAL-KAŠ.LUL=*rab šāqê*) as a personal name (רַב־שָׁקֵה), i.e., without the definite article.

himself as the mediator of the king's words (18:27) and presented his message not as his own, but as a message coming from the mouth of the king himself.[31] He invited the Judahite crowds and their representatives to listen to the very words of the Assyrian king, thus forcing them to enter into dialogue with Sennacherib.[32] Because Rab-shaqeh's words derived their credibility from the source he had quoted, the Assyrian king, to refute Rab-shaqeh's message would require refuting Sennacherib himself. The desired psychological effect of such a technique was obvious: to leave the intimidated audience paralyzed. This effect was achieved by employing quotation formulas to introduce the king's words (כֹּה־אָמַר),[33] by exhorting the crowd to listen to the king's words,[34] by using 1st person singular forms to refer to the king and 2nd person forms for the audience, and by accumulating royal titles (הַמֶּלֶךְ 'the king', הַמֶּלֶךְ הַגָּדוֹל 'the great king', מֶלֶךְ אַשּׁוּר 'the king of Assyria'),), by employing quotation formulas to

[31] Investing the message with the authority of the government is a generally recognized tactic of PsW officers; thus, novice propagandists in the U.S. army were strongly recommended not to "make promises to persons in occupied territory, to friendly guerillas, to underground movements, or to enemy troops when those promises are not backed up by word-for-word quotations from the head of his government or someone of Cabinet rank"; see Linebarger, *Psychological Warfare*, 52.

[32] For an audience acquainted with prophetic speeches, the choice of the quotation marker כֹּה־אָמַר (18:19.29.31) instead of the combination of the finite form of verb אמר followed by לֵאמֹר underlines the authoritative value of such speech. All 463 occurrences of the expression כֹּה־אָמַר, "thus said," in the Bible indicate that an important authority is being quoted. In 436 of the cases (94.4%), this phrase introduces a direct quotation of God. It is to be noted that in the prophetic literature, the phrase is almost exclusively used for marking the beginning of God's words. The exceptions are our chapters in Isaiah (Is 36–9) and Am 7:11 (the phrase introduces the words of the prophet). In those cases when the phrase does not function as a quotation marker marking the beginning of God's words, the phrase still maintains its authoritative quality, marking the beginning of the words of a king (Ex 5:10; Judg 11:15; 1 Kgs 2:30; 20:3, 5; 22:27; 2 Kgs 1:11; 9:18, 19; 18:19, 29, 31; 19:3; 2 Chr 18:26; 32:10; 36:23; Ezr 1:2; Is 36:4, 14, 16; 37:3), a prophet (Nm 22:16; 1 Sm 9:9; Am 7:11), or an important personage (Gn 32:5; 45:9; Nm 20:14).

[33] It is important to note that the beginning of the quotation is always clearly marked by the formula כֹּה־אָמַר; however, the end of the quotation is not similarly marked.

[34] Like the phrase כֹּה־אָמַר so also the phrase שִׁמְעוּ דְּבַר־ was not a neutral expression for an audience acquainted with prophetic exhortations. In all cases (24 occurrences) but one (the present passage) the phrase commands close attention to the words of God שִׁמְעוּ דְּבַר־יְהוָה, "listen to the words of the Lord!"; thus it signals the beginning of an authoritative speech.

introduce the king's words (כֹּה־אָמַר),[35] by exhorting the crowd to listen to the king's words,[36] and by using 1st person singular forms to refer to the king and 2nd person forms for the audience.

2.1.2.2 Verbal imagery

The use of verbal imagery was the second psychological technique that the biblical redactors credited to the Assyrian propagandists.[37] Since the Assyrians did not have at their disposal efficient visual media such as television and the press, the best tools for influencing an enemy were vivid verbal images. In 2 Kgs 18–19 the biblical narrator displays the Assyrian mastery of verbal imagery in the context of propaganda.

The first image, that of a broken reed (18:21), draws its penetrating power from the interchangeability of the words בטח, שען (the root of מִשְׁעֶנֶת), and סמך. All three verbs can take the preposition עַל. The noun מִשְׁעֶנֶת and the verb סמך determine the linguistic nuance of the verb בטח. מִשְׁעֶנֶת 'support, staff' was a symbol of confidence or power in the hands of a king, a shepherd, or a sick or aged person. Thus, Rab-shaqeh played with a familiar image deeply rooted in ancient Near Eastern culture: the image of the leader's scepter (Nm 21:18), the shepherd's walking/defense staff (Ps 23:4), the traveler's walking stick (2 Kgs 4:29, 31), the angel's wand (Judg

---

[35] It is important to note that the beginning of the quotation is always clearly marked by the formula כֹּה־אָמַר; however, the end of the quotation is not similarly marked.

[36] Like the phrase כֹּה־אָמַר so also the phrase שִׁמְעוּ דְבַר־ was not a neutral expression for an audience acquainted with prophetic exhortations. In all cases (24 occurrences) but one (the present passage) the phrase commands close attention to the words of God שִׁמְעוּ דְּבַר־יְהוָה, "listen to the words of the Lord!"; thus it signals the beginning of an authoritative speech.

[37] Soviet analysis of pathological syndromes developed under protracted siege demonstrated the occurrence of a common condition called sensory deprivation. Such deprivation causes a great need for and heightens susceptibility to any sensual stimulation; see Krysko, *Sekrety psikhologicheskoj vojny*, 50. Combined with other negative factors that are usually present under siege, such as shortages of food or sleep, etc., sensory deprivation can cause a variety of pathological behaviors. These include depression, hallucination, and possibly suicide. Studies of sociological pathologies during the siege of Sarajevo demonstrated an increased suicide rate; see M. Mikovic, *Samoubistva u okruzenom Sarajevu: Prilozi socijalnoj patologiji* (Sarajevo: Studentska stamparija Univerziteta, 1998), 62–78. People deprived of regular sensory stimulation naturally become vulnerable targets for enemy propaganda officers seeking to sap their resistance.

6:21), or the cane of the elderly and sick (Zec 8:4; Ex 21:19). The verb סמך in the niphal means 'to lean upon someone or something, to transfer one's weight to or to rely upon someone or something else' (Judg 16:29; Ps 71:6). Thus, the act of trusting in 18:21—בטח—can be defined as relying on someone in a moment of need, transferring the weight of problems upon someone, looking for security while leaning against someone, relying on someone else for military help, or making oneself partly dependent on someone else. The novelty of the image fully emerges only in the second part of the simile. The staff is but a reed, the symbol of Egypt, whose sharp edge easily cut through the hand of those who leaned against it. Thus, the audience was left with the repugnant image of a bleeding palm with a broken reed protruding from it. Hearing that "such is Pharaoh, the king of Egypt, to all who rely on him" (18:21b), the audience must have associated this hair-raising image with a profound feeling of deception. Rab-shaqeh's masterly use of imagery began by luring the audience's imagination with the innocuous image of a person leaning against a staff. Twisting this innocuous image into the repugnant image of a bleeding palm, Rab-shaqeh fixed this image in the memory of the audience. Once the image had been stored in memory and associated with resentment at being betrayed by an ally, it could easily be evoked when least expected.[38] And once evoked, it could undermine the defenders' confidence in Egypt and sap the bravery of the Judahite representatives.[39]

The second two images (2 Kgs 18:27, 31–32) appealed to a basic human instinct, food. During his private speech (18:26–27), Rab-shaqeh claimed that the besieged Jerusalemites were doomed to eat their own dung and drink their own urine. This disgusting image was intended to evoke the

---

[38] This three-step psychological technique belongs to the traditional strategies of PsW and corresponds to three basic activities of human memory: perception, fixation, and the evocation of an image; see Baroni, *La Guerra Psicologica*, 191.

[39] The process of eroding the bravery of the people by implanting in their minds a powerful image is well illustrated by the case of the siege of Kumassi (Ghana) in 1900. British soldiers besieged by the Ashanti tribe learned from a very unreliable source that the British army suffered a defeat. Even though they had many reasons not to trust the woman who brought this message, the colonels who heard the news could not help ruminating about it. In the evening, "everyone avoided the subject uppermost in his mind, and although each was wondering if the others had heard the dismal rumour, no one wished to be the first to spread it … so evening passed with a greater show of gaiety than usual, and with cheerfulness that hid heavy hearts"; M. A. Y. Hodgson, *The Siege of Kumassi* (New York: Longmans, 1901), 159.

memories of other sieges the Israelites had experienced themselves (2 Kgs 6–7) or inflicted on others (2 Kgs 3; Dt 20:10–20).[40]

The diary of a British colonel in Kumassi is very useful for reconstructing the psychology of a people under siege.[41] The shortage of food pushed the price for any food article to an astronomical sum.[42] People ate anything—rats, poisonous herbs, and even their own excrement. Slow starvation robbed the people of courage and strength. People became sick from constantly eating bad food, and epidemics broke out. The news about the first death from starvation prompted people to desert and to choose slavery with food over freedom with starvation. Some became apathetic, too weak to care for anything; others lost their reason and became mad. The biblical writers preserved similar stories about the desperation to which an enemy siege reduced the people. Some of them even turned to situational cannibalism and devoured their own children (Dt 28:53; 2 Kgs 6:24–31).

Rab-shaqeh emphasized that this destiny would belong not only to refugees looking for protection within the walls of Jerusalem, but also to the Judahite representatives to whom he addressed these words (2 Kgs 18:27). Presented at the beginning of the war, this image of all Jerusalemites doomed to eat their own dung and drink their own urine attacked a sensitive point—the responsibility of Judahite representatives not only for their own future, but also for the future of their fellow Jerusalemites.

In contrast to the repugnant image of a food shortage, Rab-shaqeh sketched for the Jerusalemites an image of a promised land abundant with

---

[40] P. Xella claimed that verse 2 Kgs 18:26, "the people sitting on the wall, who are doomed with you to eat their own dung and to drink their own urine," cannot be taken literally. He suggested reading this verse in the light of some Egyptian and Akkadian inscriptions. According to Egyptian funerary inscriptions, the expression "to eat one's excrements and to drink one's urine" referred to food to be consumed in the afterlife. Thus, by this phrase Rab-shaqeh referred to the afterlife of Jerusalemites doomed to eternal damnation; see P. Xella, "Sur la nourriture des morts: Un aspect de l'eschatologie mésopotamienne," in *Death in Mesopotamia: XXVIe Rencontre assyriologique internationale,* ed. B. Alster (Copenhagen: Akademisk Forlag, 1980), 151–60. However, P. Xella did not provide sufficient arguments to prove that this verse cannot be read literally as well. The combination of P. Xella's interpretation with the literal interpretation underlines even more the psychological impact of Rab-shaqeh's speech.

[41] Hodgson, *The Siege of Kumassi,* 144–95.

[42] In Kumassi, after several months of siege, the people were ready to offer 10 shillings for a rat; see ibid., 180.

food (2 Kgs 18:31–32). Rab-shaqeh cited a list of food sources that included food articles (bread, olive oil, water, and honey), fruit plants (fig-trees, olive-trees, and vines), and cultivated grounds (vineyards). This image addressed to the citizens standing on the city walls was meant to evoke the peaceful image of an agrarian society in which farmers owned and tilled their own fields, cultivated their own vineyards, and dug their own wells. The persuasive power of this positive image was augmented by juxtaposing negative and positive images. Thus, the lifestyle of the people over here (in Jerusalem) was juxtaposed to the lifestyle over there (in the new land given to them by the Assyrian king). The trials of war over here were contrasted with the peaceful agrarian life over there, eating dung with eating the desirable fruit of the earth, drinking urine with drinking water fresh from the well. This series of juxtapositions culminated in the final choice the Jerusalemites were to make, that between death over here and life over there. Thus, Rab-shaqeh tried to replace the negative image of deportation with the positive image of a new beginning in a new promised land. The juxtaposition of the negative and positive images turned the Promised Land (Israel) into a cursed land, and a foreign land (a new land to be given to the deportees) into a new promised land. Such a strategy could weaken the resistance of the Jerusalemites, and Rab-shaqeh let them entertain the idea of surrender.[43] If the right choice were made, this idyllic future might become theirs.

It is important to note that appeals to hunger on their own have never been sufficient to compel people to surrender. The strategy of appealing to hunger must be properly timed in order to reach the desired effect.[44] It can be counterproductive, if used when the besieged people still have a sufficient amount of food or a good military position. For example, W. E. Daugherty's study indicates that during World War I, shortly after the food situation deteriorated, German civilians were able to motivate themselves to acts of great altruism. Their morale increased, because their

---

[43] Krysko, *Sekrety psikhologicheskoj vojny*, 32.

[44] The exemplary usage of this strategy in proper time can be demonstrated by the example of British propaganda against the Central Powers in World War I: "as soon as evidence began accumulating of hunger or privation among the enemy, Northcliffe brought ... the picture of the land flowing with milk and honey which lay behind the encircling Allies lines and in which even prisoners of war waxed fat and were contended"; see Rogerson, *Propaganda in the Next War*, 17.

military position still gave them some hope.[45] Thus, combining food appeal images with the images of the actual military position tends to strengthen the final impact on the enemy. Enemy troops under siege are usually deprived of information and often fail to understand why they should surrender, since their own propaganda keeps them informed only about the successes of their army. In such a situation, it is useful to send them a map showing them plainly what their situation is, or a list of cities which were well fortified but still unable to resist the siege of the victorious army. Thus, positioning the appeal to hunger next to two lists of destroyed cities (2 Kgs 18:34; 19:12–13), and combining that picture of ruin with a positive description of the future available to those who surrendered, might have been a very powerful tactic of Psyops.

2.1.2.3 Undermining trust

The transformation of natural tendencies, such as the natural inclination to trust one's own rulers and the military commanders of one's country, has been an important psychological warfare strategy throughout the centuries.[46] In fact, the inclination to trust one's own rulers is rather shallow, and can easily be undermined by denouncing the leaders as incompetent, lying, and exploitative. Once this has been achieved, the enemy camp is split into factions and open to collaboration. The process of undermining trust in one's own leader has been studied by P. M. A. Linebarger.[47] According to his study, one of the psychological dimensions of war is the shift in the motivation and evaluation of both civilians and soldiers involved in war. The cruel futility inherent in war is so plain to all civilized human beings that when war does come, people overcompensate for it by fostering illusions about the noble motives of their leaders. Thus, the role of propagandists is to tear down such "inflated personages" by attributing normal human motives to the leaders of the enemy:

> The propagandist thus has an ideal situation. In the enemy country everyone is trying to be more noble, more unselfish, more hard-working. Everyone applies a higher standard of ethics and performance than in peacetime. Businessmen are not supposed to

---

[45] W. E. Daugherty, *A Psychological Warfare Casebook* (Baltimore: Johns Hopkins University Press, 1958), 99.

[46] Krysko, *Sekrety psikhologicheskoj vojny*, 32–33.

[47] Linebarger, *Psychological Warfare*, 155.

> make too much money, politicians are supposed to work around the clock, officials are supposed to cooperate ... The ground is ready for rumor, for tearing down inflated personages, for breaking the illusion by the simple process of attributing normally selfish motives in wartime.[48]

The biblical redactors depict the Assyrians as having a good command of this psychological technique as well.[49] The belittling of Hezekiah was achieved by placing Hezekiah's kingdom in its international context: even the least of the Assyrian governors had much more power than the king of Judah (18:23–24). Rab-shaqeh's first speech presented Hezekiah as a loser and an incompetent king: his rebellion was useless, his international policy had failed since he relied on unreliable Egypt, his army was not able to measure up to the Assyrian troops, and his religious reform made God angry (18:19–25). That the war continued, that the innocent people kept suffering, that further defeats occurred, and that further blood was spilled were all due to Hezekiah's unreasonableness. The people were not guilty; the real problem was their king, who deceived his people and made them trust in a god who was unable to save them (18:30, 33–34).

2.1.2.4 Shocking knowledge

The impression of being omniscient was another psychological technique attributed to the Assyrians in the biblical accounts. Rab-shaqeh's self-confident speeches created an impression that nothing, not even the most secret actions of the enemy, could be hidden from the king's eyes and ears. Above all, Rab-shaqeh was aware of the fact that the Egyptians backed Hezekiah's insurrection against Assyria. He bolstered the impression that he knew everything by recounting some further (though admittedly generally known) details about Egypt, some 1,500 km distant from Assyria, such as its political structure (Pharaoh, the king of Egypt; 18:21), its military power (chariotry and cavalry; 18:24), its low reliability (18:21), and its symbol (the reed; 18:21). As for the domestic situation in Judah, Rab-shaqeh displayed knowledge of Hezekiah's rebellion (18:20), his real political power and military resources (18:23–4), and his slogans and promises.[50]

---

[48] Ibid., 156.

[49] Gallagher, *Sennacherib's Campaign*, 176–77.

[50] Hezekiah probably used slogans to gain the support of the Jerusalemites, such as trust in God or that God would not deliver his city to the hands of his enemy (18:30, 32; 19:10).

Rab-shaqeh not only knew which dialect was used by the common people in Judah but also was able to speak it (18:26–27).

However, the most shocking thing for the Jerusalemites should have been Rab-shaqeh's detailed knowledge of their religious matters. He summarized the main aspects of Hezekiah's reform: the centralization of the cult around the altar in Jerusalem and the removal of the high places and altars (18:22). He used the correct terminology (the noun בָּמָה,[51] and the verbs בטח[52] in qal and סור in hiphil[53]). He was even familiar with major Judahite theological themes and prophetic controversies: Rab-shaqeh skillfully used the rhetoric of exodus, Promised Land, and curses and blessings (18:31–32).[54] He competently constructed his argument against the reliability of Egypt upon prophecies that declared the futility of any alliance with Egypt and condemned those who would rely on human factors such as horses and chariots (18:20–24).[55] Even more shocking must have been Rab-shaqeh's acquaintance with prior prophetic denunciations of the sins of Israel and Judah and consequent predictions of their punishment, including the particular prediction that the invading Assyrians were the Lord's punitive instrument, compelling Israel and Judah to repent for their sins,[56] and that the destiny which met several other cities would also meet Israel and Judah, if they did not repent.[57] Thus, by giving the impression that they knew all about their enemies, the Assyrians established their psychological superiority over the Judahites.[58] Combining psychological

[51] The בָּמָה was the symbol of idolatry; see 1 Kgs 11:7; 12:32; 2 Kgs 12:4; 14:4; 15:4, 35; 16:4; 17:9, 11, 29, 32; 18:4; Mic 1:5; Hos 10:8.

[52] 2 Kgs 18:5.

[53] 2 Kgs 18:4; 23:19; see Gallagher, *Sennacherib's Campaign*, 172.

[54] For similarities between Rab-shaqeh's speech and the theme of blessings and curses, see Dt 11:26; 28:1–68; 30:1. For similarities with the Promised Land and exodus theme, see for example Ex 3:8.17; 13:5; 33:3; Lev 20:24; Nm 13:27; Dt 6:3; 8:7–9; 33:28.

[55] For the futility of alliance with Egypt, see Is 28:14–15; 30:1–17; 31:1–4; Hos 7:11–16; 12:2. For the failure of Egyptians to help Israel and Judah, see 2 Kgs 17:4; Jer 37:5–8. For the unreliability of Egypt, see Ez 29:2–7.

[56] See Is 5:26–30 (Assyria as a lion); 7:20 (Assyria as a razor); 10:1–6 (Assyria as a rod); Hos 10:5–6 (exile in Assyria).

[57] Am 6:2; Is 10:9; possibly Mic 1:10–16. It is important to recognize that the enumerative argument was not only a biblical feature but was also used in Assyrian sources for demonstrating the irresistibility of Assyrian might. For Assyrian parallels, see C. Cohen, "Neo-Assyrian Elements in the First Speech of the Biblical Rab-šaqe," *IOS* 9 (1979): 36-7.

[58] A similar strategy was successfully used during the Cold War for acquiring collaborators within the Soviet block; see Codevilla, *Informing Statecraft*, 82.

superiority (the possession of shocking knowledge) with military and economic superiority (18:23–24) was another powerful psychological tool in Assyrian hands.

2.1.2.5 Cognitive dissonance

By the term "cognitive dissonance" is understood a disagreement between the intellectual-cognitive and other components of the human being.[59] Creating such dissonance, if it is properly timed and combined with other techniques of PsW, can undermine human enthusiasm, diminish human productivity, and make people more vulnerable to defection and collaboration. Generally speaking, whereas crowds are more prone to collaborate when a message appeals to their basic feelings and instincts, an audience used to logical argumentation is more open to collaboration when the flaws in the logic of their own official propaganda are clearly demonstrated, i.e., through the creation of cognitive dissonance.

The first speech of Rab-shaqeh (18:17–25) occurs in the context of a meeting between Assyrian and Judahite top officials: the Assyrian commander-in-chief (תַּרְתָּן, *turtānu*), chief eunuch (רַב־סָרִיס, LÚ.GAL–SAG=*rab ša-rēši*), and chief cupbearer (רַב־שָׁקֵה, LÚ.GAL–KAŠ.LUL=*rab šāqê*), ranged against the Judahite Eliakim, son of Hilkiah, who was in charge of the palace (אֲשֶׁר עַל־הַבָּיִת), Shebnah the scribe (הַסֹּפֵר), and Joah, son of Asaph, the recorder (הַמַּזְכִּיר). All of them were well-educated people presumably accustomed to logical argumentation. Rab-shaqeh's iron logic demonstrated obvious flaws in the rationale upon which Judahite resistance was grounded. If Hezekiah as well as the Judahite representatives had made the decision to oppose Assyria on certain logical grounds,[60] then the Assyrian representatives had to undermine that logic and create cognitive dissonance. If the premises on which Hezekiah's logic was based could be proved false, then the basis for resistance against the Assyrians would collapse.

Rab-shaqeh's whole argument proving the unreasonableness of Hezekiah's resistance is held together by a fourfold repetition of the

---

[59] Krysko, *Sekrety psikhologicheskoj vojny*, 30.
[60] Ben-Zvi, "Who Wrote the Speech," 83.

conjunction עַתָּה (18:20, 21, 23, 25)[61] and a sixfold repetition of different grammatical forms of either the verb בטח 'to trust' (18:19.20.21.22.24) or its cognate noun בִּטָּחוֹן (18:19). This repetitive structure, combined with a series of rhetorical questions, focused the attention of the audience on the main question: "What is your resistance based on?"[62] By investigating all possible answers to this question, Rab-shaqeh gradually eliminated all possible reasons for Judahite resistance: their troops were not sufficient to combat the superior Assyrian army, Egypt would not come to help them, and even their God had turned against them. This conclusion resulted from a magnificent combination of manifold rhetorical devices, such as contradiction, comparison, a wager, and a simile.

First, the futility of Judahite resistance became clear from the contradiction[63] between Hezekiah's words and his inability to put them into practice (18:19-20). Thus, his words contradicted the reality he has to face (his lack of both the strategy and the resources necessary for conducting a war against Assyria). Second, the comparison between the Judahite king and the least significant Assyrian governor showed another flaw in Judahite reasoning: if Hezekiah was unable to turn back the least significant Assyrian governor, how could he turn back the Assyrian king himself (18:24)? Third, a powerful wager (הִתְעָרֶב)[64] contrasted the military strength of both powers: if the Assyrians possessed more horses than the Judahites possessed riders, then how could the Judahite army resist the Assyrian royal troops (18:23)? Fourth, a simile using the image of a broken reed

[61] The temporal adverb עַתָּה, especially its form וְעַתָּה, in direct speeches "introduces a shift in argumentative tack with a continuity in subject and reference"; see B. K. Waltke and M. P. O'Connor, *An Introduction to Biblical Hebrew Syntax* (Winona Lake, Ind.: Eisenbrauns, 1990), 667.

[62] This repetitive argumentation skillfully plays with the question, "Whom do you trust in?," which, according to the biblical narrator, formed the core of Sennacherib's first message (18:19–21, 24). It is worth noting that the *inclusio* formed by the king's questions encloses the dialogue between the representatives.

[63] The rhetorical device of contradiction is classified as a semi-logical argument, whose goal is to involve the logic of the audience; see M. B. Garavelli, *Manuale di Retorica* (Milano: Bompiani, 1989), 91–92.

[64] K.A.D. Smelik, "Distortion of Old Testament Prophecy: The Purpose of Isaiah XXXVI and XXXVII," in *Crises and Perspectives; Studies in Ancient near Eastern Polytheism, Biblical Theology, Palestinian Archaeology and Intertestamental Literature: Papers Read at the Joint British-Dutch Old Testament Conference Held at Cambridge, U.K., 1985* (Leiden and Boston: Brill, 1986), 78.

penetrating the palm of a person who leaned upon it discredited Egypt as a possible deliverer (see 2.1.2.2). Finally, the last source of help was the mighty Judahite God. Rab-shaqeh masterfully destroyed this argument as well, by claiming that it had been the very God of Israel who, being angry with his people, had decided to punish them by the hand of the Assyrian king (18:25).[65]

Thus, Rab-shaqeh left the three Judahite representatives without any escape from the naked reality that there was no way of opposing the Assyrian troops, and he also interpreted the religious reform that stood at the basis of the anti-Assyrian revolt as the cause of present disaster.[66] However, his rhetorical questions did not force the Judahite representatives to make the decision *hic et nunc* but rather left them with a nagging question: "Does our resistance make any sense?"

2.1.2.6 Exhortation and promises

Rab-shaqeh's second speech (18:28–35), whose primary audience was the people on the city walls, differed from his negotiation with the top Judahite representatives (see 2.1.2.5). The skeleton of this speech consisted of short repetitive exhortations and promises. Imperatives and negated imperatives organized in the concentric structure A–B–A^1 (see Table 1) lent the speech emotional force. In contrast to the list of destroyed cities in A^1, the central part depicted a peaceful promised land abounding with food. In contrast to the promises of the deceitful Hezekiah in A and A^1, the center of Rab-shaqeh's speech presented the promises of the most powerful king in the world. The exhortation not to trust Hezekiah opened and closed the speech (A and A^1) and focused attention on the core of Rab-shaqeh's speech (B)–promises to be fulfilled after the surrender of Jerusalem. If they surrendered, the Assyrian king would guarantee them safe conduct and a reasonably good future in a new land. If they surrendered, not only would

[65] In verses 18:33–35, Rab-shaqeh uses a different argument contradictory to this one, that the Lord is just as weak as the gods of other nations that the Assyrian have captured. This and other logical contradictions in Neo-Assyrian propaganda will be dealt with in detail in section 5.4.2.2.2. At this point I am interested in detailing all of the arguments for surrender by means of which Rab-shaqeh attempted to undermine the logical basis for resistance.

[66] The rhetorical device "identification and definition of the problems" is also used for undermining or confirming the logic of a given argument; see Garavelli, *Manuale di Retorica*, 93–94.

they escape harm, but they would also enjoy the advantages of the Neo-Assyrian Empire.

Table 1. Concentric structure of Rab-shaqeh's second speech

A (18:29-31a)	Do not let Hezekiah deceive you! (18:29)	אַל־יַשִּׁיא לָכֶם חִזְקִיָּהוּ
	Do not let Hezekiah make rely you on the Lord! (18:30)	אֶתְכֶם חִזְקִיָּהוּ אֶל־יְהוָה אַל־יַבְטַח
	Do not listen to Hezekiah! (18:31)	אַל־תִּשְׁמְעוּ אֶל־חִזְקִיָּהוּ
B (18:31b-32a)	Make peace with me! (18:31)	עֲשׂוּ־אִתִּי בְרָכָה
	Come out to me! (18:31)	צְאוּ אֵלַי
	Eat! (18:31)	אִכְלוּ
	Drink! (18:31)	שְׁתוּ
	Live, do not die! (18:32)	חְיוּ וְלֹא תָמֻתוּ
A^1 (18:32b-5)	Do not listen to Hezekiah when he deceives you! (18:32)	וְאַל־תִּשְׁמְעוּ אֶל־חִזְקִיָּהוּ כִּי־יַסִּית אֶתְכֶם

2.1.2.7 Audience adaptation

The Assyrians seemed to be aware of the fact that in order for their PsW to be effective, it had to be tailored to a specific audience. According to the biblical redactors the Assyrians addressed their propaganda to three distinct groups: the Jerusalemites on the city walls listening to Rab-shaqeh's speech, the top Judahite courtiers negotiating with the Assyrian representatives, and the Judahite king himself, who received Sennacherib's letter.

According to the biblical redactors, both Rab-shaqeh in his speech (18:34) and Sennacherib in his letter (19:12–13) used a similar list of cities destroyed by the Assyrians as the basis for their argumentation.[67] The

[67] A number of scholars have observed the similarity between the lists of cities destroyed by Assyrian kings in B^1 (18:34) and B^2 (19:12–13) and concluded that source B^2 was a duplicate of source B^1. S. W. Holloway and N. Na'aman demonstrated that the list in source B^2 reflects the list of cities destroyed by the Babylonians and proposed considering source B^2 a post-exilic addition to pre-exilic sources A and B^1; see S. W. Holloway, "Harran: Cultic Geography in the Neo-Assyrian Empire and Its Implications for Sennacherib's 'Letter to Hezekiah' in 2 Kings," in *The Pitcher Is Broken: Memorial Essays for Gösta W. Ahlström*, ed. S. W. Holloway and L. K. Handy (Sheffield, England: Sheffield Academic Press, 1995), N. Na'aman, "New Light on Hezekiah's Second Prophetic Story (2 Kgs 19,9b–35)," *Biblica* 81 (2000), and idem, "Updating the Messages: Hezekiah's Second

success of the propaganda does not lie only in the quality of the argument but also in the persistent bombarding of the audience with the same argument with slight modifications. This strategy reflects an old Slovak saying: "A lie, after being repeated one hundred times, becomes the truth." Thus, the final version of the biblical narrative suggests that the Assyrians kept bombarding their listeners with the same argument. The differences between the lists of destroyed cities in Rab-shaqeh's speech and Sennacherib's letter illustrate how the Assyrians tailored their argumentation to their audiences.

As for the first list of the destroyed cities (18:34), its primary audience was the Jerusalemites sitting on the city wall. Rab-shaqeh reminded them of the destruction of their northern neighbor Samaria, of which they had certainly heard. Moreover, out of five cities mentioned in 18:34, three—Hamath, Sepharvaim, and Awa/Iwah—were cities from which deportees had been brought and settled in Israel after the fall of Samaria (2 Kgs 17:24). Since these deportees were settled in the Israelite kingdom twenty years before the siege of Jerusalem, we can assume that the Judahites learned from them about the sad destiny of Hamath, Sepharvaim, and Awa, and about the hardships connected with their deportation. Consequently, in order to understand Rab-shaqeh's rhetorical questions—"Where are the gods of Hamath and Arpad? Where are the gods of Sepharvaim, Hena and Ivvah? Have they delivered Samaria from my hand?" (18:34)—the Jerusalemites on the city walls did not have to consult the Assyrian annals, because they must have already known what had happened to these cities, their gods, and their inhabitants.

As for the second list of destroyed cities (19:12–13), Sennacherib is depicted as adding four more cities which were supposedly destroyed by his predecessors. Since the target of Sennacherib's letter was Hezekiah himself, who must have had some familiarity with the history of Assyria, the effect of the new list of destroyed cities was to cause Hezekiah to reflect on the history of his northern neighbors. The destruction of Gozan, Haran, Rezeph, and Telassar carried out by Sennacherib's predecessors confirmed that the recent Assyrian conquests of Hamath, Arpad, Sepharvaim, Hena, and Ivvah were not random victories, but represented a typical pattern of Assyrian

---

Prophetic Story (2 Kings 19.9b–35) and the Community of Babylonian Deportees," in *"Like a Bird in a Cage": The Invasion of Sennacherib in 701 BCE*, ed. L. L. Grabbe (London and New York: Sheffield Academic Press, 2003).

expansion over the preceding several centuries. If history thus attested that the Assyrians were always victorious, then what was the point of Hezekiah's resistance?

Another change was introduced in the construction of the argument that named the destroyed cities. The word "gods" was replaced by the word "king" in rhetorical questions, i.e., "Where is the king of ...?" (19:13) instead of "Where are the gods of ...?" (18:34). Consequently, the Assyrian argument no longer alluded to the sad destiny of local gods, but rather addressed Hezekiah's own future. If he did not surrender, he would end up like the kings of the cities destroyed by the Assyrians: he would certainly lose power and possibly be executed.

The last change introduced into the argumentation in order to tailor it to Hezekiah entailed a shift in the identity of the deceiver. In Rabshaqeh's second speech it was Hezekiah who deceived the Jerusalemites, whereas in the letter it was God who deceived Hezekiah. Thus, in both cases the same strategy was applied. The audience was not guilty; rather, the people had simply been deceived by their respective overlords: the people by Hezekiah, and Hezekiah by his God.

2.2 Biblical texts and Neo-Assyrian military and political intelligence

In section 2.1.2.4, I demonstrated that according to the biblical texts the Assyrians used the PsW technique of "shocking knowledge." Assyrian propaganda agents could shock an audience with the quality and quantity of information they had at their disposal about their enemies. Thus, the biblical redactors depicted Neo-Assyrian propaganda as containing accurate knowledge of the political, military, and religious situation in Judea. In the following sections I present other aspects of military and political intelligence that can be retrieved from the biblical sources.

2.2.1 Military intelligence

The biblical texts do not present the Assyrian invasion as a casual, disorganized attack, but rather as a carefully planned military operation. It would be impossible to organize such a large-scale military operation as was Sennacherib's invasion without basic military intelligence. The nature and types of this military intelligence can be reconstructed from the biblical texts only indirectly.

First, the Assyrians attacked Lachish (2 Kgs 18:14) and laid siege against Jerusalem (18:17ff.). The very selection of these two cities suggests that the Assyrians realized their value for Judah and that they had mapped out the fortresses of Judah and decided which of them to attack.

Second, according to the biblical texts, Sennacherib first laid siege against Lachish and then sent his officials to negotiate with Hezekiah in Jerusalem (2 Kgs 18:13–8). This indicates that the Assyrian troops came from the west and moved towards the east, taking the route along the coast southwards and then eastwards. Sennacherib's choice of this easier route presupposes a sufficient knowledge of the terrain and roads of Palestine that allowed him to avoid major obstacles in the terrain while moving his troops.

Third, Rab-shaqeh offered the Judahite representatives 2,000 horses, asking the Judahite representatives to set riders on them (2 Kgs 18:23–4). If Hezekiah had had at his disposal a cavalry of several thousand riders, then Rab-shaqeh's challenge would not have been merely ineffective but rather even counterproductive. Thus, it makes sense to conclude that the Assyrians were informed about the military capabilities of Jerusalem, and in particular about its cavalry and number of soldiers.

The last aspect of Neo-Assyrian military intelligence, as presented in the biblical texts, concerned Egypt. Sennacherib learned, while besieging the Judahite cities, that the Pharaoh Tarhaqa had set out from Egypt to attack him (19:9).[68] When Sennacherib heard about the approaching Egyptian army, he left Lachish and joined battle at Libna. This information presupposes that the biblical redactors understood that the Assyrians were

---

[68] The question of the historical value of this passage has been much debated by biblical scholars. To give credit to both the biblical story and the extrabiblical sources mentioning Tarhaqa, who ascended the throne in 691 B.C.E., some scholars suggested that Sennacherib conducted two campaigns against Judah. For a review of both positions, see Grabbe, L. L. *"Like a Bird in a Cage": The Invasion of Sennacherib in 701 BCE.* (London and New York: Sheffield Academic Press, 2003), 23 and K. A. D. Smelik, *Converting the Past: Studies in Ancient Israelite and Moabite Historiography* (Leiden and New York: Brill, 1992), 96. For the purposes of this study, what is important is that the biblical redactors attributed to the Assyrians knowledge of the whereabouts of the Pharaoh, no matter whether Sennacherib engaged in one or two campaigns.

receiving reports from scouts and intelligence agents watching the movements of the Egyptian army.

2.2.2 Political intelligence

The goal of Neo-Assyrian political intelligence was to monitor Assyrian vassals and their loyalty to Assyria. Since the Assyrians did invade Judah to punish Hezekiah's disloyalty, they must have been informed that such a rebellion had taken place. The biblical texts allow us to reconstruct some of the warning signs of Hezekiah's declining loyalty that the Assyrians would have perceived. First of all, Hezekiah stopped being Sennacherib's servant (2 Kgs 18:7b);[69] then he started to expand his territory at the expense of Philistia (2 Kgs 18:8) and to reclaim the territories of northern Israel lost to Assyria by sending a letter to Israel, Ephraim, and Manasseh (2 Chr 30:1-2). He undertook suspicious building activities (2 Chr 29:3;[70] 32:5),[71] reorganized his army (2 Chr 32:6), and built up a substantial arsenal (2 Chr 32:5b). On the international level, he welcomed the messengers of the rebellious Babylonian king Merodach Baladan (2 Kgs 20:12–19).[72] Moreover, he reorganized the cult in Jerusalem, demolished the symbols of idolatry, and consecrated new priests and Levites (2 Kgs 18:4–7; 2 Chr 29–31). His religious reform gained the

---

[69] The phrase "he (Hezekiah) would not serve him" (2 Kgs 18:7b) probably indicates Hezekiah's refusal to pay tribute to Assyria. For a detailed description of the signs of rebellion, see section 3.6.

[70] The fortification of the temple gates constituted a sign of declining loyalty, if it is understood in the context of Hezekiah's preparation for the Assyrian punitive invasion.

[71] The destruction of buildings annexed to the wall as a preparatory activity for defense has always been one of the privileges of the governor of the city; he could demolish any building during a state of siege (which could only be declared by the king); see V. Deguise, *Attaque et Défense des Forteresses: Tactique de la Guerre de Siège* (Bruxelles: Polleunis et Ceuterick, 1898), 4–5. For the historicity of the Chronicler's account, see A. G. Vaughn, *Theology, History, and Archaeology in the Chronicler's Account of Hezekiah* (Atlanta, Ga.: Scholars Press, 1999).

[72] According to several scholars, the story of Merodach-Baladan's ambassadors visiting Hezekiah is out of chronological order. The story was most likely contemporaneous with Hezekiah's rebellion; see P. R. Ackroyd, "Isaiah 36–39: Structure and Function," in *Von Kanaan bis Kerala: Festschrift für Prof. Mag. Dr. Dr. J.P.M. Van der Ploeg O.P. zur Vollendung des siebzigsten Lebensjahres am 4. Juli 1979*, ed. W. C. Delsman and J. P. M. van der Ploeg (Kevelaer: Verlag Butzon & Bercker; Neukirchen-Vluyn: Neukirchener Verlag, 1982), 10–11 and J. Blenkinsopp, *Isaiah 1–39: A New Translation with Introduction and Commentary* (New York: Doubleday, 2000), 458.

support of certain religious circles (2 Kgs 18:3–6).[73] Finally, the analysis of Neo-Assyrian PsW in sections 2.1.2.4 and 2.1.2.5 indicates that the biblical redactors wanted the reader to believe that the Assyrians knew about most of these anti-Assyrian activities.

2.3 Evaluation

As stated in the introduction, the concern of this chapter is not to resolve old problems, such as reviewing the compositional history of Hezekiah's story or finding the various *Sitze im Leben* of the different stages of the story. Rather, this chapter attempts to reconstruct the image of Neo-Assyrian intelligence as presented by the biblical redactors.

From the preceding analysis of the biblical texts, it is clear that the biblical redactors were mainly interested in describing the impact of Neo-Assyrian PsW—i.e, "intelligence" understood as an activity. The biblical redactors presented the Assyrians as masters of propaganda. To enhance the impact of their propaganda, the Assyrians employed high-ranking military and administrative representatives as their propaganda agents. According to the biblical sources, their PsW masterfully combined multiple strategies, psychological tactics, and superb rhetoric. By attacking important human components such as faith, logic, feelings, and instincts, the Assyrians aimed to change the attitudes of the Judahites. By undermining both the reliability of Egypt and the authority of Hezekiah, they tried to pit Judah against Egypt, the Judahite people and their emissaries against the king, and all of them against their god. The goals of Assyrian PsW can be captured by the words of a World War I propagandist:

> In wars between peoples there must be hatred of the enemy, there must be confidence in one's own cause and one's own leaders, there must be every effort to undermine the morale of the enemy and to strike terror into him.[74]

---

[73] An Assyrian interest in monitoring cultic activities does not prove, however, that the Assyrians attempted to impose their cult in the subdued territories, see S. W. Holloway, *Aššur is King! Aššur is King!: Religion in the Exercise of Power in the Neo-Assyrian Empire* (Leiden and Boston: Brill, 2002).

[74] Rogerson, *Propaganda in the Next War*, 11.

From the biblical texts it is also possible, though indirectly, to draw some conclusions regarding the interests of Neo-Assyrian intelligence. The Neo-Assyrian intelligence services were primarily interested in obtaining information about the situation in subdued territories (political intelligence), such as the loyalty of vassals, the formation of anti-Assyrian alliances, etc. The Neo-Assyrian intelligence services also provided information necessary for preparing and leading military campaigns (military intelligence). No conclusions, however, can be drawn from the biblical texts regarding the structures by means of which the Assyrians gathered needed information.

3

Case-studies in Neo-Assyrian military and political intelligence

Analyzing the biblical texts, especially 2 Kgs 18–19, I have demonstrated that the biblical redactors presented the Assyrians as the masters of PsW. Moreover, I also proposed that, according to the biblical sources, in order to lead efficient PsW and to organize successful military campaigns, the Assyrians had to have at their disposal basic intelligence about the military capabilities of their enemies, as well as intelligence about the most recent developments in subdued territories.

The story recounted in 2 Kgs 18–19 is probably the best-known example describing Neo-Assyrian intelligence operations on the ground. The Neo-Assyrian archives unearthed in Nineveh and Nimrud have brought to light other examples of Neo-Assyrian intelligence operations. In the following two chapters I will reconstruct some of the intelligence operations that were conducted in the territory of the Neo-Assyrian Empire. For this reconstruction I will use the first-hand reports of the Neo-Assyrian intelligence officials as preserved among the Neo-Assyrian archives. Thus, we shall have at our disposal two reconstructions of Neo-Assyrian intelligence. On the one hand, the analysis of the biblical texts (chapter 2) gives us an idea of how the Neo-Assyrian intelligence services were perceived by the biblical redactors. On the other hand, the first-hand material, including both dispatches of field agents and instructions from the Assyrian royal court, gives us an idea of how Neo-Assyrian intelligence operated on the ground (chapters 3 and 4). In chapter 5 I shall compare the reconstruction of Neo-Assyrian intelligence based on the analysis of 2 Kgs 18–19 with that based on the Neo-Assyrian sources and draw conclusions regarding the significance of the reconstruction of Neo-Assyrian intelligence services for an understanding of 2 Kgs 18–19.

The goal of the following two chapters is to provide a sufficient number of case studies to illustrate what kind of information the Assyrians were interested in and how they gathered and processed it. For practical reasons, I organize these case-studies geographically, moving clockwise from northwest to southeast to consider the most influential of Assyria's neighbors: Urartu (3.1), Elam (3.2), Babylonia (3.3), and the Arabs living in the desert (3.4).

3.1 Monitoring Urarto-Assyrian conflicts

The first series of case studies deals with the activities of the Neo-Assyrian intelligence services operating along the northern frontier of Assyria, from modern Elaziğ (eastern Turkey) to Miandoab (western Iran). This frontier was under constant pressure from neighboring Urartu. The strategies used to monitor the frontier depended on the varying degrees of proximity between Assyria and Urartu: along the upper Tigris, the Assyrian provinces directly bordered Urartu, whereas farther east, Assyria and Urartu were separated by buffer states such as Šubria, Kumme, Ukku, and Mannea.

3.1.1 Urarto-Assyrian standoff in the Upper Tigris

The area of the upper Tigris forms a triangle between the modern cities of Diyarbakır, Elaziğ, and Bingöl (eastern Turkey). The limits of this triangle are set by the Euphrates and Murat Rivers in the north and the upper Tigris in the south. During his second, fifth, and tenth campaigns, Ashurnaṣirpal II gained a steady foothold in the upper Tigris and turned the city Tušhan (Ziyaret Tepe) into the capital of a new Assyrian province. Even though Ashurnaṣirpal II was unable to conquer Amidi (modern Diyarbakır), the capital of Bit-Zimani, this region acted as a loyal Assyrian vassal during the campaign of his successor Shalmaneser III in 856 B.C.E.[75] Thus, by the beginning of the ninth c. B.C.E., the Assyrians already controlled the fertile plains along the upper Tigris and had concentrated their presence in four major cities: Amidi, Sinabu, Tidu, and Tušhan. During Sarduri II's reign (764–735 B.C.E.), the Urartian kingdom expanded westward along the banks of the Euphrates. This expansion was stopped only by Tiglath-pileser III at the battle at Kummuh. The silence of Sargon II's royal inscriptions regarding the upper Tigris indicates that Sargon II did not conduct any major campaigns in this region. Judging from textual (see below) and archaeological evidence, it is possible to conclude that the Urartians dominated the banks of the Murat river and the upper Euphrates,

---

[75] Parker, *Mechanics*, 159–218 and R. B. Wartke, *Urartu: Das Reich am Ararat*, (Mainz am Rhein: P. von Zabern, 1993), 11–58.

whereas the Assyrians controlled the valleys of the upper Tigris. The distribution of the Assyrian and Urartian finds confirms this pattern. W. Kleiss's catalogue lists 19 Urartian sites along the banks of the Murat,[76] and 44 Assyrian sites were identified during B. J. Parker's survey of the upper Tigris and its tributaries: the Bohtan River (Bitlis Çay), the Garzan River (Yanarsu Çay), and the Batman River (Batman Çay).[77] However, the frontier between Urartu and Assyria did not constitute a strictly delineated border, but rather a transitional region between the upper Euphrates and the Murat River. A conflict of interests in this area resulted in armed clashes between the Urartian and Assyrian governors, forcing the inhabitants of this transitional area to change their political affiliation accordingly. Archaeological finds in Eğil and at the source of the Tigris confirm that the towns situated in this transitional area changed their overlords more then once: W. Kleiss identified an Assyrian inscription as well as an Urartian tunnel with steps in Eğil.[78] Similarly, at the source of the Tigris, close to the modern city of Lice, Tiglath-pileser I carved a rock relief[79] and Shalmaneser III erected two stelae[80] next to what W. Kleiss identified as the foundations of an Urartian fortress with a tunnel and steps.[81]

The abundant intelligence reports covering the situation in this transitional area are preserved in the correspondence of four Assyrian officials: Liphur-bel, the governor of Amidi who was in office in 705 B.C.E., Aššur-dur-paniya, the governor of Mašenu, and two officials of Tušhan, Ašipâ and Ša-Aššur-dubbu, the latter having been the governor of Tušhan in 707 B.C.E.[82] Judging from Ašipâ's greeting formula, which is identical to that of Ša-Aššur-dubbu, and from tablet V 21, in which Ašipâ refers to the Urartian province Pulua using the same determinative as Ša-Aššur-dubbu—"opposite us," B. J. Parker identified Ašipâ as a high official

[76] W. Kleiss and H. Hauptmann, *Topographische Karte von Urartu: Verzeichnis der Fundorte und Bibliographie*, (Berlin: Reimer, 1976), 9–23.
[77] Parker, *Mechanics*, 295–313.
[78] Kleiss and Hauptmann, *Topographische Karte*, 18. During my survey of the fortress I found pieces of Urartian Red-Burnished Ware.
[79] A. T. Shafer, "The Carving of an Empire: Neo-Assyrian Monuments on the Periphery" (Ph.D. diss., Harvard University, 1998), 334.
[80] Ibid., 184–88.
[81] Kleiss and Hauptmann, *Topographische Karte*, 21.
[82] SAAS II, 48.

of Tušhan.[83] Liphur-Bel's intelligence reports covering the developments on the Urartian western frontier can be dated to the reign of Argišti II (V 3:15). Since Liphur-Bel's letters indicate that his governorship overlapped with the terms of Ašipâ and Ša-Aššur-dubbu (V 15:r.2 and 4:r.1 respectively), it can be safely concluded that all three Neo-Assyrian officials were in office during the reign of the Urartian king Argišti II.[84]

The spectrum of events that these Assyrian officials reported on varied from solely administrative matters such as agriculture (V 3:r.19-20; 21:18-21), water problems (V 26), building activities (V 15:r.5-12), tax collection,[85] and logging, to intelligence briefings on the Urartian mobilization and reports of spies sent out to reconnoiter in Urartu (see below).

---

[83] Parker, *Mechanics*, 224. S. Parpola suggested that Ašipâ's "seat of office was the neighboring city Tidu"; SAA V, XXXIV. K. Kessler convincingly argued that Tidu was part of Amidi province; see K. Kessler, *Untersuchungen zur historischen Topographie Nordmesopotamiens: Nach keilschriftlichen Quellen d. 1. Jahrtausends v. Chr.* (Wiesbaden: Reichert, 1980), 99–105. If both B. J. Parker and K. Kessler are correct, then Ašipâ could not have been the governor of Tidu.

[84] B. J. Parker dates Ašipâ's letter V 21 to the period preceding Sargon II's eighth campaign in 714 B.C.E. The reason for such a claim is that the year 714 B.C.E. marked the decline of Urartu and therefore the imminent Urartian threat described in V 2 would have been typical for the Urartian king Rusa II before 714 B.C.E. but not after 714 B.C.E., when the Urartian kingdom passed its prime; see Parker, *Mechanics*, 222–23. I prefer to date letter V 21 and the rest of Ašipâ's correspondence to the period after 714 B.C.E., i.e., to the period of Argišti II's attempt to reconquer the territories lost to Assyria. This claim can be supported by the following arguments: first, according to the correspondence of Liphur-Bel, whose eponym is 705 B.C.E., the Urartian governor opposite Liphur-Bel not only dared to defy Sargon II's messengers but also captured some Assyrian fortresses (V 2) and threatened the Amidi province by positioning his troops along the Urarto-Assyrian frontier (V 3). These two letters prove that the Urartians also posed a serious threat to the Assyrian installations along the Upper Tigris after 714 B.C.E.; see SAA V, XV and M. Salvini, *Geschichte und Kultur der Urartäer* (Darmstadt: Wissenschaftliche Buchgesellschaft, 1995), 101–2. Second, Ašipâ is mentioned as a contemporary of Liphur-Bel (V 15:r.2); Liphur-bel purchased from Ašipâ's subjects some fields on which he built a city and fortress. This purchase happened "[x] years" before letter V 15 was send to the king, but after Liphur-Bel became the governor of Amidi (eponym 705 B.C.E.). These facts indicate that the border tension described in V 21 should be dated after 714 B.C.E. and attributed to Argišti II, who did his best to reconsolidate a kingdom heavily shaken by Sargon II's eighth campaign.

[85] Taxes in the form of straw and barley as well, as exemption from taxes, are mentioned in V 16.

As far as the extant reports permit us to conclude, Urarto-Assyrian relations alternated between standoffs in which both parties respected each other's territorial sovereignty (V 1) and overt armed conflicts such as the Pulua (V 21) and Harda crises (V 2 and 3). Thus, the main task of the Assyrian officials was to monitor the Urartian frontier and to warn the royal court about an impending insurrection (V 33).

3.1.1.1 Report on the Pulua crisis

A report on the Pulua[86] crisis has been preserved in the form of Ašipâ's dispatch:

> The 'third man' of the king, my lord, who came, told me: "Your guard should be strong!" The guard is very strong.
> Three governors in Pulua and another three in Danibani are gathered with pack animals opposite us. We are keeping watch opposite them. All the people are inside fortified places; the oxen and sheep are on this side [o]f the river. We are standing by and keeping wa[tch] in [...]. (V 21:7–22)

According to lines V 21:7–9, this report is only one among many reports informing the court about the tension on the Urarto-Assyrian frontier. The king was already well aware of the escalating tension and ordered Ašipâ to keep a close eye on events. Watching carefully, he provided the royal court with the following intelligence: six Urartian governors with pack animals took their position along the banks of the Murat; thus he communicated intelligence on the rank, number and location of the Urartian military commanders and on the combatant core of the Urartian troops. The last information provided by Ašipâ was an account of his defensive countermeasures: he moved his people into the fortified places and the domestic animals to the other side of the river (most likely the Tigris). Furthermore, he strengthened his guard and took advantage of the situation by asking the king to supply another five hundred men from Guzana to enforce his own guard (V 21:r.15-20).

[86] K. Kessler has suggested that ancient Pulua be identified with the modern city of Palu; see Kessler, *Untersuchungen*, 65.

3.1.1.2 The Harda crisis

Three reports relating a similar escalation of tension in Harda came from the governor of Amidi, Liphur-Bel (V 1, 2, 3). Information about the crisis was acquired from two sources: a diplomatic envoy and spies.

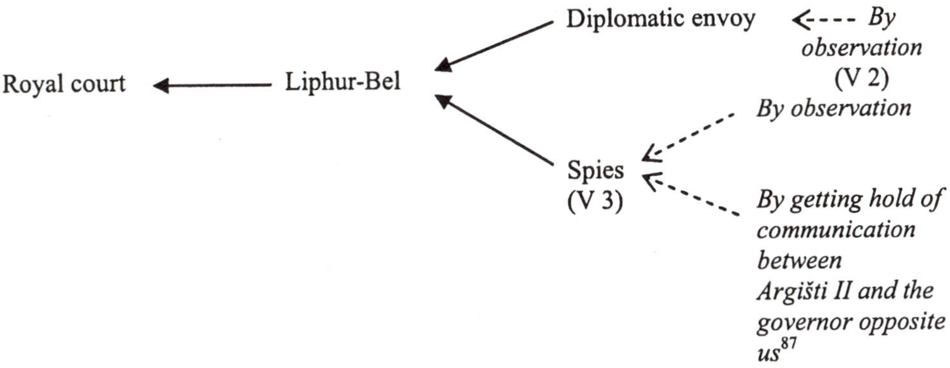

Figure 1. Information flow related to Harda crisis

Table 2. Comparison of the contents of tablet V 2 and V 3

	Tablet V 2	Tablet V 3
Commanders	The governor opposite me (Liphur-Bel) is in Harda.	The governor opposite us (Liphur-Bel and his officials) and his deputy governor are in Harda.
Army	His troops are assembled with him in Harda.	Levied troops are positioned town by town in battle array as at Ṭurušpa; the Urartian king ordered them to stop working and feed their horses.

The development of the crisis can be sketched as follows. The Urartians made a foray into the territory under Assyrian control and captured some border fortresses (V 2). The foray was organized under the auspices of the Urartian governor and his deputy "opposite" Amidi province

[87] This interpretation is based on Deller's translation: "*Ein Bote des Argišti ist (zu dem 'Statthalter') gekommen (mit folgender Nachricht)*"; K. Deller, "Ausgewählte neuassyriche Briefe betreffend Urartu zur Zeit Sargons II," in *Tra lo Zagros e l'Urmia: Ricerche Storiche ed Archeologiche nell'Azerbaigian Iraniano*, ed. P. E. Pecorella and M. Salvini (Roma: Edizioni dell'Ateneo, 1984), 113.

(V 2:8; 3:9). The Urartian city of Harda[88] became the center in which the Urartian troops were assembled and from which the Urartian frontier was closely watched.

As for the extent of the foray, it was not a simple local border clash. Liphur-bel reported that the "levied (Urartian) troops are positioned town by town in battle array as far as Ṭurušpa" (V 3:13–14). The mobilization was ordered by the Urartian king himself: "As to the work I ordered you (the governor of Harda)[89] to do, don't do it! Feed your horses until I send you a messenger!" (V 3:16–20). This interruption of assigned work constituted a clear warning that an attack could shortly befall the Assyrians.

Lines V 3:13–14 of Liphur-bel's briefing can be illuminated by V. Sevin's archaeological survey,[90] which demonstrated that during the second

---

[88] In order to locate the city of Harda, it is first necessary to locate the Urartian province involved in the Harda crisis. The location of this Urartian province is determined by the position of the Assyrian governor responsible for the Harda crisis, Liphur-Bel, because this Urartian province was opposite the Assyrian province governed by Liphur-Bel. Consequently, this Urartian province might have been located within the valleys spread out along the road connecting Elaziğ with Bingöl. The Asvan and Keban archaeological projects as well as surveys in these valleys have provided a sufficient amount of Urartian finds to prove that the region flourished during the Iron Age; see for example R. Duru, *Keban Projesi Degirmentepe Kazisi 1973; Keban Project Degirmentepe Excavations 1973*, ed. Projesi Keban Bölgesi Tarihî Kurtarma ve Degerlendirme (Ankara: Türk Tarih Kurumu Basimevi, 1979), D. A. Günay, *Keban Baraj Gölü Yöresi Halkbilim Arastirmalari*, 1. baski. (Ankara: Türk Tarih Kurumu Basimevi, 1980); A. McNicoll and R. Fletcher, *Taskun Kale: Keban Rescue Excavations, Eastern Anatolia* (Oxford, England: B.A.R., 1983), S. Mitchell, *Asvan Kale: Keban Rescue Excavations, Eastern Anatolia* (Oxford, England: B.A.R., 1980) and Y. A. Shibl, *The Aswan High Dam* (Beirut: Arab Institute for Research and Publishing, 1971). Because of the mountain ranges that separated the Assyrian and Urartian settlements, such a foray could have occurred only along two roads: first, along the ancient road connecting Malatya (ancient Melidi) with Diyarbakır (ancient Amidi); second, along the road connecting modern Bingöl with Diyarbakır. Since the latter passes through Šubrian territory, which was under the control of Tušhan province, the former route is preferred by the present author (the modern road linking Malatya, Elaziğ, Maden, Ergani, and Diyarbakır). Only limited survey material is available for this region; however, the presence of Assyrian fortresses overseeing the major trade and logging road (see below) around the Maden river (upper Tigris, Dicle) can be logically assumed. For this reason, we may assume that the crisis as described in these tablets refers to the escalating tension along the Maden river.

[89] "*... zu dem Statthalter;*" see ibid.

[90] V. Sevin, "The Oldest Highway: Between the Regions of Van Elaziğ in Eastern Anatolia," *Antiquity* 62 (1988).

half of the eighth c. B.C.E. the Urartians built a highway connecting their westernmost peripheries with the Lake Van region. For the most part, this ancient highway followed the modern highway: it started at Elaziğ, crossed the Murat at Palu, then ran northwards to Bingöl. The bridges identified by V. Sevin's survey in the Bingöl Dağ (a range of mountains about 3,000 m high) indicate that the Urartians were able to overcome this natural obstacle, and their highway wound through the rocky terrain to connect the Bingöl valley with the Muş province. A series of forts and fortresses, constructed at intervals of 30–35 km, secured this highway. Thus, the positioning of "the troops town by town in the battle array" (V 3:13) most likely entailed the mobilization of the forts, fortresses, and fortified cities located along the highway connecting Elaziğ with Lake Van and consequently with the Urartian capital, Ṭurušpa. The road stations, when put on high alert, assured fast communication between Ṭurušpa and the western peripheries and could facilitate the transport of the Urartian army to the west, in case the Assyrians decided to retaliate.

On the basis of the extant written sources, the Assyrians did not retaliate, but limited their response to negotiations (V 2) and strengthening their guards. Liphur-Bel was ordered to send his messengers to reproach the Urartian governor for violating the Urarto-Assyrian treaty: "Why do you capture our forts, while we are at peace?" (V 2:12–15). The arrogant answer of the Urartian governor indicates that Liphur-Bel's mission failed.

3.1.1.3 Logging problems

Urartian expansion southwards resulted in the loss of some Assyrian fortresses. One of the purposes of such fortresses was to secure water transportation for logs, as depicted on two Neo-Assyrian reliefs from Khorsabad,[91] demonstrated by the location of the Eğil fortress, and described in the Eziat episode (see 3.1.1.3.1). The Assyrians and Urartians were probably interested in this relatively remote district (the triangle formed by Ziyaret Tepe, Elaziğ, and Bingöl) because the region was traditionally considered one of the richest resources of raw materials such as timber and metal. Logging for the purposes of the acquisition of timber, necessary for the construction of buildings and used as a fuel for smelting ore, had been documented since the third millennium B.C.E.[92] Since no

[91] See *Monument de Ninive*, pl. 32, 34.

[92] M. B. Rowton, "The Woodlands of Ancient Western Asia," *JNES* 26 (1967).

dramatic climactic change can be supposed in this area during the last 4,000 years,[93] the area between the Murat and the upper Tigris must have contained undisturbed forest, and thus it is possible to reconstruct, at least partly, the ecological habitat inherited by the first millennium B.C.E. inhabitants of this region. The region south of the upper Tigris around modern Urfa and Adiyaman had been deforested for some centuries and used for the cultivation of crops, whereas the area north of the upper Tigris–including the Ziyaret Tepe-Elaziğ-Bingöl triangle–was still forested by oak and poplar.[94]

Textual evidence referring to Assyrian logging (V 3; 4; 5; 6; 7; 8; 25; 32; 33; 34; 39; 43) proves that Sargon II's administration not only knew about these timber resources, but also duly took advantage of them. In Sargon II's time, timber represented an indispensable raw resource necessary for the military industry in particular, for building chariots, siege shields, siege machines, and battering rams. However, Sargon II's interest

---

[93] W. van Zeist, R. W. Timmers, and S. Bottema, "Studies of Modern and Holocene Pollen Precipitation in Southern Turkey," *Palaeohistoria* 14 (1968): 37.

[94] Excavations conducted on four sites in the area of Asvan near modern Elaziğ have produced a large quantity of charcoal recovered by water-sieving and trench-sampling. Analysis of charcoal of the Chalcolitic, Early Bronze, and Hellenistic layers demonstrated that the habitat consisted mainly of *Quercus, Salicaceae,* and *Ulmaceae*; see G. H. Willcox, "A History of Deforestation as Indicated by Charcoal Analysis of Four Sites in Eastern Anatolia," *AS* 24 (1974): 128. A research team under the leadership of W. van Zeist reached similar results by analyzing the pollen seeds from the sediment core taken from Lake Gölbasi and Bozova (south of the Tigris). The area contained undisturbed forest consisting of oak, juniper, and pistachio until the beginning of the second millennium. The sediments dated by carbon analysis to the second millennium displayed a significant drop in pollen counts, indicating the gradual disappearance of the forest. Since no dramatic climactic changes are attested between the third and the second millennium B.C.E., W. van Zeist suggested that such a decrease in forestation was caused by human agency; see van Zeist, Timmers, and Bottema, "Pollen Precipitation," 38. W. van Zeist's team also analyzed surface samples in the area between the Murat and the upper Tigris. The best-represented species were oak, juniper, and pistachio; see ibid., fig. 2. The mapping of the forested area as reconstructed from data of the nineteenth c. C.E. and from military maps of the Soviet Union dated to 1942 indicates that the area between the Murat and the upper Tigris was still forested in the nineteenth and twentieth c. C.E.; see A. J. Tsvetkov, "Turtsija; J-37-X, XI, XVI, XVII, XXI, XXIII" (Moscow: Generalnij Shtab, 1942). Even though there is little data available on the eighth c. B.C.E., undisturbed forest has been sufficiently attested for the second millennium, Hellenistic period, and the nineteenth c. C.E. Since no radical climactic change can be proved in the last 4,000 years, then one can reasonably infer that the area in question was forested during Sargon II's reign.

[94] van Zeist, Timmers, and Bottema, "Pollen Precipitation," 37.

was, above all, in timber suitable for his colossal construction projects. Oak and poplar, growing in this transitional frontier area, were particularly suitable as roofbeams (GIŠ.ÙR=*gušūru*) and door-beams (GIŠ.ŠÚ.A=*šibšutu*) able to span even large halls.[95] The high numbers of door-beams (2,000 in V 7, [*1*],200 in V 6, and 3,000 in V 26) and roofbeams (500 in V 7, [*1*],200 in V 6, 500 in V 33, 500 and [*x* thousand *x*] hundred in V 34) prepared for transport, as well as the high number of woodcutters deployed in the mountains ("all my people" in V 25:r.4'-7' and 100 men in V 33:r.9'), indicate that Sargon II's troops were clear-cutting the forest.

Sargon II's logging did not differ greatly from early-twentieth-century C.E. logging.[96] First, Sargon II's inspectors were sent out to evaluate the quality of the wood and count the suitable trees (I 100 and 101). According to I 100, the trees were divided into five categories: heavy beams (the highest quality); second-, third-, and fourth-size trees; and damaged trees. Selected trees were cut down by troops of woodcutters (LÚ.*na-ki-su-te;* I 98:11). After cutting down the trees, haulers dragged and piled the timber at river banks.[97] The logs were then thrown into the river and floated down to one of the fortified installations where the logs were stacked, counted, and transported to one of the major centers.[98] There the

---

[95] Both species are even now used for the construction of the houses; Willcox, "History of Deforestation," 121. V 294 provides a list of the trees needed for the construction (probably destined for Dur Šarrukin).

[96] This claim is based on the comparison of textual evidence, in particular V 33, with the personal communication of a woodcutter named Roy in Allagash Forest, Maine, in August 2003.

[97] As was also the case for the woodcutters at the beginning of the twentieth c. C.E., the timbers had to be ready before "melting snow in the high mountains provided ample water to allow a successful drive"; see Parker, *Mechanics*, 227. For this reason, troops of woodcutters also worked in the winter and the log-driving season was restricted to the spring.

[98] The stages of log transportation are differentiated linguistically by the usage of several technical verbs: for the whole process of transportation, the G-form of the verb *zabālu* 'to transport' is used (V 25:r.3'; 34:r.7); for the prior inspection of the trees, the G-form of the verb *amāru* 'to see' is used (V 34:r.29; I 62:6; I 98:10); for the selection of the trees, the G-form of the verb *nasāqu* 'to select, to choose' is used (V 33:r.3'–4'); for cutting down the trees, the G-form of the verb *nakāsu* 'to cut' is used (V 25:r.7'; 33:5'; 34:r.6.19); for dragging the trees to the riverbanks, the G-from of the verb *šadādu* 'to haul' is used (V 8:r.5'; 127:10); and for piling the trees on the riverbanks, the G-form of the verb *karāru* 'to lay' is used (V 33:6'). Two different stages of timber's progress in the water are distinguished by the expression *ina nāri karāru*, "to throw into the river," (V 33:10') (in

logs were bound into rafts similar to Arab keleks[99] or loaded on boats. Two reliefs of Khorsabad in the Louvre[100] depict flotillas loaded with wood driving logs to ports in the Assyrian heartland where they were unloaded and towed, if necessary, to their final destination (I 63; 100–2).

Because of the strategic value of the timber, the reports on logging listed above not only were administrative records, but conveyed to the royal court engaged in building a new capital, Dur-Šarrukin, important strategic intelligence concerning access to a key natural resource. This may be illustrated by the case of the Eziat crisis.

3.1.1.3.1 Eziat crisis

Three reports mentioning Eziat (V 3:r.1–9; 4; 5) recount the successful solution of difficulties with log transport. When enemy troops withheld logs in Eziat, Liphur-Bel sent a group of soldiers, under the command of the village inspector, to get the logs moving.[101] The quarrel evolved into an armed conflict that cost the Assyrians nine soldiers who, together with the deputy of the village inspector, were shot by bows whereas the Assyrians wounded only three enemy soldiers (V 3:r.1–9). Liphur-Bel, in order to secure the fortified installation against further problems, moved 90 soldiers to Eziat fortress (V 5). Information about the development and the results of the crisis was obtained from the report of the soldiers returning from the combat—a first-hand post-factum briefing that Liphur-Bel forwarded to the royal court.

Eziat was situated on the bank of a river which, at least during the spring, contained enough water to float the logs (V 3; 4).[102] The Assyrian

---

contrast with *ina šiddi nāri karāru*, "to pile at the bank of the river") and the Š-form of *etāqu* 'to float' (V 3:r.4; 4:r.9; I 63:r.12).

[99] Parker, *Mechanics*, 81–82.

[100] See *Monument de Ninive*, pl. 34, 35.

[101] The omission of the typical phrase "what are the king's orders" indicates that the solution of this local problem was left to Liphur-Bel, who did not fail to resolve it.

[102] The location of Eziat can be narrowed down as follows. The report on the Eziat logging crisis came from the governor of Amidi. Since none of his extant reports (twenty letters) deals with logging problems in Šubria, it seems that Liphur-bel reported on logging problems in the area northwest of Amidi (Diyarbakır), whereas Ašipâ and Ša-Aššur-dubbu reported on logging problems in the Šubrian territory (the logs were floated down the Batman, Garzin, and Bohtan Rivers). From the geographical point of view, the contents of the reports follow the administrative division of the area into the Amidi and Tušhan

installation in Eziat contained a large watchtower able to house at least sixty soldiers (V 5). Thus, the site would qualify as one of the fortified installations in the upper Tigris area. The news that this strategically important fortress had fallen into enemy hands meant not only that Urartu had extended its dominion further south,[103] but also that access to such a key strategic raw material as timber was now seriously obstructed.

3.1.2 Untangling Šubrian foreign policy

The second series of case studies on intelligence services operating along the northern frontier of Assyria will deal with Šubria, the territory between the Batman River and the Ambar Çay. These case studies demonstrate how closely the Assyrians monitored their vassal kings. Thanks to the reports, which Assyrian provincial officials sent to the royal court, the Assyrians were able to see through the tangled web of Šubrian foreign policy. Since Assyrian vassals and collaborators were required to turn over runaways, the way in which the Šubrian king Hu-Tešub dealt with Assyrian runaways became the tell-tale indicator of his declining loyalty.[104]

The Assyrian officials governing this area experienced an ongoing problem of desertion among their subordinates. The two most common types of runaways were military personnel and forced laborers (V 52:16–r.1). Since the runaways were not only single individuals, but also entire groups, a large desertion could have a devastating effect on the Assyrian provinces. The Neo-Assyrian archives preserve reports on two large

---

provinces. The rivers Ambar Çay (northern tributary of the Tigris) and Göksu Çay (southern tributary of the Tigris) formed a natural frontier between the two provinces; see Kessler, *Untersuchungen*, 121. Study of the maps covering the area of the upper Tigris and my survey of the region indicate that the forested region would have corresponded to the area around the upper Tigris (the Maden River) and its northern tributaries, Hançayı Çay, Yalnızdanılar Çay, and Berklin Çay. The dams on the upper Tigris prohibit any conclusions regarding the water volume of the latter two rivers (Yalnızdanılar Çay and Berklin Çay). My survey of Hançayı Çay, conducted during the late spring of 2004, indicates that its water table, especially during spring, contains enough water to float the logs. Furthermore the surrounding hills, even though now scarcely forested, still contain poplar and oak. Consequently, the Eziat fortress should be sought on the banks of the upper Tigris and its three tributaries. From among these rivers, Hançayı Çay is the best candidate.

[103] Since the Harda crisis and the Eziat conflict are reported in the same letter (V 3), it is possible to assume that the crises were connected.

[104] The Assyrian vassals were often bound by treaty to surrender fugitives (II 1:13–4). Consequently, by falling short in this duty, vassals were guilty of breaking the treaty.

desertions. During the first one Ša-Aššur-dubbu, the governor of Tušhan, lost at least fifty people:

> [in] (the month of) Kanun (X), 10 soldiers, (all) cavalrymen, deserted there (to Šubria); [recently], 40 soldiers from [...]ri took their people with them, pulled out their grinding slabs, and went there. (V 35:r.1–6)

Another large desertion was reported from Halziatbar province. Aššur-belu-da''in, probably the governor of Halziatbar, forwarded the desperate report of his mule stable attendant, who said that more then four hundred people escaped:

> The mule stable attendant whom I (Aššur-belu-da''in) brought forth in search of the runaway people of the country has brought forth men from my neighborhood and given them to me. All Halziatbareans have run away in great numbers and are (scattered) all over the countries. The mule stable attendant is desperate, saying: "It is an impasse."
> Now Nabû'a, the mule stable attendant who was appointed in charge of the Chaldeans, has brought me 380 persons; a number of them remain in Yasumu[105] and in Bit-Zamani. (V 79:4–r.6)

The large number of runaway laborers and soldiers were not only a loss as such to Assyria; they could also be interrogated by her adversaries to obtain valuable information on Assyria. For this reason, Assyria's enemies and their allies willingly offered asylum to the Assyrian runaways. The same was true in reverse. The Assyrians willingly offered shelter to Urartian runaways, from whom they obtained necessary information. Therefore, both powers exercised high pressure on the buffer states caught between them to hand over enemy runaways and to return their own runaways. In consequence, treatment of Assyrian and Urartian runaways was a good indicator of how loyal a given buffer state was to Assyria. A good example of such a buffer state is Šubria. The following episodes bear witness not only to how difficult it was for Šubria to maneuver between these two

105 S. Parpola identified Yasumu with modern Karaça Dağ, a mountain 1,957 m high situated about 50 km east of the ancient provincial center Amidi (modern Diyarbakır); see SAA V, 246.

powers, but also to how closely the Assyrians monitored Šubrian runaway policy.

3.1.2.1 Ambush (V 32, 33)

Some Assyrian runaways were held in the Šubrian city of Penza. After some negotiation, the Assyrian delegation, consisting of four officials and six soldiers, departed to escort the runaways back to Assyria. The runaways were handed over to the Assyrians, and the pact was sealed by a ritual meal in which the brother of the Šubrian king also took part. After dining together, the escort set out for Assyria. To their surprise, the Assyrians found themselves ambushed by the Šubrians shortly after their departure.[106] The fight with the Šubrians ended in the capture of six Assyrian soldiers and two officials; out of ten Assyrians escorting the runaways, only two cohort commanders managed to escape. Ša-Aššur-dubbu, who was responsible for the whole transaction, immediately sent a letter to the Šubrian king asking him to release the Assyrian soldiers without delay. Though Hu-Tešub refused to assume responsibility for the ambush, he assured Ša-Aššur-dubbu that the matter would be investigated, and that if the Assyrians were found in his country, they would be returned to Ša-Aššur-dubbu. Such a downplaying of the event spurred Ša-Aššur-dubbu to undertake his own investigation, during which he found out that the captured soldiers had been already moved to one of Hu-Tešub's fortresses. The result of his investigation was reported to the Assyrian king, who recommended taking a severe countermeasure: to kidnap the same number of Šubrians.[107] Unfortunately, the Neo-Assyrian archives do not

---

[106] KUR.*šub-ri-a-a šu-ub-tú ina pa-na-*⌜*tú*⌝*-š*[*ú-nu*], "the Šubrians were ambushing [them] from ahead" (see also I 244:9). Contrast the expression denoting ambush from behind: [... *šu*]*b-tú ina ku-ta-li-ni* [*ú-se-ši*]*b*, "they ambushed us from behind" (I 175:16). Thus, the Šubrian ambushers took the Assyrians by surprise in a frontal attack (see I 244:8–10).

[107] Different governments have taken different countermeasures against similar terrorist and paramilitary acts. An "interesting" countermeasure was taken by the Soviets in 1984 when a Shia Muslim faction in Beirut kidnapped several officials of the Soviet Embassy: some members of Syrian intelligence (at that time closely collaborating with the KGB) "kidnapped a member of that faction. The following day his family received his severed genitals, and word spread in the neighborhood where he had lived that if the Soviet officials were not released immediately, Syrian forces would turn that neighborhood into another Hama–Syria's third largest city, a large part of which the regime of Hafez Assad turned to rubble in 1981. The Soviets were released forthwith." Codevilla, *Informing Statecraft*, 47.

preserve further tablets enabling us to evaluate the efficiency of this Assyrian countermeasure.

3.1.2.2 Asylum for an assassin (V 53)

An Assyrian military official (a commander-of-fifty), commanding a unit composed of Gurrean soldiers (an Aramean tribe), assassinated the mayor of the city of Meturna. Then, he and his people stopped performing their work (*dullu* 'service') and shortly after, together with fifteen soldiers, he left for Urartu. Aššur-dur-paniya, the governor of Masennu, immediately ordered Il-dalâ to arrest the fugitives.[108] Diligent searching through the mountains and mountain passes was to no avail. Finally, Il-dalâ learned that the trespassers had found shelter in one of the royal fortresses belonging to the Šubrian king.[109] Negotiations with the assassin brought no result. On the contrary, the trespassers, aided by a hundred Šubrian soldiers, attacked Il-dalâ's troops on the road. Since the Assyrian soldiers were on high alert, they wounded the assassin (the commander-of-fifty), but no Assyrian life was lost. Further negotiations with the Šubrians about the extradition of the trespassers caused Aššur-dur-panyia another frustration: the Šubrians agreed to hand over the trespassers, but instead of handing over the assassin and his companions, they handed over "old subjects of the king, my lord, who have been living there" (V 53:r.9–11).

3.1.2.3 Hu-Tešub the god-fearer (V 35)

The ambiguous policy of Hu-Tešub, the king of Šubria, was reflected in the different treatment of Urartian and Assyrian runaways. Lines V 35:15–16[110] indicate that the Assyrians made an attempt to capture

---

[108] The tablet permits a reconstruction of hierarchical relationships among the subjects: Aššur-dur-panyia > Il-dalâ > mayor of Meturna > the commander-of-fifty. Such a reconstruction is based on the use of possessive pronouns: Aššur-dur-paniya called the commander-of-fifty "my commander-of-fifty" (V 52:27) and at the same time he called the rebels "your (Il-dalâ's) servants" (V 52:12). Since Aššur-dur-paniya gave orders to Il-dalâ, he must have been Il-dalâ's superior.

[109] The expression ᵐDINGIR–*da-la-a e-ta-am-m*[*a*]*r-šú,* "Il-dalâ saw him (the commander-of-fifty)," employing the verb *amāru* 'to see', which is often used to describe spies' activity, suggests that this information might have been acquired as the result of intelligence activity.

[110] Letter V 35 is a summary of several events that can be individuated as follows:

an Assyrian runaway who was hiding in Šubria. The attempt failed because the Šubrians defended the Assyrian runaway with force. The case of an escaped Urartian chief-scout, who might have been a priceless source of information on Urartu, had an even more unfortunate outcome. The Šubrians, instead of handing him over to Assyria, captured him, "put iron shackles to his arms and feet and returned him to the [Urarti]an (king)" (V 35:27–29). Hu-Tešub justified his actions by citing his fear of the gods.[111] Such an answer coming from Hu-Tešub's mouth upset Ša-Aššur-dubbu, who denounced his falsehood and called him names—because it was the same "god-fearer" Hu-Tešub who did not hesitate to offer shelter to the Assyrian runaways.

3.1.2.4 Sick king (V 35; 52)

Ša-Aššur-dubbu took due advantage of Hu-Tešub's deteriorating health. His angry letter denouncing Hu-Tešub's falsehood hit the nail right on the head. Though unwillingly, Hu-Tešub, swearing in the Šubrian language, finally conceded and handed over the Assyrian runaways (V 35:r.11–12).

While Hu-Tešub was sick, some Šubrians showed up in Šabirešu willing to negotiate the extradition of the Assyrian runaways who had escaped during the previous three years (V 52). The emissaries were not the brother of the Šubrian king and his deputy, as Ša-Aššur-dubbu expected, but

---

- An Assyrian attempt to capture a runaway was frustrated by the Šubrians, who did not hesitate to use force to prevent the Assyrians from meddling in their affairs (V 35:15–16).
- The Assyrians protested against the protection that Hu-Tešub provided for the Urartian deserters (V 35:17–22).
- Hu-Tešub justified his act by a pious lie: "I fear the gods" (V 35:23).
- Ša-Aššur-dubbu denounced Hu-Tešub's falseness and called him names (V 35:30–32).
- A large group of Assyrian soldiers deserted to Šubria (V 35:35–r.6).
- Ša-Aššur-dubbu learned about Hu-Tešub's illness and asked him to extradite the runaways (V 35:r.8–9).
- Hu-Tešub unwillingly consented (V 35:r.10–11).

[111] Most likely having made a treaty with Urartu, Hu-Tešub swore by the name of his gods to extradite Urartian fugitives.

two low-ranking officials from the towns near the Urartian border.[112] This and Aššur-dur-paniya's previous experience with the Šubrians were the reason why he recommended caution: "They (the Šubrian emissaries) are coming (to the royal court), but (when) they read the said tablet to the king, my lord, it is not the whole truth" (V 52:r.10–11).

To conclude, the Assyrians were well-informed about Hu-Tešub's double standard: in dealing with the Urartians, he voluntarily handed the Urartian runaways back to Urartu and prevented the Assyrians from getting hold of valuable sources of information, but when dealing with the Assyrians, he found all kinds of excuses not to return the runaways to Assyria. Thus, many of the Assyrian runaways found asylum under the protective wing of the Šubrian king who hid them and gave "them fields, gardens and houses, (and) settle(d) them in his country" (V 52:r.5–6).[113]

A double standard in dealing with runaways was only one aspect of Hu-Tešub's ambivalent foreign policy. As a buffer state, Šubria was obliged to keep both lords satisfied, at least outwardly: on the one hand, Hu-Tešub compiled a detailed report for the Urartian king,[114] but on the other hand, he sent to the Assyrian king a report on the Urartian invasion of Mannea, indicating Urartu's intention to attack Zikirtu, as well as a report on the troops dispatched in Hubuškia (V 45; 44 respectively). Moreover, he had to maintain the impression of good diplomatic relations with both powers; and so just as he welcomed the emissaries coming from Urartu (35:33–34), he also sent his emissaries to Assyria (V 40:r.2–3; probably V 31[115] and V 75:4–6).

Had Assyrian knowledge of Šubrian affairs been limited simply to the impression that Hu-Tešub had created through his diplomatic relations with Assyria, Hu-Tešub would have been perceived as a faithful Assyrian

[112] The fact that these two low-ranking officials could hardly represent the Šubrian interest is further underlined by their origin. Their names, Yata and Abi-yaqa, were Aramean, whereas Hu-Tešub was a Hurrian name; see Parker, *Mechanics*, 230.

[113] According to S. Parpola Šubria became "the sanctuary for fugitives"; SAA V, 48.

[114] V 25; see Parker, *Mechanics*, 229.

[115] *"In ihm wird geschildert, dass der Statthalter der assyrischen Provinz Tušhan* (Ša-Aššur-dubbu) *in diplomatischen Kontakt zu Šupria stand"*; see Kessler, *Untersuchungen*, 107–8. Unfortunately, the tablet is too damaged to prove K. Kessler's claim.

vassal. He paid due respect to the king,[116] he promptly answered the king's questions, he informed the king about whatever he had heard (V 45:3–8), and he sent his emissaries to the king as royal etiquette required (V 40; 75). Naturally, he had nothing to do with ambushing the Assyrian escort and he even showed his good will by investigating the event. However, it was the Neo-Assyrian intelligence network that was able to show that Hu-Tešub was two-faced. The provincial officials disclosed that Hu-Tešub was behind the ambush of the Assyrian escort and the arrest of another messenger (V 31:r.22'–4'), and that he maintained intensive diplomatic relations with Urartu,[117] applied a double standard in dealing with runaways, and was reluctant to collaborate in logging (V 34:r.3–7). Thanks to this information, the Assyrian royal court was aware that, at least during a certain period, Hu-Tešub, despite his overtly good relations with Assyria, was favoring Urartu. Knowing this, the Assyrians could exercise caution when relying on his reports and dealing with the Šubrian emissaries. Unfortunately, there are no extant reports on the basis of which we could reconstruct how this knowledge affected Assyrian tactics and strategy toward Šubria.

3.1.3 Monitoring buffer states and regions

The third series of case studies deals with Kumme and Ukku, located north of modern Cizre along the Hizel Çay.

3.1.3.1 Historical introduction

During the lull before Tiglath-pileser III ascended the Assyrian throne, Urartu, under the kingship of Sarduri II, had expanded its influence over Kumme, Ukku, and Ulluba. Tiglath-pileser III's defeat of the Urartian troops in Ulluba marked the definitive change of overlordship in the Cizre Valley (ancient Ulluba). The Assyrians settled down in Ulluba, built two administrative centers (Aššur-iqiša and Šabirešu), and set up a few smaller garrisons.[118] The royal palace in Aššur-iqiša became the seat of a newly appointed governor over the region. Šabirešu[119] became the junction of two

[116] He greeted the Assyrian king: "The very best health to the king, my lord. Your servant Hu-Tešub" (V 44:1–2; 45:1–2).
[117] The Urartian king gave orders to a Šubrian priest (V 31:6–11). Moreover, lines v 25:7–9 can be interpreted as a report compiled by the Šubrian king for the Urartian king; see Parker, *Mechanics*, 229.
[118] Parker, *Mechanics*, 78.
[119] B. J. Parker identifies it with Basorin Höyük; see ibid., 79.

major trade routes and an important crossing point on the Tigris. The entire region was attached to the Masennu province and governed by Ṭab-šar-Aššur, the treasurer (LÚ.IGI.DUB=*masennu*). The Cizre Valley was repopulated by Phoenician and Syrian deportees[120] in order to turn the fertile plains of Ulluba into a new source of grain, as indicated by archaeological surveys of the Cizre plain. These surveys demonstrated the presence of several larger sites and numerous smaller sites whereas medium-size sites were absent. B. J. Parker suggested that the larger sites housed the Assyrian administration, whereas the smaller sites contained the houses of deportees working in the fields.[121]

The entire region was monitored by three top Assyrian officials: Sennacherib (the crown prince), Ṭab-šar-Aššur (the treasurer), and Gaba-ana-Aššur (the palace herald). However, the most important source of information was Aššur-reṣuwa (the Assyrian delegate in Kumme), who reported directly to the king and was also in close contact with other officials (V 113). Besides the Assyrian officials, other sources of information were the Kummean vassal king Arije, the Kummean high official Ariṣa, and the Ukkean king.

3.1.3.2 Kumme

Kumme was situated northwest of Ulluba. During Sargon II's reign it became a full-fledged Assyrian vassal, and the Kummean royal family was granted the privilege of staying in power.[122] As a full-fledged vassal, the Kummean king Arije had to pay tribute, draft soldiers for the Assyrian military campaigns, and keep his Assyrian lords posted about the political situation in the region. The royal delegate Aššur-reṣuwa and several Assyrian garrisons scattered around the country made sure that Assyrian interests were faithfully pursued. The Assyrians felt free to build new fortresses, exploit Kummean natural resources, namely timber (V 111), and relocate its inhabitants (V 105 and I 233).

---

[120] Ibid., 54.
[121] Ibid., 83.
[122] Ibid., 90.

3.1.3.2.1 Revolt

Heavy Assyrian demands on the local economy[123] and the careless relocation of people from one place to another lay at the roots of an uprising in Kumme. The first sign of dissatisfaction was reported by the governor Nabû-uṣalla. Three powerful Kummeans did not observe the traditional order of communication (V 104): local informer → Assyrian provincial official → the royal court. They refused to report their news to the governor or the royal bodyguard, as was the custom, and requested an audience with the king.[124] When the delegation returned from the audience, they expressed their loyalty to Assyria (V 106:12'–16'). But the uprising was growing larger. Its center became the city of Kumme, whose inhabitants "could not stand the royal delegate (Aššur-reṣuwa)" any longer (V 106:14'–15') and revolted against their pro-Assyrian king Arije. Moreover, rumors concerning a plot to kill the Assyrian delegate, Aššur-reṣuwa, were brought to Aššur-reṣuwa himself (V 107). Thus, both Assyrian officials, Aššur-reṣuwa and Nabû-uṣalla, were well informed about the upheaval, and Aššur-reṣuwa suggested a secret removal and execution of four major protagonists:

> [Aššur]-reṣuwa has said: "[There are] four men [who should be] removed; they must not walk (free) in my presence while I [am] here; they are inci[ting] the country."
> [In f]act, he (Aššur-reṣuwa) told me (Nabû-uṣalla): "T[hey] should stay with you and be provided with [foo]d and drink; when the ti[me is right] let them disappear." (V 106:17'–21')

---

[123] Ibid., 91.

[124] Three letters inform us about the careless relocation of the Kummeans (I 233, V 104, V 105). I 233 presents a royal order to compile a list of all Kummeans living abroad and to move some of them away from Zarana (unknown location, probably in eastern Syria). However, the execution of this order was delayed. Letter V 105 presents the public reading of a similar royal order. The response of the Kummeans listening to this royal order bespeaks the submissive attitude of vassals who had but one choice: "The king, our lord, is the lord of all; what can we say? The king, our lord, may take all the Kummeans who hold houses in (other) countries to wherever it is appropriate;" (V 105:11–15). If the request of three powerful Kummeans is read in the context of the careless relocation of the Kummeans abroad, then it is possible that the matter to be discussed with the king concerned the Kummean discontent with the policy of moving their people. This hypothesis can be further buttressed by the first line of the speech of three powerful Kummeans: "Our people may go where the king said, but your messenger should take us to the Palace." (V 104:10–13).

On the other hand, the Urartian king Argišti II took advantage of resentments the Kummeans had harbored against their Assyrian overlords over several years and sent them an invitation to resume normal diplomatic relationships:

> [... "Ever s]ince [I ha]ve been on the throne, there has not really been (anybody) you have sent to greet me (Argišti II); (everybody) comes to me [in the na]me of Aššur and your gods."[125] He further said: "I have heard that you are scar[ed]; why are you scar[ed]? Even Rusa did not speak about destroying [your country; nor have I] spoken about it." (V 95:3–10)

The answer of the Kummeans can be read as both an expression of their loyalty to the Assyrians and an expression of the bile they had to swallow while serving their Assyrian overlords:

> They responded like th[is]: "Since we are subjects [of Assyria], a foreman of cavalry is [our su]perior. (Only) the houses of Kumme are left to us; [*we have authority*] *over them (only)*, we cannot put our feet anywhere." (V 95:11–8)

The Assyrians, aware of Argišti II's attempt to foment unrest in Kumme, watched carefully the Urartian frontier with Kumme and Ukku. For this reason, Aššur-dur-paniya (the governor of Masennu) placed his spies in the mountains to capture the Urartian messengers. The following lines illustrate the efficiency of this web of spies:

> My [sco]uts in the m[ountain] have captured an informer [who] was g[oing from A]rgistiani t[o Ar]iye, over the mountain. [I as]ked him about [the ne]ws of the Urartian], and he informed me (rest broken away). V 55:4–10

Thus, the Assyrians were informed about the uprising, the people's resentments, and the rumors passing among the mob. They knew who the main inciters of the uprising were and where its epicenter was. Intercepting communications between Urartu and Kumme, they also learned that the Urartian king had tried to press the Kummeans to join his camp.

---

[125] That greeting someone in the names of the Assyrian gods was a sign of the loyalty of a vassal king is attested in V 146. Urzana blessed the king in the name of the Assyrian gods.

3.1.3.2.2 Smugglers

Even though customs services are separated from intelligence services in many Western countries, this has not always been the case. It is sufficient to mention the role of the KGB and the Czechoslovakian ŠtB in controlling black-market trade with Western Europe.[126] The case presented below illustrates that the same officials who were responsible for intelligence gathering were also involved in compromising a large smuggling network run by Kummeans. Smuggling activity was first discovered in the Kummean city of Arzabia, which was under the control of the Assyrian treasurer. The traded objects were called *ṣahittātu* 'the objects of value'.[127] The unknown sender of I 46 suggested that the smugglers should be arrested.

A similar, though much more sophisticated, network of smugglers was compromised by Aššur-reṣuwa, the Assyrian royal delegate in Kumme (V 100).[128] The network was run by six Kummean runaways; two of them were under the jurisdiction of the Kummean king, Arije, and four under the jurisdiction of Arisa (a high official of Kumme, most likely Arije's son). The first trafficking route[129] was quite well mapped by the Assyrian intelligence services: the inhabitants of Bususu, a city located in the chief cupbearer province (LÚ.GAL–KAŠ.LUL=*rab šāqê*), acquired the objects of value in Calah and Nineveh. They sold the objects to the Kummean smugglers, who smuggled them to Urartu. The smugglers' network was well disguised. On the one hand, Calah[130] and Nineveh were Neo-Assyrian

---

[126] K. Kaplan, *Nebezpečná Bezpečnost: Státní Bezpečnost 1948-1956*, 1. vyd. (Brno: Doplnek, 1999), 8.

[127] The noun *ṣahittu* is derived from the verb *ṣahātu* 'to wish, desire'; see SANTAG 5, 331. Thus, *ṣahittu*, besides meaning "wish, desire," designates also a desired object such as in V 37:20 GUD.MEŠ *ša ṣa-hi-ti*, "the oxen of desire" or "precious/desirable oxen". If the fragmentary tablet V 101 is connected with the smuggling cases, then the objects of value were various utensils made out of bronze and leather.

[128] From the fact that all the verbs in lines V 100:9-r.5 are in durative form, it is possible to deduce that the smuggling activities were still going on when the letter was filed.

[129] It would make little sense, first, to ask the Bususeans to acquire the goods from Calah and bring them up to Bususu, and after purchasing the goods in Bususu to bring the goods back to the Calah province and only afterwards up to Urartu. For this reason, I prefer to read tablet V 100 as describing two at least partly independent trafficking routes run by the same group of Kummeans–one located on the periphery and the other nested in the Assyrian heartland.

[130] Tablets I 116, 117 and 118 mention mercantile activities taking place in Calah.

trade centers, and so a group of people from the chief cupbearer's province who were purchasing objects of value would not appear suspicious. On the other hand, Kumme was administratively under Masennu province, which bordered on the chief cupbearer's province.[131] So the Kummean merchants would not appear suspicious in the chief cupbearer's province.

The second trafficking route can be only partly reconstructed from the extant sources. The base of the two-way traffic in valuables between Urartu and Assyria was Aira, a city located in Calah province. Thus, the smuggling activities of this network took place in the Assyrian heartland itself. When the smuggling network was compromised, Aššur-reṣuwa recommended that the king write a letter to Saniye, who was the city lord of Aira, and ask him to arrest the smugglers. The order was issued but the smugglers managed to escape (V 103).

The priorities of the Assyrian officials were to identify the smugglers, their local connections, and the smuggled goods. The questions to be put to the smugglers after their arrest indicate where the Assyrian interest lay: 1) Where did they buy these valuable objects? (Urartian and Assyrian sources); 2) Where did they sell them? (destination); 3) Who received the objects? (local contacts); and 4) Who let them pass the border? (border contacts). When letter V 100 was filed, some of the questions were already partly answered: the local contacts were Bususeans and Aireans, and the main figures of the smuggling network had been already identified (six Kummeans). The area in which the smuggling networks operated turned out to be quite large; it extended from the treasurer's province and the chief cupbearer's land (both controlling the Assyrian northern frontier) down to the provinces of Nineveh and Calah (the Assyrian heartland).

3.1.3.3 Ukku

Ukku was situated north of Ulluba beyond Mount Nippur (Cudi Daği). Its rugged mountain terrain prevented the Assyrians from turning Ukku into a vassal state, and the Ukkeans maintained their partial independence from both Assyria and Urartu. Ukku directly bordered on the Urartian provinces governed by Kaqqadanu (V 87) and Sunia (V 88). Such a geographical location attracted the interest of both powers, which made great efforts to control as much of Ukku as possible. Besides its

[131] For the location of both provinces see SAAS XI, 18–20, 48–51.

advantageous location, the economic interest of its lucrative timber resources provided another incentive for keeping Ukku submissive (V 111 and 129).

The first task of the Neo-Assyrian intelligence network that monitored Ukku was to keep track of shifts in Ukkean allegiances. The Assyrians closely observed Ukkean foreign relationships with Assyria, Urartu, and Ukkean other neighbors. The Ukkean king maintained a regular diplomatic relationship with Assyria. He sent his messenger to Ṭab-šar-Aššur (I 42) and to Sennacherib (I 31:8-20). Moreover, the briefing that the Ukkean king sent to the latter played an important role in clarifying the results of the Urarto-Cimmerian war (see 3.5.2). As for Ukku-Urartu relationships, Ṭab-šar-Aššur reported that the Urartian governor opposite Ukku visited the Ukkean king (V 286) and that the Ukkean king paid a visit to the Urartian king (I 41). As for the relationships of Ukku with its other neighbors, the Assyrians received information that the Ukkean king had paid a visit to Arije, the king of Kumme, and forwarded him the message of the Urartian king (I 41). Letter I 29 suggests that Sennacherib was also informed about Ukkean expansionist tendencies and intervened to protect a ruler of Arzabia (unknown location).

3.1.3.3.1 Mini "Cuban crisis"

The Assyrians, in order to strengthen their position in the territory close to the Urartian frontier, decided to build a fortress in Kumme. The construction of such a military base might have reinforced the overwhelming Assyrian presence in Kumme, reined in the resisting factions, and curbed Urartian influence.[132] On the other hand, if the Urartians had been able to stop the construction of this fortress, they would have disrupted Assyrian control of the region, and the Assyrian governors who were taken hostages would have constituted an important source of intelligence as well as a valuable negotiating tool.

The fact that several Assyrian governors were involved in this construction indicates that construction of the fortress was one of the major

---

[132] The psychological impact of the presence of an occupying force in a conquered territory can be illustrated by the case of Czechoslovakia in the early seventies of the last century. The overwhelming presence of Soviet troops ostensibly moving from city to city paralyzed opposition movements for a few decades.

priorities of the regional officers. However, seen from the overall imperial perspective, such a fortress was of medium or even low importance.[133]

Analysis of the structure of tablet I 29 can serve as a window on the Neo-Assyrian intelligence network. As sketched below (Table 3), the tablet is Sennacherib's summary report to his father and overlord, the Assyrian king Sargon II, containing three reports and some administrative matters.

Table 3. Literary structure of tablet I 29

Content	Text
Presentation of the addressee and sender	[To] the king, my lord: [your servant] Sin-ahhe-riba.
Sender's greeting	Good health to the king, my lord! [Assyri]a is well, [the temp]les are well, all [the king's forts] are well. The king, my lord, can be glad indeed.
Kumme crisis	
Sennacherib's introduction	They are working on [the fort in Kumme; their] work [... is mak]ing [good progress].
Arije's report	
I. Opening clause	A messen[ger of Arije] has come [into] m[y presence] (with the following message):
II. Body	
Intercepted [Ukku]-Urartu communication	"[The (ruler) of Ukku has written to] the Urartian king [that the govern]ors of the king of Assyria are building [a fort in Kumme],
Intercepted Urartu-Urartu communication	The Urartian king has [give]n his governors (the following) order: 'Take your troops, go and capture the governors of the king of Assyria alive from the Kummeans, and bring them to me.'
Arije's comments	I do not have the full details yet; as soon as I have heard more, I shall write by express to the crown prince that they should rush troops to me."
III. Closing clause	This was the report of Arije.

[133] The comparison of tablet I 29 with I 31, which Sennacherib dedicated entirely to a briefing about the Urarto-Cimmerian war, indicates that the "Cuban crisis" in Kumme was not perceived in Nineveh as tragically as it was presented by Arije who was directly exposed to the Urartian imminent attack. Furthermore, Sennacherib assumed that a short introduction to Arije's message was needed so that the Assyrian king might understand the importance of the report. From these indications it is possible to deduce that the construction of the Kumme fortress was not a top priority on the imperial level.

Aššur-reṣuwa's briefings on Urartu

I. Opening clause	On the 11th of Elul (VI) I got a letter from Aššur-reṣuwa.
II. Body	
A. News on the Urartian king	
Urarto-Zikirtean raid	"The Urartian (king) did not achieve anything on the venture on which the Zikirteans took him, but had to return empty-handed; he went with his troops to Waisi, entered the city and left his forces there.
Urartian invasion of Mannea	Taking but a few troops with him, he set out and entered the territory of the Manneans. I have not heard about the invasion yet, but I shall write you as soon as I have heard more.
B. News on the governor "opposite" Kumme	
Whereabouts	The governor opposite me was (also) in Waisi; I have heard that he left and went off after the king's departure, but nobody has seen him come out of Waisi.
Suspicious building activities	They are improving the roads leading to me and constructing bridges; as soon as I have heard what it is all about, whether he is coming with his troops or whether he is 'clean,' I shall immediately write to the crown prince."
III. Closing clause	This was the report of Aššur-reṣuwa.

Ukkean conflict with the ruler of Arzabia

I. Opening clause	The (ruler) of Arzabia has written to me thus:
II. Body	"The (ruler) of Ukku must be kept away from me; why do you keep silent while he is trying to destroy me?"
III. Closing clause (substituted by Sennacherib's intervention)	I have sent my bodyguard (with this message): "Do[n't ar]gue with the Arzabian! [Until the ki]ng comes, [I will ar]bitrate between you!"

Concluding section

Administrative matters	
Tribute from Mannea	A messenger of the Mannean … I put a silver bracelet on his arm.
Tribute from Ashdod	The tribute of the Ashdodites was brought to Calah …
Date	I am sending this letter to the king, my lord, on the 11th of Elul.

The first report on the "Cuban crisis" in Kumme was sent to Sennacherib's office by Arije, the king of Kumme. According to Arije, the Urartian king received news that the Assyrians were building a fortress in

Kumme.[134] This intelligence was highly appreciated by the Urartian king, who immediately ordered his governors to organize an attack. When Sennacherib sent the tablet to the king, the information about the Urartian attack had not yet been verified; if it proved correct, Arije recommended to Sennacherib that he sent his troops to aid the endangered Assyrian military base that was under construction.

The second report came from Aššur-reṣuwa, the Assyrian royal delegate in Kumme. According to Aššur-reṣuwa, the Urartian king returned empty-handed from a raid organized by the Zikirteans. After returning and leaving part of his army in Waisi, he undertook a small raid in Mannea. Moreover, the governor "opposite" Kumme, after meeting the king in Waisi, supposedly returned to his province. The final part of Aššur-reṣuwa's report related some suspicious construction in the vicinity of the Kummean border.

The third report came from the ruler of Arzabia (unknown location) who complained about trouble from the Ukkean king and urged Sennacherib to intervene.

Sennacherib's briefing, which combines all three reports, gives us a clue as to how intelligence was gathered and processed. It is possible to identify three steps in processing the intelligence data: first, local agents gathered raw intelligence; second, the provincial officials (Arije, Aššur-reṣuwa) processed raw intelligence and sent it to the royal court; third, the crown prince, Sennacherib, reevaluated intelligence received from the provincial officials and sent it to Sargon II.

The local agents were able to intercept communications between the Ukkean and the Urartian kings (following S. Parpola's reconstruction) and between the Urartian king and the governors of the Urartian provinces close to Kumme. This level of intelligence network was run by Aššur-reṣuwa and Arije. Arije, after receiving intelligence, compiled it, evaluated it as "not yet verified," and suggested a course of action, if this intelligence proved correct. Aššur-reṣuwa's agents provided information about the whereabouts and activities of the Urartian governor of the territory neighboring on

[134] According to S. Parpola's reconstruction, the Urartian king learned it from the Ukkean king (I 29:11).

Kumme. The tablets do not offer any information about the local agents and the way this intelligence was acquired by Arije and Aššur-reṣuwa.[135]

Arije, the Arzabian ruler, and Aššur-reṣuwa, as noted, operated at the middle level of collecting and processing the data. They received the data, evaluated it, and sent it to Sennacherib. If we compare Arije and the Arzabian ruler's reports with that of Aššur-reṣuwa, it is possible to see the differences between local and Assyrian informers. The main priority of the Arzabian ruler was not to report on the Ukkean king, but to get Sennacherib involved in his problems. Similarly, though more moderately, Arije reported the intercepted communication. Presenting the Urartian governors as the enemies threatening the Assyrian building project, he urged Sennacherib to intervene. On the other hand, Aššur-reṣuwa's report had the touch of a professional. Above all, his report contained primarily data and not complaints or requests, as was the case with Arije and the Arzabian ruler. The intelligence network run by Aššur-reṣuwa had a much greater reach, extending some 300 km from his seat (Zikirtu) and penetrating into the Urartian heartland (Waisi). He sent to Sennacherib a concise summary of several smaller reports sorted into two groups: the first group was about the Urartian king and the second concerned the Urartian governor "opposite" Kumme. His professional touch can be discerned through his double-checking of the information received from local agents. According to one source, the governor "opposite" Kumme left Waisi, but double-checking the news, Aššur-reṣuwa informed Sennacherib that no one had seen the governor leaving Waisi.

The last stage of processing this intelligence was Sennacherib's duty. Arije's report was introduced by Sennacherib's short comment, which placed it in context. Sennacherib inserted a copy of Arije's message among the dispatches of Aššur-reṣuwa and the Arzabian ruler, labeled their beginning and end, and together with some other administrative matters, sent them to the king.

---

[135] However, lines V 105:16-23 speak about Kummean spies who were used for gathering intelligence in Urartu. These Kummean spies were relocated by the Assyrians along with other Kummeans. The unknown sender of V 105 urged the king to return these spies to Kumme because they were needed to gather information in Urartu. This indicates that at least part of this level of the intelligence network consisted of Kummean agents sent out to spy on Urartu.

Seen in the light of Aššur-reṣuwa's and the Arzabian ruler's reports, Arije's warning gains more importance and prominence. First, the Ukkean was an unreliable king, proving his disloyalty to Assyria by harassing the Arzabian ruler and forcing Sennacherib to intervene. Therefore, Arije's message that the Ukkean king had passed strategic information to the Urartian king, though it bore the mark of Arije's self-interest, was not to be overlooked. Second, Arije reported that the Urartian governors were ordered to attack the Assyrian fortress under construction. Independently, Aššur-reṣuwa reported that the Urartian governor "opposite" Kumme was improving roads and building bridges. This activity made Aššur-reṣuwa suspicious about whether the governor would use the roads for a military campaign against Kumme. Even though, when Sennacherib sent his briefing to the king, it was not clear whether suspicious construction at the Kummean border was the result of the order given to the Urartian governors by the Urartian king, Sennacherib's compiling of these three independent reports (Arije's, Aššur-reṣuwa's and the Arzabian ruler's) provided the king with important comparative data which alerted him to the increasing tension at the Urarto-Kummean frontier.

3.1.4 Urartian takeover of Muṣaṣir

The fourth case study treats the Urartian reconquest of the Urartian national sanctuary Muṣaṣir, located in the southeastern corner of Turkey.[136] Sargon II conquered this sanctuary during his eighth campaign. This case study will investigate the role of the Neo-Assyrian intelligence services in monitoring the city containing the sanctuary and its king, Urzana.

3.1.4.1 Historical introduction

Three groups of sources concerning the Urarto-Assyrian conflict have been preserved: Neo-Assyrian royal inscriptions describing Sargon II's campaigns in the north,[137] Urartian royal inscriptions describing Rusa I's

---

[136] The identification of Muṣaṣir with modern Muğaisir proposed by R. M. Boehmer is generally accepted in the scholarly literature; see R. M. Boehmer, "Forschungen in und um Mudjesir (Irakisch-Kurdistan)," *AA* 4 (1973); idem, "Zur Lage von Musasir," *BagM* 6 (1973).

[137] The conflict over Muṣaṣir is mentioned in Sargon II's annals and in Sargon II's letter to Aššur. For detailed bibliography, see G. W. V. Chamaza, "Der VIII. Feldzug Sargons II. Eine Untersuchung zu Politik und historischer Geographie des späten 8. Jhs. v. Chr. (I)," *Archäologische Mitteilungen aus Iran* 27 (1994): 91–92.

invasion of Muṣaṣir,[138] and the cluster of Neo-Assyrian letters describing Urartian military and cultic activities regarding Muṣaṣir.[139] Absolute dating can be established only for Sargon II's eighth campaign, which occurred in 714 B.C.E.[140] The rest of the Assyrian and Urartian documents can be dated only relatively on the basis of their relation to Sargon II's eighth campaign.

This study will follow the division of the historical events described in Assyrian and Urartian sources into three phases: pre-campaign, campaign, and post-campaign.[141]

Pre-campaign phase. Rusa I had been upset by Urzana's pro-Assyrian political orientation for a long time, and he finally organized a military expedition against Muṣaṣir (to be dated sometime before 714 B.C.E., and described in the Topzawä stele). Urzana prepared his troops to defend Muṣaṣir but was defeated and sought refuge in Assyria. Rusa I annexed Muṣaṣir to Urartu and imposed a heavy tribute on the citizens. Despite Urzana's previous pro-Assyrian orientation, Rusa I reinstalled Urzana on the throne. The resulting elimination of Assyrian influence on Muṣaṣir was not well received in Nineveh and is reflected in Sargon II's eighth campaign letter to Aššur, where he vilifies Urzana with all kinds of derogative epithets (ll. 309–10).

Campaign phase. This situation was radically altered when Sargon II suddenly changed the course of his eighth campaign and invaded Muṣaṣir. The sanctuary and Haldi's temple were plundered, Urzana's family deported, and the city annexed to Assyria.

Post-campaign phase. The Assyrian dominion did not last very long, however. According to V 147, shortly after the departure of the Assyrian troops an unnamed Urartian king reconquered Muṣaṣir and turned it again into the Urartian national sanctuary. Since Rusa I committed suicide shortly

---

138 Two Urartian steles—Topzawä and Mergeh Karvan—describe Rusa I's intervention in Muṣaṣir; see M. Salvini, "La Bilingue Urarteo-Assira di Rusa I," in *Tra lo Zagros e l'Urmia: Ricerche Storiche ed Archeologiche nell'Azerbaigian Iraniano*, ed. P. E. Pecorella and M. Salvini (Roma: Edizioni dell'Ateneo, 1984) and N. V. Arutjunjan, *Korpus Urartskich Klinopisnych Nadpisej* (Jerevan: Gitutjun, 2000), 289–94.

139 Tablet V 147 and a cluster of related letters: V 88, 89, 112, 146, and 148.

140 Salvini, *Geschichte*, 82. For a discussion regarding the date of Sargon II's eighth campaign, see section 3.5.2.1.

141 "Campaign" is understood Sargon II's eighth campaign in 714 B.C.E.

after Sargon II's eighth campaign, the reconquest of Muṣaṣir should be attributed to his successor, Argišti II, who, according to Neo-Assyrian letters (see below), devoted a good part of his reign to reconsolidating the Urartian kingdom and reconquering the territory lost to the Assyrians.

According to this division, the historical context for the cluster of the intelligence reports connected with V 147 is the period of Argišti II's reconsolidation of the Urartian kingdom after Sargon II's eighth campaign. The cluster of reports connected with V 147 consists of tablets V 88, 89, 112, 136, 139, 146, and 148. Tablets V 136, 139, 146, and 148 describe Urzana as subordinate to Assyria: V 136 describes the stages of Urzana's journey to Assyria; in V 146, Urzana justifies the delay in the delivery of his tribute; V 148 mentions the visit which Urzana's brother paid to Šulmu-beli; and V 139 mentions the Muṣaṣirian men summoned by the order of the (Assyrian) king. Urzana was under Assyrian dominion twice: for the first time before Rusa I's intervention (Topzawä stela), and for the second time after Sargon II's eighth campaign. Since V 139 and 136 are attributed to Šulmu-beli, the deputy of the Assyrian palace herald to whom Muṣaṣir was annexed after Sargon II's eighth campaign, tablets V 136, 139, 146, and 148 can be dated to the interval when Muṣaṣir was under Assyrian dominion, i.e., between Sargon II's eighth campaign and Argišti II's reconquest of Muṣaṣir. Tablets V 88, 89, 112, and 147 belong to different stages of Argišti II's reconquest of Muṣaṣir. Tablet V 88 can be associated with V 147 on the basis of geographical similarities: according to V 147, two Urartian governors (the governor of Waisi and the governor next to Ukkean) entered Muṣaṣir as the rest of the governors and the king were on their way from Waisi to Muṣaṣir. Similarly, tablet V 88 mentions that the governor opposite Ukku and Settini, namely, the governor opposite Aššur-reṣuwa, set out towards Muṣaṣir. Details regarding the Urartian king in V 147 and V 88 also match.[142] In the former, the king stayed in Waisi and was about to go (to Muṣaṣir); in the latter, "the king is in Waisi; he will be going but has not yet departed" (V 88:r.5–8). V 112 mentions Urzana in the contest of a military purge. The heavily damaged tablet V 89 does not provide any solid grounds for its dating. If S. Parpola's reconstruction is correct, then this tablet describes the very end of Argišti II's reconquest of Muṣaṣir: Urzana was seized and his people were taken to Waisi.[143]

---

[142] SAA V, XVII.
[143] SAA V, 73.

3.1.4.2 Assyrian monitoring of the Urartian reconquest of Muṣaṣir

In the interval between Sargon II's eighth campaign and the beginning of Arigišti II's reconsolidation process, Urzana ruled as the king of Muṣaṣir. The region was under Assyrian control, being administered by Gabbu-ana-Aššur (the palace herald, LÚ.NIGÍR–É.GAL=*nāgir ekalli*) and his deputy Šulmu-beli, who together with Aššur-reṣuwa (the Assyrian delegate in Kumme) were responsible for monitoring Muṣaṣir. Shortly after the Assyrian conquest, the Assyrians' surveillance of Muṣaṣir was limited to watching how Urzana complied with the imposed yoke, which involved such obligations as tribute delivery (V 136 and 146), summoning the people (V 139), and regular visits to Assyria (V 136[144]). Non-fulfillment of any of these requirements, lest it be understood as a sign of Urzana's disloyalty, needed to be adequately explained. Thus, when Urzana delayed the tribute and did not pay regular homage to the Assyrian king, he tried to justify his absence by blaming the climate (V 146).

Furthermore, in order to keep an eye on Muṣaṣir, the palace herald, well aware of the religious and symbolic meaning of this national sanctuary, declared that "Nobody may take part in the (religious) service (in Muṣaṣir) without the king's (Sargon II's) permission" (V 147:r.3–7). Since worship in Urartu was usually connected with the gathering of several local governors (V 84:r.4–8; 85:r.1'–2'), the Assyrians, by prohibiting such a cultic gathering, prevented the fomenting of Urartian religious and nationalistic feelings and imposed a clever preemptive measure whose transgression would constitute a clear warning sign of increasing Urartian resistance.

The content of the reports changed dramatically when the Urartian king Argišti II began to reconsolidate his beleaguered kingdom. There are four letters that report on the renewed political aspirations of Urartu (V 88, 89, 112, and 147). The news brought by these letters provided the king with details as to the whereabouts of the Urartian king: his actual location, the location he was currently approaching, and the location he next intended to approach. Another important piece of information was the number of soldiers participating in military movements and the types of animals used

[144] The reverse of the tablet, even though badly damaged, says: "We have se[nt ...] 56 horses, [x oxe]n, and 2,000 sh[eep]; 100 [...], the audience gift, [...];" (V 136:r.2'–6'). This determines the goal of Urzana's visit–the tribute delivery.

(V 88).[145] According to these reports, Waisi became the center of the Urartian offensive against Muṣaṣir.[146] V 88 relates that two Urartian governors set out towards Muṣaṣir. V 147 names two governors who reached the city and defied Assyrian sovereignty by performing religious actions without the king's permission. Urzana did not pose any resistance, and if S. Parpola's reconstruction of V 89 is correct, Urzana was captured and taken before Argišti II arrived in Waisi.[147] This reconquest by the Urartians may have ended with some kind of purge (V 112).[148] There is no indication that Sargon II intervened, and it seems that he limited himself to observing the loss of Muṣaṣir through the eyes of his officials.

3.1.5 Eastern provinces

The last series of case studies concerning conflicts along the Urarto-Assyrian frontier deals with the region located southeast of Lake Urmia (western Iran).

3.1.5.1 Historical introduction

Sargon II had to stage four military interventions in the region located southeast of Lake Urmia in order to pacify the rebellious kings and annex their kingdoms to Assyria. The westernmost parts of this region, Mazamua and Mannea, were annexed to Assyria during five military expeditions at the end of the ninth c. B.C.E. Thenceforth, Mazamua was ruled by Assyrian governors and became the point of departure for Sargon

---

[145] "3,000 foot soldiers, their prefects, and the commanders of the *kallāpu* troops of Setini, the governor opposite me, have set out towards Muṣaṣir and crossed the Black River. All the pack animals of Setini are with him." (V 88:4–11)

[146] Waisi or Uais has not yet been identified with certainty. Van Loon proposed to identify Waisi with the site of Qalatgah; see van Loon, "The Inscription of Ispuini and Meinea at Qalatgah, Iran," *JNES* 34 (1975). This proposal was followed by A. I. Ivantchik; see A. I. Ivantchik, *Les Cimmériens au Proche-Orient* (Fribourg: Editions Universitaires, Vandenhoeck & Ruprecht, 1993), 33. However, M. Salvini identified Waisi with the Urartian fortress Qal'eh Ismail Aqa, situated close to Urmia Lake; see M. Salvini, "La Storia della Regione in Epoca Urartea," in *Tra lo Zagros e l'Urmia: Ricerche Storiche ed Archeologiche nell'Azerbaigian Iraniano*, ed. P. E. Pecorella and M. Salvini (Rome: Edizioni dell'Ateneo, 1984), 50.

[147] See SAA V, 73.

[148] "I have [not y]et heard what happened to [tho]se men, [wheth]er they [have] been killed [or] deported." (V 112: 6'–r.2)

II's campaigns. Mannea was turned into a vassal state governed by a pro-Assyrian king at the end of the ninth c. B.C.E.

Sargon II's first military intervention was required to pacify a rebellion against the pro-Assyrian Mannean king Iranzu (S II Ann 58-68). Two cities bordering the pro-Urartian kingdom, Zikirtu (Šuandahu and Durdukka), and three cities bordering Urartu (Sukkia, Bala, and Abitikna) revolted against Mannean sovereignty. The Urartian king Rusa I and the Zikirtean king Mitatti provided moral and military support for the rebels. The rebellion was suppressed and part of Urartu (Wišdiš) and Zikirtu was added to the territory of the new Mannean king Aza, Iranzu's son. These territories became the epicenters of the second revolt sponsored by Rusa I (S II Ann 78–94) in 716 B.C.E. During this revolt, the coalition of Wišdiš and Zikirtu defeated pro-Assyrian Mannean troops and Aza died in the battle. Sargon II rushed to help the Manneans. The rebellious coalition was defeated, Bagdatti, the king of Wišdiš, was flayed, and the territories of Wišdiš and part of Zikirtu were entrusted to the hands of the new Mannean king Ullusunu, the brother of Aza. Ullusunu, shortly after his enthronement, instead of furthering Assyrian interest, allied himself with the anti-Assyrian coalition led by Rusa I and supported by Itti, the king of Allabria, and Aššur-le'i, the king of Karalla. Sargon II promptly intervened for the third time and captured the Mannean capital Izirtu and two other fortified cities. While the allies suffered severe repercussions—Itti was deported and Aššur-le'i flayed—Ullusunu managed to get reappointed to the Mannean throne. Despite the defeats, Rusa I did not give up and attempted a direct attack on the Mannean border (S II Ann 101–19, 127–65). Capturing twenty-two Mannean fortresses and taking the son of Dajukku, the governor of one of the Mannean cities, as a hostage, Rusa I was able to regain control over Northern Mannea. Sargon II's intervention partly pacified the rebels, but a more radical expedition was required to make the region completely submissive. This took place in 714 B.C.E. when Sargon II on his eighth campaign penetrated deeply into Urartian territory, and Rusa I, shortly after the defeat, committed suicide.

3.1.5.2 Reconstruction of the intelligence activities

In order to pacify these four upheavals, Sargon II adopted a straightforward strategy: first, he promptly destroyed the epicenters of the rebellion, then he severely punished their supporters and attached their territories to the Mannean kingdom. This strategy culminated with the eighth campaign (714 B.C.E.), which paralyzed Urartu, the backbone of all the rebellions. Such a strategy and the course of the campaigns required from the Neo-Assyrian intelligence services the answer to two strategically important questions: where were the epicenters of the rebellion (Mannea, Wišdiš, Zikirtu), and who supported the rebels (Urartu, Zikirtu, Mannea)? This was possible thanks to a ramified intelligence network through which the royal court and provincial officials were constantly updated with current information.

3.1.5.2.1 Intelligence network

Information flow between the royal court and the provincial officials was a two-way process. On the one hand, the king communicated his orders (V 200, 203, 215), requested clarifications (V 199), or suggested solutions (V 203). The king communicated with the provincial officials via messengers, most often by means of his royal bodyguards, or in some cases via special emissaries. On the other hand, the king and his officials received information through three channels: 1) through the ambassadors visiting the court, 2) through the people sent to the court, and 3) through provincial information hubs (see Appendix 1).

Regular visits—known as "inquiring about the king's health"—were required from the vassal and buffer kingdoms. The visits were often connected with tribute delivery. These emissaries (I 32, V 40, and V 52), the crown princes (V 171), and the vassal kings themselves provided first-hand information about the situation in their region.

The second source was those persons of interest to the Assyrians who were sent by the provincial officials to the court to be interrogated. The following examples can illustrate the scale of Assyrian interests: arrested Urartian messengers who had tried to influence the Zikirtean king (V 169), the merchant Bel-ahhe (V 218), and captured criminals and their accomplices who threatened the trade routes in Arzuhina province (V 227 and 228).

However, the most important channels through which information flowed to the king were the peripheral information hubs. Appendix 2 lists the peripheral information hubs in the eastern provinces where information was processed and from which it was forwarded to the king. Thus, for example, information about Mannea reached the king through at least eight different information hubs (Arzuhina, Birate, Kumme, Mazamua, Parsua, Šubria, the treasurer's land, and the so-far-unidentified seat of Aššur-belu-uṣur).

The officials at the centers of the information hubs gathered intelligence through different sources: through regular reviews of the regions under their control (V 230, 234, and XV 54), through the reports of their subordinates or colleagues (mule express attendants, fellow provincial officials; V 210, 211, 213, 214, and 218), through the interrogation of refugees (Aššur-le'i's eunuch who fled to Mazamua; V 218), through informers (V 164), through the testimonies of messengers returning from missions (V 202, 204, 217), through interrogations conducted by officials (interrogation of criminals; V 227), and through merchants and trade officials (V 218 and XV 58).

3.1.5.2.2 Verification of information

The variety of sources, the side-interests of provincial officials, and the changing loyalty of vassal kings required a close inspection of the reported data. The first way of verifying the data may be modeled as a fourfold feedback (FB) system that allowed the royal court to track the execution of the royal command. This sophisticated system of feedback can be sketched as follows:

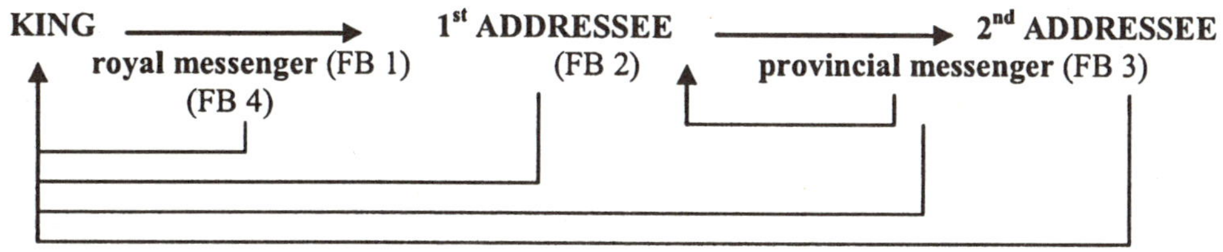

Figure 2. Feedback system

Letters V 204, 217, and 226 illustrate how this feedback system served to verify the communication between the king and the provincial officials.[149] The first type of feedback (FB 1) represents the report of a messenger carrying a royal message to the first addressee. Thus, the royal envoy (bodyguard Nabû-ahu-uṣur) was asked to report on the results of his mission and the reactions of the provincial officials (V 226). The second type of feedback (FB 2) represents the report of the first addressee. Thus, Adad-issiya and Šarru-emuranni reported how the royal order was executed (sending Šamaš-ukin to Mannea; V 204). The third type of feedback (FB 3) represents the report of the messenger sent by the first addressee to the second addressee. Thus, Adad-issiya expected the return of his third man from Mannea after having accomplished the mission (V 217). The fourth type of feedback (FB 4) represents the report of the second addressee. The intensive diplomatic contacts with Mannea and the exchange of emissaries, as well as information acquired through Mannean tribute bearers, indicate that the king received information both from Mannean (the second addressee) and Assyrian sources.[150]

Thus, court officials were informed not only about the final results of the mission but also about the difficulties encountered during the realization of every single phase of the project.

Another system of verifying the data was to compare information about the same event coming from independent sources (information hubs). The reliability of an information hub official was determined not only by the reliability of the data he offered, but also by the data he did not report. This is illustrated by tablet V 221. The king learned that the Mannean king

---

[149] V 204: The king sent his bodyguard Nabû-ahu-uṣur to Šarru-emuranni, the governor of Mazamua, asking him to undertake the diplomatic mission in Mannea. Šarru-emuranni chose Šamaš-ukin "a trustworthy and chosen man … able in words" (V 204:15–17), "implanted" the king's words in his mouth (V 204:r.1–3), and sent the messenger to Mannea. Šarru-emuranni promised to inform the king about the results of the mission as soon as Šamaš-ukin returned.
V 217: The king sent his emissary Nergal-belu-uṣur to Adad-issiya, the governor of Mazamua prior to Šarru-emuranni, with the order to set out for the military campaign. Adad-issiya sent his third man to the Mannean king to join him in the campaign, but the Mannean king found all kinds of excuses to avoid the campaign.
V 226: The king sent his bodyguard Nabû-ahu-uṣur to the magnates, namely, the delegate of Mazamua (Nabû-hamatua) and the governor of Mazamua (Šarru-emuranni). Nabû-ahu-uṣur in this letter communicated the result of this mission and the reaction of the addressees of the king's order.

[150] Letters I 84 and 179 also indicate that provincial officials were aware of the possibility that the king might receive information directly from their subordinates.

offered his sacrifices at the border (probably with Assyria). Since Adad-issiya, the governor of Mazamua, was obligated to get hold of this information and forward it to the court officials, the king rebuked him for failing to do so.

The fact that the court officials continuously received information about the same event from different sources put constant pressure on the local officials to give full and accurate reports, if they did not want to be accused of negligence. Such constant pressure developed a servile syndrome well known among modern communist secret services. Officials became servile officers motivated by fear, ready to denounce everyone and to report on everything. At the same time, they did not despise the material and social benefits they obtained from this service.[151]

The governor and the delegate of Mazamua, Šarru-emuranni and Nabû-hamatua, may be considered good examples of such submissive servants (V 199–214). Their first goal was to present themselves as industrious servants who faithfully and promptly fulfilled the king's requirements. If they failed in this duty, they had to provide valid justification for their actions as quickly as possible. They promptly informed the king about missions in progress and about whatever they heard or saw. However, for our purposes the most important characteristic of the "submissive servant" was his willingness to denounce the misbehavior of other officials and vassals. This improved the image of the submissive servant at the royal court, especially if his own exemplary behavior could be contrasted with the misbehavior of his fellow officials. Thus, Šarru-emuranni informed the king that the king of Allabria mobilized people for the campaign, and he did not forget to add that these people were not the best men of the Allabrian king (V 199 and 200). Such denunciation provided the royal officials with an important piece of information about the loyalty of the Allabrian king, Bel-iddina, and the quality of the troops the Assyrians could count on. Bel-iddina's lack of support for the king, when contrasted with Šarru-emuranni's willingness to give up his best servants for the king's mission, definitely improved Šarru-emuranni's image at the court (V 204, 211). Moreover, Šarru-emuranni presented himself not only as a passive reporter but also as an active supporter of the king's interests by

---

[151] Frolík, *Špión vypovídá.*

suggesting how to deal with Bel-iddina's unwillingness to participate in the campaign (V 200).

These three mechanisms of control—the feedback system, verification of the completeness of reports, and mutual denunciation among the officials—gave court officials the tools they needed to assure that complete information would promptly flow to the king.

3.1.5.3 Reported issues on Mannea

Numerous reports on Mannea dated to the period before Sargon II's eighth campaign underline the importance of Mannea[152] as a key state for reining in Urartian expansion to the southeast. For if such an expansion were to take place, the first target of the Urartian king would be the buffer state Mannea. For this reason, the Assyrians closely monitored the situation along the Urarto-Mannean border. The Assyrian intelligence network informed the king about at least two Urartian military invasions of Mannean territory (I 29 and V 45)[153] and at least one Mannean raid in southern Urartu (V 84).

Intelligence on Mannea reached the royal court through at least eight different information hubs (see Appendix 2) and covered two Mannean vassal kings, Aza (killed in 716 B.C.E.) and his brother Ullusunu, enthroned after Aza. As for the former, Sargon II's annals present him as a loyal king who paid with his own life for his loyalty to Assyria. Unfortunately, the only letter mentioning his name is badly damaged (V 216). As for Ullusunu, Sargon II's annals describe him as a vassal king who three times shifted his allegiance between Assyria and Urartu. If the only source of information had been the Mannean emissaries, then Ullusunu would have been considered a faithful vassal king who paid regular visits to the Assyrian

[152] R. B. Wartke suggests locating Mannea south of Lake Urmia in the region of modern Mahabad; see Wartke, *Urartu*, 41.

[153] Since tablet I 29 describes Zikirtu as an Urartian ally whereas in V 45 both Mannea and Zikirtu are the object of the Urartian attack, tablets I 29 and V 45 do not describe the same event. Line I 29:r.22 mentioning the tribute of Ashdodites provides a clue for dating the tablet. Ashdod paid tribute to Assyria before 714 B.C.E. and after 712 B.C.E.; see Ivantchik, *Cimmériens*, 33. Since Zikirtu, according to I 29:25, was an Urartian ally—which was the case before 714 B.C.E.—then I 29 can be dated to the period prior to Sargon II's eighth campaign. It describes one of the Urartian attacks against Mannea before 714 B.C.E.

court and brought audience gifts (I 29 and 32). However, Adad-issiya, the governor of Mazamua, was able to pinpoint two signs of Ullusunu's declining loyalty: first, Ullusunu looked for excuses when asked to assemble his troops and to participate in the campaign together with Mazamuean troops (V 217). Second, Ullusunu attempted to bribe Aššur-le'i, the king of Karalla, who was one of the leading figures during the anti-Assyrian insurrection in 716 B.C.E. (V 218).[154] Even if the Assyrians had received no other warnings, these reports might have been enough to guarantee that the Assyrians were not taken by surprise when Ullusunu allied himself with Aššur-le'i and Itti against Assyria.

Intelligence on Mannea in the period after the eighth campaign, as preserved in the archives, was gathered by the governor of Mazamua, Šarru-emuranni, and the royal delegate in Mazamua, Nabû-hamatua.[155] The first group of reports can be classified as strategic military intelligence necessary for leading local campaigns organized by the provincial officials.[156] Thus, Šarru-emuranni reported on logistical problems, such as difficult terrain and the obstacle posed by a strong river current (V 199), on the results of ration collections (V 203), and on difficulties connected with the conscription of troops and their unwillingness to cooperate (V 199 and 200).

Tablet V 202 can be classified as a piece of economic intelligence. The region under the jurisdiction of Šarru-emuranni was an important breeding place of horses, a valuable commodity for the Assyrian army.[157] Delay in the delivery of horses was not tolerated and, in order to enforce delivery, Šarru-emuranni sent soldiers to put villagers "on the mouth of the iron sword" (V 202:r.9'). After such an act of terror, the villagers gave up

---

[154] The third warning sign can be partly reconstructed from tablet V 221. It came from a source, now impossible to identify because of the broken condition of the tablet, reporting that the Mannean king was offering sacrifices at the border (V 221). For the strategic role of such sacrifices see section 3.5.1.1. From the fact that the king rebuked the sender because he did not report on the sacrifice of the Mannean king, it can be deduced that this sacrifice had strategic meaning for the Assyrians.

[155] Dating letters V 199–210 to the post-eighth-campaign period is based, above all, on Šarru-emuranni's eponym—712 B.C.E.; see SAAS II, 60. Furthermore, the letters deal with Bel-iddina, who became king of Allabria after deportation of Itti in 716 B.C.E.

[156] The local campaigns were organized with a certain regularity; see V 199 and 200.

[157] According to reports V 169, 171, 224, 226 and XV 53, 59 the entire region south and east of Lake Urmia was known as a source of high-quality horses.

their resistance and Šarru-emuranni imposed a deadline of delivery upon them.

These reports indicate that in this period, before Sargon II's eighth campaign, Neo-Assyrian intelligence operations were limited to controlling typical warning signs, such as tribute delivery, the conscription of troops, and gathering rations for the campaigns. As far as the reports show, the most troublesome area during this period was Allabria, though Sargon II's annals do not mention it.

3.1.5.4 Reported issues on Zikirtu

Similarly, the archives preserve a few reports depicting shifts in the political orientation of Zikirtu—from a pro-Urartian ally to a forced, and thus not very reliable, pro-Assyrian vassal. Sennacherib received news about an Urarto-Zikirtean raid from Aššur-reṣuwa. The Zikirtean king took advantage of his protection by Urartu and talked the Urartian king into a small raid, which, however, did not bring too much booty (I 29). Another piece of intelligence demonstrates the Assyrian ability to intercept communications between Urartu and its two allies, Zikirtu and Andia (V 164). When the Assyrians took off on a punitive campaign, the Zikirtean and Andian kings asked Urartu for help. Bel-iddina, the Allabrian king and sender of V 164, informed the Assyrian royal court about this request and the Urartian response–namely, that Rusa I had immediately set out together with the Hubuškian king. This report contains another strategically important piece of information: the coalition between the Hubuškian and Urartian kings who marched down to help out their endangered allies had dissolved during the march, and the Hubuškian king ordered his magnates to organize their troops (V 164:r.9–10). After Zikirtu was turned into an Assyrian vassal state, the Zikirteans not only updated Assyria about the recent situation in Urartu (V 188), but also captured Urartian messengers sent by the Urartian king to negotiate with Zikirtu and brought them to Assyria (V 169). On the other hand, the Zikirteans were looking for all possible excuses to avoid selling horses to Assyria, and judging from the tone of V 169, the Assyrians considered it a sign of resistance.

3.2 Monitoring Elamite-Assyrian conflicts

Elam was another major power that competed with Assyria for the control of vassal and buffer states along the eastern frontier of Assyria (southeastern Zagros). The following sections will focus on the role of Neo-Assyrian intelligence services in one of the states in this region, Ellipi, during the last two decades of the eighth c. B.C.E.

3.2.1 Historical introduction[158]

At the beginning of Sargon II's reign, the southeastern Zagros (modern western Iran) threw off the Assyrian yoke. The upheaval was triggered by the expulsion of Kibaba, the pro-Assyrian mayor of Harhar. The rest of the local governors took advantage of ebbing Assyrian control and stopped paying tribute. Ellipi, the southernmost locale under Assyrian sway in the Zagros range,[159] followed a similar policy: Dalta, the Ellipian king, forced to pay tribute since 737,[160] "made himself great" (S II Ann 96a) and enjoyed independence for four years. In 716 B.C.E. Sargon II invaded the region, and by turning the city Harhar into the Assyrian provincial capital Kar-Šarrukkin, he set up a firm foothold in the southeastern Zagros.[161] Ellipi was annexed to the province of Kar-Šarrukkin, and its king Dalta became an Assyrian "submissive servant" (Prunk 117). When another anti-Assyrian rebellion stirred up the southeastern Zagros three years later (713 B.C.E.), the Ellipian king did not join it, and Sargon II rewarded his faithfulness by keeping him in power.

---

[158] This historical introduction is based on SAA XV, XIII-XXXIX, SAAS VIII, 81–96, G. Frame, "The Inscription of Sargon II at Tang-i Var," *Or* 68 (1999), A. Fuchs, *Die Inschriften Sargons II. aus Khorsabad*, 1. Aufl. ed. (Göttingen: Cuvillier, 1994), 373–405, A. Kuhrt, *The Ancient Near East, c. 3000-330 BC*, vol. 2, (London and New York: Routledge, 1995), 578–82, and D. T. Potts, *The Archaeology of Elam: Formation and Transformation of an Ancient Iranian State* (New York: Cambridge University Press, 1999), 263–88.

[159] Ellipi is "thought to be coterminous with modern Luristan and the area south of Kermanshah"; see Potts, *Elam*, 267. For the location of Ellipi, see also SAAS VIII, 112.

[160] Fuchs, *Inschriften*, 408.

[161] The rebellion against Assyria in 716 B.C.E. ignited the whole region. "Aššur-le'i of Karalla and Itti of Allabria were led into rebellion against Assyrian overlordship by Ullusunu, the ruler of the Manneans who was acting with the support of the Urartian king Rusa I. In response to this rebellion, Sargon II conducted his sixth campaign into the mountains and defeated them. Ullusunu was pardoned and allowed to remain the ruler of Manneans, but Itti and his family were deported"; Frame, "Tang-i Var," 49.

After the death of Dalta in 708 B.C.E.,[162] his two nephews, Ašpa-bara and Nibê,[163] drew the country into a war of succession. The strategic importance of the region as a buffer state between Elam and Assyria helped Nibê to gain the support of Elam and to seize the throne. However, he enjoyed his kingship for only one year. In 707 B.C.E. his brother Ašpa-bara, who had been ousted from Ellipi, returned with a superior Assyrian army. The Assyrians took advantage of the quarrel between the brothers and sent their troops, led by seven magnates, to help Ašpa-bara. The Assyrian troops besieged the Ellipian capital, Murabištu, which was protected by 4,500 Elamite archers whom Šutur-Nahundi had sent to secure Nibê's kingship. The city, despite its inaccessible location on the top of a cliff, quickly fell into Assyrian hands. Ašpa-bara was appointed to the throne, the Elamites had to pull back, and the Ellipians enjoyed the *Pax Assyriaca*. Ašpa-bara was only a short-term ally of Assyria. After the death of Sargon II, he turned against the Assyrians, and Sennacherib once more had to intervene in the Zagros.[164]

3.2.2 Pre-war intelligence

Neo-Assyrian intelligence activities before the death of Dalta (708 B.C.E.) are illustrated by the reports sent by two local Assyrian officials, Nabû-belu-ka''in, governor of Harhar, and Nergal-eṭir, probably another governor.[165]

After the suppression of the rebellion of the southeastern Zagros in 713 B.C.E., Sargon II imposed a substantial tribute upon the region.[166] Thus, the first task of Assyrian officials was to control the material expression of Dalta's loyalty towards the Assyrian overlordship—regular payment of tribute, especially in the form of much-needed horses (XV 65; 66; 68; 83; 84). Despite some problems in the delivery of tribute,[167] which

---

[162] SAA XV, XXX.

[163] Neo-Assyrian archives contain only one report mentioning Nibê (XV 3).

[164] L. D. Levine, "Sennacherib's Southern Front," *JCS* 34 (1982): 38.

[165] According to letters XV 65–68 and 84, Nergal-eṭir's major responsibility was to collect tribute and supervise the *ilku* assignments. Supervision of these tasks usually fell under the responsibility of a governor.

[166] Sargon II's annals mention that Dalta had to pay 4,609 horses, (together with) mules, bulls and countless sheep/goats (S II Ann 191–94).

[167] The tribute had to be delivered on time and under any circumstances. The case of Nabû-belu-ka''in, who was asked to deliver the tribute collected from Kar-Šarrukin in Shebat

were immediately reported by Nabû-belu-ka''in ("I have heard that he (Dalta) is collecting the rest of the tribute. I shall harness[168] him to deliver it"; XV 84:3'–5'), the Assyrian annalists considered Dalta loyal enough to give him an honorable mention in Sargon II's annals: "Dalta, the king of Ellipi, a submissive servant (ARAD *kan-še*)" (Prunk 117).

The spectrum of events on which the Assyrian officials operating in southeastern Zagros were supposed to report was quite large. Besides reporting on tribute collection and detecting surprise attacks, the Neo-Assyrian intelligence services kept the king posted about the situation at the Ellipian court,[169] quarrels between Assyrian officials,[170] and the difficulties caused by a change of mayor in the Ellipian city, Uriakka.[171]

3.2.3 War of succesion

After Dalta's death, the tenor of Neo-Assyrian intelligence reports radically changed. The first warning came from the deputy governor of Der, Nabû-belu-uṣur, who reported on an Elamite effort to raise support among

---

(January/February) 708 B.C.E. when the roads were covered with snow, is an example of this imperative. During a similar delivery one year earlier, some of the horses died in the snow (XV 83).

[168] ⌜*a*?-*ṣa*?*me*⌝-*su* is derived from *ṣamādu* 'to harness'. Besides its literary meaning of harnessing animals, the verb also had a ceremonial meaning: to harness a defeated king to the king's chariot and consequently acquired a figurative meaning: to subdue someone and oblige him to serve his master as a harnessed ox; see *CAD* 16, 90–91.

[169] In XV 84:3'–4', Nabû-belu-ka''in reported: "As to the news of Dalta, he is not leaving (his) house and nobody is entering into his presence." Such a report about Dalta's health informed the Nineveh court that Dalta's health had worsened and his capability of exercising power had lessened.

[170] The following lines illustrate a quarrel over spoils between Nergal-eṭir and an unknown Assyrian official. Such a report was an important piece of information to be included in the personal files of the provincial officials.

> It is true; why does he brag about his [...] work assignment? By [the god o]f the king, my lord, it is not a work assignment of the palace or anybody. He has been assigned but 30 courses of brick. This accomplishment is altogether that of Nergal-eṭir. They argued about the house of Hunanu as long as it existed. Now they are arguing about Kar-šarrukin. Not a day passes without their quarreling about the spoils. (XV 84:7–18)

[171] XV 85:6–13 informed the royal court that the Urriakeans had a problem with accepting a new governor imposed by the Assyrians and had presented their petition for a change of the governor. However, such a change never happened. When Manu-ki-Ninua became the governor of Kar-Šarrukin, Rametî was still the governor and the city kept its rebellious attitude (XV 101).

Assyrian allies in the Yadburu region (XV 130). Even though the tablet is heavily damaged, it is still possible to recover the gist of Nabû-belu-uṣur's report. The Elamite king Šutur-Nahundi visited the Pilattu sheiks in person and invited them to participate in a military campaign against Ellipi. The Pilattu tribe, which had recognized Assyrian sovereignty during Sargon II's expedition into Yadburu (710 B.C.E.), turned down the Elamite invitation: "We will not go to battle" (XV 130:22).[172]

Nabû-belu-uṣur's second report contained even more alarming news: the Elamite king asked Parsumaš, situated about 300 km east of Susa, to participate in the anti-Assyrian campaign (XV 129:7–8), and requested that Bit-Bunakki (situated close to the Ellipian border) raise provisions for the troops.[173] The combination of this information with the news that the Elamite king had set out to the northwest (XV 129:12–13) was a clear warning sign of the imminence of Elamite intervention. When tablet XV 129 was filed, it was not yet clear what the Elamites really intended. Nabû-belu-uṣur evaluated different possibilities and proposed possible military responses so that the Assyrians would not be caught by surprise: mobilizing soldiers (XV 129:30–34), fortifying the city walls and bastions of Der in case the Elamites intended to attack Der (XV 129:38–r.4),[174] and raising provisions around Meturna to support the Assyrian army in case the

---

[172] S. Parpola and A. Fuchs restore line XV 130:6 thus: [*ma-a* LUGAL KUR.NIM.MA.K]I *e-mu-qi i-d*[*a-ak-ki*], "[the king of Ela]m is mob[ilizing] the troops." Since the only secure word of this line is *e-mu-qi* 'troops' it is impossible to decide this issue, though this emendation fits the military tone of the letter and agrees with XV 129:7–9.

[173] The phrase "raising provisions" is based on the restoration of line XV 129:9–11: ᵐ*um-man–mi-na-a* LÚ*.NIGÍR[*x x x* TA ᵐ*bu*]*r-si-la-a ina* URU.É–*bu*-[*na*]-*k-ka re-eš* ZÍD.[DA KASKAL.2. *i-na-á*]*š-ši-iu,* "Umman-minâ, the herald, [...and Bu]r-Silâ [are rai]sing pro[visions for the expedition] in Bit-Bunakka." Even though the lines are broken, the restoration of the phrase "are raising provisions" is almost sure. The expression *rēš* ZÍD.DA KASKAL.2. *našûm,* "to raise provisions," is a well attested idiom, for example in XV 30:15; 129:r.12. Thus, the phrase starting with *rēš* ZÍD can be only a variant of the idiomatic phrase "to raise provisions."

[174] Besides describing the Assyrian king, the word LUGAL without any modifier (XV 129:r.2) was also used to describe the Elamite king, and thus the verses may refer to the possibility that the Elamite king could invade the Assyrian provincial capital. The reasons for such a claim are the following: first, the preferred formula referring to the Assyrian king is LUGAL *be-lí-ia,* "king, my lord"; and second, in line 14 Nabû-belu-uṣur used the term LUGAL without the modifier KUR.NIM.MA.KI 'Elam' for the designation of the Elamite king. For this reason, I take the term LUGAL in line r.2 as referring to the Elamite king and not to the Assyrian king. Consequently, lines XV 129:38–r.4 raise the possibility of an Elamite attack on Der.

Assyrians counterattacked (XV 129:r.9–18). To complete the picture of the Elamite threat, his superior Šamaš-belu-uṣur provided the Assyrian royal court with detailed geographical information about the distance between Hunnur[175] and Der, thus estimated the time remaining for the Assyrians to get ready for an eventual military encounter with Elamite troops:

> How many stages are there [from] Hun[nur] to [Bit-Bunakki?
> [From Hun]nur to Bubilu it is [x stages,
> fr]om Bubilu [to Madaktu one stage,
> [from Madaktu t]o [Malak]ka [...]....
> [from Mal]ak [to Bit-B]unakki [x stages,
> and from] Bit-Bunakk[i to] me three stages. (XV 111)

The tense situation in Ellipi caused both intelligence services, Elamite and Assyrian, to be put on high alert and to strive to acquire as much information about the enemy as possible. The following lines allow us to reconstruct the intricate relations between both intelligence services:

> [^{m}*xxx*] has written to me: "[The king of] Elam heard [that a] citizen of Babylon has written to [Assyr]ia: "[Concern]ing the news of the king of Elam, tell your [lord] that [...... as f]ar as [...]" (XV 111:r.4–10)

This damaged tablet allows the following interpretation. An Assyrian intelligence agent—"a citizen of Babylon"—provided the Assyrian royal court with some information about the king of Elam.[176] The Elamite intelligence network learned the content of this dispatch. Another Assyrian informer, [^{m}*x x x x*], found out that the Elamites had discovered that "a citizen of Babylon" had provided the Assyrian royal court with some information about the king of Elam, and immediately informed his superior,

---

[175] Hunnur was situated near modern Arjan, roughly midway between Susa and Anshan; see Potts, *Elam*, 124.

[176] The letter of "a Babylonian" contains the imperative [*ma-a x x*]-*ka qi-bi-i*, "tell your [x x]" (XV 111:r.9). This line indicates that the addressee was to report the message to [x x], his superior. Therefore, the letter was not addressed to the king, because the Assyrian officials did not use the imperative in their communications with the king, and it was most likely a communication between two local officials. Unfortunately, the lines are too fragmentary to determine further details.

the governor of Der,[177] about this information leak.[178] Thus, the Assyrians knew that the Elamites knew.

After the Elamite not very successful effort to raise support among southern tribes, the Elamite king Šutur-Nahundi set out against Ellipi. Three Assyrian officials closely watched his movements and reported them to the Assyrian court so that the Assyrian military high command could have information about Šutur-Nahundi's precise location at any given time.

Table 4. Šutur-Naḫundi's whereabouts during the war of succession in Ellipi

Location	**Date**	**Source**	**Tablet**
The king of E[la]m set out. He is go[ing forth to] Bit-Bunakka. The spearhead of [his] ch[ariotry has] gone [with] the king to Bit-[Bunakka].	Received on X/Y/Z	Nabû-duru-uşur	129:6–14
The king of E[lam … is] in Bit-Bunakka.		Šamaš-belu-uşur	112:13–4
He entered Bit-Bunakka.	11th of Tammuz 707	Šamaš-belu-uşur	113:7–22
(He) left it (Bit-Bunakka) and went up to the mountain (marching to Burati).	13th (of Tammuz) 707		
The king of Elam is in the mountain, in the town Burati. He has not set out, he is still there.	Received on X/Y/Z	Šamaš-belu-uşur	114:6–11
He is in the mountain.	Received on X/Y/Z	Šamaš-belu-uşur	115:7–8
[*News*] of the Elamite (king): [*he is*] *i*[*n* …].	Received on X/Y/Z	Mannu-ki-Ninua	98:8

[177] The beginning of the tablet containing the name of the addresse and sender is broken away. A. Fuchs and S. Parpola attributed the tablet to the governor of Der, Šamaš-belu-uşur; see SAA XV, XI.

[178] Because of the fragmentary status of this tablet, it is impossible to determine whether the Elamites intercepted an Assyrian letter and thus came to know the content of this dispatch, or whether [^{m}*x x x x*] learned about the information leak in another way.

The first reports came from the Derian officials[179] who were monitoring Šutur-Nahundi's movements along the Assyrian-Elamite frontier. Once the Elamite troops entered the mountains, they were out of reach of the Derian intelligence network, and so the next report came from Mannu-ki-Ninua, governor of Kar-Šarrukkin.

3.2.4 Sargon II's intervention

Only a few reports have been preserved from the Assyrian expedition organized to support Ašpa-bara of Ellipi.[180] The best-preserved is a communication between the Assyrian high command and the field commanders:

> [I (the king) am writing to you (field commander)] right now: this suggestion, the [way he put it], is extremely good. You [know] that this pass [leading to] Urammu is [ver]y difficult [to march

[179] M. W. Waters has dated tablets XV 113 and 115 to 710 B.C.E. on the basis of the eponym list; see SAAS XII, 19–20. According to this list, Šamaš-belu-uṣur was the governor of Arzuhina with the eponym entry for 710 B.C.E.; see SAAS II, 60, 118. However, a connection between the Šamaš-belu-uṣur of XV 113 and 115 and the one of the eponym list cannot be maintained for the following reasons. Šamaš-belu-uṣur was a common name and there were at least four Neo-Assyrian high officials bearing the same name; see SAAS II, 117–18. The Šamaš-belu-uṣur of the eponym entry for 710 B.C.E. who is mentioned in the legal transactions of the royal court in Nineveh (VI 13; 28; 29) was the governor of Arzuhina. On the other hand, the Šamaš-belu-uṣur mentioned in letters XV 113 and 115 was the governor of Der. This claim is based on the fact that the opening greeting of these two letters refers to the city Der: "The city of Der and the fort are well" (XV 112, 113, 114?, 115, and 117?). Moreover, these letters report on the situation in Der and its vicinity. Thus, the structure of the opening greeting and the content of the letters prove that the Šamaš-belu-uṣur mentioned in letters XV 113 and 115 was the governor of Der and not the governor of Arzuhina, as assumed by M. W. Waters. However, there are another three letters (XV 121, 122, and 123) that are also attributed to Šamaš-belu-uṣur but contain a different opening formula: "Good health to the king, my lord!" These letters deal with issues connected with the Labdu territory distant only 100 km from Arzuhina (Der is about 350 km from Arzuhina). Therefore, letters XV 111–28, which S. Parpola and M. W. Waters attributed to the governor of Der (Šamaš-belu-uṣur), should be attributed to two different persons bearing the same name: letters XV 111–20 should be attributed to Šamaš-belu-uṣur, the governor of Der, whereas letters XV 121–28 should be attributed to the Šamaš-belu-uṣur, the governor of Arzuhina.

[180] S. Parpola and A. Fuchs have reconstructed lines XV 76:r.3–4 as pitching a camp in Sumurzu. Sumurzu was located close to Urammu and thus tablets XV 76 and I 13 would refer to the same event. However, the tablet is too badly damaged to make any certain pronouncement about this issue.

> through]; there is absolutely no way the Elamite [troops] will be able to get at you.
> Don't be afraid; at the city of Urammu where you are to pitch the camp [there is] a plain which is [very] good for encamping; it is also [very] good for reconnaissance expeditions, there is [much] grass there, and it is a [good] place to rest. (I 13:5–19)

This communication presupposes that the Assyrian high command had the following data at hand: first, a detailed knowledge of the terrain at stake (geographical characteristics of the terrain and the cities, the accessibility of mountain passes, the type of terrain and its flora); second, information about the exact position of the Elamite king and an evaluation of the possibility that an Elamite surprise attack would be launched against the Assyrian camp; third, judging from the phrase "Do not be afraid!," they also had information about the morale of the Assyrian camp.

3.2.5 After the war

Once the Ellipian capital was conquered by the Assyrians, Ašpa-bara was appointed king (I 16) and the territory was divided among pro-Assyrian leaders (XV 69). Three governors monitored the region: Mannu-ki-Ninua, governor of Kar-Šarrukkin; Aššur-belu-uṣur, governor of Kišešim[181] or Bit-Hamban;[182] and Marduk-šarru-uṣur, a delegate in Babylonia who was appointed governor in Šangibutu. These governors faced an extremely delicate task—to penetrate the entangled relationships of hatred and servility and distinguish overt loyalty from covert undermining of the Assyrian regime.

Despite the change in regime, the entire region was far from being completely pacified (XV 62, 100, and 101). One of the Ellipian dynasty, Nibê's brother, Lutû (called also son of Dalta), refused to collaborate with the Assyrians. His initial defiance of the Assyrian officials—when Lutû refused to take action against the fugitives of the king—was reported by Aššur-belu-uṣur:

---

[181] SAA XV, XI.

[182] According to XV 60 and 61, Aššur-belu-uṣur collected tribute from Bit-Hamban and delivered it to Babylon.

> The servants of the ki[ng, my lord, who ...], have escaped, and are staying [*with* ...] of Lutû [in ...]. I have written to [Lutû], telling him to [deliver] the tr[aitors], and he (responded): "Come; let you and me g[o] and bring them out (together)." I fear the king; what is it that the king commands? (XV 62:4–11)

After his brother Ašpa-bara turned Ellipi into an Assyrian vassal state, Lutû openly attacked his troops:

> As to the news of Lutû, he and Ašpa-bara are engaged in battle against each other in Hadalpa and killing each other's men. (XV 101:10–14)

To pacify Lutû, the Assyrian court officials orchestrated an exemplary covert action. Šarru-emuranni, the governor of Babylon, kidnapped Lutû's son (XV 100). Once Lutû's son was in Assyrian hands, the Nineveh officials asked Mannu-ki-Ninua to meet Šarru-emuranni in a mountain pass and to transfer Lutû's son secretly to Kar-Šarrukkin. The operation was performed according to plan. Once Lutû's son was under guard within the walls of Kar-Šarrukkin, the Nineveh officials asked Mannu-ki-Ninua to write an angry letter voicing the king's strong disapproval of Lutû's behaviour.[183] Having his kidnapped son in their hands, the Assyrians could dictate their terms.[184]

Not even this intervention brought peace to the region. Marduk-šarru-uṣur, an experienced official whose skill had been tested during a difficult reconsolidation of Babylonia after Merodach-Baladan's defeat, was appointed to control Šingubutu, the region directly bordering on Ellipi. The division of the region between him and Ašpa-bara curbed the authority of the local potentates, Kibabiše and Dasukku, who turned to Ašpa-bara hoping to involve him in an upheaval against the Assyrians. Ašpa-bara, aware that he was closely watched by the Assyrian informers, publicly turned down their request:

---

[183] A similar action was performed by the SIS (Slovak intelligence services) in 1994 when they kidnapped the president's son and transferred him to Austria in order to stop the political movement that he supported.

[184] Line XV 70:r.5' *ma*[!]*-a* DUMU[!]*-a-a bi-la-ni*, "… saying: 'Bring me my son!' " could be Lutû's response to the Assyrian conditions. Unfortunately, the letter is too poorly preserved to determine whether the son in question is really Lutû's son.

> [Concerning the n]ews of the district, they told me [previously: "Ašpa-ba]ri [has t]old Kibabiše and Dasukku: 'The king gave Ellipi to me and I shall enjoy it. He gave Šangibutu to Marduk-šarru-uṣur. It is your towns that have been snatched away. If you (want to) fight, do so, or leave it; I am not involved in it.'"
> He spoke thus before the people of the country. (XV 69:5–18)

The next lines of tablet XV 69 indicate that Kibabiše and Dasukku did undertake an action against the Assyrians by *ka-a-a-ma-nu pu-tu-[u-a] i-du-lu*, "constantly running about opposite [me (Marduk-šarru-uṣur)]"[185] (XV 69:22–23). Since the overall number of the cavalrymen of Kibabiše and Dasukku did not exceed twenty, Marduk-šarru-uṣur investigated the composition of the band harassing his frontier and reported to the Assyrian court:

> Now Kibabiše and Dasukku are constantly running about opposite [me] with a hundred cavalrymen. The king, [my] lord, [knows] that their own [cavalrymen] are (only) twenty (in number); [x of them] are Lutu's, and the rest [of the cavalrymen are] Ašpa-bari's. They do not openly show [that] they are run[ning around] with them. (XV 69:19-r.4)

Thus, Ašpa-bara publicly refused to collaborate with Kibabiše and Dasukku, but at the same time he secretly offered the support of his cavalrymen in the actions of Kibabiše and Dasukku along the Šangibutu frontier. Thus, the same Ašpa-bara who was fighting against his brother Lutû was ready to collaborate with his cavalrymen when the harassment of

---

[185] S. Parpola and A. Fuchs translated the verb *duālu* 'to run about'. From the semantic point of view, the basic meaning of the verb *duālu* is synonymous with a moving around with or without any purpose, such as the wandering of a dog (XV 288, XVI 34, and XIII 190); see *CAD* 3, 58–59. This meaning branched into two directions: first, it describes an idle wandering around (XVI 63; I 153; 154); second, it denotes the walking around of an attendant serving his lord (V 171; XVI 33). Applied to the military, the verb assumes several nuances: first, it designates the walking around of a victorious army (X 104), plundering the enemy territory (I 1); second, it designates the walking of troops stationed at the border whose task was not only to watch an exposed frontier (XV 156), but also to be ready for combat, if necessary (XIII 20); third, judging from its substantivized form *dayyālu* 'scout, picket', the verb describes a scout's reconnoitering activity; see *CAD* 3, 59. Thus, the line in question describes troops running about not only to watch closely the border, but also to join in combat, if disturbed by Marduk-šarru-uṣur's units.

the pro-Assyrian city of Šangibutu was at stake. Thus, this report warned the royal court about Ašpa-bara's duplicity: his overt loyalty disguised his pursuit of personal interests. Sennacherib's annals indicate that Marduk-šarru-uṣur's analysis of Ašpa-bara's duplicitous behavior was correct. For they make clear that later on, Ašpa-bara turned from being a pro-Assyrian vassal, who was secretly plotting against the Assyrians, to an overtly anti-Assyrian king. Ašpa-bara's disloyalty forced Sennacherib, while operating in Babylonia, to make a swift punitive expedition into Ellipi: he destroyed two of Ašpa-bara's royal residences together with another thirty-four cities, and attached Ellipi to the Kar-Šarrukkin province.[186] Ašpa-bara had to escape in order to save his life.[187]

The extant intelligence reports regarding the region of Ellipi allow us to trace the flexibility of the Neo-Assyrian intelligence services over the last decades of the eighth c. B.C.E. The first reports are typical of the reports coming from pro-Assyrian submissive states. Once Dalta died, the situation changed and the Neo-Assyrian intelligence services did not fail to inform the Assyrian royal court about the new developments and secret allegiances. The most important operation of the Neo-Assyrian intelligence services was the detection of the anti-Assyrian coalition and the mobilization of the Elamite king who intervened after the death of Dalta. Any modern government would highly appreciate this intelligence. The intelligence officials monitoring Ellipi also deserve recognition. After the intervention of the Neo-Assyrian troops, the region was apparently pacified. However, the Neo-Assyrian intelligence services were able to monitor new secret allegiances formed under a veneer of pro-Assyrian sentiment. Most modern intelligence services are ready to spend a good part of their budget for reports that clarify who is really an ally and who only looks like an ally.

---

[186] SAAS XII, 24.
[187] Senn Ann II:10–32.

3.3 Assyro-Babylonian conflicts

Most of the intelligence reports among the Neo-Assyrian letters deal with Assyrian control of Babylonia, especially during the reigns of Sargon II and Sennacherib. The complexity of the political situation in Babylonia during this period requires a short historical introduction.

3.3.1 Historical introduction[188]

After the demise of Tiglath-pileser III, the Babylonian king Merodach-Baladan expelled the Assyrian troops and, with Elamite and Aramean support, reestablished the Babylonian kingdom. During the shorter and militarily less aggressive reign of Shalmaneser V, Merodach-Baladan aspired to extend his influence beyond the borders of the territory of his home tribe, Bit-Yakin, to other Chaldean and Aramean tribes. After the death of Shalmaneser V, Sargon II ascended the throne in Assyria. Merodach-Baladan took advantage of Assyrian internal problems and usurped the throne in Babylon.[189] In order to quell opposition, he confiscated property from the citizens of several Babylonian cities and imprisoned some of their leading men.[190]

In 720 B.C.E., Sargon II attempted to recover the territories lost to Merodach-Baladan, but the decisive battle at Der resulted in a draw and for the next ten years, Assyrian presence in the region was limited to three outposts: Der, Dur-Šarrukku,[191] and Dur-Kurigalzu. Ten years later (710

---

[188] The introduction to the political history of Babylonia between 710-700 B.C.E. relies on the following sources and discussions: ABD 4, 732–77; CAH^2 3, 67–88; SAA V, XIII–XXX; SAA XV, XIII–XLII; SAA XVII, XV–XXXVII; SAAS XII, 16–24; Fuchs, *Inschriften,* 373–405; A. K. Grayson, *Assyrian and Babylonian Chronicles* (Locust Valley, N.Y.: J. J. Augustin, 1975), 1–65; Kuhrt, *The Ancient Near East, c. 3000-330 BC,* vol. 2, 493–539, 576–88; Mayer, *Politik und Kriegskunst der Assyrer,* 316–96; Potts, *Elam,* 259–308; G. W. Vera Chamaza, "Der VIII. Feldzug Sargons II. Eine Untersuchung zur Politik und historischer Geographie des späten 8. Jhs. v. Chr. (I)," *Archäologische Mitteilungen aus Iran* 27 (1994); idem, "Der VIII. Feldzug Sargons II. Eine Untersuchung zur Politik und historischer Geographie des späten 8. Jhs. v. Chr. (II)," *Archäologische Mitteilungen aus Iran* 28 (1996).

[189] A. T. Olmstead, *History of Assyria* (Chicago: University of Chicago Press, 1975), 250–51.

[190] Ibid., 252.

[191] There is no evidence as to when Dur-Šarrukku passed into Assyrian hands. Tiglath-pileser III did not list the city among the captured cities and Sargon II's second campaign

B.C.E.) Sargon II launched his second military offensive against Babylonia. The ultimate goal of the campaign was the capture of Babylon. To achieve this, Sargon II set out on a rather elliptical course designed to neutralize Merodach-Baladan's Aramean allies, and to block potential support from the Elamite king Šutur-Nahundi.[192] By this strategy Sargon II intentionally avoided a frontal attack on Babylon, and, even though he now headed a better-equipped and more experienced army,[193] he opted for a more secure, though more complicated, route along the north Tigris.[194]

News of the Assyrian army marching down along the north Tigris route mobilized the anti-Assyrian coalition. The Aramean tribes crossed the Tigris to meet Sargon II's troops. Merodach-Baladan fortified the major north Tigris fortress Dur-Athara and conscripted the Aramean tribe Gambulu. Once the Assyrian royal army reached Dur-Athara, the city had little hope of being able to resist their sophisticated siege machinery and quickly fell into Assyrian hands. The rebels were deported and the city was turned into the capital of the new province of Gambulu, governed by an Assyrian eunuch (Dur-Athara phase).

When the sheiks of the Aramean tribes living along the banks of the Uqnu river heard about the defeat of Dur-Athara, eight of them surrendered. The rest of the sheiks, however, sought refuge in the inaccessible terrain of the Uqnu river. The difficult terrain prohibited Sargon II from deploying his chariotry and cavalry against the rebels. Therefore, he blocked the Tubliaš river, their food supply, and starved the rebels out. Some of them surrendered, but a group of recalcitrant sheiks escaped to the marshes of the Uqnu river. The Assyrians resorted to cutting down the orchards and date palms and thus compelled another fourteen cities to surrender. As a result, the Uqnu region was attached to the Gambulu province (Uqnu phase).

---

was limited only to Der. However, before Sargon II launched his twelfth campaign against Babylonia, the city was already in Assyrian hands. Consequently, the city must have passed into Assyrian hands sometime between 720 and 710 B.C.E.

[192] The Babylonian Chronicle uses the form Ištarhundu and the Elamite sources render his name as Šutur- or Šutruk-Nahhunte; see SAAS XII, 2. Since the following chapters primarily deal with the Neo-Assyrian sources, I use the form "Šutur-Nahundi".

[193] J. Scurlock, "Neo-Assyrian Battle Tactics," in *Crossing Boundaries and Linking Horizons: Studies in Honor of Michael C. Astour on his 80th Birthday*, ed. G. D. Young and R. E. Averbeck (Bethesda, Md.: CDL Press, 1997).

[194] This bespeaks his worries of a repeat of the battle at Der ten years ago; see Potts, *Elam*, 265.

Once the Uqnu region was in Sargon II's hands, the Assyrian troops moved towards Yadburu, which was under Elamite control. The fall of two major Yadburu fortresses, Bab-Duri and Sam'una, made six Yadburean sheiks surrender. The inhabitants of these regions were deported and their cities demolished. Three cities (Lahiru, Sulaja, Gurmuk), together with the land of the Pillatu tribe and the territory along the banks of the Naditu river, were attached to the Assyrian administrative orbit (Yadburu phase).

After having secured the border with Elam by establishing a series of fortresses, Sargon II's army turned back and passed through Raši along the piedmont road. Because the Elamite king avoided a pitched battle with Sargon II and opted to retreat into the Hamrin mountains, Sargon II had to satisfy himself with passing through evacuated cities and appointing an Assyrian delegate over the region.

Only then did Sargon II venture to cross the Tigris. By moving his troops into central Babylonia, he drew a wedge between Babylon and its Chaldean allies. Merodach-Baladan, isolated from the rest of his allies, had but two choices: to escape or to face the Assyrian attack. Choosing the former, Merodach-Baladan fled Babylon by night. After his nocturnal flight, the Chaldean tribes, left to their own devices, quickly surrendered. A small expedition to Sippar pacified the remnants of the rebels. Sargon II's victorious entrance into Babylon and offerings to the Babylonian deities crowned the end of his twelfth campaign (Chaldean phase).

In Iyyar (April/May) of 709 B.C.E., Sargon II moved against Bit-Yakin. Merodach-Baladan prepared his capital for the decisive battle: he fortified the city, dug a moat 100 m wide and 9 m deep, and flooded the area with waters diverted from the Euphrates[195] in order to prevent Sargon II from using his chariotry and cavalry. Sargon II built a ramp across the swamps and burned down the city. Merodach-Baladan once again managed to escape and found refuge in Elam. The inhabitants of Dur-Yakin were deported and the last part of Babylonia was attached to the Assyrian administrative orbit (Bit-Yakin phase).

Babylonia remained in the harsh hands of Assyrian governors until Sargon II's ignominious death in Tabal triggered a wave of insurrections all

---

[195] M. A. Powell, "Merodach-Baladan at Dur-Jakin: A Note on the Defense of Babylonian Cities," *JCS* 34 (1982).

around the empire. Sargon II's son Sennacherib inherited an empire torn by internal strife and external rebellions. Merodach-Baladan, of course, took advantage of the situation and returned to Babylon (intermediate phase). Once again he managed to gain the support of most of the Aramean and Chaldean tribes living in Babylonia. Sennacherib's first campaign was directed against Babylon (704/3 B.C.E.), but Merodach-Baladan managed to escape to Elam yet again. Sennacherib installed a viceroy in Babylon, Bel-ibni, to watch over the rebellious region. However, finding him unfaithful, Sennacherib removed Bel-ibni from office during his second campaign against Babylonia in 700 B.C.E. This campaign ended with a massacre of rebels in the swampy area of southern Babylonia. The last and definitive defeat of Merodach-Baladan's allies took place in 698 B.C.E. when Sennacherib attacked the remnants of the rebels seeking a refuge in southern Elam (final phase).

3.3.2 Intelligence preparing and supporting Sargon II's campaigns

Timely and accurate gathering of all accessible information on the capabilities and intentions of the enemy has always been a good test of the quality of intelligence services. Neo-Assyrian intelligence did not fall short in these activities during Sargon II's invasion. It was responsible for the careful monitoring of the enemy's whereabouts and for providing timely and accurate information from within enemy territory.

3.3.2.1 Enemy whereabouts

The crucial task of Neo-Assyrian intelligence was to monitor the enemy's whereabouts during Sargon II's invasion of Babylonia. Thus, Sargon II's intelligence network reported on Merodach-Baladan's movements and on Merodach-Baladan's most important ally, the Elamite king Šutur-Nahundi. As for the Aramean tribes, their movements were monitored only when they participated in larger military operations (XV 186).

Among the tablets containing information about the whereabouts of Šutur-Nahundi and Merodach-Baladan, only a few also contain time information (XV 118; 155; 217). Most of the tablets contain neither an exact timetable of enemy movements nor the date when the tablets were dispatched. Although we do not have access to the dates when the tablets were dispatched, court officials could easily ascertain the exact date when a given tablet was received, and estimate how much time the messenger had needed to deliver it.[196] Tables 5, 6, and 7 show how closely the movements of Merodach-Baladan and his allies were monitored. According to the collected data, Assyrian military officials had precise information as to where the enemy and his troops were located at a given time. This data allowed the military commanders to create an accurate "map" of enemy movements and assess their intentions.

Since each tablet sent to the royal court contained the name of the sender, and quite often also the source through which the information was acquired, the court officials, having at their disposal the "personal files" of the senders and informers, could evaluate the reliability of that information. Thus, the final decision-making process could take into consideration the time and location of the enemy, as well as the reliability of the sources.

Table 5. Merodach-Baladan's whereabouts during Sargon II's twelfth and thirteenth campaigns

Location	*Reconstructed date*	Sender/source	Tablet
Leaving Cutha T[o] the river	*On the 5th of [xxx]/710*	Il-yada'	XV 155:6–9.r.2–7
Entering [...]	*On [yyy]*	Il-yada'	
T[o] the river	*After [yyy]*	Il-yada'	
Crossing Tigris at Bab-bitqi	*Received on X/Y/710*	Ra'iwanu Šamaš-abu-uṣur *Il-yada'*	XV 186:7–9
(He) returned from *the other side of the Tigris* into his country (Babylon).	*Received on X/Y/710*	Il-yada'	XV 156:r.23
In Babylon	*Received on X/Y/710*	Nabû-belu-ka''in	XV 30:r.11
In Babylon	*Received on X/Y/710*	Il-yada'	XV 157:9'–11'
In Babylon	*Received on X/Y/710*	Il-yada'	XV 158:7–9
In Babylon	*Received on X/Y/710*	Il-yada'	XV 160:5'–6'
In Babylon	*Received on X/Y/710*	Il-yada'	XV 161:7–8
In Babylon	*Received on X/Y/710*	Il-yada'	XV 162:r.11–14
In Babylon	*Received on X/Y/710*	Aššur-belu-taqqin	XV 178:3'

[196] The time needed to deliver a tablet varied depending on the location and the difficulty of the terrain. XV 61:7–8 indicates that the arrival dates of letters were closely watched.

Left Babylon for Dur-Yakin	*On the 11th day of Marchesvan (VIII) 710*	Nabû-bel-šumate	XVII 10:10–11
Going to Borsippa	*Received on X/Y/710*	Nabû-belu-ka''in	XV 33:r.3'–5'
In Nippur	*Received on X/Y/710*	Aššur-belu-taqqin	XV 177:4–5
In Hiuru (Puqudu)	*Received on X/Y/710*	Šarru-emuranni (Int. coming from a seized spy)	XV 218:r.4–7
In Puqudu or in Uruk	*Received on X/Y/710*	Šarru-emuranni	XV 219:5–9
Going to [xxx]	*Received on X/Y/710 or 709*	Unattributed	XVII 181:r.1–3
In Dur-Yakin	*Received on X/Y/709*	Aššur-belu-taqqin	XV 179:9–10
Location broken away	*Received on X/Y/Z*	Aššur-belu-taqqin	XV 180:11
In Elam	*On the 3rd day of [Shebat]/709*	Ana-Nabû-taklak	XVII 68:r.22–24

Table 6. Whereabouts of Merodach-Baladan's army during Sargon II's twelfth and thirteenth campaigns

Location	*Reconstructed date*	Sender/source	Tablet
Kiš	*Received on X/Y/710*	Il-yada'	XV 162:r.12
Moving towards Bab-bitqi	*Received on X/Y/710*	Bel-iqiša	XVII 22:6–18
In most cases Merodach-Baladan's army stayed with the king.			

Table 7. Šutur-Nahundi's whereabouts during Sargon II's twelfth and thirteenth campaigns

Location	*Reconstructed date*	Sender/source	Tablet
He has set out […] and gone […]	*Received on X/Y/Z*	Unattributed	XV 202:r.5'–8'
Bit-Imbî crossing over	*Received on X/Y/Z*	Unattributed	XV 209:r.3'–10'
He returned to […]	*Received on X/Y/Z*	Nabû-belu-ka''in	XV 33:r.7'–8'
[*xxx*]	*Received on X/Y/Z*	Nabû-belu-ka''in	XV 36:4–5
Bit-Imbî	*14th of Kislev 710*	Šamaš-belu-uṣur	XV 118:r.4'

3.3.2.2 Monitoring communications within the enemy coalition

Another important task of Neo-Assyrian intelligence services was monitoring communications within the enemy coalition. Above all, an intercepted communication allowed Sargon II to estimate whether or not enemy coalition troops would come to the assistance of a city under siege (XV 199, see below) or intervene in a military operation, such as the entrance into Babylon (XVII 84:1'–4'). Of particular interest were communications between two major axes of the enemy coalition: the Elamite king Šutur-Nahundi and the Babylonian king Merodach-Baladan.

Neo-Assyrian intelligence was able to intercept at least one of Merodach-Baladan's letters sent to Šutur-Nahundi (XV 200). In this letter a provincial official, whose name has not been preserved, referred to the king's words:

> [Concerning wh]at the king, my lord, wrote to me (a provincial official): "The son of Yakin has written to the king of Elam: 'The king of Assyria [is ma]rching aga[inst me]. You [...]' (XV 200:r.1–6)

Such a quote implies that the Assyrians were able to get hold of what Merodach-Baladan wrote to Šutur-Nahundi, viz., that the king of Assyria was marching against him (XV 200:r.5). S II Ann 309 also confirms that Merodach-Baladan asked Šutur-Nahundi for help but to no avail.[197]

In another letter, Nabû-belu-ka''in described the content of messages exchanged between Merodach-Baladan and Šutur-Nahundi's brother-in-law (XV 32). Merodach-Baladan sent two messengers to Šutur-Nahundi's brother-in-law asking him to move to the city of Har (unknown location). Šutur-Nahundi's brother-in-law, operating at the Elamite frontier, refused to go to the city of Har without the explicit permission of the Elamite king. Therefore, Merodach-Baladan sent a messenger to Šutur-Nahundi, probably to get permission for Šutur-Nahundi's brother-in-law to come to Har. In the second part of the letter (XV 32:r.3–8), Nabû-belu-ka''in reported that the letter of Šutur-Nahundi's brother-in-law was

---

[197] Tabtlet XVII 84 is another report coming from an unknown informer that confirms that the king of Elam will not oppose Sargon II (XVII 84:1'–4').

intercepted. Thus, tablet XV 32 indicates that the Assyrians monitored three channels of communication: Merodach-Baladan – Šutur-Nahundi, Merodach-Baladan – Šutur-Nahundi's brother-in-law, and Šutur-Nahundi's brother-in-law – Šutur-Nahundi. Unfortunately, the tablet is too damaged to reconstruct the contents of the reports.

There is also one letter that Šutur-Nahundi sent to Merodach-Baladan (XV 201). The tablet is too damaged to reconstruct its contents.

These letters, and several dozen fragments containing the names of both kings, indicate that Neo-Assyrian intelligence considered the acquisition of dispatches exchanged between enemy allies as one of its priorities.[198]

3.3.2.3 News from within enemy territory

The Assyrian presence in Babylonia before Sargon II's twelfth campaign was limited, as noted before, to the vicinity of three outposts: Dur-Kurigalzu, Dur-Šarrukku, and Der. At the outset of the campaign, probably right after the conquest of Dur-Athara, Sargon II strengthened Assyrian presence in the region by sending his chosen soldiers to establish a garrison at Dur-Ladini (S II Ann 304–5; XVII 22:r.19–20).[199] This fortress was to watch Sargon II's back while the rest of his army was operating in the east and to maintain its efforts to subvert Merodach-Baladan's kingdom. The presence of the Assyrian troops and Sargon II's victorious advance in

---

[198] According to letter XVII 22, the Assyrian informers working in Babylonia were also able to intercept communications between Merodach-Baladan and his Chaldean ally, Bit-Dakuri (see below).

[199] A. Fuchs noticed the awkward wording in lines 304–305 of Sargon II's Annals and suggested that the lines are a later reformulation of the previous events. The difficulty is that if the Assyrian troops were already in Babylonia, why, then, should Sargon II have left his troops in Dur-Ladini? On this difficulty, see Fuchs, *Inschriften*, 331, who suggests that Sargon II's annals describing the twelfth campaign did not follow the chronological order of events, and so the establishment of the garrison in Dur-Ladini might have happened after the conquest of Dur-Athara and not after the return from Yadburu. Lines XVII 22:r.19–20 confirm A. Fuchs' intuition: "I ... have built a powerful fortress on the border of the lands." Because Bel-iqiša, the sender of the tablet, urged Sargon II to intervene at Bab-bitqi against the coalition led by Merodach-Baladan, the tablet must be dated before Sargon II's crossing of the Tigris. There is no evidence that any other Assyrian fortress might have been built in the region before 710 B.C.E.; thus, it is possible to conclude that the fortress mentioned in XVII 22 was the garrison of Dur-Ladini.

the north-Tigris phase brought pro- and anti-Assyrian sentiments to the boiling point. Merodach-Baladan and his supporters were not willing to give up easily and used every opportunity to harass Assyrian officials (XVII 156:r.2'–20') and installations in Babylonia (XVII 63:3–r.5). The fatigue that the Assyrian officials serving in the triangle Dur-Kurigalzu–Dur-Šarrukku–Dur-Ladini experienced is illustrated by the dispatch of Bel-iqiša: "I have written to the king because I am desperate! The king should not hesitate, for we are now at our limits" (XVII 22:r.20–23). Such fatigue is also conveyed by the ironic letter of Nabû-taklak, serving in Borsippa:

> As to what my brother (Gadiya') wrote: "May you be in good spirits!" How could I be in good spirits! The enemy has pitched camp over against us, we [assemble] for fight [day and] night, and none of yo[u] has co[me] to my aid! I am not in good [spirits] at all! (But) really, you must be in good spirits yourself! You live in [your] lords' house, you eat bread and drink [beer] comfortably in [the house of your lord]! (XVII 63:3–r.5)

Sargon II, aware of the difficulties his officials had to experience, encouraged them to keep their guard strong: "For these two months (while Sargon II was fighting the Aramean tribes and Elam in the East) be attentive (Il-Yada') and keep your guard strong, until I (Sargon II) come" (XV 156:8–10). Besides the fatigue caused by service in this triangle, these reports show that timely intelligence about enemy plans was demanded not because of Sargon II's curiosity to learn what was going on at his back;[200] rather, it was a matter of life and death for the Assyrian officials operating in the triangle of Dur-Kurigalzu–Dur-Šarrukku–Dur-Ladini.

A good illustration of this are the reports on the operation at Bab-bitqi (XV 186 and XVII 22).[201] Tablets XV 186 and XVII 22 represent two independent reports on this crisis. The core of XV 186 is captured in the following lines:

---

[200] See SAA XVII, XVI.

[201] The importance of accurate and timely intelligence for this triangle can be compared with the role that timely intelligence plays in present-day Israel. Since accurate intelligence is a question of survival, the intelligence services are highly appreciated by citizens; see W. Laqueur, *A World of Secrets: The Uses and Limits of Intelligence* (New York: Basic Books, 1985), 221.

The son of Zerî (Merodach-Baladan) is crossing over at Bab-bitqi.
The Itu'u, the Rubu'u, and the [Li]ta'u [have c]rossed [over be]fore them [at] the town Apallâ.
The Rahihu [are spen]ding the night at the town Nunak. (XV 186:7–r.6)

The report says that enemy troops, divided into three units, had crossed the Tigris at three points. The first unit, under the command of Merodach-Baladan, crossed the Tigris at Bab-bitqi. Bab-bitqi was a ferry station on the Tigris in the vicinity of the city Upis (I 94:6–17). If we combine the contents of tablets XV 155, 186, and 189,[202] it is possible to reconstruct some details of Merodach-Baladan's itinerary: his unit departed from Babylon, stopped at Cutha, crossed the Tigris at Bab-bitqi, and moved towards Dur-Šarrukku. Thus, the reports warned the king about an imminent threat that Merodach-Baladan's crossing of the Tigris at Bab-bitqi posed for one of the key Assyrian installations—Dur-Šarrukku, only a dozen kilometers from the Bab-bitqi ferry. The second unit was composed of three Aramean tribes and crossed the Tigris at Apallâ. The third unit was formed by the Rahihu tribe and spent the night in the city Nunak. Unfortunately, it is impossible to locate either Apallâ or Nunak. In sum, tablet XV 186 represents an important warning about the crossing of a large group of hostile troops into Assyrian territory, which directly endangered at least one of the major Assyrian centers.

However, tablet XV 186 was not the only report about the crisis at Bab-bitqi which the king received. The Babylonian pro-Assyrian circles coordinated by Bel-iqiša sent several reports[203] warning the king about the negotiations between Merodach-Baladan and Bit-Dakuri. The king did not pay attention to these warnings and preferred to listen to "the leading men"

---

[202] The connection of tablets XV 155 and 186 is based on the following arguments: Merodach-Baladan's seat was Babylon, and therefore it is possible to assume that his unit departed from Babylon and moved towards Bab-bitqi. Since Cutha is halfway between Babylon and Bab-bitqi and tablet 155 also mentions "the (Tigris) river," then Merodach-Baladan's movements described in XV 155 followed the route Babylon–Cutha–Bab-bitqi. Finally, by continuing the itinerary north of Babylon–Cutha–Bab-bitqi, one reaches Dur-Šarrukku. It is not impossible that such a crossing was prompted by Marduk-šarrani's advice (XV 189, see below).

[203] Lines XVII 22:6–7 read *dib-bi mah-ru-ti ma-la a-na* LUGAL *be-lí-ia ni-il-tap-ra*! LUGAL *ul iš-me,* "As for the previous messages, as many as we had sent to the king, the king did not listen (to them)."

of Babylonia, who followed their own interests (XVII 22:19–24). This mistake almost caused Babylonia to slide out of the king's hands (XVII 22:r.23–24). Lines XVII 22:8–19, besides proving that Bel-iqiša's warnings were correct, describe the results of the military operation at Bab-bitqi. The complexity of the syntax requires a short presentation of these lines.

en-na
A LÚ.TIL.LA.GÍD.DA.MEŠ *šá* URU.É–^{m}*da-ku-ri a-na* 1-*en pi-i ki-i i-tu-ru*
B *a-na* ^{d}AMAR.UTU–DUMU.UŠ–SUM-*na ki-i iš-pu-ru*
C LÚ.GÚ.EN.NA $^{md+}$AG–Á.GÁL LÚ.GAR–UMUŠ *ù e-muq šá* É–^{m}*ia-a-ki-ni*
it-ti-šú-nu a-di UGU (KÁ)–*bit-qa ki-i il-li-ku-ni*
D LÚ.*šak-nu* LÚ.*ki-zu-ú*.MEŠ *šá* URU.É–^{m}*da-ku-ri* LÚ.*a-ra-mu ù* ERIM.MEŠ *šá* URU.É–^{m}*da-ku-ri a-na* UGU-*hi-šú ki-i ú-tir-ru*
E LÚ.*qí-pa-nu ki-i ip-la-hu* *is-sak-tu*
F *ul-lu-ti ki-i iš-mu-ú* *ana ku-tal-li it-te-eh-su*

Now
A after the delegates of Bit-Dakuri had become of one accord,
B (and) after they had written to Merodach-baladan,
C when the *šandabakku* and Nabû-le'i, the commandant, and together with them the troops of Bit-Yakin, marched to (Bab)-bitqi,
D (and) after the prefect had turned the charioteers of Bit-Dakuri, the Arameans and the troops of Bit-Dakuri, against him/it,
E (and) after the delegates had become afraid, they became silent,
F (and) after those had heard, they retreated.

Sections A and B indicate that the delegates of Bit-Dakuri at last reached agreement on their attitude towards Merodach-Baladan. By a written message, they confirmed their willingness to participate in the Bab-bitqi operation. The coalition consisted of Bit-Yakin units (most likely led by Merodach-Baladan himself), Borsippean units lead by Nabû-le'i, a Chaldean unit led by a *šandabakku* (C),[204] and some Arameans (D). According to XV 186 at least four Aramean tribes were involved. However, the prefect of Bit-Dakuri, instead of joining the coalition, turned his units against him/it[205] (D). Thus, the coalition split and "those," i.e., the Chaldean

---

[204] The title *šandabakku* was most often used in Nippur; see SAAS IV, 50-5.
[205] The expression *a-na* UGU-*hi-šú* can be interpreted as turning "against him," namely, against Merodach-Baladan, or "against it," possibly against the city of Babylon; see XVII 21.

units led by the *šandabakku* and Nabû-le'i,[206] retreated (E and F). This split brought the country to the verge of anarchy. Deceitful messages were spread about and each magnate started to fortify his own town (XVII 22:24.r.5–8). Obviously, the news that Merodach-Baladan's coalition had split and was unable to go on with the operation at Bab-bitqi was probably some of the best news Sargon II ever received.

Since tablets XVII 21, 75, and 84 are dated to the same period,[207] it is reasonable to connect them with the chaos into which Babylonia had plunged before Sargon II's crossing of the Tigris. After the split of the coalition, the prefect of Bit-Dakuri ventured an attack against the city of Babylon (XVII 21:r.2–5); the land was plundered (XVII 24:1920), and Borsippa was caught in the flames of an insurrection that ended with a massacre (XVII 75:10–r.10) and the desertion of its inhabitants (XVII 84:r.3–9). Thus, by combining information on the split of the coalition and the anarchy raging in Babylonia with Il-yada''s report (XV 156), which confirmed that Merodach-Baladan would not attack the Assyrian installation anymore, Sargon II could safely complete his north Tigris operations and had enough data to organize the Chaldean phase of his campaign.

In conclusion, the Neo-Assyrian intelligence services before and during Sargon II's twelfth and thirteenth campaigns were responsible for monitoring the enemy's whereabouts, for intercepting communications between enemy troops, for detecting imminent surprise attacks (strategic military intelligence), for informing on rebellions and splits within the enemy camp, for reporting on military actions of the enemy, for providing accurate data about the capabilities of the enemy army (structure, ethnic composition, weaponry, etc.), and for providing basic tactical data (tactical military intelligence). Timely gathering of such data facilitated the Assyrians' military operations and saved many lives.

3.3.2.4 The active involvement of Neo-Assyrian intelligence service

The Neo-Assyrian intelligence services were not only "passively" reporting the news about Assyrian enemies but also "actively" collaborating in bringing Sargon II's campaigns to a successful end. According to the

---

[206] Nabû-le'i was Merodach-Baladan's governor of Bit-Dakuri; see SAA XVII, XXV.
[207] See SAA XVII, XXII–XXVI.

extant Neo-Assyrian archives, the Neo-Assyrian intelligence services established contacts with pro-Assyrian factions, organized special actions, and compromised the enemy intelligence sources.

3.3.2.4.1 Establishing contacts with pro-Assyrian factions

The apex of Sargon II's invasion was the conquest of Babylon (Chaldean phase). However, the economic, political, and religious importance of this Mecca of ancient Mesopotamia called for the employment of other strategies than the iron fist used to subordinate the recalcitrant Aramean tribes. First of all, the takeover of Babylonia had to be carefully timed. Sargon II decided to enter Babylon only after he learned about Merodach-Baladan's flight from Babylon (XVII 10:10–11), when he was sure that the king of Elam would not intervene (XVII 84:1'–4'), and after the Bit-Dakurians retreated to the marshes (XVII 84:r.3–5).[208] Besides this crucial military intelligence, the complex ethnic composition and social stratification of Babylonia required that the Assyrians gain the support of some influential groups in Babylonia. Thus, the Neo-Assyrian intelligence services carefully mapped and established close contact with groups dissatisfied with the current leadership and assured them Assyrian support. These resistance groups penetrated all social strata of Babylonian society: from the nobility of the city of Babylon through the clergy and craftsmen down to the plebs (S II Ann 311–13). The cells of resistance were scattered all around Babylonia; the major Babylonian cities such as Babylon, Sippar, Nippur, and Borsippa became the epicenters of the resistance against Merodach-baladan (see Table 8 and 9).

[208] Dating tablet XVII 84 before Sargon II's entrance into Babylon is based on taking "the king of Assyria" as the subject of lines XVII 84:5'–6' *ù ki-i ana* KÁ.⸢DINGIR.RA⸣.KI *il-la-ka*, "and if he (the Assyrian king) comes to Babylon." Thus, the Assyrian king had not yet entered the city of Babylon at the time when this tablet was dispatched. In the following lines (XVII 84:5'–r.2), an unknown sender encouraged an unknown addressee to enter Babylon. The last lines of the tablet (XVII 84:r.3–9) describe the retreat of the inhabitants of Bit-Dakuri into the marshes. Thus, the tablet describes political unrest and troop movements that preceded the entrance of an Assyrian king into Babylon. Consequently, the tablet could be dated to either Sennacherib's or Sargon II's entrance into Babylon. My preference for the latter is based on M. Dietrich's arguments (SAA XVII, XXV–XXVI): first, the ductus of the writing supports the attribution to Ana-Nabû-taklak, the commander of Borsippa before and during Sargon II's invasion; second, tablet XVII 84 is closely connected with XVII 85, which mentions Šumaya, son of Nenê. Šumaya is also mentioned in XVII 30:3', written by Bel-iqiša, whose letters are safely dated to Sargon II's period.

Table 8. Factions loyal to Sargon II during his twelfth and thirteenth campaigns

Loyal factions	**Location**	**Description of loyalty**
Babylonian nobility	Babylon	"Certain Babylonians, members of the nobility, friends, who are loyal to the king and the vizier..." (XVII 20:7–12).
All Babylonians	Babylon	"When will the king, my lord, come here and establish the protection of Babylon? All Babylonians have daily confidence in this ... the whole of Babylon raises its hands towards my lord" (XVII 21:13–r.2, r.5–6).
Guzummaneans living in Babylon	Babylon	Informing about Merodach-Baladan's escape from Babylon (XVII 10:7–14).
Some priests of Esaggil and Ezida temple	Babylon	The tablets originated from priestly circles voicing the discontent of certain priestly faction with the current leadership[209] (XVII 20, 21, 23, 24, and 67).
Some Larakeans under Da'ini	Chaldea	Lareakans loyal to Assyria were asked to march to Larak (XVII 22:r.10–11).
"Their people"	A Chaldean city (XVII 27:4)[210]	"... their men, who are devoted to nobody, will follow our commands. The king will handle them easily; the king's name is settled upon them" (XVII 27:20–24).
All the people of the land of Akkad	Bit-Dakuri	"[...] all the people of the land of Akkad [...] await the [kin]g, my lord, and bless the king, [my lord]..." (XVII 67:22–24).
Five high-ranking Daratian officials	Darati (Chaldea)	Five Daratians offered collaboration in digging tunnels under the city walls (XV 199).
Merodach-Baladan's opponents in Chaldea	Sippar, Nippur, Babylon, Borsippa	Some inhabitants of these cities were arrested by Merodach-Baladan and kept in chains (Prunk 134; XVII 21:5–15; S II Ann 311–13).
[The elders of S]ippar	Sippar	Report of Radmanu, sheik of Opis about the situation in Sippar (XV 158:10–16).
Isuqaeans (Aramean tribe)	Arranu (unknown location in Babylonia)	Ten Isuqaeans came to negotiate the condition of peace with Il-yada' (XV 162).

[209] G. W. Vera Chamaza, *Die Omnipotenz Assurs: Entwicklungen in der Assur-Theologie unter den Sargoniden Sargon II., Sanherib und Asarhaddon* (Münster: Ugarit-Verlag, 2002), 29.

[210] U[R]U.*kal-du* is translated as "a Chaldean city" instead of "city *conquered.*"

Table 9. Factions opposing the Assyrians in Babylonia during Sargon II's twelfth and thirteenth campaigns

Opposing factions	Location	Description of disloyalty
Chaldean leaders[211] pretending to be Sargon II's collaborators	Chaldea; outside of Babylon	"But the leading men who do not keep the land in order and to whose words the king has listened ... are sending deceitful messages and fortifying their cities" (XVII 22:19–24).
Some Babylonians	Babylon	Since Belšunu described the Babylonians who provided him with information as those loyal to the vizier and the king (XVII 20:7–12), this indicates that there were some Babylonians who were not expecting Sargon II's entrance into Babylon with joy.[212]
Starving Aramean tribes (Lihuteans, Rabileans, Hamaraneans, and Hatalleans)	Vicinity of Sippar	List of starving tribes is in XVII 7:10–13; the discontent of Lihuteans and Hamaraneans is voiced in the following lines: "We shall not make peace until ..." (XVII 8:11'–4').
Aramean tribes (Ita'u, Rubu'u, Lita'u, and Rahihu)	Northern Chaldea	Four Aramean tribes crossed Tigris with Merodach-Baladan (XV 186:7–r.6).
Partly preserved list of people	Region north of Tigris under Il-yada''s watch	They were plotting on Merodach-Baladan's behalf to kill Ani-nuri (XVII 156:r.2–6)

Several letters originating in temple circles[213] demonstrate that the Assyrians found their most collaborative assistants in Merodach-Baladan's seat, Babylon. The most valuable contact the Assyrians were able to establish constituted a group of priests connected with the Nabû and Bel temples of Babylon.[214] Once this contact was established, Sargon II got hold of crucial information about Babylonian sentiment regarding Sargon II's eventual takeover of Babylon. Thus, he learned that the priests of Esaggil and Ezida were unhappy with Merodach-Baladan's leadership because he was negligent in supporting the temple (XVII 21:r.7–10).[215] Moreover,

[211] ERIM.MEŠ *mah-ru-ti šu-nu-ma šá*, "they are leading men who" (XVII 22:19-20).

[212] Vera Chamaza, *Omnipotenz*, 32.

[213] XVII 20-24; 67; 145; 158.

[214] Vera Chamaza, *Omnipotenz*, 21.

[215] G. W. Vera Chamaza suggests reading this difficult passage in the context of the leadership's negligence of its obligation to support the cultic activities in Babylon; see ibid., 29. This interpretation can be supported by reading lines XVII 21:r.7–10 in the

Sargon II's informers kept him posted about the religious interpretation of some recent events and about the instability of the political scene in Babylon. The situation in Babylon was considered serious. The Babylonians were "being handed over to the dogs"[216] (XVII 21:r.4), the city of Babylon was being destroyed (XVII 21:r.11), many bad omens appeared, rare steppe animals entered into the center of the city (XVII 24:25–8), and an "evil enemy who does not fear the gods" (XVII 24:17) plundered and burned the land of Akkad (XVII 24:19). Sargon II was also informed that this disaster was interpreted as Marduk's punishment. He also learned about the reaction of the Babylonian king, namely, that once the king of Babylon heard about the woes pronounced about his wrong deeds—in particular, that the dynasty of the Sealand would disappear,[217]—he reconciled himself with Marduk (XVII 24:21–24). Finally, these contacts helped Sargon II to make the final decision about his entrance into Babylon. Though fighting the Babylonians, the Assyrians venerated the ancient Babylonian religious traditions[218] to the point that Sargon II's magnates attempted to talk him out of entering into Babylon despite all of the reports favoring this symbolic step. His contact with the temple personnel helped Sargon II to clarify the question. The most important information came from Belšunu's report on Bel's oracle, according to which the god Bel declared his intention to oust Merodach-Baladan and guarantee Sargon II's entrance into Babylon (XVII 20:r.1'–

---

context of lines XVII 21:r.1–10 and 23:r.–8, according to which the successful entrance into Babylon was closely connected with the quality of Sargon II's offerings.

[216] The identity of the "dogs" destroying Babylon is far from clear. The fragmentary condition of the tablets allow several possible reconstructions. If the destruction of Babylon is read from tablet XVII 22's point of view, then the "dogs" were the group led by the prefect of Bit-Dakuri who, after the split at Bab-bitqi, turned "against him" (XVII 22:16), i.e., against Merodach-Baladan. Taking advantage of Merodach-Baladan's crumbling power, the Bit-Dakurian troops attacked Babylon. Another possibility would be to connect the "dogs" destroying Babylon with the "evil enemy who does not fear gods ... (who) plundered and bu[rned] the land of Akkad [..] Esaggil, Babylon [...]" (XVII 24:17–20). Since we do not know the identity of this evil enemy, no further conclusions are possible. Finally, the dogs could be identified with the Aramean tribes around Sippar (XVII 7; 8). After their lords let them starve, they rebelled, plundered the land, and attacked Babylon; see ibid., 30–31.

[217] The expression URU-*šú* TIN.TIR.KI, "his city, Babylon," repeated twice in lines XVII 24:22–23 suggests that the object of the woes was the king of Babylon, i.e., Merodach-baladan, whose dynasty, i.e., the dynasty of the Sealand, was doomed to die out. For the identification of Merodach-baladan's dynasty with the Sealand dynasty, see R. Follet, "Une nouvelle Inscription de Merodach-Baladan II," *Biblica* 35 (1954): 423.

[218] J. A. Brinkman, "Sennacherib's Babylonian Problem: An Interpretation," *JCS* 25 (1973): 90.

11'). Independently, the commander of the fortress in Birati, Ana-Nabû-taklak, reported that the gods opened for Sargon II a passage to Borsippa and Babylon(?)[219] (XVII 67:r.3–4). Finally, the report of the prelate Bel-iqiša defined the conditions of a successful entrance into Babylon:

> If you come, (as) [a king who] disposes of the leftovers (of the gods), [who] restores peace (and) [...] to Esaggil (and) Babylon, establishes a pact of protection [and] concludes it with the inhabitants of Babylon, [who reple]nishes [the trea]suries of Esaggil and Ezida–Bel and Nabû will grant (you) a long life, good health and happiness. (XVII 23:r.1–8)

Thus, it is possible to conclude that the Neo-Assyrian intelligence network informed Sargon II when Babylonia was ready for his solemn entrance into Babylon. These reports assured the king that his entrance would be welcomed by the Babylonian gods. Being in close touch with most of the Assyrian sympathizers and adherents, the Assyrians also knew which groups were dissatisfied with Merodach-Baladan's reign and thus were open to collaboration and would welcome Sargon II's entrance into Babylon, and which groups opposed the Assyrians completely or conditionally. Combining these pieces of information with reports about Merodach-Baladan's flight from Babylon, the retreat of militants from Bit-Dakuri to the marches, and assurances that Šutur-Nahundi would not intervene, Neo-Assyrian intelligence services helped Sargon II to make a final decision about his entrance into Babylon.

3.3.2.4.2 Special operations

Modern manuals of intelligence discuss at length whether covert actions, special operations, and paramilitary activities should be classified as intelligence operations or rather as the covert interventions of police or military forces.[220] Since the main element of special operations is the use of

---

[219] M. Dietrich reconstructs the lines as follows: [*x x* $^{d+}$EN] $^{d+}$AG *u* DINGIR.MEŠ *ša* LUGAL KASKAL.2 *šá* LUGAL *be-lí-iá* [*a-na* TIN.TIR.KI *u*] BÁR.SIPA.KI *ip-te-tu-ni,* "[Bel and] Nabû will open the passage of the king, my lord, [to Babylon and to] Borsippa." (XVII 67:r.3–4)

[220] R. Godson, "Covert Action in 1990s: Neither Exceptional Tool nor Magic Bullet," in *Covert Action in the 1990s*, ed. R. Godson, R. J. Kerr, and E. R. May, *Working Group on Intelligence Reform Papers* (Washington, D.C.: Consortium for the Study of Intelligence, 1993), 4–7.

information normally unavailable, I will follow A. Shulsky and G. J. Schmitt[221] in considering these activities a part of intelligence services and present two examples of special operations preserved in the Neo-Assyrian archives.

Local traitors helping the Assyrians to conquer a city

SAA XV 131; ABL 1093; 81-2-4,59
Date: North-Tigris phase (710 B.C.E.)
Location: Der province

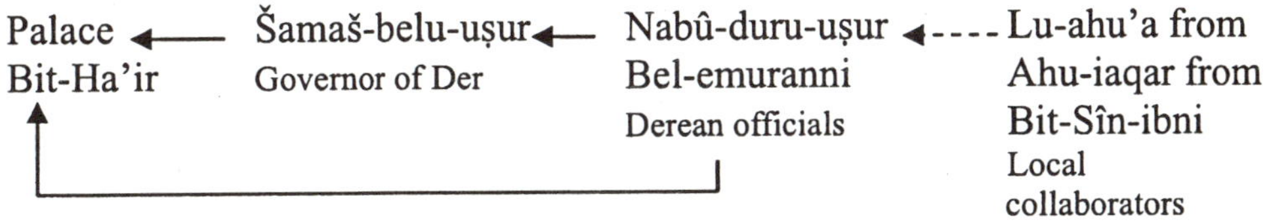

Figure 3. Information flow

Two local collaborators, Lu-ahu'a and Ahu-iaqar, offered to collaborate with the Assyrian officials Nabû-duru-uṣur and Bel-emuranni in capturing the city of Bit-Ha'ir (located in the vicinity of Der[222]). Nabû-duru-uṣur immediately informed his superior Šamaš-belu-uṣur, the governor of Der, about the offer, hoping that the governor would approve it and that the gods would bless it (XV 131:r.12ff). From the fact that this letter was found in Nineveh, it may be concluded that Šamaš-belu-uṣur sent the original, or a copy, to the royal court. At the same time, Nabû-duru-uṣur sent his official, Bel-emuranni, with another letter to the Palace (XV 131:r.9–11). Thus, the royal court received two letters describing the offer: the first one sent via Šamaš-belu-uṣur, the second one via Bel-emurani. The court could compare both letters in order to guard against a possible deception (see Figure 3.).

The letter sent via Šamaš-belu-uṣur starts with a description of the offer:

> [C]ome with al[l the men] in yo[ur] hands, [gather] wha[tever can] go with y[ou t]o Bit-Ha'ir, all those w[ho] are devoted to Eṭiru and

[221] Shulsky and Schmitt, *Silent Warfare: Understanding the World of Intelligence*, 75–97.
[222] Waterman 3, 297

[do not g]o with the Elamites, and come! [W]e shall give up the city [and deliv]er it [into your hands]! (XV 131:10–19)

The offer guarantees that the Assyrians could count on local support, and it also provides an estimate of the extent of the military operation: the local collaborators asked the Assyrians to bring in all the troops standing at Nabû-duru-uṣur's disposal—in particular, the troops devoted to Eṭiru.

Should such a special operation take place, it would have to be approved by Šamaš-belu-uṣur, the governor of Der, whose responsibility it was to decide which units should be dispatched into the front line (*ina* ŠÀ-*bi;* XV 131:r.17), and which units should form the rear of the army (*ina ku-*[*tal-l*]*i*[!]*-en-ni;* XV 131:r.19). Knowing that Šamaš-belu-uṣur had to consult the king about the operation, Nabû-duru-uṣur, in order to facilitate the process, sent another letter with a description of the same offer to the royal court via Bel-emuranni, who was expected to furnish further details in person.

There is no evidence as to whether the operation was approved and carried out successfully, though according to Sennacherib's annals, the city fell into Elamite hands during Sargon II's reign, and was recaptured only in 693 B.C.E. by Sennacherib (Senn Ann IV:54–61). This evidence might indicate that this special operation never took place.

Digging tunnels under the city wall

SAA XV 199; ABL 222; K 186
Date: Chaldean or Dur-Yakin phase[223] (710/9 B.C.E.)
Location: Darati (unidentified site in Babylonia)
Information flow: Local correspondence[224]

---

[223] The whole operation could be dated to the Chaldean or Bit-Yakin phase because Marduk-šarru-uṣur assumed the office of the governor of Babylon only after the conquest of the north-Tigris.

[224] The letter does not start with the sender's traditional greeting. L. Waterman calls it "a community document … a kind of manifesto, a joint report of conditions, proposals, and requests"; see Waterman 3, 90. From the fact that the tablet was found in Nineveh, it is possible to conclude that the dispatch was sent to an Assyrian official who forwarded it to the royal court.

The tablet is an excellent example of a secret military operation. Five traitors offered Marduk-šarru-uṣur, the Assyrian prefect in Babylonia, assistance in capturing the city Darati (unknown location). The operation was to be carried out by means of underground tunnels dug under the city's walls.

The report first established the identity of the collaborators: Sapiku, Aqaba, La-baši, Zaqiru, and Bel-le'i. All of them were inhabitants of Darati and the phrase *a-nin-ni pu*$^{!}$*-tuh*[225] URU.*da-ra-a-te na-ṣa-ni,* "we bear responsibility for the city" (XV 199:3–4), indicates that they belonged to the city's ruling class. Because Merodach-Baladan refused to get involved in the defense of the city, a group of city rulers, realizing that the city could hardly resist the Assyrian siege, if left on its own, opted for secret negotiations with Assyria.

The collaborators proposed a detailed plan for the operation:[226] tunnels would be dug from inside of the city in the house of one of the loyal people. Once the tunnels were finished, Sa'eru and his people would be brought secretly into the city. Meanwhile Marduk-šarru-uṣur's army would surround Atâ's wing of the city. The operation itself would start *a-ki dib-bi lam-ma-du-u-ti ina* ŠÀ-*bi* URU.*da-ra-a-ti e-tar-bu*, "after one of them (?) has entered Darati by learned words" (XV 199:r.2–4).[227] Once Sa'eru and his troops were inside the city and Marduk-šarru-uṣur's army outside, the city should quickly fall into Assyrian hands.

As good politicians, the collaborators were aware that such an offer would be scrutinized in order to rule out a trap, and so they provided important supportive intelligence: "Merodach-Baladan will not come to their (Daratian) help" (XV 199:r.17–19). This information came from the mouth of a man who took part in the earlier negotiations with Merodach-

---

225 This study will take *pu*$^{!}$*-tuh* as a bound form of *putu(h)hu* used in the Neo-Assyrian idiom *putu(h)hu našû* meaning "to bear responsibility for" (see von Soden 2, 885), as suggested by S. Parpola (SAA XV, 130), instead of L. Waterman's reading: "We are bringing the overseer(?) of the city Darati" (see Waterman 1, 151).

226 Iconographic representation of a similar operation can be found on relief WA 124 554, dated to 865 B.C.E.; see SAA XV, 131.

227 The adjective *lam-ma-du-u-ti* is derived from the D-stem of the verb *lummudu* meaning "to teach someone (a craft or skill) in apprenticeship context"; see *CAD* 9, 53. Such a meaning would describe an activity of a person whose training enables him or her to deliver a convincing speech.

Baladan about support for the city,[228] and it aimed at convincing the Assyrians that Merodach-Baladan's army would not ambush the Assyrian troops.

Even though the final decision about the operation would be taken in Nineveh, the provincial center played a decisive role in it. Its role can be summarized thus: the provincial center acted as the mediator between the royal court and the collaborators; it reported the details of the offer and supportive data; and if the project were approved, it would be the responsibility of the provincial center to carry it out.

3.3.2.4.3 Neo-Assyrian counterintelligence

Whether knowledge acquired through an intelligence network, through penetration into enemy camps, or through intercepted communications is a useful asset for a hostile intelligence service depends, above all, on whether the enemy knows that the hostile force knows. A. Codevilla illustrates this basic principle of counterintelligence with the following example:

> They know. It's all right–we know they know. No, they know we know they know. It's all right–we know they know we know they know–and so on, ad infinitum. But in real life such chains are finite, and the most useful knowledge about the enemy is knowledge of which the enemy is not aware.[229]

Even though the term "counterintelligence" belongs to our modern vocabulary, the reality it represents is much older, perhaps indeed a human universal. The Neo-Assyrian archives present several cases of counterintelligence on both sides.

---

[228] Lines r.14–s.3 have a common subject: "he (Sapiku) says … he (Sapiku) says … I (Sapiku) have." It is quite possible that the subject of these verbs is one of the five collaborators who played the leading role in the conspiracy. Since line r.16 mentions Sapiku's name and Sapiku is listed as the first of five collaborators, he probably led the Duratian delegation asking Merodach-Baladan for his military support. Thus, information that Merodach-Baladan would not get involved in the defense of the city was coming from a first-hand source. Moreover, the line "there are no men who are not loyal to Sa'eru in Sapiku's house" indicates that Sa'eru's people would be safe when entering the city through the tunnels because Sapiku's house was loyal to Sa'eru.

[229] Codevilla, *Informing Statecraft*, 29.

An Assyrian official in Merodach-Baladan's service

SAA XV 189; ABL 1024; K 5333B
Date: Pre-campaign phase (early 710 B.C.E.)
Information flow: Local communication[230]

Tablet XV 189, in its restored form, contains at least two quotations from an Assyrian official, Marduk-šarrani. In the last quotation[231] Marduk-šarrani passed important strategic intelligence to Merodach-Baladan:

> He (Marduk-šarrani) has (also) said to the son of Yakin (Merodach-Baladan): 'There is no water in Dur-Šarrukku. If you (Merodach-Baladan) come and launch an attack on it, you will take it in a matter of a day.' (XV 189:r.9'–13')

Marduk-šarrani, being an Assyrian provincial official, had access to important strategic data concerning the region west of Der, such as the extent of arable fields, taxes, and the hydrology of the Diyala river. Thus, passing information about the severe drought in Dur-Šarrukku to Merodach-Baladan would reveal the vulnerability of a key Assyrian outpost situated about 80 km north of Babylon. Capturing Dur-Šarrukku would give Merodach-Baladan a strategic advantage: it would allow him to secure his northern border, confine Il-yada''s influence to Dur-Kurigalzu, and drive a wedge between Šamaš-belu-uṣur's province (Der) and Il-yada''s territory.[232]

---

[230] The letter does not start with the usual opening greeting typical of the reports sent by provincial officials to the royal court. The opening "he says" is typical of communications between local officials, such as those found in the Governor's Archives; see SAAS IV, 84–106. That the letter was found in Nineveh indicates that this is an original or an exact copy of a report exchanged between two local officials.

[231] L. Waterman interprets the second speech as "a copy of a treasonable letter" of Marduk-šarrani; see Waterman 3, 283.

[232] There are two other letters sent by Marduk-šarrani to the king (XV 187 and 188). According to these letters, Marduk-šarrani was a medium-rank Assyrian official in charge of cultivation work and tax collection in the Labdudu region, west of Der. The identification of Marduk-šarrani, the sender of XV 187 and 188, with the Marduk-šarrani of XV 189, suggested by S. Parpola (SAA XV, XIX), can be further supported by the facts that all three letters deal with the same territory (west of Der) and by the linguistic connection between the verb *dabābu* ("plotting against/litigating with (Marduk-šarrani)"; see XV 189:3) and *mahāru* ("the appeal about which the king wrote to Marduk-šarrani"; see XV 188:4–6). Since the connection between the legal terms *dabābu* 'to contest, litigate'

Even though the first quotation is heavily damaged, it is still possible to reconstruct one of Marduk-šarrani's motivations for betraying Assyria. His question—"Who is the one who is plotting against me in Assyria?" (XV 189:2–3)—suggests that Marduk-šarrani got into trouble at the royal court and that Merodach-Baladan came to know about his problems. From this report it is impossible to conclude whether Merodach-Baladan came to know about Marduk-šarrani's problems and shrewdly took advantage of his shaky position at the court, or whether Marduk-šarrani, motivated by frustration, jealousy, and a desire for vengeance, willingly offered his services to Merodach-Baladan.[233]

If we connect this tablet with tablets XV 186 and 155, which report on Merodach-Baladan's movements, it is possible to surmise that Merodach-Baladan followed Marduk-šarrani's advice and crossed the Tigris at Bab-bitqi with the intention of attacking Dur-Šarrukku (see 3.3.2.3).

We know that they know what we are doing

SAA XV 157, ABL 1041, Sm 30
Sender: Il-yada' (Assyrian official operating north of the Tigris and Nar-Šarri canal)
Date: 710 B.C.E. (Dur-Athara or Diyala phase)

Though tablet XV 157 presents an excellent example of Neo-Assyrian psychological warfare (see 4.2.1.2), it also illuminates the intricate relations between Merodach-Baladan's intelligence and Neo-Assyrian counterintelligence. In it we learn that Merodach-Baladan's local informers reported on a subversive Assyrian mission conducted among the Aramean

---

and *mahāru* 'to appeal' is known from other letters (XV 15; 24), it is possible that Marduk-šarrani understood the appeal of Nabû-šarru-ibni and [Mak]kame to the king (XV 188:5–6) to mean that they were contesting/plotting against him in Assyria (XV 189:3).

[233] According to the motivations which enable foreign intelligence services to recruit an agent from among enemy officials, M. Lloyd divides intelligence agents into six groups: (1) the ideologist (acting from patriotic, political or religious conviction); (2) the agent of conscience (acting to save world peace); (3) the non-achiever (motivated by frustration, jealousy, desire for vengeance); (4) the agent under pressure (subject to blackmail or compromising traps); (5) the mercenary (possessing financial motivations); and (6) the adventurous (those who like danger in itself); see M. Lloyd, *The Guinness Book of Espionage* (New York: Da Capo Press, 1994), 106–112. If the reconstruction of the tablet proposed above is correct, then Marduk-šarrani would belong to group three or four.

tribes loyal to Merodach-Baladan. The description of Merodach-Baladan's informer as "one of [his] broth[ers]" (XV 157: 9') indicates that the anti-Assyrian faction of the tribe provided Merodach-Baladan with information about Assyrian attempts to gain Aramean support. Because the Assyrian mission was not undertaken in secret but was aimed at the general public, Merodach-Baladan's informer probably did not have to make too much of an effort to get hold of this information. However, the Assyrians immediately came to know that their subversive activity had been reported to Merodach-Baladan, and lines 9'–11' even report the message sent to Merodach-Baladan word for word.[234]

Capture of an enemy spy

SAA XV 218, ABL 763 + ABL 1213; 81-2-4,125 + 81-2-4,126
Date: Chaldean phase
Reported information: capture of Merodach-Baladan's informer in Larak; Merodach-Baladan's whereabouts.

Figure 4. Information flow

Merodach-Baladan's intelligence agent was sent by [^{m}x]*x-ha-a-a-ú* to spy on the city of Larak. The agent was compromised and brought to Šarru-emuranni, who conducted two series of interrogations. The first aimed at proving the spy's identity and the second one aimed at determining Merodach-Baladan's whereabouts (see Figure 4.).

234 Merodach-Baladan's intelligence services and the Neo-Assyrian counterintelligence networks operated in Chaldea in a similar way, as illustrated by tablet XVII 62, dated to 710/9 B.C.E. (Chaldean or Bit-Yakin phase). Nabû-taklak (shortened form of Ana-Nabû-taklak, the commander of the fortress in Borsippa) visited the city Marad; thus the Assyrians knew that Nabû-taklak went to the city of Marad. The Maradians sent a messenger to [NN], and thus the hostile forces learned that Nabû-taklak visited Marad. The Assyrians learned that the hostile forces learned that Nabû-taklak visited Marad. This interpretation is based on M. Dietrich's reconstruction of the obverse of the tablet; see SAA XVII, 60. That NN was part of a hostile group can be deduced from the reverse of the tablet, when Nabû-taklak complains that the people of Bit-Dakuri refused to obey him. Unfortunately, the tablet is broken in the crucial places and thus the reconstruction presented above is far from the only possible interpretation.

Merodach-Baladan's agent came to Larak under cover of a Babylonian envoy. The Larakeans recognized him as a Nippurean[235] and called him a crook and liar.[236] At that time, Babylon was already under the Assyrian governor Šarru-emuranni. Therefore, there was no reason to be suspicious of a traveler coming from Babylon to Larak. The fact that Merodach-Baladan imprisoned the pro-Assyrian Nippureans, who were liberated only in the last phase of the war (S II Ann 373), suggests that Merodach-Baladan still had some control over Nippur during the Chaldean phase. Since both Nippur and Babylon contained Chaldean minorities,[237] a Chaldean Nippurean could easily pass for a Chaldean Babylonian and thus be used for espionage purposes after Merodach-Baladan had to withdraw from Babylon. Therefore, a Chaldean Nippurean disguising himself as a Chaldean Babylonian was rightly suspect.

Once the spy's disguise was revealed, he underwent an interrogation during which he revealed that Merodach-Baladan was stationed in Hiuru of Puqudu. Merodach-Baladan's presence in this territory, which had already been incorporated into the Gambulu province, would represent an important piece of intelligence about Merodach-Baladan's secret negotiations. Šarru-emuranni sent the captured spy to the king for further investigation. Displaying the traits of an experienced intelligence coordinator, Šarru-emuranni, after having received news contradicting the spy's testimony, sent his own agents to Sapia to inquire about Merodach-Baladan's whereabouts (XV 219), in case the captured Nippurian tried to deceive him.

---

[235] Line XV 218:r.1 can be reconstructed in the following way: "EN.LÍL.KI-*a-a* [*šu-u*]," "[he is a] Nippurean."

[236] The common practice of each security agency (usually an operational branch of intelligence services) is to screen intruders to uncover their true identity. Once a false identity is recognized, the person is immediately suspect and the security organs are allowed to take adequate actions or hand over that person to other branches of intelligence services for further interrogation. A false identity may be penetrated during the interrogation of immigrants (e.g., Joseph's brothers Gn 42:5–17), if their accent betrays them, or if they are unable to produce the requisite documents.

[237] SAAS IV, 23–44.

3.3.3 Neo-Assyrian intelligence in the post-war period

3.3.3.1 Intermediate phase

Several reports dated to the period after Sargon II's twelfth and thirteenth campaigns give the impression that the situation in Babylonia had stabilized. The king's assignments were proceeding according to plan (XVII 101:r.10'-2'), tribute was delivered (V 257:2'–8'), the temples were examined (XVII 43:6–r.8) and placed under control (XV 241:4–11), informers guaranteed the delivery of intelligence (XVII 146:1'–r.10), some local quarrels were settled (XVII 155:4–r.18), Bit-Dakuri was finally pacified (XVII 68:5–10; 73:4–r.4), no bad news was coming from Elam (XVII 49:11–r.1), and the situation was generally characterized as stable (XVII 68:8; 86:6–r.2).

Only petty wars between local officials stirred up the seemingly calm waters of Babylonia. The royal court received several reports about such petty conflicts. On the one hand, officials were denouncing each other and struggling to obtain the king's favor.[238] For instance, Amel-Nabû (a Babylonian official) accused his colleague Mannu-ki-Urbail of burning his fields and denying him food and seed grain (XVII 48); and Sin-duri, prelate of the Eanna temple in Uruk, complained about being turned into a laughing stock by his colleague, Qištiya (XVII 130:13–14). On the other hand, the accused officials asked the king not to trust their accusers (XVII 52:5–20; 164:r.1'–6'). The report on Batulu's raid (XV 168), sent to the king by the Assyrian official, Il-yada', illustrates these small-minded conflicts. Batulu was an Assyrian official[239] working for an Assyrian governor whose name has not been preserved. Batulu shrewdly took advantage of his position at the royal court and slandered Am-yata', the Assyrian delegate, before the king. Then, with the help of two hundred and fifty Chaldeans, he looted Am-yata''s city, molested slave girls, slaughtered pigs, destroyed vines, and captured royal servants. Because Am-yata''s town was under Il-yada''s jurisdiction, Il-yada' sent his official to reestablish order and to arrest Batulu. The transgressors resisted; however, the Assyrian posse managed to arrest them and bring them to Il-yada'. Knowing that the best defense is a

[238] For an example of an effort to secure a good appointment, see XVII 86.

[239] Since Batulu could visit and influence the king, he probably belonged to the high-ranking officials.

good offense, Batulu at the royal court accused Il-yada' of mistreating him. Tablet XV 168 furnishes Il-yada''s explanation of the problem.

Although several reports give the impression that the situation in Babylonia was under control, hostilities against the occupying forces resurfaced as soon as the royal army moved away (XVII 172:4–r.6). The heavy burden imposed on the tribes quickly aroused resistance not only among those tribes that still harbored a preference for Merodach-Baladan (XVII 142), but also among the Assyrian allies (V 63). The settling of new ethnic deportees in Babylonia and the ravishing of the local bands added to the border instability of the region. The Neo-Assyrian intelligence services reported the results of these hostilities: some Babylonians were murdered (XVII 92:4–9); the people from the Tubliaš region were running away to Elam (XVII 149:5–12); some cohort commanders were killed during one skirmish (XV 35:12–7); and in another conflict an Assyrian royal bodyguard was chased away (XV 369:1'–3'). Moreover, despite the rehabilitation of Bit-Dakuri, Nabû-taklak complained about the disobedience of Bit-Dakuri (XVII 62:r.6') and reported that the guards in Bit-Dakuri still had to be on high alert (XVII 68:9–10).

The reports coming from the Elamite border informed the king that the situation along the Assyro-Elamite frontier was far from stable. Above all, the Assyrian officials had to face raids along the trade routes. For instance, letter XV 37 reports the worries of an official from the vicinity of Der who recommended delaying the delivery of oxen because bandits were looting caravans carrying tribute. A Meturnian official, however, insisted on the delivery, and the caravan set out from Der, accompanied by a cohort of soldiers. But after one league the caravan had to return because "the enemy was attacking them" (XV 37:14'–15'). The caravan could pass through only five days later.

Not only the commercial roads but also the Assyrian installations along the Assyro-Elamite frontier were exposed to the raids of bandits, whose subversive activity was often supported by Elam (XV 116; 118).[240]

---

[240] The frontier looting strategy was also adopted some by the Czechoslovakian intelligence services at the West German-Czechoslovakian border between 1952 and 1956. The armed ŠtB units (Czechoslovakian intelligence services) plundered West German border villages, imprisoning or even executing the villagers. The raids were known collectively as "akce Kámen" (Operation Stone); see Frolík, *Špión vypovídá*, 108–13.

Tablet XV 116, sent by the Assyrian official, Šamaš-belu-uṣur, describes a group called Gar[...eans] who raided the city of Gabê, located somewhere along the piedmont of the Hamrin range between Meturna and Der. The pro-Assyrian Gabeans were panic-stricken; one half of them fled to the mountains and the other half took refuge in the inner city. The Assyrian official, Nabû-belu-ka''in, sent his troops to pacify the city. Along the same lines, tablet XV 118 provided the court with news on a foray by a band supported by Elam.[241] The leader of the raiders—the Elamite herald[242]—attacked the city of Malak, located at the Raši border. The raid was successful: the bandits plundered Zera-iddin's household, took a heavy booty, and imprisoned some of the Malakeans. The rest of the Malakeans managed to escape to Der. The general tone of Šamaš-belu-uṣur's letter is very calm, and there is no sign of panic. This indicates that, up to that point, the raiders did not intend to attack Der but rather limited themselves to the looting of border towns. The intelligence provided in both reports (XV 116 and 118) can be divided into four clusters: identification of the raiders (local bands supported by Elam); an estimate of losses and captured booty; the reaction of the local inhabitants (in both cases the local inhabitants were scared[243] and escaped); and a report on the results of Assyrian punitive interventions (in both cases the Assyrian troops were able to recapture the cities). Monitoring the raids along the Assyro-Elamite frontier also provided the royal court with information about the security of the strategically important road[244] between Meturna and Der, which was used as the main artery for moving tribute from the Der province (XV 27:r.1'-6').

The main task of intelligence in the post-war period did not change too much in comparison with the pre-war and war periods. Its highest priority still remained guaranteeing the security of the region by detecting surprise attacks. Besides small local skirmishes and raids by bands, the

---

[241] Elamite backing of the raid is deduced from the fact that the letter reported on the position of the Elamite king (XV 118:r.2–4).

[242] A. Fuchs suggested identifying the herald with Umman-minâ of XV 129:9–10; see SAA XV, XXXV.

[243] Both letters describe the reaction of the people with the same verb *qarāru* 'to grovel, to writhe' (XV 116:r.8'; 118:8').

[244] The strategic importance of this road was noticed by H. W. Saggs. He suggested that by this road "the Assyrians could rapidly bring military forces against any point in Babylonia and by-pass the concentration of the cities at the neck formed by the convergence of the Euphrates and Tigris"; W. F. Saggs, "The Nimrud Letters, 1952—Part I," *Iraq* 17 (1955): 46.

Assyrians had to deal with large-scale enemy military operations. Letter XV 88,[245] coming from the hand of the Assyrian governor, Nabû-belu-ka''in, describes the successful detection of a Puqudian plan to carry out a surprise attack against Assyrian-controlled Babylonia, and demonstrates that the Puqudu tribe kept harassing Assyrian establishments for several years after the fall of Dur-Yakin. As far as the fragmentary status of the report permits, the following reconstruction may be proposed: Belšunu and his Puqudian companions,[246] whose names are not preserved, "went down" to the territory under Nabû-belu-ka''in's jurisdiction. PN, Nabû-belu-ka''in's official, heard about the Puqudian plans. When Belšunu and his people saw that their plans were revealed, they returned to Puqudu. Thus, a timely warning prevented the Assyrians from being caught by surprise.

While most of the small-scale attacks and raids were reported post factum, failing to detect large-scale Elamite operations beforehand could easily have had disastrous consequences for the provinces of Der and Gambulu. An important warning came from merchants trading wool with Bit-Imbi. According to their information, "the (Elamite) palace herald and the entire army of Upper Elam are at Bit-Imbi. They *are crossing* a ford on the river Abani" (XVII 136:r.2–5). The sender of the letter, Marduk-naṣir, asked the vizier to organize the army and station it opposite the Elamite troops. In another report, Nabû-šuma-lišir and Aqar-Bel-lumur, commanders in Gambulu, listed the countermeasures taken once they received warning of an imminent Elamite invasion (XVII 120:8–13). At the command of the messenger from Der, the people from Der as far as the river Nergal were mobilized and asked to move to the fortified places. The region returned to normal when it was learned that "there is nothing to worry about" (XVII 120:r.11–21).

---

[245] Three letters, XV 35, 37, and 88, can safely be attributed to Nabû-belu-ka''in (III), i.e., to the period when Nabû-belu-ka''in finished his tenure as the governor of Kar-Šarrukki and became active in the area southeast of Der; see SAA XV, XXXIX. A. Fuchs based his claim on the following argument: Nabû-belu-ka''in was the governor of Kar-Šarrukin before Manu-ki-Ninua. The change of governors must have happened before Nibû, Dalta's son, usurped the throne (probably 708 B.C.E.) and therefore can be dated to the post-war period; see SAA XV, XLIII.

[246] Identification of Belšunu and his companions as Puqudians is based on the assumption that the subjects of the verbs *i-tu*[!]*-ur*[!]*-du* (XV 88:8) and *e-ma-ru-u-ni* … *it-ta-ab-bu* [*i-su-uh*]-⌜*ru*⌝ … (XV 88:10–13) are Belšunu and his companions, who returned to Puqudu.

Thus, in the post-war period, it was the task of intelligence to assess correctly such warning signs as local unrests, upheavals, riots, or skirmishes, which, if unnoticed and unpunished, could easily grow into open rebellions. A surprise invasion of Elamite troops could result not only in the plunder of the Assyrian provinces but also in their loss.

3.3.3.2 Final phase

The content of the intelligence reports sent from Babylonia changed after Sargon II's infamous death. A series of reports coming from two commanders stationed in Gambulu informed the king, now Sennacherib, about Merodach-Baladan's return to Babylonia. Reports XVII 106, 107, 110, 112, and 113 came from Aqar-bel-lumur, and reports XVII 115, 117, and 118 came from Aqar-bel-lumur and his colleague Nabû-šumu-lišir.[247] The informers reported that Merodach-Baladan was back in Babylon (XVII 55:7;[248] 106:5; 115:10; 116:9–10; 118:9),[249] and that he had become involved in the celebration of a festival during the month of Nisan (XVII 110:5'–10'; 115:9–16). From the strategic point of view, report XVII 106 was probably the most important dispatch on the situation at the beginning of Sennacherib's reign. The strategic importance of this report can be summed up in five points: 1) Merodach-Baladan's return to Babylon (XVII 106:5); 2) the march of anti-Assyrian troops to Litamu (XVII 106:6–10); 3) their intention to attack Bit-Dakuri (XVII 106:10–15); 4) the reaction of Babylonia to this march (XVII 106:15–r.1); and 5) the rules of the anti-Assyrian alliance (XVII 106:r.2–6). The Assyrian court received a warning that enemy troops led by Nabû-hamatua[250] had marched downstream to the

---

[247] According to M. Dietrich's reconstruction, there are two more reports mentioning Merodach-Baladan, XVII 109 and 116; see SAA XVII, 96, 103. However, these reports are very fragmentary.

[248] This report was dispatched by Bel-ibni, whose identity still remains doubtful; see J. A. Brinkman, "Bel-Ibni's Letters in the Time of Sargon and Sennacherib," *RA* 77 (1983). However, M. Dietrich's research suggests that Bel-ibni, mentioned in letters XVII 52-7, can be identified with high probability as the viceroy of Babylonia appointed by Sennacherib; see SAA XVII, XXIV, AOAT 253, 83. There are other letters coming from Bel-ibni (XVII 56 and 57) that also mention Merodach-Baladan's name; unfortunately, they are too fragmentary.

[249] If M. Dietrich's reconstruction is correct, then reports XVII 109, 113, and 118 also contained information about Merodach-Baladan's whereabouts; see SAA XVII, 96, 101, 105.

[250] The troops were led by Nabû-hamatua. K. Kessler identified the Nabû-hamatua mentioned in tablet XV 179 with the Nabû-hamatua mentioned in tablet XVII 106; see

territory of the Aramean tribe Lita'u[251] and intended to attack the cities of the Chaldean tribe Bit-Dakuri. After a series of rebellions, Bit-Dakuri had been pacified by Sargon II shortly after 709 B.C.E. Between Sargon II's and Sennacherib's campaigns, Bit-Dakuri was controlled by the Assyrians, who used the region as a base for extinguishing anti-Assyrian hostilities. Thus, Nabû-hamatua's march and his intention to attack Bit-Dakuri could have seriously undermined the Assyrian foothold in Babylonia. The tablet indicates that the Bit-Dakurians welcomed Nabû-hamatua's march.[252]

In sum, Sennacherib was promptly informed about Merodach-Baladan's reconquest of Babylon, about the details of the anti-Assyrian alliance,[253] and even about the death of Merodach-Baladan's wife (XVII 112:7).

Prosopography 2/II, 833–34. M. Dietrich suggested dating tablet XVII 106 to the reign of Sennacherib, at the time when Merodach-Baladan again attempted to recover Babylon (705 B.C.E.), whereas tablet XV 179 must be dated to the Bit-Yakin phase (709 B.C.E.). However, the dating of the tablets does not exclude the possibility that it was the same associate of Merodach-Baladan who once mustered the troops in Puqudu and later on marched with his troops "downstream all the way to Litamu" (XVII 106:6–9).

[251] The variant spelling of the name of this Aramean tribe is Li'tta'u; see E. Lipinski, *The Aramaeans: Their Ancient History, Culture, Religion* (Leuven and Sterling, Va.: Peeters, 2000), 467. Lita'u was an Aramean tribe which was subdued during the north-Tigris phase of Sargon II's campaign (Prunk 18–19).

[252] This reconstruction is based on the following interpretation of the obscure syntax of lines XVII 106:15–r.1. It must be noted that the syntax permits more than one interpretation of the reaction to Nabû-hamatua's march. *šá-ni-ia-a' um-ma a-mat-su-nu i-ba-áš-ši šá il-li-ka ul ṭa-bu-ú ki-i ih-hi-su-nu a-na* TIN.TIR.KI *n*[*i*!]-*ter-bu-nu,* "secondly, there are their words (of Bit-Dakurians) as follows: 'Isn't it good that he (Nabû-hamatua together with his army) came here? When they (the Assyrians or Nabû-hamatua and his troops) retreat, we (Bit-Dakurians) can enter Babylon.'"
The expression *ki-i ih-hi-su-nu* can be taken as 3rd p. sing. or as 3rd p. pl. with a Babylonian subjunctive marker. If taken as 3rd p. sing., then the expression can refer to Nabû-hamatua. If taken as 3rd p. pl., one possible interpretation is that when Nabû-hamatua enters Bit-Dakuri, the Assyrians will have to retreat and then Bit-Dakurians can reenter Babylon. In a similar way, Bit-Dakuri took advantage of Sargon II's army fighting in north-Tigris, and the prefect of Bit-Dakuri turned his troops against Merodach-Baladan and entered Babylon, if the "dogs" in XVII 21:r.4 are to be identified with the Bit-Dakurians.

[253] The anti-Assyrian allegiance was enforced under a threat of punishment (XVII 106:r.2).

3.3.4 Information network

The recent publication of SAA and Neo-Assyrian Prosopography volumes allows a partial reconstruction of the intelligence network covering Babylonia during the reigns of Sargon II and Sennacherib.

3.3.4.1 Agents

According to the preserved sources, from the time before Sargon II's invasion until Sennacherib's campaigns, the royal court was informed about matters in Babylonia by at least 112 agents.

Table 10. Intelligence network in Babylonia during Sargon II's and Sennacherib's reigns

Northwestern Babylonia
Assyrian officials:
1-EW The elders of Sippar (XV 158–59)
2-CW Nabû-ahhe-lumur; Sippar (XVII 7–9)
3-LW Nabû-bel-šumati; Birati (XVII 10–16)
4-GW Il-yada'; (?)(XV 155–76)
5-GU Marduk-šuma-iddina; (?) (XVII 17–19)
6-UB Aššur-belu-taqin; (?) (XV 177–83)
7-UW Marduk-šarru-uṣur; (?) (XV 184–85)
8-UW Marduk-šarrani; (?) (XV 187–88)
Local:
9-SW Radmanu; Opis (XV 158–59)
10-UW Ra'iwanu (XV 186)
11-UW Šamaš-abu-uṣur; (?) (XV 186)

Babylon and its vicinity
Assyrian officials:
12-OP Bel-iddina (XVII 43–44)
13-UP Amel-Nabû (XVII 48–50)
14-UU Arad-Ea (XVII 51)
15-VP Bel-ibni (XVII 52–57)
16-UP Bel-ibni's opponent (XVII 52)
17-CW Ha'il-il (XVII 59–61)
18-CW Zabdi-il (XVII 59–61)
19-UW Ahi-nuri (XVII 156)
21-CU Gabbarru (XVII 157)
22-UW Marduk-apala-iddina (XVII 158)
23-GP Šarru-emuranni (XV 21739)
24-CU NN, the cohort commander (XVII 168)
25-UW Šamaš-taklak: (?) (XV 180)

Temple personnel:
26-TW Eṭiru (XV 161)
27-TW Belšunu (XVII 20)
28-TW NN from Babylon (XVII 21)
29-TW Bel-iqiša (XVII 22–31)
30-TB Qišti-Marduk (XVII 39–42)
31-TP Ina-tešî-eṭir (XVII 32–33)
32-TP Rimutu (XVII 47)
33-TP Nabû-šumu-lišir (XVII 34–38)
34-TP Nabû-šuma-iškun (XVII 39; 46; 133)
35-UU Ilu-ipuš (XVII 45)
Local:
36-UW Leading people of the land (XVII 22)
37-NW Gu[zummaneans] (XVII 10)
38-UW A Babylonian informer, if found (XV 159)
Unidentified
39-UU Nabû-ili (XVII 159)
40-UU Nabû-[...] (XVII 160)
41-UW Naṣib-il (XVII 161–63)
42-UP Šuzubu (XVII 164)
43-UU Ullubaya (XVII 165)

Southern Babylonia
Assyrian officials:
44-CW Nabû-taklak/Ana-Nabû-taklak; Borsippa (XVII 62–72)
45-CW Nabû-šar-ahhešu; Borsippa (XVII 75–76)
46-CW Da'ini; Larak (XVII 22; 88)
47-GB Nabû-le'i; Bit-Dakuri (XVII 88)
48-UP Bulluṭu; Uruk (XVII 132)
49-CU Nabû-dan; Uruk (XVII 133)
50-UU Sillaya; Uruk? (XVII 134–35?)
51-UP Marduk-naṣir; (?) (XVII 136)
52-UA Šuma-ukin; Uruk (XVII 139)
53-UP Nabû-ušallim; Uruk (XVII 140–44)
54-UU [*xxx*]-eššir; Uruk (XVII 138)
55-UU Nergal-naṣir, Uruk (XVII 139; 147)
56-UP Nabû-ereš; (?) (XV 226)
Temple personnel:
57-TW Marduk; Borsippa (XVII 77–80)
58-TW Šullumu; Dilbat (XVII 86–87)
59-TU Sîn-Duri; Uruk (XVII 39; 129–31)
60-UU Nabû-zera-iddina; Uruk (XVII 137)
61-CW Sîn-iddina; Ur (XV 234)
62-TU Kinâ; Nemed-Laguda (XVII 145;147)
63-TW Kinnâ; Nemed-Laguda (XVII 148)
64-TU Ereši; Nemed-Laguda (XVII 145)
65-UW Aššur-bel-šarrani; (?) (XV 240)

66-UW Sin-ila'i; (?) (XV 241)
Local:
67-NP Barsipitu; Borsippa (XVII 73)
68-RW Balassu; Borsippa (XVII 74)
69-MP Fifteen citizens of Borsippa (XV 226)
70-MP Hamureans; near Borsippa (XVII 81)
71-RP *Šandabakku* from Nippur (XVII 89–91)
72-SW Sapiku; Darati (XV 199)
73-SW Aqaba; Darati (XV 199)
74-SW La-baši; Darati (XV 199)
75-SW Zaqiru; Darati (XV 199)
76-SW Bel-le'i; Darati (XV 199)
77-UW NN, a Chaldean; (?) (XV 221)
78-UU A manservant; (?) (XV 222)
Unidentified:
78-UU NN; (?) (XVII 83)

Northern and Northeastern Babylonia
Assyrian officials:
80-GB Nabû-belu-ka''in; Lubda (XV 24–28; 30; 32-3; 36; 41)
81-UW Naṣibi; Lubda? (XV 36)
82-GB Šamaš-belu-uṣur; Der (XV 111–28)
83-DB Nabû-duru-uṣur; Der (XV 129–35)
84-CW Nabû-šumu-iddina; Lahiru (XV 136–39)
85-CW Nabû-balliṭanni; Lahiru (XV 140–41)
86-UB Lanšê; Gambulu (XVII 92–100)
87-CW Badâ; Gambulu (XVII 101-2)
88-CP Nabû-šumu-lišir; Gambulu (XVII 115–26)
89-CP Ahu-ila'i; Gambulu (XVII 69)
90-UW Nabû-iqiša; Lubda? (XV 32)
91-CP Kalbi-Ukû; Gambulu (XVII 127–28)
92-CP Aqar-bel-lumur; Dur-Abhara (XVII 103–20)
Local:
93-SU Abi-yaqiya; Tubliaš (XVII 149; 151–52)
94-SU Bel-epuš; Tubliaš (XVII 150–51)
95-SU Nabû-zera-ušabši; Tubliaš (XVII 150–51)
96-SU Il-ya[tanu]; Tubliaš (XVII 150–51)
97-SU Adgi-hi'il; Tubliaš (XVII 150)
98-SU Mar-[...]; Tubliaš (XVII 150)
99-SU Nakkia; Tubliaš (XVII 150)
100-SU Kudurru; Tubliaš (XVII 150)
101-SU Bel-l[išir]; Tubliaš (XVII 150)
102-SU Iddin-aha; Tubliaš (XVII 150)
103-SU Nabû-šuma-ereš; Tubliaš (XVII 151)
104-SU Adgi-hinna; Tubliaš (XVII 151)
105-SU Nabû-ušallim; Tubliaš (XVII 151)
106-SU Abi-yadi'; Tubliaš (XVII 152)

107-SU Zerutu; Tubliaš (XVII 152)
108-SU Šulluma; Tubliaš (XVII 152)
109-SU Ahi-abigayanu; Tubliaš (XVII 152)
110-SU Šuma'gunu; Tubliaš (XVII 153–55)
111-SU Ummaniša; Tubliaš (XVII 155)
112-AP Elamite envoys; Elam (XVII 52; 53; 54)

First letter (type of agent)
A-envoy; C-commander of troops; D-deputy governor; E-elders; G-governor; L-legate; M-magnates; N-nobility; O-overseer of the temples; P-prelate; R-local ruler; S-sheik; T-temple official; U-unidentified; V-viceroy
Second letter (period)
A-pre-war; B-both during and after war; P-post-war (after Sargon II's campaigns); U-unidentified; W-war (Sargon II's campaign)

Table 10 groups the agents according to the location and time in which they operated.[254] However impressive this list might seem, it is far from being exhaustive and even statistically representative. The preserved reports are only a fraction of the actual communications between the Assyrian officials working in Babylonia and the royal court.[255] Moreover, that there are only a few reports coming from local informers indicates that local informers communicated their intelligence orally. Though incomplete, this reconstruction is quite illustrative; in particular, it can reveal some important dynamics of gathering and transmitting intelligence.

As for the intelligence officials, the king received, besides reports from the officials themselves, information and complaints about the officials. Thus, the king and his courtiers could compile dossiers on the senders. The following example of Nabû-belu-ka''in's troubles illustrates the tensions between governors and what the royal court knew about him.

Before and during the invasion, the most valuable information came from the governors Il-yada', Nabû-belu-ka''in, and Šamaš-abu-uṣur. All three officials were put on high alert and required to "keep watch" (XV 27:r.3'; 30:r.6; 119:s.4). Nabû-belu-ka''in, the governor of Lubda, and

[254] The classification of the agents is based on SAA XV, SAA XVII, and *Prosopography*, vols. 1–3.
[255] The region Raši may be cited as an example of that has no reports associated with it. Sargon II appointed a royal legate (XVII 152:r.1617) to control this region. It is possible to assume that this legate sent several reports informing the king about the situation in his region which, immediately after the retreat of Sargon II's troops, was exposed to the threats of the Elamites. Yet not one of them has been preserved.

Šamaš-abu-uṣur, the governor of Der, were responsible for monitoring the road connecting Lubda with Der at the piedmont of the Hamrin range. Nabû-belu-ka''in controlled the northern part of the road from Lubda to Dur-Bel-ila'i (south of Meturna) and Šamaš-abu-uṣur controlled the area around Der. Nabû-belu-ka''in's correspondence, dated to 710 B.C.E.,[256] deals mainly with security problems along the piedmont of Hamrin. The first problems occurred north of Meturna. His colleague Il-yada' informed him that a group of 3,000 men with horses had invaded the region. A quick joint expedition reestablished Assyrian control.[257] The next skirmish took place south of Lubda. Nabû-belu-ka''in successfully reestablished order, set up his guard, and imposed a treaty on the cities "below Lubda" (XV 28:1'–6'). Despite his quite successful furthering of Assyrian interests in the Hamrin piedmont, Nabû-belu-ka''in did not enjoy the favor of the royal court. The king reproached him several times for disobedience (XV 30:8–11). In response, Nabû-belu-ka''in's letters voiced his difficulty in pleasing a king who was issuing self-contradictory commands (XV 24). He found himself caught in an impasse: he was asked to perform the work required by the court and at the same time to keep watch over troublesome regions (XV 30). His colleague Il-yada' helped to deepen this rift even more. Despite an outwardly good collaboration in military operations and the sharing of intelligence, neither governor had much sympathy for the other. Il-yada' shrewdly took advantage of Nabû-belu-ka''in's vacillating position at the court, and during his regular visit to the court waited until Nabû-belu-ka''in had left. In his absence, he accused Nabû-belu-ka''in of illegally

---

[256] The dating of the whole series of letters (XV 24; 25; 26; 27; 28; 30; 32; 36; 116) to 710 B.C.E. is based on their connection with XV 30:r.10–11, according to which Merodach-Baladan was still in Babylon.

[257] This reading connects tablet XV 25 with XV 36. Tablet XV 25 contains Il-yada''s warning about the invasion of 3,000 men and tablet XV 36 describes an appropriate action taken by Nabû-belu-ka''in in order to reestablish order. This reading is based on the following arguments: first, XV 25 and 36 are the only tablets that mention the collaboration of Il-yada' with Nabû-belu-ka''in, who were otherwise at odds. Second, both tablets deal with the same region: XV 26 refers to the invasion of Zabban, located in the Daduni region (north of Meturna), and XV 36 refers to the expedition northwards of Dur-Bel-ila'i (located south of Meturna). Third, both tablets convey the concept "to set guards" using the D form of *etāku*, which appears primarily in the G form (out of eighteen occurrences, fifteen are in G stative forms, and one in G precative; only in tablets XV 25 and 36 is the verb in the D durative and D stative, respectively). Linguistic and geographical similarities are the basis of the claim that the expression "I went as far as Meturna with Il-yada'" (XV 36:r.7–8) could be understood as a joint military response to the threat presented in tablet XV 25.

appropriating some territory in the province of Arrapha. Nabû-belu-ka''in, in response, wrote an angry letter to the court and requested a new hearing:

> He (Il-yada') should have appealed while I (Nabû-belu-ka''in) was [the]re (at the court), and we should have spoken with each other. Why did he appeal to the king only when I had come here (to Lubda province)? Now the king, my lord, should write to Il-yada' that he come [t]o the review. I shall come too and bring my witnesses with me. Nashur-Bel should come and arbitrate between us. Let us litigate with each other, and let the king decide between us. (XV 24:8-20)

3.3.4.2 Three branches of the intelligence network

The intelligence network in Babylonia was organized into three sub-networks: 1) the Assyrian network; 2) the local network; and 3) the temple network. The first network followed the Assyrian administration structures imposed upon other conquered territories and, as far as the records allow, most information was gathered through this network. The first tier of this intelligence network included the top Assyrian officials, such as governors and the viceroy, who oversaw the flow of information between their territories and the court. The second tier of this intelligence network included high- and medium-ranking Assyrian officials such as deputy-governors, legates, and magnates. The third tier included local officials, such as commanders of the troops and fortresses. The second intelligence network was also organized according to the hierarchical rules of a given local group. The most important information came from the upper tiers, such as city rulers in the case of Chaldean cities, magnates and the nobility in the case of Babylon, and sheiks in the case of the Aramean tribes. Local informers also played an important role. In cases where the upper tiers of the society were oriented against Assyria, these local informers provided valuable information about their lords. This network was closely linked with the Assyrian administration: local officials and informers sent their reports to Assyrian officials. Temple officials formed the third intelligence network, organized according to the temples in Babylonia, which enjoyed a certain independence from the local and Assyrian administration. All three networks were interlinked with each other, as demonstrated by the following chart:

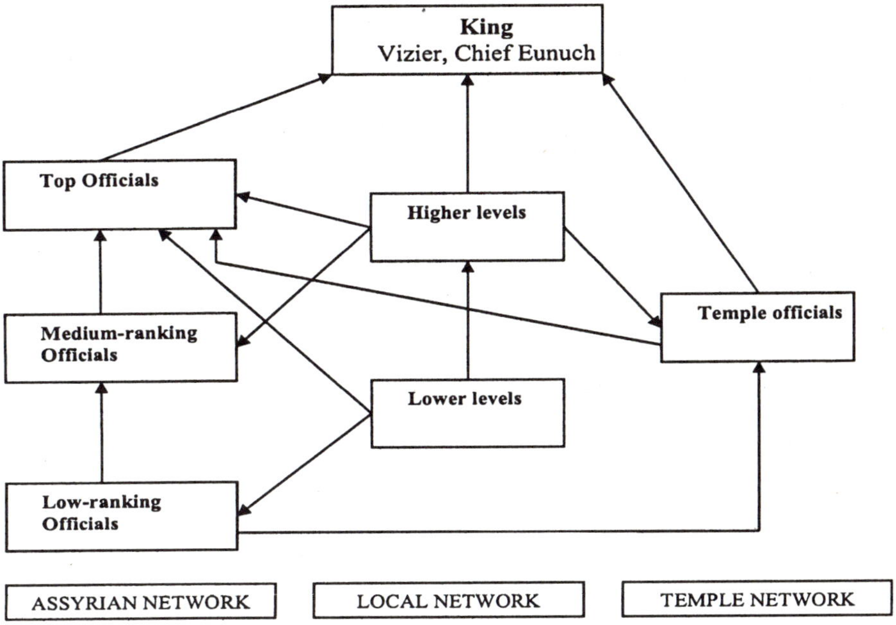

Figure 5. Intelligence network in Babylonia during Sargon II's and Sennacherib's reigns

The Neo-Assyrian archives contain several letters that illustrate this network.[258] The best example of gathering intelligence on the local level is tablet XV 186. It was addressed to the governor, most likely Il-yada' or Šamaš-belu-uṣur:

Palace ←	Governor ← Top Assyrian Official	Šamaš-abu-uṣur ←--- Local provider	Ra'iwanu Local informer from Nagiati

Figure 6. Information flow

[258] Communications within the Assyrian network are illustrated by reports XV 32:4–5, 131:1–5 and 186:1–2; the communication between higher local officials and top Assyrian officials, by XV 131:6–19 and 158:10–16; between higher and lower local officials, by XV 158:10–16; between higher local officials and medium-ranking Assyrian officials, by XVII 10; between higher local officials and temple personnel, by XV 20:7–16; between temple personnel and top-ranking Assyrian officials, by XV 161:9–15; between low-ranking Assyrian officials and temple personnel, by XVII 22:r.5–16; between lower local officials and low-ranking Assyrian officials, by XV 186:3–6; and between lower local officials and top-ranking Assyrian officials, by XV 221:r.3.

In the last line of this tablet, Šamaš-abu-uṣur asks the governor to pass information to the king; the fact that the tablet was found in Nineveh indicates that this governor sent the entire tablet, or its copy, to the king. Šamaš-abu-uṣur received the message from the local informer Rai'wanu, the nephew of Bel-iddina from the region Nagiati. According to S II Ann 279l, Nagiati was situated between the Surrapu and Tubliaš rivers, about 100 km east of Der. Before Sargon II's 12th campaign, which is when tablet XV 186 is to be dated, the most eastern outpost of Assyria in Babylonia was Der; thus, this report may indicate that the local informer, who bore an Aramean name, was recruited from among the Aramean tribes nestled in the midst of the enemy heartland.

Tablets XV 158 and XVII 20 illustrate the flow of information on the upper levels:

XV 158						
Palace	←	Il-yada'	←	Radmanu	←	[The elders of S]ippar
		Governor		Sheik of Opis		Higher local level
XVII 20						
Palace	←	Belšunu	←	Babylonian nobility		
		Temple official		Higher local level		

Figure 7. Information flow

If we take into consideration the rest of the letters referring to Babylonia published in SAA V, XV, and XVII, it is possible to conclude that the Neo-Assyrian intelligence network covered quite a large area (approximately 45,000 km^2). In the north, Assyrian intelligence monitored the Elamite border—in particular, the strategically important road between Meturna and Der at the piedmont of the Hamrin range—and covered also a part of the Elamite region of Raši. In the east, the Assyrian intelligence network covered the regions along the banks of the Tigris and Uqnu inhabited by major Aramean tribes: the Itu'u, Rubu'u, Lita'u, Rahihu, and Ru'ua. In the south, Assyrian spies penetrated the very heart of enemy territory between the Tigris and the Euphrates.

3.4 Control of the Arabs

From their first contact with the Arabs[259] in 853 B.C.E.,[260] the Assyrians kept stockpiling ethnographic information about the tribes, which in turn was used for controlling them and for leading punitive campaigns, as well as for Esarhaddon's unprecedented crossing of the Sinai desert. Even though no ethnographic manuals have been found within the Neo-Assyrian archives, the extant sources suggest that Assyrian leaders possessed sufficient ethnographic data for controlling these tribes.

3.4.1 Intelligence sources

Data was obtained from a variety of sources. Most of the information was acquired from first-hand experience during military campaigns.[261] Further data flowed to Niniveh on a regular basis through the information channels of the Assyrian provincial centers established in Damascus (Bel-duri), Zobah (Bel-liqbi), Hamath (Adda-hati), Assur (Ṭab-ṣill-Aššur), Babylonia (Nabû-šumu-lešir), Rasappa, Laqê, and Suhu.[262] Another source of information was the Arabs themselves, who furnished the Assyrians with information about their fellow Arabs (I 177:r.7–15). Important pieces of information were also obtained through the interrogation of captured Arab militants (ABL 262) or Assyrian soldiers who survived Arab raids (ABL 260), as well as through some unidentifiable sources.[263]

---

[259] The present author adopts the terminology of I. Eph'al, for whom the term "Arabs" refers "to all the populations in the deserts of northern Sinai and northern Arabia and in the Syro-Arabian desert"; see I. Eph'al, *The Ancient Arabs: Nomads on the Borders of the Fertile Crescent, 9th–5th Centuries B.C.* (Jerusalem: Magnes Press Hebrew University, 1982), 5–6.

[260] RIMA 3, 2:ii 94.

[261] RIMA 3, 2:ii 94; TP III Summ 4:19'–34'; 8:24'–27'; Senn A1:28; H5:r.22–27.

[262] Even though the correspondence of the governors of Rasappa, Laqê, and Suhu published in the SAA series does not mention the Arabs, because this region directly bordered with the Syrian Desert, it stands to reason that these governors also sent some information about the Arabs. Moreover, the archives of the governor of Suhu and Mari mention an ambush on an Arab caravan; see A. Cavigneaux and B. K. Ismail, "Die Statthalter von Suhu und Mari im 8. Jh. v. Chr.," *BagM* 21 (1990): 346.

[263] The fact that the king received some information from as-yet-unidentified sources is deduced from the king's reproach of provincial officials, according to which the king had learned about a raid on Sippar and the trade in iron from other sources (I 84 and 179).

3.4.2 Ethnographic encyclopedia

One of the tasks of the Assyrian information hubs was to provide a basic ethnographic picture of hitherto unknown people living in the desert. Piecing together the information in the royal inscriptions and the archives yields the following picture of what Assyrian policy-makers knew about the Arabs. The Arabs were depicted as camel breeders and camel riders.[264] According to the Neo-Assyrian reliefs they rode the one-humped camel (*Camelus dromedarius*[265]), with the saddle placed on the top of the hump.[266] Because of their use of camels, which permitted them to survive in the otherwise uninhabitable desert, the Arabs became the main traders of goods coming from Arabia. Trade was indeed one of the sources of their wealth (e.g., the wealth of Samsi[267]). Besides being camel breeders (true nomads), the Neo-Assyrian letters also presented Arabs as semi-nomadic or semi-sedentary pastoralists, and as hired agricultural laborers.[268] Thus, the tribal leader Ammili'ti not only owned 300 camels (I 175:4–10), but also had at his disposal gardeners and farmers who probably worked as hired laborers (I 179:10–19).[269] The most important source of sustenance for the Arabs was the herding of sheep and goats (semi-nomadic pastoralists; I 82). This

---

[264] See RIMA 3, 2:ii 94; TP III Summ 4:20'; Sargon II Ann 124.

[265] I. Köhler-Rollefson, "Camels and Camel Pastoralism in Arabia," *BA* 56 (1993): 180.

[266] See ibid., 186.

[267] See TP III Summ 4:19'–26'.

[268] For the classification of nomads, see R. Cribb, *Nomads in Archaeology* (Cambridge, England and New York: Cambridge University Press, 1991), 15–22; and A. M. Khazanov, *Nomads and the Outside World* (Cambridge: Cambridge University Press, 1984), 17–25. Archaeological surveys in the Byzantine Negev demonstrated the differences in Bedouin lifestyles. Generally, nomad settlements could be classified as those showing evidence of farming and those with very little or almost non-existent farming. The archaeological remnants of such communities were identified in several surveys in Negev; see Köhler-Rollefson, "Camels and Camel Pastoralism in Arabia"; S. A. Rosen, "Nomads in Archaeology: A Response to Finkelstein and Perevolotsky," *BASOR* 287 (1992); and S. A. Rosen and G. Avni, "The Edge of the Empire: The Archaeology of Pastoral Nomads in the Southern Negev Highlands in Late Antiquity," *BA* 56 (1993).

[269] Several modern studies on the dynamics of dimorphic societies indicate that neither farmers nor herders can be understood in isolation. Thus, an older model contrasting the desert versus the sown has been replaced by the model of "a continuum" encompassing both the desert and the sown; see Cribb, *Nomads in Archaeology*, 65, and D. C. Hopkins, "Pastoralists in Late Bronze Age Palestine: Which Way Did They Go?," *BA* 56 (1993): 205.

highly mobile group[270] lived in tents (I 82:r.14) while their herds grazed the fringes of the settled territories. Because they relied on a variable source of sustenance, they oscillated between times of prosperity and times of hunger (I 82:9) that were often connected with epidemics and plagues (I 172:14–15; 180:10'–13').[271] Another characteristic of the Arabs was their bellicose nature, which often found expression in raids. The various groups of Arabs were organized in tribal structures without too much unity among themselves.[272]

3.4.3 Monitoring Assyrian control and Arab resistance

Having these ethnographic data at their disposal, the Assyrians attempted to control the Arabs on four levels—administrative, political, economic, and military. However, like all powers attempting to dominate the essentially uncontrollable Arabs,[273] the Assyrians also experienced several difficulties. The role of the intelligence services in controlling the Arabs was to provide as accurate information as possible about the efficiency of Assyrian control and about Arab resistance.

To control the Arabs, Sargon II's administration imposed a well-known bureaucratic system upon the territories bordering the regions settled by the Arabs. The cities and villages, even those of the desert, were recorded (I 172:12–14). The territory was partitioned accordingly and assigned to the administration of Assyrian eunuchs (LÚ.SAG; I 82:r.10), governors (LÚ.EN.NAM; I 82:r.8; 172:4) and their deputies (LÚ.2-*u*; I 177:20) or prefects (LÚ.GAR-*nu*; I 177:10). Some of these administrators were directly installed by the king (I 171:3–5);[274] others were appointed by

---

[270] The mobility of the Arabs was described by the expression "coming and going"; see I 177:r.7–9 and 178:10–11.

[271] As proposed in R. Byrne's reconstruction of Ammili'ti's raids; see below. For models of fluctuation due to unfavorable weather changes, see J. Portugali, "The Theoretical Speculations on the Transition from Nomadism to Monarchy," in *From Nomadism to Monarchy: Archaeological and Historical Aspects of Early Israel*, ed. I. Finkelstein and N. Na'aman (Jerusalem: Yad Izhak Ben-Zvi Israel Exploration Society; Washington: Biblical Archaeology Society, 1994).

[272] According to the royal inscriptions, the Assyrians knew the names of the Arab tribes; see TP III Summ 4:27'–8'; 7:r.3'; S II Ann 120–5; Zyl 20.

[273] I 82 reflects this bias against the Arabs.

[274] Sargon II installed Ilu-mušezib, who was a baker of Bel-emuranni, in the city of Hatarikka (I 171:3–5). He was most likely assigned to the office of governor or city-

a responsible provincial official. On the provincial level, these officials answered directly to the king and had at their disposal scribes (LÚ.A.BA; I 171:s.1) responsible for the execution of their reports. On the city level, Assyrian control was administered by Assyrian city-overseers (LÚ.*šá*–UGU–URU; I 176:r.32) and gate-guards (LÚ.Ì.DU$_8$; I 176:r.32), whereas the villages were overseen by village managers (LÚ.GAL–URU.ME-*te*; I 177:21). The checkpoints and waystations were controlled by Assyrian postmasters (LÚ.GAL–*kal-li-e*; I 177:6) and commanders of recruits (LÚ.GAL–*rak-si*; I 176:6). In one case, a local tribe leader (Ammili'ti) was also assigned to administer a part of the territory and was the administrative equal of an Assyrian governor (Bel-liqbi).[275] A special case involved an Arab tribe (Idibi'ilu) that was entrusted to supervise and check the entrance to Egypt (TP III Summ 4:34'; 7:r.6').[276] Another quite efficient administrative measure was to repopulate certain regions in order to break down anti-Assyrian resistance;[277] thus Sargon II moved the Arab tribes of the Tamudi, Ibadidi, Marsamani, and Haiapa to Samaria around 715 B.C.E. (Zyl 20).

Assyrian economic control had two aspects: exploitative and tolerative. As for the former, the Assyrian interest in the petty Levantine states was motivated, above all, by the profit derived from trade along the ancient commercial routes.[278] The fabled wealth of the Arabs flowing from the desert—exotic spices, precious stones, and textiles[279] carried by Arab caravans—was subject to tolls. For this purpose, the Assyrians established a network of toll-points, usually placed at city gates (I 179:r.7–12). Another sort of Assyrian exploitation followed the regular Assyrian pattern of

---

overseer. Another example is the case of the Arab Queen Samsi: an Assyrian delegate (*qēpu*) was assigned to monitor her (TP III Summ 4:26').

275 Since Ammili'ti was able to threaten the governor of Zobah, it is possible to conclude that he had attained a certain measure of influence in Niniveh and was able to convey his side of an incident regarding the molestation of farmers to the king by means of his own communication channel, independent from those of the governor of Zobah (I 179). R. Byrne deduced from this story that Ammili'ti might even have had his own scribes; see R. Byrne, "Early Assyrian Contacts with Arabs and the Impact on Levantine Vassal Tribute," *BASOR* 331 (2003): 16.

276 For a discussion of the duties of "gate-keepership," see Eph'al, *Arabs*, 93.

277 See S II Ann 120–23; Prism iv 42; I 177:4–16.

278 See map in Eph'al, *Arabs*, 241.

279 The incident described on the clay tablet of the governor of Suhu (prob. dated to Tiglath-pileser III) lists the booty that the ambushers of the caravan acquired; see Cavigneaux and Ismail, "Statthalter von Suhu," 346–47.

domination: governors had to collect regular tribute and guarantee the flow of gifts to Assyria (TP III Summ 7:r.5'; TP III Ann 14:2; S II Ann 120–25), raise food and fodder from the villages of the desert (I 172:3–8), and conscript people for construction projects (I 176:r.34–39).[280] Arabs were also employed as agricultural hired laborers (I 176:10–19).[281] Moreover, the Assyrians took advantage of the Arabs' knowledge of camel breeding and of the desert. According to I. Eph'al, Arab knowledge of the desert routes and water resources in the Sinai wilderness, as well as the levying of camel corps, was one of the reasons for Esarhaddon's successful crossing of the Sinai desert.[282]

As for the tolerative aspect of Assyrian economic control, the Assyrians tolerated the Arab semi-pastoralist lifestyle under the condition that Arab shepherds graze only the territories assigned to a given tribe (I 82). The Assyrians, aware of Arab dependence on "the sown,"[283] also controlled the Arab market—in particular, the trade in grain and metals (I 179:20–r.6).

Assyrian political control of the Arabs was exercised, above all, by means of treaties. Two treaties concluded between Arab rulers and Assyrian kings are mentioned in the Neo-Assyrian documents. The first was negotiated between Queen Samsi and Tiglath-pileser III,[284] and the second was imposed upon the Qederite tribe by Ashurbanipal (II 10). Moreover, the Assyrians attempted to control the Arabs by helping a pro-Assyrian candidate ascend the throne (Esarhaddon's backing of Ia'lu)[285] or by delegating to tribal leaders power over their kinspeople and other tribes. Thus, Queen Samsi was granted punitive authority over Arab criminals,[286] the sheik of the city of Laban was put in charge of deportees,[287] sheik

---

[280] Since the construction took place in the desert, it stands to reason that Adda-hati conscripted people living in the desert as well as in the hills.

[281] They might also have been present among the harvesters laboring in Laba'u (I 176:20–33).

[282] Eph'al, *Arabs*, 141.

[283] C. Nelson, *The Desert and the Sown: Nomads in the Wider Society* (Berkeley, Calif.: Institute of International Studies University of California, 1973).

[284] Tiglath-pileser III accused Queen Samsi of breaking her oath; TP III Ann 23:18'.

[285] Eph'al, *Arabs*, 128.

[286] Byrne, "Assyrian Contacts," 18.

[287] *VA* 8424 ii, 1–7; see Eph'al, *Arabs*, 93.

Badi'ilu was granted special privileges for pasturing (ND 27173:6–8[288]), and Jarapa and Hataranu were employed as Assyrian captains (LÚ.GAL–*ki-ṣir*; ABL 631:9–10).

If all political, economic, and administrative tools failed, the Assyrians resorted to the use of military force in order to pacify the rebels. According to the Assyrian royal inscriptions, the Arabs participated in all of the major anti-Assyrian rebellions.[289] Besides the "regular" destruction of Arab troops, execution, and deportation, the Assyrians also took their divine images to Assyria[290] and deported Arabian princes and princesses as hostages to Nineveh, where they were "educated" and at an opportune time nominated as tribal leaders.[291]

It was the task of the Neo-Assyrian intelligence network to monitor the loyalty of the Arab tribes and to pinpoint Arab resistance. The Assyrian attempt to control Arab trade quickly met with strong resistance. When a toll-collector was installed at the city gate of Zobah, the Arabs simply avoided the Assyrian agent; thus Bel-liqbi reported that "the Arabs are leaving and not coming anymore because they had been frightened" (I 179:r.9–10). Similarly, the Assyrian king was informed that the Arabs were able to get around the trade restrictions that limited their access to iron (I 179:20–r.2). If the king's sources were right, then the Arabs managed to trade in iron behind Bel-liqbi's back.

Two ways of earning a living open to the Bedouins–raising livestock and raiding–became the major points of Arab resistance to Assyrian control, as reported by the Neo-Assyrian intelligence network. Regarding livestock, the king ordered the governor of Assur to restrict the grazing of Arab flocks to certain areas. When the governor of Assur tried to put the king's order into practice, his effort was met with strong Arab resistance. He assigned a chief-scout to control Arab grazing, but the Arabs simply ignored him:

[288] *CTN 5*, 175–76.
[289] For detailed descriptions of the Assyrian campaigns against the Arabs and the pertinent cuneiform and biblical sources, see Eph'al, *Arabs*, 21–169.
[290] Tiglath-pileser III seized the divine images of Samsi, and Sennacherib seized the Arab divine images, which were returned by Esarhaddon; see ibid., 126–27; and Tadmor, *Inscriptions of Tiglath-Pileser III*, 226.
[291] Eph'al, *Arabs*, 122.

> I (Ṭab-ṣill-Ešarra) am going to Hinzanu (Hindanu), (but) they (Arabs) (are sure to) leave the territory I am assigning to them, move further downstream and plunder; they pay absolutely no heed to the chief-scout I have appointed. (I 82:r.1–7)

Ṭab-ṣill-Ešarra, well aware that any effort to constrain the Arabs was doomed to failure, tried to shift the responsibility onto the shoulders of the governor of Calah. The governor of Calah, he argued, should be responsible for keeping Arab grazing within the limits imposed by the king, whereas he himself would be responsible only for granting or denying the privilege to pasture in his own territory (I 82:r.8–17).

Raiding,[292] more or less effectively denied to Arabs by each controlling power from the ancient Egyptians down to modern Arab governments, became one of the major targets of Neo-Assyrian intelligence. Local officials reported on two types of raids, those on cities and those along the commercial routes (ABL 260 and I 175). Arabs upset by the Assyrian king's attempt to regulate their grazing not only ignored the order, but also resorted to raiding. They went far beyond the regular Bedouin raids, aimed mainly at pillaging the travelers, and attacked Babylonian cities. Ṭab-ṣill-Ešarra reported: "They plunder *cities*; they never plunder sheep or camels, but they do loot people" (I 82:s.1–2). However, the situation became more serious when the king learned that the city of Sippar had been plundered and that not only had the legate of Birat let the looters go unpunished, he had not even lifted a finger to prevent the looting (I 84).

In the Levant, looting was, as far as the archives report, restricted to raiding along the commercial routes. R. Byrne has reconstructed the historical background of Ammili'ti's raid (I 175).[293] As he shows, exasperation caused by food shortages and epidemics as well as the impossibility of complying with the Assyrian yoke lay at the basis of

---

[292] "Raiding was a domain of activity involving not only gain alone, but also the demonstration of valor and fortitude ... If he (a raiding tribe member) was successful and returned with booty, ... his reputation rose in the eyes of the sons and daughters of his tribe, especially in the eyes of his young lady, if he had fallen in love with one"; J. S. Jabbur, *The Bedouins and the Desert: Aspects of Nomadic Life in the Arab East* (Albany: State University of New York Press, 1995), 354.
[293] Byrne, "Assyrian Contacts," 16–17.

Ammili'ti's decision to take matters into his own hands.[294] According to S. Parpola's reconstruction of line I 175:11, Adda-hati, the governor of Hamath, received intelligence about an attack planned by the Arabs on the convoy transporting tribute from Damascus to Assyria. Together with his fellow governor, Bel-iqbi, he went to meet the convoy. However, Ammili'ti learned about the Assyrian attempt to protect the convoy, ambushed the Assyrians, and engaged them in battle. After the armed encounter, Ammili'ti made off to the desert with about 3,000 sheep.[295] Even though the Assyrian governors in Syria received intelligence about Ammili'ti's plans to ambush the convoy, the Assyrian posse returned empty-handed because the terrain became unsuitable for chariots and horses.[296] The raid, followed by a retreat to the safety of the desert that was inaccessible to pursuers, was one of the pillars of Arab life,[297] which gave the Arabs an advantage over the settlers.

Another preserved report on Arab raids was dispatched by Nabû-šumu-lešir (ABL 260). He reported that Amme'ta ambushed a caravan departing from Niba'ati. During the ambush some of the people were killed and some were taken captive:

> As for the caravan which went forth from Naba'ati, when Aiakamaru, the son of Amme'ta of Mash, attacked them, killed and captured (some) people, and when one of them (one of the caravan) escaped, he entered the royal city. Now I have sent him

---

[294] This reconstruction follows a well-known pattern of alternation between violent and peaceful cohabitation of settlers and nomads. When drought and other natural calamities hit the population of the desert hard, "hungry" Arabs encroached on the settled zone and resort to raids; see Eph'al, *Arabs*, 13.

[295] J. S. Jabbur describes the strategy of such a retreat: "If raiders mounted a surprise attack on the herdsmen of a tribe and stole their camels, for example, they would split into two groups and send the stolen camels with one group to herd and continue on with them, and leave the other group waiting in ambush for the camel-owners' pursuit party, in order to obstruct its search for their livestock. When the ambush party retreated, some of its members would fall back, protected by others who remained in their positions until those who had withdrawn regrouped in a position behind them, after which the ones who had remained in place fell back to a position behind their comrades. This process of alternating stages of retreat continued until the pursuers became exhausted and the stolen camels were too far away to be overtaken. At that point, the raiders reunited and drove the stolen camels before them back to their own territory"; Jabbur, *Bedouins*, 352.

[296] Byrne, "Assyrian Contacts," 17.

[297] Jabbur, *Bedouins*, 43–189.

to the king, my lord. May the king hear (about it) from his own lips. ABL 260:11-r.10

The Assyrians employed three preemptive measures to combat the Arab raids: the adaptation of their army for desert conditions, the establishment of checkpoints along the commercial routes, and the restriction of the iron trade. The Assyrian intelligence network reported not only about the raids but also about the efficiency of these three preemptive measures.

The advantage enjoyed by the Arabs lasted only until the Assyrians were able to adjust their units for desert fighting (Sennacherib's campaign against Adummatu[298]), and it was completely lost when Esarhaddon conscripted the first Assyrian camel corps, after which the desert was no longer a safe refuge for the Arab raiders.[299]

The second preemptive measure imposed to secure the trade arteries in the Levant against raiders was control of the routes.[300] Since the Arabs were ill equipped to overtake the fortified settlements,[301] the most efficient way of controlling the trade was to establish fortified outposts of various sizes: fortified cities in the desert (10 URU.MEŠ É–BÀD *ina madᵈ-bar;* I 176:r.37), fortresses (*birāti*; see for example ND 2644:23), checkpoints (*maṣṣarāte*; see for example I 176:r.41), and waystations (*mardiāte*; see for

[298] For details see Eph'al, *Arabs*, 118–23.

[299] Similar difficulties were experienced by the French colonists at the beginning of the twentieth c. C.E. in the Middle East. The decisive air strike, during which the French airplanes bombed several Bedouin tribes, pacified the revolting tribes, who realized that the desert was no longer a safe refuge against the French colonists; see D. Chatty, *From Camel to Truck: The Bedouin in the Modern World*, 1st ed. (New York: Vantage Press, 1986), 21–36.

[300] According to R. Byrne, trade in the ninth and eighth c. B.C.E. between Assyria and Arabia moved along the Levantine routes. His analysis of the written sources suggests that the alternative routes around the Nafud desert were used only later; see Byrne, "Assyrian Contacts."

[301] A similar countermeasure was employed during the Byzantine control of Palestine. Small city walls and fortifications were often sufficient to protect the towns and cities against Arab raids; see P. Mayerson, "The First Muslim Attacks on Southern Palestine (A.D. 633–634)," in *Transactions and Proceedings of the American Philological Association*, ed. D. W. Prakken, *Muslim Attacks* (Ithaca, NY: Cornell University Press, 1964), 176.

example I 172:r.31; 177:4).[302] Information coming from these points kept the Assyrian court up-to-date about Arab movements ("coming and going," I 177:r.7–9; 178:10-11; 179:7-12; "entering the interior of the province," 178:6–8; "settled on the other side of the Hadina river" I 179:5–6), about the whereabouts of their leaders (Ammili'ti, I 180: r.10'–12'; son of Ašapi, I 177:r.13–14), about the hostility of the local inhabitants among whom the Assyrian officials operated ("they are constantly hostile," I 176:r.40), about the state of the waystations (the waystation in Hêsa lacked people, I 177:4–16; problems maintaining the road stations in the province of Damascus, I 172:r.30-36), and about the quality of the guards (I 173:4–8; 174:4–10; 176:r.41–42). Thus, the reports provided the king with sufficient updates about the situation of the Arabs in the newly conquered states of the Levant.

The last preemptive measure taken to control the Arab raids was the imposition of restrictions upon the trade in iron. The Arabs could buy only copper, whereas iron was sold exclusively to the settled deportees. By this measure the Assyrians controlled Arab weapon production. Since weapons made of iron were superior to those made of copper, the settled deportees possessed better weaponry than the Arabs. When the Arabs attempted to purchase iron illegally, the Assyrian king, through an unidentifiable source, learned about the Arab iron trade in the city of Huzaza. Since the city was under Bel-liqbi's control, the governor was severely reproached for his negligence (I 179:20-r.2).

The Neo-Assyrian intelligence network informed the king not only about tensions and violent encounters, but also about peaceful cohabitation between the Arabs and the Assyrians. Several "situation-is-under-control" reports indicate that the Arab nomadic nature was often within tolerable limits. Bel-liqbi, satisfied with the state of affairs, repeatedly assured the king that everything was fine (I 177:r.9.13). In a similar way, it is possible to assume good intelligence collaboration between the Assyrians and the Ibidi'ilu tribe, which was assigned to watch the brook of Egypt. This almost traditional task of the nomadic tribes—to guard the entrances of the desert—spared the Assyrians the high cost that maintaining outposts in the desert would require and at the same time kept the Arab tribes under control. If we compare the Arab role of guarding the entrances into the

[302] See Eph'al, *Arabs*, 94–95.

desert with a similar role they performed for the Romans,[303] it is possible to conclude that the Assyrians offered some remuneration for the provided services.[304]

3.5 Penetration into the enemy heartland

While expanding in every direction of the compass, the Assyrians encountered not only the resistance of petty states but also the opposition of major powers: Egypt, Phrygia, Urartu, and Elam. Consequently, the Neo-Assyrian intelligence services were responsible not only for relaying information about the Neo-Assyrian provinces and vassals but also for gathering information about the intentions and inner affairs of these four powers. Thus, one of the tasks of Neo-Assyrian espionage was to penetrate into the enemy heartland. No significant report relaying military or political intelligence about Egypt has been preserved. As for the reports concerning Phrygia, tablet I 1 represents a rare example of a letter from the king instructing his governor on how to organize intelligence operations in Phrygia.[305] In contrast to the scarce information about Egypt and Phrygia, numerous fragments of tablets mentioning Elam have been preserved. Most of them have already been treated in sections 3.2 and 3.3. The most exhaustive reports preserved in the Neo-Assyrian archives relate how Assyrian spies penetrated into the Urartian heartland. The Assyrian intelligence network was able to gather information about Urartian inner affairs and even to provide important pieces of information about the situation on the far northern and northeastern Urartian frontier.

---

303 According to Theophanes, a Roman eunuch refused to pay a money allowance to the Arabs guarding the entrances of the desert. As revenge, the upset Arabs went to their compatriots and showed them the desert route to Gaza; see Mayerson, "The First Muslim Attacks on Southern Palestine (A.D. 633–634)," 156–59.

304 Eph'al, *Arabs*, 93.

305 In 709 B.C.E. Sargon II established friendly political relationships with the Phrygian king Midas; see Kuhrt, *The Ancient Near East, c. 3000–330 BC*, 498. However, this political treaty between Assyria and Phrygia did not mean that the Assyrians withdrew their informers. Sargon II sent the following instructions to the governor of the province of Que: "I am now writing to (tell) you that you should not cut off your messenger from the Phrygian's presence (the Phrygian king Midas). Write to him (Midas) in friendly terms and constantly listen to news about him ..." (I 1:13–15).

3.5.1 Urartian affairs

The contents of the reports on Urartian affairs can be divided into three categories:

- Reports on Urartian religious matters.
- Reports on Urartian inner politics.
- Reports on the whereabouts of the Urartian king and his governors.

3.5.1.1 Religious matters

The reports concerning Urartian religion were limited to observations on the offering of sacrifices, especially those offered by the Urartian king and his officials (V 84:r.4–8; 85:r.1'–2'; 147; 165:4–9). The Urartian royal inscriptions preserve a complete list of the offerings to be performed in temples, in front of steles, or before divine statues at a given time and season. If we compare the offerings in these royal inscriptions to the ones mentioned in the Assyrian reports, it is clear that the Assyrians were interested only in those sacrifices performed in Urartu that had strategic meaning.[306] When the Urartian king (V 84:r.4–8) offered his sacrifices, Urartu had been invaded from the southeast by the Manneans and one part of the Urartian troops had already set out to watch the Urarto-Mannean border. Thus, the sacrifices of the Urartian king in Ṭurušpa could have been readings of omens or sacrifices concerned with purifying the camp and blessing troops that had been sent out.[307] The special meaning of these sacrifices is also underlined by the fact that "all the governors participated in the sacrifices in Ṭurušpa" (V 84:r.7–8). Similarly, S. Parpola's reconstruction of line V 165:8 suggests that the Urartian king

[306] The long list and the detailed descriptions of sacrifices to be offered in a given place (Urartian royal inscriptions no. 30, 36, 38, 38b, 39a, 82, 270, and 424) bespeak the role that sacrifices played in Urartian society. This is also reflected in a nuanced vocabulary; there are several words used for sacrifices: *atqanari, urbu*(*e*), and the Assyrian loan word *naqû*. These examples are evidence that the Assyrian reports on sacrifices performed in Urartu did not refer to the ordinary sacrifices performed in the Urartian temples on a regular basis.

[307] Unfortunately, the Urartian royal inscriptions do not preserve any description of such sacrifices. The only equivalent could be the prayer of the king at the outset of the campaign (*hutia;* see inscription no. 173 I:3; 173 II:8; 174 A1:23; 174 A4:19; etc.). However, it is impossible to determine the nature and the meaning of this prayer. Equivalents of such sacrifices are mentioned in Sennacherib's annals (Senn F1:79–80) and in Saul's cycle (1 Sam 13:8–15).

offered sacrifices "wi[th his magnates]" after setting off for the campaign. Since this kind of sacrifice most likely represented one of the last steps before setting out on a campaign, the Assyrian officials who reported on them provided the royal court with important warning signs.

3.5.1.2 Urartian inner affairs

Four extant tablets bear witness to the fact that the Assyrians had at their disposal quite a good picture of what was going on in Urartu itself (V 91; 93; 166; 179). Unfortunately, only tablet V 91 has been sufficiently preserved.

Punished conspiracy (V 91)

The tablet allows the reconstruction of the following correspondence between Aššur-reṣuwa and Sargon II: Aššur-reṣuwa sent a factual report on the conspiracy in Urartu (V 91:3–6); the king replied asking further questions (V 91:21–r.3); Aššur-reṣuwa answered the questions and updated the king about the revolt in Ṭurušpa (V 91).

Aššur-reṣuwa's breaking news about the conspiracy contained, above all, data about the conspirators. Royal chief-tailor Naragê and twenty eunuchs orchestrated a conspiracy. The revolt was quickly crushed and the conspirators were arrested. Aššur-reṣuwa's second report relayed news about the purge that followed the suppression of the revolt. The king entered Ṭurušpa and initiated investigations resulting in the execution of a hundred people, some of whom were eunuchs and "bearded courtiers." During the second round of investigations, the deputy commander-in-chief and the governor of Muṣaṣir were interrogated and found not guilty of treason. This bloody purge following the king's entrance to Ṭurušpa quelled the last flames of the rebellion and also caused that the Assyrian court officials lost track of some important personages, such as Iṣiye, so that they did not know whether he survived the purge.

From this intelligence report, the Assyrians learned about a faction in the Urartian royal court that was discontented with the current leadership. Moreover, the Assyrians could infer that whereas the Urartian periphery governor(s) (Muṣaṣir) and some military commanders remained faithful to the king, most of the conspirators were high-ranking court officials. Thus, the revolt was not a *coup d'état* but rather a *révolution de palais*. Finally, the Assyrian officials could estimate the consequences of such a revolt and purge for the administration of the Urartian empire.

3.5.1.3 Reports on the Urartian whereabouts

As illustrated in tables 11–14, the Neo-Assyrian intelligence network closely monitored the whereabouts of the Urartian kings. The main interest of the provincial officials seems to have been concentrated not only on mapping the king's movements, but also on mapping the whereabouts of the Urartian army, the commander-in-chief and his deputy, some major governors, and even army commanders, such as unit commanders, prefects of the soldiers, and commanders of *kallāpu*[308] troops. The Assyrian interest in mapping the movements not only of the king and his army but also of his governors was necessitated by the relatively less centralized Urartian state, and demonstrates the flexibility of the Neo-Assyrian intelligence services. P. Zimansky showed that the Urartian centers of habitation were concentrated around arable patches of land in the valleys.[309] Because of the mountainous terrain, each valley was isolated from the others for a good part of the year. These climatic conditions forced each valley to establish a certain level of independence from the capital. Such independence was reflected in the organization of the army as well. Each valley was responsible, to some extent, for its own defense. In times of war, the local governors were required to make themselves available, together with their army, to their king.[310] Thus, any royal campaign required the mobilization of a large number of local governors and their concentration in a certain place. This pattern is confirmed by the Assyrian documents, which show that almost every large military operation undertaken by the Urartians was a "national" enterprise (V 87; 88; 90). Consequently, for intelligence purposes, monitoring the movements of the local Urartian governors was just as important to the Assyrians as mapping the movements of the Urartian king and his commander-in-chief.

[308] A *kallāpu* was a member of the light troops (a special military formation); see *CAD* 8, 77.

[309] P. E. Zimansky, *Ecology and Empire: The Structure of the Urartian State* (Chicago: Oriental Institute of the University of Chicago, 1985).

[310] T. Özgüç, *Altintepe II*, *Türk Tarih Kurumu Yayinlarindan-V* (Ankara: Türk Tarihi Kurumu Basimevi, 1969), 59.

Table 11. Whereabouts of the Urartian king during the reigns of Sargon II and Sennacherib

Text	Source	Tablet
"He is still over there; nobody has come from there."	Liphur-Bel	V 1:11–r.2
"If [things have gone badly] for him, he will be sta[ying] in Mannea; [i]f things have gone well for him, he will have attacked the Zikirteans."	Hu-Tešub	V 45:r.3'–5'
"The Urartian is in Ṭurušpa, making his sacrifices."	Aššur-reṣuwa	V 84:r.4–6
"[The ki]ng of Urartu has left Ṭurušpa [on the fir]st of Nisan (1) and gone to Elizzada."	Aššur-reṣuwa	V 86:5–7
"The king has moved out of Ṭurušpa and gone to Wazaun."	Aššur-reṣuwa	V 87:19–20
"I have heard that the king is in Waisi; he will be going but has not yet departed."	Aššur-reṣuwa	V 88:r.5–8
"Their king, however, escaped secretly on a lone (horse) and took to the mountains."	Aššur-reṣuwa	V 90:r.1–3
"The king of Urartu has now entered Ṭurušpa."	Aššur-reṣuwa	V 91:7–8
"Ne[ws of] the king: he is [in] Ṭurušpa."	Aššur-reṣuwa	V 92:r.15'–16'
"The king entered the city [af]ter him (to Waisi)."	Unattributed	V 112:3'–5'
"The Urartian did not achieve anything on the venture on which the Zikirteans took him, but had to return empty-handed; he went with his troops to Waisi, entered the city and left his forces there. Taking but a few troops with him, he set out and entered into the territory of the Manneans."	Aššur-reṣuwa	I 29:24–32
"The Urartian king is in the province of Wazaun."	Aššur-reṣuwa	I 31:r.2–3
"The Urartian has not come out of Ṭurušpa."	Gabbu-ana-Aššur	V 113:r.3–5
"The king of Urartu has assembled his army in Wazana; I have [n]ot heard where he intends to go."	Gabbu-ana-Aššur	V 114:3–6
"The king is on his way; he is staying in Waisi."	Urzana	V 147:13–15
"He set out to Zikirtu, he himself with his troops."	Bel-idinna	V 164:12–r.2
"He is encamped in … within Uluaza."	Ada	V 168:r.6
"He has taken the governor with him to Turuš[pa]."	Unattributed	V 179:3'–5'
"He himself has escaped and entered his country."	Nabû-le'i	I 31:r.13–14
"[The king of] Urartu is in the city of [...]arda."	Ṭab-šar-Aššur	I 43:7

Table 12. Whereabouts of the Urartian governors during the reigns of Sargon II and Sennacherib

Region	Text	Sender/Source	Tablet
Ṭurušpa	"All the governors are with him (in Ṭurušpa)."	Aššur-reṣuwa	V 84:r.7–8
	"[Fo]ur governors are coming down to [Ṭurušpa] to do service (in the temple)."	Aššur-reṣuwa	V 85:r.1'–2'
	"He has taken the governor with him to Turuš[pa]."	Unattributed	V 179:3'–4'

	"When Abliuqnu (the governor of Muṣaṣir) came to Ṭurušpa."	Aššur-reṣuwa	V 91:16–7
Western provinces	"The governor opposite us is keeping watch with the deputy governor in the city Harda, opposite the Vizier."	Liphur-bel	V 3:9–11
	"He (the Urartian governor opposite Liphur Bel) is keeping watch in Harda."	Liphur-Bel	V 2:r.7
	"Three governors in Pulua and another three in Danibani are gathered with pack animals opposite us (Tušhan)."	Ašipa	V 21:11–4
	"The messenger of the governor of Waisi] has gone to Urzana for [help], saying: 'Let yo[ur] troops come to (aid) the people of Pulia and Suriana.' "	Urda-Sin	V 145:14–r.5
Southeastern provinces	"[Five] governors of the Urartian] have ent[ered] Waisi: Setinu, the governor o[ppo]site us; Ḳaqqadanu, the one opposite the Ukkeans; Sakuata of Qaniun; Siplia of Alzi; Tuki of Armiraliu: these are their names."	Aššur-reṣuwa	V 87:4–12
	Governors Setini and Suna have departed for Muṣaṣir.	Aššur-reṣuwa	V 88:4–r.4
	"Abaluqunu, the governor of Muṣaṣir, and Tunbaun, the governor of Kar-sipar[ri], have gone to the Mannean border, to guard (it)."	Aššur-reṣuwa	V 84:9–r.3
	"The governor opposite me was (also) in Waisi."	Aššur-reṣuwa	I 29:r.1–2
	"The governor of Waisi and the governor next to the Ukkean have come … and further governors are coming to Muṣaṣir to do the service."	Urzana	V 147:9–r.2
	"When the governor of Waisi en[tered] Muṣaṣir."	Liphur-Bel	V 11:r.6'–7'
Unidentified region	"The gov[ernor oppo]site me is here;"	Unattributed	V 41:1'–2'
	"This governor has come to Mount Kirmesi—it is not so, he has not come but is still there."	Nabû-šarru-uṣur	V 83:r.2'–7e
	"[The governor] opposite him came from Ur[artu] and they spen[t] the night together [in the town] Irmuna."	Ṭab-šar-Aššur	V 286:5'–6'

Table 13. Whereabouts of the top Urartian officials during the reigns of Sargon II and Sennacherib

Official	Text	Sender/Source	Tablet
Commander-in-chief	"Kaqqadanu, his commander-in-chief, has gone to Waisi."	Aššur-reṣuwa	V 86:8–9
	"The right-hand commander-in-chief, of the family [of Sarduri, [...] but has [not y]et entered Ṭurušpa."	Aššur-reṣuwa	V 93:6'–r.3
	"Kaqqadanu, his commander-in-chief, has been taken prisoner."	Aššur-reṣuwa	I 31:r.1–2
	"His commander-in-chief, has been taken prisoner."	Ukkean king	I 31:13
	"The city Kar-siparri has revolted against him, and his commander-in-chief is engaged in [bat]tle [the]re."	Bel-idinna	V 166:r.1–5
	"[B]efore [him, Kaq]qa[danu had en]tered Wai[si] in Tishri (VII)."	Unattributed	V 112:1'–5'
	"[The] Urartian [commander]-in-chief has gone [to he]lp with [his troops ...]."	Unattributed	V 131:4'–5'
Deputy commander-in-chief	Ursene, the deputy commander-in-chief, brother of Abliuqnu, was likewise arrested in Ṭurušpa."	Aššur-reṣuwa	V 91:13–16
Military officers	"Each of the prefects of the Urartian oppo[site me] has gone to (his) country."	Ša-Aššur-dubbu	V 34:r.23–24
	"They have entered Waisi with three unit commanders. Now, after their (arrival), they have raised the levies of the country, and are keeping the army in readiness."	Aššur-reṣuwa	V 87:13–18
	"3,000 foot soldiers, their prefects, and the commanders of the *kallāpu* troops of Setini … have set out towards Muṣaṣir and crossed the Black River. All the pack animals of Setini are with him. The troops of Suna, the governor opposite Ukku, have also set out towards Muṣaṣir."	Aššur-reṣuwa	V 88:4–r.4
	"The cavalrymen [under the command of Šar]ru-lu-dari have disappeared and are on the run in Urartu."	Urzana	I 30:r.3–5
	"As to Isiye about whom the king, my lord, wrote me, nobody knows where he is; I keep inquiring, but nobody can tell me whether he is alive or dead."	Aššur-reṣuwa	V 91:21–r.3

Others	"I have [not y]et heard what happened to [tho]se men, [wheth]er they [have] been killed [or] deported."	Unattributed	V 112:6'–r.2
	"Sarduri is […] in Ṭurušpa."	Urda-Sin	V 145:11–12
	"The Hubuškian too went with him, for five stages. (Then) he turned back and ordered his magnates: 'Organize your troops, I shall array myself against the Assyrian king.'"	Bel-idinna	V 164:r.3–10

Table 14. Whereabouts of the Urartian troops during the reigns of Sargon II and Sennacherib

Text	Sender/Source	Tablet
"His (the Urartian governor opposite Liphur Bel) troops are assembled with him (in Harda)."	Liphur-Bel	V 2:r.5–6
"Levied troops (of the governor opposite Luphur-Bel) are positioned town by town in battle array as far as Ṭurušpa."	Liphur-bel	V 3:12–4
"The whole Urartian army is marching [t]o Elizzada, following the king."	Aššur-reṣuwa	V 86:10–12
"The king of Urartu has assembled his army in Wazana; I have [n]ot heard where he intends to go."	Gabbu-ana-Aššur	V 114:3–4
"His son Melarṭua, and Aba[l]iuqunu, the governor[of ...], together with [their] tro[ops ...]."	Gabbu-ana-Aššur	V 114:7–11
"His (king's) army has not yet arrived (back)."	Nabû-le'I	I 31:r.14–15

Only reports V 86:4–7 and 112:3' contain the exact time when such a movement happened. Most of the tablets contain neither an exact timetable of the Urartian movements nor the date when the tablets were dispatched. Although we do not have access to the dates when the tablets were dispatched, court officials could easily ascertain the date when a given tablet was received, and estimate how much time the messenger had needed to deliver it. Thus, Assyrian military officials had information as to where the Urartian king and his governors were located at a given time. This data allowed the military commanders to the movements of the Urartian king and his governors and assess their intentions.

3.5.1.4 Monitoring the Urarto-Cimmerian War

Neo-Assyrian officials did not limit their reports to news about the Urarto-Assyrian frontier but also relayed information about several disastrous events that befell Urartu. As far as the preserved records show, one of the most important achievements of the Neo-Assyrian intelligence services was their coverage of the Urartian defeat during the Urarto-Cimmerian war.

3.5.1.4.1 Historical introduction

After reconquering and reconsolidating a kingdom deeply troubled by Tiglath-pileser III's invasion, the Urartian king Rusa I tried to resume the expansionistic politics of his predecessors.[311] His first campaigns were oriented towards the north and followed in his father's footprints. He attacked Adahni, Uelikuhi, Lueruni, and Arquqini. This invasion was successful. Then he tried to regain Mannea,[312] and sometime later he attempted another campaign against the Cimmerians. This campaign, ending in a great fiasco, stirred up the interest of the Assyrian court. Since the celebrative character of the Urartian royal inscriptions leaves no room for the description of Urartian failure, Rusa I's defeat is not mentioned in them. By contrast, this information was highly prized by the Assyrians.

Most scholars agree that the mention of Sargon II's daughter, Ahat-abiša, who married Ambaris, the king of Tabal, is a sufficient argument for dating the Urarto-Cimmerian war before 714 B.C.E.[313] According to I 31:r.26–29, the majordomo of Ahat-abiša sent a letter to Sennacherib, who then forwarded it to Sargon II. Ambaris, who plotted against Sargon II, was dethroned and exiled in 713 B.C.E. (S II Ann. 194–201), and Ahat-abiša

---

[311] This historical outline is based on the following introductions to the history of Urartu: R. D. Barnett, "Urartu," in *The Cambridge Ancient History*, ed. J. Boardman and Edwards I. E. S. (Cambridge: Cambridge University Press, 1982); Deller, "Briefe"; Salvini, *Geschichte*, 56–103; and Wartke, *Urartu*, 35–46.

[312] M. Wäfler, "Die Auseinandersetzungen zwischen Urartu und Assyrien," in *Das Reich Urartu: Ein altorientalischer Staat im 1. Jahrtausend v. Chr*, ed. V. Haas, (Konstanz: Universitätsverlag Konstanz, 1986), 93.

[313] This idea was first proposed by F. Thureau-Dangin, *Une Relation de la Huitième Campagne de Sargon (714 av. J.- C.)* (Paris: Paul Geuthner, 1912), XIV–XV. W. Mayer's argument for the later dating of the Urarto-Cimmerian war were successfully addressed by Ivantchik, *Cimmériens*, 24–25 and Salvini, *Geschichte*, 85.

probably had to return to Assyria. In consequence, tablet I 31 describes the situation before Ambaris had been dethroned, while Sargon II's daughter was still in Tabal. Thus, the Urarto-Cimmerian war may be dated shortly prior to Sargon II's eighth campaign during the reign of the Urartian king Rusa I.

An evaluation of Assyrian intelligence operations in the Urarto-Cimmerian war is presented here in two parts: an analysis of intelligence sources and a comparative study of the content of the reports.

3.5.1.4.2 Intelligence sources

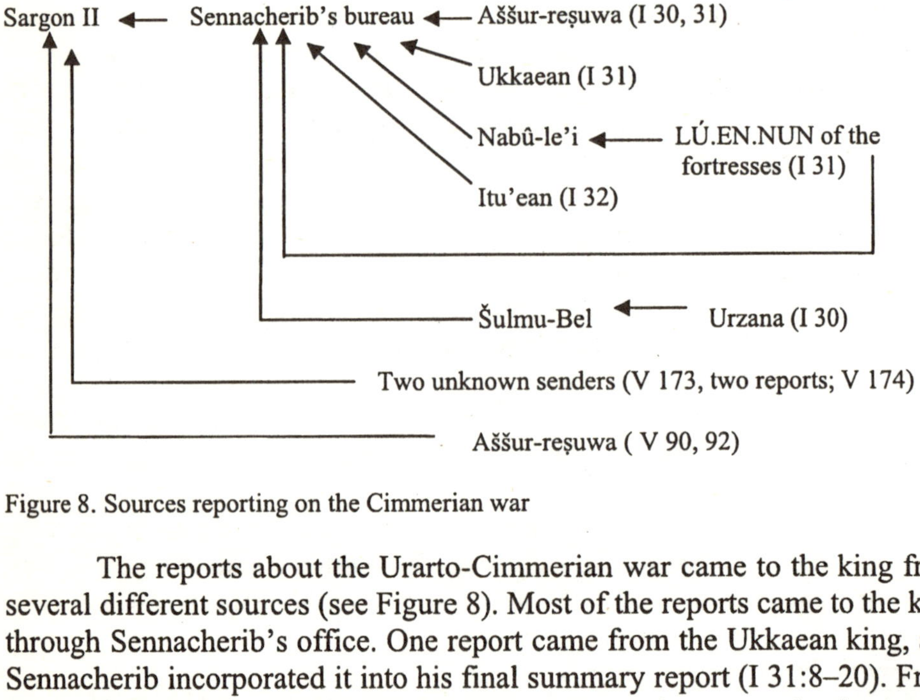

Figure 8. Sources reporting on the Cimmerian war

The reports about the Urarto-Cimmerian war came to the king from several different sources (see Figure 8). Most of the reports came to the king through Sennacherib's office. One report came from the Ukkaean king, and Sennacherib incorporated it into his final summary report (I 31:8–20). From the hand of Aššur-reṣuwa came two other reports that were also integrated into Sennacherib's summary reports (I 30:1'–2'; I 31:21–r.4). Aššur-reṣuwa's second letter confirmed his previous report,[314] which may be either tablet V 92 or the unpreserved part of I 30:1'–2'. There were also two secondhand reports: Urzana's message, which Šulmu-Bel forwarded to Sennacherib (I 30:4'–r.2), and Nabû-le'i's report on the news coming from

[314] The idiomatic expression *šu-tú-u-ma šu-ú* literally means "it is itself," and K. Deller suggests the translation: "*hat sich vollinhaltlich bestätig*"; see Deller, "Briefe," 99.

the captains of the fortresses at the very border with Urartu (I 31:r.5–16). The almost exact repetition of the expression LÚ.EN.NUN URU.*bi-ra-a-te ša ina* UGU *ta-hu-me*, "the guards of the forts along the border," which occurs in two different places (I 31:r.7–8 and I 31:r.23), indicates that the captains of the fortresses sent two messages with similar contents: one to their direct superior, Nabû-le'i, and the other directly to Sennacherib. Besides the information coming from these sources, Sennacherib's bureau obtained unexpected intelligence through the interrogation of an Itu'ean (I 32:8–16). Thus, the archives show that Sennacherib's bureau received at least seven different dispatches reporting on the Urarto-Cimmerian war. Moreover, the king received probably two messages directly from Aššur-reṣuwa (V 90[315] and 92). The fragmentary condition of reports V 173 and 174 does not permit the determination of their sources and their addressees.

3.5.1.4.3 Comparison of the contents of the reports

Chronologically, intelligence on the war can be divided into three stages: letters reporting not-yet-clarified data, letters clarifying previous data and supplying further details, and letters compiling the final results.

Not-yet-clarified data

Tablets I 30, V 173, and V 174 represent the first set of reports on the war, written at a time when their senders did not yet have detailed information at hand. I 30 was the first summary report on the Urarto-Cimmerian war, sent to the king by his son Sennacherib. S. Parpola includes letter I 30 among Sennacherib's letters sent to the king. Even though the beginning of the tablet is broken away, S. Parpola's claim can be substantiated by the fact that the sender of this tablet must have been a very high official to whom even the Assyrian delegate in Kumme, Aššur-reṣuwa, and the deputy delegate of the palace herald felt obliged to report. Furthermore, two very similar summary reports came from Sennacherib's office (I 29; 31). All three reports share a similar structure which, as far as the Neo-Assyrian archives permit us to judge, occurs only in the summary reports coming from Sennacherib's bureau (see Table 15).

[315] Since most of Aššur-reṣuwa's messages were addressed to the king, it is possible that V 90 was addressed to the king as well (the beginning of the tablet is broken away).

Table 15. Syntax of letters I 29, 30 and 31

Source	Structure	I 29	I 30	I 31
1	Opening clause	A messen[ger of Arije] has come [into] m[y presence]:	Broken away	The Ukkaean has sent me (this message):
	Body	"[The (ruler) of Ukku …"	"[I] appointed…"	"The troops…"
	Closing clause	This was the report of Arije.	[Thi]s was the report of Aššur-reṣuwa.	[Thi]s was the report of the Ukkaean.
2	Opening clause	On the 11th of Elul I got a letter from Aššur-reṣuwa:	[Šulmu]-Bel … came into my presence:	Aššur-reṣuwa has written to me thus:
	Body	"The Urartian…"	"Urzana …Birate …"	"The previous report …"
	Closing clause	This was the report of Aššur-reṣuwa.	Rest broken away	This was the report of Aššur-reṣuwa.
3	Opening clause	The (ruler) of Arzabia has written to me thus:		Nabû-le'i the governor of Birate has written to me:
	Body	"The (ruler) of Ukku … "		"I have written …"
	Closing clause	Missing, because Sennacherib directly intervened.		This was the report of Nabû-le'i.

The preserved part of the record relays information that the Urartian royal army was defeated and the governor of Waisi was killed. Tablet V 173[316] adds two new pieces of information: the Urartian king and [x] his magna[tes] were killed (V 173:6–7). V 174 is heavily damaged and only seven lines have been preserved.[317] According to Parpola's restoration, this tablet reports that "all [his governors and his troops] were kil[led; n]ot [one] has returned [from there]" (V 174:4'–5'). Thus, the first set of data differs substantially regarding how many Urartian governors died in the war and what happened with the Urartian king (see Table 16).

---

[316] This tablet is very fragmentary, and the preserved lines do not specify either the subject or the object of the massacre. However, the idiomatic expression *bēt alāku,* "to march" (V 173:4'), which was consistently employed in the description of the Urarto-Cimmerian war, and the mention of [KUR P]AB-*ra* 'the Cimmerian (king)' led K. Deller to include the letter in the corpus of the letters dealing with the Urarto-Cimmerian war; see Deller, "Briefe," 100.

[317] The reason for including the tablet in the corpus dealing with the Urarto-Cimmerian war is again the variant of the idiomatic expression *bēt alāku* (V 174:2'–3').

Stage of reporting	**Not yet clarified data**		
Number	**I 30**	**V 174**	**V 173**
Sender	[Sennacherib]	?	?
Report type	Summary report	?	?
Source of information	1. Aššur-reṣuwa (not preserved) 2. Šulmu-Bel reported Urzana's message	?	? This is already the second report of the sender.
Reliability	Not yet verified; second hand report	?	Not yet verified.
Defeat description	The Urartian army was defeated on their expedition against the Cimmerians.		Their king and [their magnates] utterly killed on the expedition. N.B.: Uncertain whose are "their."
King		Killed	Killed
Governors/ Magnates/ Army	The governor of Waizi was killed	-[a to]tality of [...] was killed.	[x] of his magnates were killed.
Other information	The cavalrymen [under the command of Šar]ru-lu-dari have disappeared and are on the run in Urartu.		
Preservation state	Beginning and end are broken away.	Very fragmentary	Beginning and end are broken away.

3.5.1.4.4 Clarification and further details

The syntax as well as the details of Aššur-reṣuwa's next preserved report indicate that V 92 represents the second stage in gathering intelligence on the Urarto-Cimmerian war. Tablet I 30 presents the result of the conflict—the Urartian defeat—in the main clause, whereas the march against the Cimmerians is in the subordinate clause. V 92 puts both facts into the subordinate clause, and further details are added in the main clause:

I 30:6'–r.1 (earlier stage)		V 92:8–11 (later stage)	
[*ina* KUR.PA]B$^{!}$-*ir*$^{!}$ *bé-et il-lik-ú-ni*	When the Urartian king marched against [Cimmeria]ns,	…*a-ki-i* KUR.URI-*a-a ina* UGU KUR.*ga-mi-ra il-lik-u-ni*	When the Urartian king marched against the Cimmerians
[*ma*]-*a* LÚ*.*e-mu-qe-e-šú de-e-ka*	then his troops were killed	*a-ki-i a-bi-ik-tú ina* ŠÀ KUR.URI-*a-a ta-áš-šá-ki-nu-ni*	and when defeat was inflicted upon the Urartian king,
[*m*]*a-a* LÚ*.EN.NAM *ša* URUR.*ú-a-si de-e-ke*	and the governor of Waisi was killed		
ma-a qu-di-i-ni ba$^{!}$-*ti*$^{!}$-*iq-tú la-a ni-har-ra-ṣa*	and we do not have a detailed report yet	LÚ*.ERIM.MEŠ *a-mar* TA* *ma-ka* …	(then) whatever troops from there … (and)
[*ma*]-⸢*a*⸣ …	and …		

This suggests that the reader of I 30 was already informed about the Urartian march against Cimmerians, whereas the result of the war was a new piece of information. On the other hand, by putting the result of the war into the subordinate clause as well, the writer of V 92 presupposed that the reader knew not only about the campaign but also about its result.

Tablet V 92 clarifies the result of the war: the Urartian king did not die as claimed in V 173, but survived and returned to Ṭurušpa. Moreover, the tablet clarifies what happened to the rest of the Urartian army: some of the troops were killed, others were taken captive, and the rest escaped to the land of Guriania (see table 17.). Not expecting the royal officials to know where the land of Guriania was located, Aššur-reṣuwa prefixed his report with a short geographical introduction locating Guriania between Cimmeria and Urartu. Guriania became the Urartian vassal state during Sarduri II's reign and afterwards paid tribute to Urartu.[318] This vassal state not only remained loyal to Urartu, but also provided refuge for the escaping Urartian troops.

Another report (I 32),[319] also attributed to Sennacherib,[320] provided the king with information coming from an Itu'ean, an unexpected source

[318] Arutjunjan, *Korpus*, 243–45.

[319] The tablet contains two elements indicating that it should be numbered among the group of tablets dealing with the Urarto-Cimmerian war: first, the names of the kings: KUR.URI-*a-a* 'Urartian' (I 32: 11,17) and KUR.PAP-*ir*$^{!}$ 'Cimmerian' (I 32:12); second, a variant of the idiomatic expression *bēt alāku,* "to march": KUR.URI-*a-a* [LÚ.GAL.MEŠ-*šú a-na*]

independent of the established Neo-Assyrian intelligence network (see Table 17). The tablet added a new piece of information useful for evaluating the aftermath of the war:

> … and they are very much afraid of the king my lord. They tremble and keep silence like women, and nobody […] the forts of the king, my lord. They are very quiet. (I 32:13–16)

Table 17. Comparison of the contents of the tablets describing the Urarto-Cimmerian war II

Stage of reporting	**Further data**	
Number	**V 92**	**I 32**
Sender	Aššur-reṣuwa	S[ennacherib]
Report type	Simple report	Simple report
Source of information	Unspecified	Interrogation of an Itu'ean
Reliability	Second hand report	The reliability of Itu'ean testimony should be proved.
Defeat description	The defeat was inflicted upon the Urartian king.	The Urartian king [and his … were defeated] on their expedition [against] the Cimmerians.
King	In Turušpa	
Governors/ Magnates/ Army	Some taken captive, some killed, some escaped to Guriania.	
Other information	1. Location of Cimmeria 2. Tribute 3. 8,000 soldiers 4. Snow	The Urartians tremble and keep silent like women; the situation is very good; Mannean king […] oxen and sheep
Preservation state	Reverse is very fragmentary.	Reverse is very fragmentary.

KUR.PAP-*ir*[!] *bé-et il-li-k*[*u*]-*ni*, "the Urartian king [and his magnates] marched against the Cimmerians"; cf. I 30:5'–6' and I 31:9–10.

[320] The attribution of the tablet to Sennacherib is based on its greeting formula, characteristic of Sennacherib's letters (see the greeting formulas in I 29–38): "[To the king, my lord: yo]ur servant S[ennacherib. Good health to the king, m]y lord! Assyria [is well], the temples [are well], all the [forts o]f the king [are well; the king, my lord], can be glad indeed" (I 32:1–7).

3.5.1.4.5 Final reports

The last of the extant reports about the war are Sennacherib's post-factum summary report (I 31) and Aššur-reṣuwa's final report (V 90). The structure of the former might be outlined as follows:

1) Greetings
2) Reports
   a) Ukkayan's report:
      i) The Urartian king went to Cimmeria.
      ii) His army was utterly defeated.
      iii) Eleven of his governors together with his army (soldiers) were impaled.[321]
      Restored parts:
      iv) The Urartian commander-in-chief and two governors *were taken captive* (restored on the basis of Aššur-reṣuwa's report; see I 31:r.1-2).
      v) *The Urartian (king) saved his life by escaping* (very fragmented).
   b) Aššur-reṣuwa's report:
      i) Confirmation of his former news about the Urartian king.
      ii) There was a lot of bloodshed.
      iii) The description of the results and the situation in Urartu after the war:
         (1) The magnates returned home.
         (2) The Urartian commander-in-chief was captured.
         (3) The Urartian king fled to the land of Wazaun (probably an alternative spelling of Waisi)
   c) Nabû-le'i forwarded the report coming from the border forts:
      i) The Urartian king went to Cimmeria.
      ii) His army was slaughtered.
      iii) Three magnates were killed and their troops destroyed.
      iv) The Urartian king escaped and returned to his country.
3) Sennacherib's additions:
   a) A list of the people who went to see the Urartian king and to wish him good health:

[321] Translation of I 31:12 *še-e-lu-u* "they were impaled," follows *CAD*, which gives as the meaning of the Š-stem of *elûm* 'to impale'; see *CAD* 4, 128.

   i) *Mu-ṣa-ṣir-a-a* (Urzana, the king of Muṣaṣir), his brother, and his son.
   ii) A messenger from Hubuškia.
b) All the governors from the border sent similar news to Sennacherib.
c) Nabû-le'i forwarded a letter sent by the majordomo of Sargon II's daughter, Ahat-abiša.

The first series of records (I 30, V 173, and V 174) agrees on the defeat of the Urartian army, as well as some losses even among the Urartian high officials. The unknown senders of V 173 and V 174 claimed that the Urartian king himself also died in the battle. Sennacherib maintained caution in reporting this "good news." The preserved lines of his first two reports (I 30 and 32) do not mention the Urartian king, nor do Urzana's report and the interrogation of an Itu'ean soldier provide any clear data concerning the king's whereabouts. It was Aššur-reṣuwa who clarified this question. His two preserved reports (V 92 and I 31) affirm that the Urartian king escaped from the battle. This news was confirmed by the commanders of the fortresses and probably by the Ukkean king as well. Thus, intensive intelligence gathering clarified the status of the Urartian king, and so Sennacherib, in his last summary report, could confirm that according to at least three sources the Urartian king did survive the war (see Table 18). Sennacherib's final report also clarified what happened to the Urartian commander-in-chief: according to at least two sources, the Cimmerians captured the head of the royal troops and took him as a prisoner of war. By estimating the cost and effect of the defeat, Sennacherib's final report drew a picture of Urartian defensive capabilities after the war as well. The exact number of Urartian high officials who were killed or captured during the war remained uncertain. The Ukkean king gave the highest estimate: eleven governors died and two were taken captive. An important piece of intelligence came from the commanders of the fortresses: in three cases, not only were the Urartian governors killed but their troops were also completely massacred. Moreover, the Urartian royal troops had not yet returned from the battlefield when I 31 was filed. Finally, intelligence acquired through the interrogation of an Itu'ean and gathered by Aššur-reṣuwa helped the Assyrians evaluate the morale of the Urartians after the war: the Urartians were decimated and shocked, silent like women, and afraid of the Assyrians (I 31 and 32). Such results seemed to satisfy Sennacherib deeply: "The situation is very good" (I 32:16).

Table 18. Comparison of the contents of the tablets describing the Urarto-Cimmerian war III

Stage of reporting	**Final clarifications**			
Number	**I 31**			**V 90**
Sender	Sennacherib			Aššur-reṣuwa
Report type	Summary report			Simple report
Source of information	Ukkean king	Aššur-reṣuwa	Nabû-le'i reported the news of fort commanders	Unspecified
Reliability		It confirmed his previous report.	Second hand data	
Defeat description	King's troops were utterly defeated on their expedition against the Cimmerians.	There was great bloodshed.	King's troops were utterly defeated on his expedition against the Cimmerians.	Broken away
King	*Escaped*	In Wazaun	Escaped	Escaped
Commander-in-chief	[Taken captive]	Taken captive		
Governors/ Magnates/ Army	11 governors from king's army were impaled and 2 [taken captive].	Each of his magnates returned home.	3 magnates with their troops were killed; his army not yet arrived back.	List of nine governors killed in the war.
Other information	1. Aššur-reṣuwa reports that Urartu is now quiet; 2. Sennacherib's additions: i. All the guards sent similar reports to that of Nabû-le'i; ii. The delegation of Muṣaṣir and Hubuškia in Turušpa; iii. A message from Tabal.			The rear of the army did not know that the king saved himself and enthroned his son.
Preservation state	Very well preserved			Fragmentary

A final evaluation of the losses suffered by the Urartians came once again from Aššur-reṣuwa (V 90). He presented the final results of the Urartian defeat: nine governors died in the war. Aššur-reṣuwa even identified their provinces. This information clarified which provinces were destabilized after the loss of their governors. They are listed here from west to east:

the governor opposite Ša-Aššur-dubbu (Tušhan)[322]
the governor opposite us (Kumme)
the governor opposite the chief cupbearer
the governor opposite Muṣaṣir
the governor of Wazae (probably another variant of Waisi)

Uncertain location:
two governors opposite Kar-siparri (west of Lake Urmia)

Unknown location:
the governor of Šibturu
the governor of Šattera

The next information provided by Aššur-reṣuwa's final report concerned the Urartian king. The initial confusion regarding what had happened to the Urartian king reflected the confusion in the Urartian camp itself after the defeat. The rear part of the Urartian army, not knowing that the king "escaped secretly on a lone (horse) and took to the mountains," (V 90:r.1–3) assumed that the king died on the battlefield. They "[li]fted up his son Melarṭua and [ma]de him king [al]ong the road" (V 90:r.6–8). Thus, Aššur-reṣuwa's final briefing (V 90) informed the king about the extent of the confusion both among the royal troops and in several key Urartian provinces that lost their governors.

Some scholars add four other tablets to the corpus describing the Urarto-Cimmerian war (V 147; 86; 87; 144). If M. Salvini's localization of the Urarto-Cimmerian war (south of Lake Urmia)[323] is correct, then an otherwise unknown Assyrian official Urda-Sin informed the palace herald about the very beginning of the Urarto-Cimmerian war. Thus, almost immediately after the Cimmerian king invaded Urartu from Mannea, the Assyrians were informed about the Cimmerian invasion, communications between the governor of Waisi and Muṣaṣir, and the psychological impact of the Cimmerian invasion on the local inhabitants. Moreover, the king would have received information through another source–the palace herald (Gabbu-ana-Aššur), assuming that the palace herald forwarded Urda-sin's report to the king. As a result of this reconstruction, M. Salvini added to the

[322] Ša-Aššur-dubu's eponym was 707 B.C.E.; see SAAS II, 60. This means that report V 90 reflects the very beginning of his career.
[323] Salvini, "Storia," 40–50.

corpus tablets V 86 and 87, which preserve Aššur-reṣuwa's reports on the large military movements south of Lake Urmia. Thus, the Assyrians closely monitored the early stages of Urartian mobilization south of Lake Urmia: first the governor of Muṣaṣir (V 145), then five other governors who came to Waisi (V 87), and finally the Urartian commander-in-chief and the Urartian king himself (V 86). S. Parpola added tablet V 144, in which an unknown sender reported about events immediately after the Cimmerian victory: the Cimmerian king pitched his tent in Uṣunali (unknown location, probably in the vicinity of Waisi).[324] Even though S. Parpola's proposal is very appealing, it was severely undermined by A. I. Ivantchik.[325] Since the tablets do not contain dates, some scholars have gathered convincing arguments for connecting these tablets with other events.[326]

Based on this analysis we can conclude that Neo-Assyrian intelligence on the Urarto-Cimmerian war was interested above all in answering five questions: 1) Who won and who lost? 2) What happened to the Urartian king? 3) Which high-ranking officials died or were captured? 4) How did the defeat influence Urartian defensive capabilities? 5) How did the defeat influence the morale of the Urartians? The answers to these questions had great strategic significance for the Assyrians. In dealing with the revolts in the eastern provinces, Sargon II did not limit his intervention to pacifying the rebels, but rather severely punished the rebels' supporters as well (see 3.1.5.2). Since Urartu was the backbone of all the rebellions in this region, a punitive campaign against Urartu required perfect timing. As the result of the Urartian defeat, at least nine Urartian provinces were destabilized after losing their governors, including the governor of Waisi (this region became one of the main objectives of Sargon II's eighth campaign). Moreover, the Urartian commander-in-chief was captured, three units together with their magnates were destroyed, and one part of the Urartian army was taken captive. Finally, the remainder of the army, thinking that Rusa I had died, enthroned his son Melarṭua. Knowledge of

---

324 SAA V, XX.

325 A. I. Ivantchik, "Kimmerijci i Urartu na kanune Vosmogo pochoda Sargona II," *Vestnik Drevnej Istorii* 194 (1990), Ivantchik, *Cimmériens*, 19–56.

326 Besides M. Salvini's proposal, tablets V 86 and 87 could be connected with the Mannean invasion (V 84). Thus, the concentration of the troops in Waisi would constitute the Urartian reaction to the Mannean invasion. Moreover, G. B. Lanfranchi suggested connecting these tablets with the revolt against Rusa I. Thus, these tablets would describe a punitive action of Rusa I aimed at quelling the insurrection; see G. B. Lanfranchi, "Some New Texts About a Revolt against the Urartian King Rusa I," *OrA* 22 (1983).

this confusion, and of the Urartrians' fear of the Assyrian king, would have made clear even to a less experienced strategist than Sargon II that the time was ripe for commencing the decisive intervention and punishing the heart of all the rebellions—Urartu. On these grounds, it is possible to conclude that the Neo-Assyrian intelligence network monitoring Urartu played a decisive role in setting the timing for Sargon II's eighth campaign.

3.6 Legal basis of Neo-Assyrian intelligence

Assyrian expansion assumed different forms—military, economic, cultural, and diplomatic.[327] The least costly, though not the least efficient, was expansion by means of diplomatic pacts known as the *adê* texts. S. Parpola's investigations demonstrated that these texts were not uniform loyalty oaths as proposed by I. J. Gelb,[328] but rather a variety of bilateral and unilateral treaties and pacts based on oaths sworn before the gods.[329] Such treaties, whether imposed upon or willingly assumed by local leaders (V 78 and XV 90) trying to bargain or to take advantage of Assyrian imperialism, saved the Assyrians the expense of military campaigns. Yet the treaties provided results similar to those achieved by military campaigns: they guaranteed the conscription of soldiers for the Assyrian campaigns and channeled a significant portion of the wealth of vassals to Assyria.[330] At the same time, the treaty partner became a part of the civilized (i.e. Assyrian) world[331] and enjoyed the advantages of Assyrian protection.[332] Both parties entering into the treaty had to answer to the gods if they transgressed the

---

[327] Parker, *Mechanics*, 1–35 and S. Parpola, "Neo-Assyrian Treaties from the Royal Archives of Nineveh," *JCS* 39 (1987): 161.

[328] I. J. Gelb suggested translating the term *adê* as "loyalty oaths"; see I. J. Gelb, "Rezension: D. J. Wiseman, *The Vassal-Treaties of Esarhaddon*," *BiOr* 19 (1962): 161. This notion was successfully challenged by S. Parpola, who proposed translating *adê* as "treaty"; Parpola, "Treaties," 181–83. For a detailed review of the terminology, see K. Watanabe, *Die Adê-Vereidigung anlässlich der Thronfolgeregelung Asarhaddons, Bam Bh 3* (Berlin: Gebr. Mann Verlag, 1987), 6–8.

[329] S. Parpola listed eight kinds of treaties: bilateral and unilateral treaties, nonaggression pacts, peace and friendship treaties, mutual assistance pacts, alliance treaties, treaties with exiled foreign royalty, treaties with Assyrianized foreign royalty, and treaties with submissive adversaries; see SAA II, XV–XXII.

[330] SAA II, XXIV.

[331] The chief-scribe Bel-ušezib called the Manneans "barbarians who recognize no oath sworn by god and no treaty" (X 111:15–16).

[332] Mannu-ki-Ninua promised during the treaty renewal that the Kulumaneans and Zabgageans would benefit from his protection (XV 90:r.5–6).

treaty.[333] If the party bound by the treaty fell short of the treaty obligations, it suffered heavy repercussions for such negligence. Most importantly, the negligent party called down upon itself a series of curses[334] that were usually specified at the end of each treaty. Thus, the human and divine conditions of the treaty required that the Assyrian king treat the violators of an oath sworn before the gods not only as rebels against his person and his kingdom, but as sinners[335] and offenders of the gods.[336] In practice this meant that the Assyrians rarely left broken treaties unpunished;[337] sooner or later, Assyrian troops poured into the perpetrator's country,[338] and destruction, deportation of the population, and exemplary punishment ensued.

Besides being the efficient instruments of Assyrian imperial control, the treaties also assured a regular flow of information to the royal court from the provinces and from vassal and buffer states. The Assyrians preferred not to leave the task of reporting about the most recent developments on the peripheries of the Empire as well as in the Assyrian provinces to the good will of local officials, but made it a compulsory duty and legally enforced it by means of the treaties. Consequently, failure to report was not only an administrative lapse but a violation of a treaty sworn before the gods, which allowed the Assyrian king to take action against the negligent party.

3.6.1 Imperial interests and intelligence priorities

As in every form of imperial control, the contents of the reports were determined by imperial interests and priorities. Priority number one of the royal court was to keep the king safe. For this reason, the party that

---

[333] The obligation to keep the treaty bound both sides. Thus, when Sennacherib inquired about the infamous death of his father, one possibility was to interpret the death of his father as a punishment for not keeping the treaty (III 33:17'–20').

[334] For a comprehensive study of curses, see D. R. Hillers, *Treaty-Curses and the Old Testament Prophets* (Rome: Pontifical Biblical Institute, 1964).

[335] Neo-Assyrian royal inscriptions and archives often used the verb *haṭû* 'to sin' and its active participle to talk about the rebels; see, for example, XVI 59:5, S II Ann 19, 67, and Luckenbill, 25, 32, 57, 70.

[336] SAAS VIII, 112.

[337] See for example III 44, X 199, TP III Ann 18:8', 23:18', TP III Summ 7:19, and S II Ann 256; for an example of an unpunished treaty partner, see X 316.

[338] SAA II, XXIII.

contracted a treaty with Assyria was asked to report on any plot, conspiracy, or action taken to undermine the exercise of kingship. Two extant succession treaties (II 6 and 8)[339] illustrate the legalities of the Assyrian demands: vassals (the city lord of Nahšimarti and his subordinates in II 6) as well as Ashurbanipal's brothers (II 8) were required to report on the following issues:

conspiracy, rebellion	*si-hu* (II 6:133); *šá si-hi* (8:r.3)
rebellion	*bar-tú* (II 6:133); (*šá*) *bar-te* (8:r.3)
(plan) to kill (the king)	*šá d*[*u-a-ki*]-*šu* (II 6:133); *šá da-a-ki* (8:r.8)
(plan) to eliminate (the king)	*hul-lu-qi-šú* (II 6:134); (*šá*) *hul-lu-qí* (8:r.8)
assassination	*ša-mut-ti-šu* (II 6:133)
instigation (armed rebellion)	*mu-šam-hi-ṣu-u-tú* (II 6:500)
agitation (conspiracy)	*mu-šad-bi-bu-tu* (II 6:500)
stratagem	[*ki-i nik-l*]*u la da-an-qu* (II 8:r.13)

Moreover, the treaties obliged the non-Assyrian party to report not only any rebellious actions, but also any improper, unsuitable, or unseemly speech concerning the king and the exercise of his kingship:

> [Nor] will you conceal from me anything that you hear, be it from the mouth of a king or on account of a country, (anything) that bears upon or is harmful to us or Assyria, but you will write to me and bring to my attention. (II 13 iii:10–17)

Since the Assyrian treaties were often exclusive, the party bound by the treaty was not allowed to contract a treaty with the enemies of

---

339 Most of the extant treaties published in SAA II are dated to Esarhaddon's and Ashurbanipal's reigns. S. Parpola's research indicates that this collection is only a fraction of the numerous treaties that were concluded to further Assyrian interest; see Parpola, "Treaties," 184–86. Thus, conclusions regarding the obligation to report drawn from the analysis of treaties during Esarhaddon's and Ashurbanipal's reigns will be extrapolated to the periods of Sargon II and Sennacherib periods. The validity of such extrapolation is confirmed by XV 90 and 98, which indicate that Sargon II's officials concluded treaties with their subordinates.

Assyria.[340] Thus, the Nahšimarteans were required to report on any attempt to make them enter into a new treaty:

> You shall not take a mutually binding oath with (any)one who installs (statutes of) gods in order to conclude a treaty before gods, (be it) by sett[ing] a table, by drinking from a cup, by kindling a fire, by water, by oil, or by holding breasts, but you shall come and report to Ashurbanipal. (II 6:152-6).

The following table gives a list of what treaty partners were obliged to report:

Table 19. Issues to be reported to the Assyrians

improper word	*a-bu-tú* ⌜*la*¦ *de*¦⌝*iq*-⌜*tú*⌝ (II 3:2'); *a-bat-su la* ⌜*de*⌝-*i*[*q-t*]*ú* (II 4:4'); (*a-bu-tú*) *la de-iq-tú* (II 6:108); [*a-bu-tú la*] *de-iq-tú* (II 8:r.3)
malicious whispers	*šá a-mat* MÍ.HUL *la* DÙG.GA-*tú* (II 6:501)
improper (not good)	*a-bu-tú la* DÙG.GA-*tú* (II 6:73); *la ṭa-bat-u-ni* (II 6:75); *a-bu-tú la* DÙG.GA-*tú* (II 6:108); *la ṭa-bat-u-ni* (II 6:111)
not good, not nice	*a-bu-tú la ba-ni-tú* (II 6:73), (*a-bu-tú*) *la ba-ni-tú* (II 6:109); (*šá a-mat*) *la ba-ni-tú* (II 6:501)
incorrect, unseemly	(*a-bu-tú*) *la ta-ri- ṣu* (II 6:74); *la tar-ṣa-tú-u-ni* (II 6:75); *la tar-ṣa-at-u-ni* (II 6:110)
treacherous talk	*da-bab sur-ra-a-ti* (II 6:502)
not truthful (disloyal talks)	(*da-bab*) *la ke-na-a-te* (II 6:502)
(any unseemly word) concerning the exercise of kingship	(*a-bu-tú la ta-ri- ṣu*) *ša e-peš* LUGAL-*te* (II 6:74)
favorable or not favorable thing (heard from the perpetrators of insurrection)	*du-un-qu la du-un-qu* (II 6:148)
(anything) that bears upon or is harmful to us or Assyria	(*a-bu-tú*) [*ša ina* UG]U-*hi-ni ina* UGU KUR–*aš-šur* [*qur*]-*bu-u-ni la ṭa-bu-u-ni* (II 13 iii:13-4)

Such requirements ensured that the king was informed about any hostile feelings toward him long before rebellion broke out. In the case of

[340] For an example of such a report, see XVI 21:r.4–6.

rebels, the party bound by the treaty was required to report not only their unfavorable but also their favorable words (II 6:148).

The treaties were usually tailored to the specific situation and location of the party bound by the treaty.[341] Thus, for example, Mannu-ki-Ninnua, the governor of Kar-Šarrukin, asked the Kulumaneans and Sikriseans to provide information about the Medes when it came time to renew their treaty:

> ["Just] as [you] previo[usly stood at the dis]posal of Nabû-belu-ka''[in, found out wha]tever there was to report and [to]ld it to him, [in like] manner [stan]d now at my disposal and send me whatever news [of th]e Medes you hear!" (XV 90:28–r.3)

3.6.2 Potential perpetrators

The treaties also contained exhaustive lists of potential perpetrators in the court, including the king's family, court officials, and scholars. Any Assyrian or foreigner, any ally or enemy, any human being at all was a potential traitor. If the potential perpetrators were family members, friends, or vassals of the party bound by the treaty, that party should not conceal their subversive activities but report them to the king. The following table lists potential perpetrators as presented in the Neo-Assyrian treaties.

Table 20. List of potential perpetrators

Officials	
Palace	É.GAL (II 6:198)
magnates	[L]Ú.GAL.MEŠ(II 4:5'); LÚ.GAL.MEŠ (II 6:77)
governors	[LÚ.NAM.MEŠ] (II 4:5'); LÚ.NAM.MEŠ (II 6:77)
bearded men	LÚ.*šá–ziq-ni* (II 4:6'; 6:78, 338; 8:r.21); LÚ.*šá–ziq*!*-ni* (II 8:6)
eunuchs	[1-*en* LÚ.SAG.MEŠ] (II 4:6'); LÚ.SAG.MEŠ (II 6:78; 8:r.21); L[Ú.SAG] (II 6:338)
Scholars	
scholars	LÚ.*um-ma-ni* (II 6:79)
prophet	LÚ.*ra-gi-me* (II 6:116)

[341] See, for example, II 5:15'–7' and the discussion of Ashurbanipal's treaty with the Babylonians in A. K. Grayson, "Akkadian Treaties of the Seventh Century B.C.," *JCS* 39 (1987): 140.

ecstatic	LÚ.*mah-he-e* (II 6:117)
an inquirer of oracles	DUMU *šá-'i-li a-mat* DINGIR (II 6:117)
Royal family	
his brothers	ŠEŠ.MEŠ-*šú* (II 6:76, 113, 337); PAB.MEŠ-*šú* (8:r.21)
his uncles	ŠEŠ.MEŠ–AD.MEŠ-*šú* (II 6:76, 114, 337)
his cousins	DUMU–ŠEŠ.MEŠ–AD.MEŠ-*šú* (II 6:76, 114); [DUMU–ŠEŠ].MEŠ–AD.MEŠ-*šú* (II 6:337)
his family	*qin-ni-šú* (II 6:77, 115, 337)
royal line, members of his father's line	NUMUN É–AD-*šú* (II 6:77, 115, 338); NUMUN MAN (II 8:r. 22);
Party's family and friends	
your brothers	ŠEŠ.MEŠ-*ku-nu* (II 6:115); PAB.MEŠ-*ku-nu* (II 8:r. 22)
your sons	DUMU.MEŠ-*ku-nu* (II 6:116)
your daughters	DUMU.MÍ.MEŠ-*ku-nu* (II 6:116)
your friends	EN *ṭa-ba᾿-te-ku-nu* (II 8:r. 22)
any one in the entire nation	UN.M[EŠ K]UR *gab-bu* (II 8:r. 23)
one of the kings	1-*en* LUGAL.MEŠ (II 13:iii 11)
his (king's) vassal	*sal-me-šú* (II 6:112)
General	
any human being	*nap-har ṣal-mat*–SAG.DU (II 6:79, 118, 339)
an Assyrian	DUMU KUR–*aš-šur* (II 6:338)
a foreigner	DUMU KUR *šá-ni-nim-ma* (II 6:339)
his enemy	LÚ.KÚR-*šú* (II 6:111)

3.6.3 Indicators of loyalty

Besides the obligations to report on the issues listed above and to keep an eye on potential perpetrators, the treaties included a number of other general and specific obligations and prohibitions. These obligations and prohibitions were used to monitor the loyalty of the party that was bound by the treaty. Compliance with these obligations and prohibitions was carefully watched, and transgression of any obligation or prohibition was to be reported by other officials. Issues serving as indicators of a vassal's loyalty:

OBLIGATIONS

- *The obligation to extradite rebels, enemy messengers, soldiers, and fugitives:*

- The party bound by the treaty agreed to extradite all rebels, instigators of insurrections, and those who spoke evil words against the king and his officials, or plotted against them (II 6:130–37; 9:12'–6').
- The Babylonians swore to extradite any messengers of Šamaš-šumu-ukin, king of Babylonia and brother of Ashurbanipal, or any enemy of Ashurbanipal, or any subject whom Ashurbanipal did not tolerate (II 9:6'–9', 29'–31', 36'–7').
- Mati'-ilu agreed not to hide escaped cavalrymen and chariot-fighters (II iii 2:21').
- "The king (Marduk-zakir-šumi) shall indicate to him (Šamši-Adad V) the fugitives [who] fled [*from Assyria to Babylonia*]" (II 1:13–14).

* *The obligation to take action against rebels* (II 6:123–29, 138–46, 249–58, 302–27, 340–59).
* *The obligation to participate in the Assyrian campaigns:*
    - The Babylonians agreed to muster bowmen and courageously fight against king's enemies (II 9:23'–5').
    - Aššur-nerari V imposed upon Mati'-ilu the obligation to participate in the Assyrian campaign with full loyalty (II 2 iv:1–3).
* *The obligation to be completely loyal to the king*:
    - Sennacherib's succession treaty required complete devotion to Esarhaddon (II 3:4'–5'; see also II 4:9').
    - Esarhaddon's succession treaty required Nahšimarteans to protect the king (II 6:62–67, 162–72; see also II 9:10'–11'), to always give Ashurbanipal sound advice and to smooth his way in every respect (II 6:52–53), to demonstrate absolute honesty and respect to Ashurbanipal (II 6:96), to serve him in a true and fitting manner (II 6:236), to show complete obedience to him (II 6:195; see also II 9:21'–22'), and finally to love him (II 6:266–68; see also II 9:32') and even to die for him and his family (II 6:50–51).
* *Special obligations*
    - The Qeder tribe was obliged to make every effort to kill Yauta' (II 10:r.5'–7').

- The treaty with Baal, the king of Tyre, established the rules regulating the maritime trade along the Mediterranean coast (II 5:15'–17').

PROHIBITIONS

- The prohibition against instigating or participating in any revolt, insurrection, or rebellion against the king, his kingship, and his family (II 6:55–56, 66–72, 101–7, 180–87, 196–97, 212–13, 259–65, 269–74, 302–18, 360–73; II 9:12'–16', 18'–19').
- The prohibition against helping or protecting rebels, or handing them over to the enemies of Assyria (II 6:123–29, 214–25).
- The prohibition against sending reports to the enemies of Assyria (II 9:35') or providing information about Assyrian plans (II 13 iii:1–9).
- The prohibition against invalidating the treaty by rituals (II 6:373–84) or by destruction of the treaty tablet (II 6:397–413).
- The prohibition against making another, especially anti-Assyrian, treaty (II 4:10'–11'; 6:71–72, 129, 152–61, 173–79).

In summary, the treaties established the legal foundations of the local branch of Neo-Assyrian intelligence. The party entering into a treaty with Assyria legally bound itself to inform the king of all suspicious actions and to keep an eye on potential perpetrators. Thus, the treaties assured a continuous flow of information to the royal court from the Assyrian provinces, vassal states, and buffer regions. However, the treaties were a double-edged sword. On the one hand, the party bound by the treaty to report on "everything they heard" (XVI 21:11) provided the Assyrian king with information necessary to control his subjects, and in return enjoyed the protection of Assyria and other benefits. On the other hand, the treaties gave the Assyrians a powerful instrument for controlling the party itself. The treaties outlined the obligations and prohibitions that functioned as warning signs. If the treaty partner failed to report suspicious activities, shielded perpetrators, or transgressed any of the prohibitions and obligations imposed by the treaty the king and his officials were thereby warned that that party was no longer wholeheartedly devoted to Assyria. This, consequently, justified any Assyrian punitive action, however brutal and destructive it might be, in order to bring into line the party that had broken a treaty sworn before the gods.

4

Neo-Assyrian psychological warfare

The extant letters of the Neo-Assyrian archives allow for the reconstruction of two series of case studies of Neo-Assyrian psychological warfare. The first set of Psyops was conducted under the aegis of Tiglath-pileser III in 731–729 B.C.E. and the second under the aegis of Sargon II in 710–709 B.C.E. While the Tiglath-pileser III series refers to new political and military events that have not been discussed in the previous chapters, the Sargon II series elaborates the case studies presented in section 3.3 from the PsW point of view.

4.1 Psychological warfare during Tiglath-pileser III's last campaigns in Babylonia

4.1.4 Historical introduction[1]

The reign of Nabonassar, a rather weak king of Babylonia who reigned between 747 and 734 B.C.E.,[2] was very much overshadowed by that of Tiglath-pileser III, who directed his first campaign (745–744 B.C.E.) against rebellious tribes in Babylonia in order to support Nabonassar, his ally. During this campaign Tiglath-pileser III marched through most of Babylonian territory and boasted of having subjugated most of the Aramean and Chaldean tribes. Tiglath-pileser III adopted the title "King of Sumer and Akkad," made Nabonassar his vassal king, and let him enjoy the privileges of the *Pax Assyriaca* for the next ten years. After Nabonassar's death, his son Nabû-nadin-zeri ascended the throne (733–732 B.C.E.). His reign was

---

[1] This historical reconstruction is based on ABD 4, 732–77, CAH^2 3, 32–42, J. A. Brinkman, "Merodach-Baladan II," in *Studies Presented to A. Leo Oppenheim: June 7, 1964* (Chicago: University of Chicago Press, 1964), idem, *A Political History of Post-Kassite Babylonia, 1158–722 B.C.* (Rome: Pontifical Biblical Institute, 1968), 226–45, Grayson, *Assyrian and Babylonian Chronicles*, 1–65, Kuhrt, *The Ancient Near East, c. 3000–330 BC*, vol 2., 493–539, 576–88, Olmstead, *History of Assyria*, 175–81, G. Roux, *Ancient Iraq*, 3rd ed. (Harmondsworth, Middlesex and New York: Penguin, 1992), 305–10, Saggs, "NL I", and Tadmor, *Inscriptions of Tiglath-Pileser III*, 232–84.

[2] This study will follow the chronology as reconstructed by Brinkman, *Post-Kassite Babylonia*, 73–77.

short-lived. After ruling for two years, he lost his life in a rebellion led by his provincial governor Nabû-šumu-ukin. Nabû-šumu-ukin took advantage of an insurrection which broke out in Syria and kept Tiglath-pileser III and his troops militarily engaged in the west. After having seized the Babylonian throne, Nabû-šumu-ukin (II) enjoyed a reign of only one month. Mukin-zeri, the governor of Bit-Amukani, deposed him and ruled in Babylonia for the next three years (731–729 B.C.E.). When Tiglath-pileser III finally intervened in 731 B.C.E., he did not encounter a united front of Aramean and Chaldean tribes[3] but rather a country split into numerous factions. As soon as the Assyrian troops set out for Babylonia, Mukin-zeri quickly retreated from Babylon to his tribal capital of Šapia and was decisively defeated only in 729 B.C.E. Tiglath-pileser III burned down the surroundings of Šapia and felled its date-palms. There is no evidence indicating that Šapia itself actually fell,[4] in the contrary, it seems that Mukin-zeri remained at large.[5] The Chaldean leaders (Merodach-Baladan, the governor of Bit-Yakin; Balassu, the governor of Bit-Dakuri; and Nadinu, the governor of Larak) paid tribute.[6]

4.1.5 Neo-Assyrian propaganda versus Mukin-zeri's counter-propaganda

Mukin-zeri's rebellion and the possibility of Tiglath-pileser III's military retaliation generated conflicting loyalties throughout Babylonia.[7] On the one hand, Assyrian garrisons that survived the rebellion against Assyria and some Chaldean cities such as Dilbat (ND 2717:50'-51') supported Assyria. Moreover, some parts of Aramean tribes such as the Itu'u, Ru'ua (ND 2700:9'; 2663:12'), and Lita'u (ND 2632:39–40) also remained loyal to Assyria. On the other hand, there was an anti-Assyrian faction, which included Mukin-zeri's home tribe Bit-Amukani and his tribal allies Bit-Ša'alli and Bit-Šilani,[8] as well as some Aramean sheiks and cities (TP III Summ 7:13–15). Some of the temple personnel in Babylon also

[3] Brinkman, "Merodach-Baladan," 10.
[4] Tadmor, *Inscriptions of Tiglath-Pileser III*, 163.
[5] Brinkman, *Post-Kassite Babylonia*, 238.
[6] TP III Summ 7:23–28.
[7] Brinkman, *Post-Kassite Babylonia*, 237.
[8] That Bit-Ša'alli and Bit-Šilani remained loyal to Mukin-zeri can be deduced from the brutal punishement that Tiglath-pileser III inflicted upon these tribes: Bit-Ša'alli's capital Dur-Illatayu was demolished and its governor Zakiru was taken in chains to Assyria (TP III Summ 7:19–21); Nabû-ušabši of Bit-Šilani was impaled (TP III Summ 7:15–16).

supported Mukin-zeri's rebellion, and some servants of the Bel temple in Babylon even joined Mukin-zeri in the reprisals inflicted upon the city of Dilbat (ND 2717:48'–49'). However, it seems that most of the cities and the rest of the Aramean sheiks did not want to commit themselves to one group or the other before knowing for sure whether Tiglath-pileser III would intervene. Finally, the Akkadians[9] shrewdly took advantage of the conflict and while Mukin-zeri was engaged in battle against the Assyrians in Buharu (a yet to be identified city in Babylonia), they plundered his sheep (ND 2717:46–48').[10]

A mix of conflicting interests and loyalties, diverse religious traditions and ethnic identities, as well as the varying degrees of independence of the cities factionalized Babylonia and turned it into fruitful territory for disseminating propaganda. An analysis of letters ND 2632, 2717, 2700, and 2603 will demonstrate how both sides—the Assyrians and Mukin-zeri—used PsW.

4.1.5.1 At the gate of Babylon

The first round of Psyops (ND 2632), dated before Tiglath-pileser III's invasion (731 B.C.E.), was conducted by two Assyrian officials, Šamaš-bunaya[11] and his colleague Nabû-namir. Both officials were stationed in the Assyrian garrison Kar-Nergal[12] (ND 2632:34-5). The target of their missions was the citizenry of Babylon.

---

[9] The term "Akkadians" conveys socio-cultural implications, i.e. a sedentary population of the urban centers, rather than specifically ethnic ones; see G. Frame, *Babylonia 689–627 B.C.: A Political History* (Istanbul: Nederlands Historisch-Archaeologisch Instituut te Istanbul, 1992), 34.

[10] According to ND 2717:47'-8' the Akkadians took with them 20,000 sheep from Šapia and its vicinity. This probably inflicted a significant blow on Mukin-zeri's rear guard and severely undermined the food resources of his troops. Knowing this, the Assyrians could plan their siege of Šapia.

[11] Šamaš-bunaya was the author of letters ND 2632, 2663, and 2628.

[12] Two possible locations have been suggested: according to the first proposal, the city Kar-Nergal was located on the canal linking Cutha and Sippar; see H. W. F. Saggs, "The Nimrud Letters, 1952—Part III," *Iraq* 18/1 (1956): 51.; according to the second proposal Kar-Nergal is to be identified with the modern town aṣ-Ṣuwaira; see S. Parpola and M. Porter, *The Helsinki Atlas of the Near East in the Neo-Assyrian Period* (Helsinki: Casco Bay Assyriological Institute and Neo-Assyrian Text Corpus Project, 2001), 11.

Letter ND 2632 is a summary briefing of several negotiations with Babylonian representatives.[13] The first round of negotiations is described in lines ND 2632:5–17. Šamaš-bunaya and Nabû-namir met with a Babylonian representative,[14] who was accompanied by Asinu, Mukin-zeri's official, and some citizens of Babylon. The negotiations took place in front of the Marduk gate, situated on the northern part of the east wall of Babylon.[15] Lines 13–18 report the content and the results of this negotiation.[16] Unfortunately, these lines are severely damaged and the content of the Neo-Assyrian propaganda therein can be only partially reconstructed. The Assyrians promised to grant a privileged status to the Babylonians if they agreed to collaborate. The word used to describe this status is *kidinnūtu* (ND 2632:17; XVII 21:14; 2644:r.15), which signifies protection and a privileged or exempt status.[17] Thus, the Babylonians were offered special protection[18] or exemption from certain vassal obligations (e.g., tax exemption, *ilku, dullu* duties, etc.).

The second round of negotiations was carried out in the presence of two Babylonian administrative authorities, the Five and the Ten,[19] and the above-mentioned Babylonian representative.[20] The Assyrian negotiators clearly stated that the goal of their missions was that the Babylonians

---

[13] Unfortunately, it is impossible to determine whether tablet ND 2632 describes discrete events or whether it is a report on the different steps of one diplomatic mission. However, the syntax of the letter suggests that the Assyrian officials repeated their diplomatic pressure upon the Babylonians over a certain period of time (ND 2632:5, 17–18, 22–24).

[14] [L]Ú? *babili*^{ki} mentioned in ND 2632:7 could be translated as "the Babylonian," or "the Man of Babylon"—i.e. the representative of the city; see *CTN 5*, 20. This idea is further confirmed by the usage of the 3rd p. sing. in ND 2632:24.

[15] Saggs, "NL I," 25.

[16] This assumption is based on J. Hämeen-Anttila's observation about the conjunction *ma-a*. According to his research, *ma-a* placed after a verb in the 1st p. pl. introduces direct discourse in the same way as it does when placed after a verb in the 3rd p. sing.; see SAAS XIII, 133. H. W. F. Saggs suggests that the direct report finshes in line ND 2632:18; see *CTN 5*, 21.

[17] *CAD* 8, 344; SANTAG 5, 156; see also XVII 21:14.

[18] A variant LÚ.*kiddinû* is used as a title, "a protégé" (XVII 48:r.8; 83:e.9), often in a construct chain: "the protégé of" god NN; see IX 9:1; XVI 105:r.12–3.

[19] H. W. F. Saggs suggested interpreting the expression *ṣābe*$^{me[š]}$ *h*[*a*]-*meš* *ṣābe*^{meš} X as referring to two administrative authorities in Babylon; see Saggs, "NL I," 25.

[20] His presence can be deduced from the shift from plural to singular in ND 2632:20–24; see *CTN 5*, 20–21.

should open the gate for the Assyrians (ND 2632:23).[21] This time, however, Assyrian propaganda met with strong resistance and the Five and the Ten refused even to talk to Šamaš-bunaya and Nabû-namir. The rejection of the Assyrian demand that the gates of Babylon be opened was met with new PsW strategies intended to make the Babylonians collaborate. By asking the question, "When the king himself comes, what shall I say to the king?" (ND 2632:27–28),[22] the Assyrian officials compelled the Babylonians to think about the consequences of any negative report the officials might send to Tiglath-pileser III. The shrewd Babylonian reply neutralized the Assyrian threat as reported by Šamaš-bunaya and Nabû-namir: "When the king comes, they will open the Great Gate" (ND 2632:28–29). Thus, the Babylonians did not refuse to obey the king; rather, they did not feel obliged to obey the commands of middle-ranking Assyrian officials. A comment in line 30 indicates that the Assyrian officials saw through the Babylonian strategy: being convinced that the king would never come, the Babylonians thought that they would not have to open the gate at all.

Another PsW strategy can be reconstructed from the following lines:

---

[21] Among the Neo-Assyrian archives are preserved two letters inviting a local official to open the gate of the city (ND 2632 and XVII 3). Tablet XVII 3 is a very fragmentary royal letter addressing the Urukian high-ranking official, Bulluṭu, dated to Sargon II; see SAA XVII, XXII. For dating the tablet to the reign of Esarhaddon or Ashurbanipal see *Prosopography* 1/II, 351. Although the edge of this tablet is missing, the meaning can be reconstructed with certainty: *ú ṭup-pa-ka a-na* [xxx] *liš-šu-nim-ma* KÁ *a-na* [xxx] *pi-ta-ma ki-i an-ni*[*ti-x*], "and let them bring the tablet to [xxx]. Open the gate to [xxx] and … !" The phrase KÁ *a-na* [xxx] *pi-ta-ma,* "Open the gate to [xxx]!" is a syntactic unit delimited by two coordinate conjunctives: *ma*: *liš-šu-nim-**ma*** KÁ *a-na* [xxx] *pi-ta-**ma***. Thus, the logogram KÁ, *bābu* 'gate' must be the direct object of the imperative *pi-ta-ma*, and the preposition *ana* determines the indirect object, i.e., to whom the gate should be opened. Both letters invite the representatives of their cities to open the gate to the Assyrians (XVII 3:r.2-3; ND 2632:23). However, the strategy of PsW is quite different. Šamaš-bunaya and Nabû-namir threatened the Babylonians with writing to the king about the hostilities (ND 2632:27–28, 37–38), whereas letter XVII 3 indicates that the Babylonian prelate, Bel-iqiša, an Assyrian informer in Babylonia, spoke positively (lit. "nice words") about Bulluṭu (XVII 3:4–6). Furthermore, ND 2632 is the report of Assyrian field-officials fulfilling the king's command, whereas XVII 3 is a unique exemplar of a letter in which the king attempted to manipulate directly a local official. Since no destruction of Babylon and Uruk is mentioned in the inscriptions of Tiglath-pileser III and Sargon II, it is possible to conclude that both cities accepted the Assyrian offer and opened their gates to the Assyrians.

[22] The same threat is repeated in ND 2632:38.

ki-i an-ni-i ni-iq-ṭí-ba-šú-n[u] m[a]-a ^{m}[x x x] ù ^{amēl}urdāni^{meš} ša ^{m}[mu]kīn-zēr lu en-du-ni šu-nu
then this (thing) we said to them: "[NN] and the servants of Mukin-zeri are subject to penalty." (ND 2632:31–33)

The Assyrian officials claimed that Mukin-zeri, the leader of the rebellion, and his servants deserved punishment. It is possible that by this phrase the Assyrians alluded to Mukin-zeri's violation of a treaty between Tiglath-pileser III and the Chaldean tribes that had been concluded during Tiglath-pileser III's first invasion.[23] By this strategy, the Assyrians, without regard for the real reason for the punishment of Mukin-zeri and his servants, tried to undermine Mukin-zeri's authority by claiming that he deserved punishment, which implies that he was a criminal. Thus, the Assyrians appealed to the Babylonians' dignity, hoping that they would not associate with people who deserved punishment.

Lines ND 2632:34–38 suggest that the efforts of Šamaš-bunaya and Nabû-namir to talk the Babylonians into collaborating failed and that they retreated to Kar-Nergal to await the arrival of Tigleth-pileser III. However, they did not stop working and remained in touch with the Babylonians.

4.1.5.2 Cautious Arameans

The protagonists of the second set of Psyops were Iasubaya, the commander of Assyrian cavalry, and the unknown sender of letter ND 2717. The letter reported the results of two diplomatic missions: the first mission was directed against an Aramean tribe holding an unknown city,[24] and the second against the Arameans living in Šapia.

The first mission was led by Iasubaya, whose words were underscored by his cavalry unit, in whose presence he conducted his diplomatic negotiations (ND 2717:11'–31'). He was sent to the Arameans by his superior, the unknown sender of letter ND 2717. The goal of

[23] Similarly, Tiglath-pileser III accused Zakiru, another Chaldean leader, of violating a loyalty treaty (TP III Summ 7:19).

[24] The name of the city is not mentioned in the preserved lines of the tablet. However, its location can be deduced from lines ND 2632:14'–15'. The Aramean tribe was invited to march as far as Marad. Consequently, the city held by the Arameans must have been located somewhere between Babylon and Marad.

Iasubaya's mission was to compel the Arameans to leave their city and join the Assyrians in the campaign against Mukin-zeri.[25] Iasubaya offered the Arameans a compromise: if they did not want to march with him against Mukin-zeri, at least they should march as far as the city Marad. He further emphasized that the Assyrian troops would go with them and so they would not march alone. Finally, he challenged their soldierly bravery by challenging them not to cower in the city (ND 2717:12'), i.e., to come out and behave like real soldiers. However, since there was no evidence that Tiglath-pileser III's troops were about to intervene, the Arameans refused to commit themselves and preferred to hold the city (ND 2717:20'–27').

The second diplomatic mission was directed against the Arameans living in the seat of the rebellion, Šapia. The Assyrians[26] offered to all Arameans who would defect from Šapia exemption from their *dullu* service (ND 2717:r.1'–4').

4.1.6 Mukin-zeri's counterattack

Mukin-zeri did everything he could to prevent his kingdom from falling apart. The first psychological strategy he employed was to play one ruler against another, namely, Merodach-Baladan against Balassu (ND 2603).[27] Since Balassu was sympathizing with Assyria, he sent Merodach-Baladan a letter blackening Balassu's reputation by calling him Merodach-Baladan's adversary and the destroyer of the land (ND 2603:7'–8'). The letter was brought to an Assyrian official (the unknown sender of ND 2603)

---

[25] The fragmentary state of the obverse of the tablet allows only speculation about the nature of arguments the Assyrians used to compel the Arameans to collaborate. According to line ND 2717:8', the Assyrians were informed about the situation in Mukin-zeri's camp. He was confined to a certain territory and could no longer move back and forth. The Assyrian commanders wanted to take advantage of this situation and attack Mukin-zeri's camp. However, for such an attack they needed the help of the Arameans. To this end, the Assyrians shared intelligence with the Arameans, hoping that by plainly depicting Mukin-zeri's position, they might compel the Arameans to join them in the campaign.
Another Assyrian argument might be reconstructed from lines ND 2717:5'–6'. The sender of the letter suggested that if the Arameans joined the Assyrians, they would not have to march in the front lines and thus would not be exposed to heavy losses. The sender generously offered to have his own units march first. The Arameans refused the offer for fear of Mukin-zeri (ND 2717: 4'); see *CTN 5*, 22–25.

[26] Probably the sender of letter ND 2717.

[27] Saggs, "NL I," 48.

and read out in front of Balassu (ND 2603:9'–10').[28] Hearing it, Balassu became terrified. This reveals Mukin-zeri's shrewdness. Balassu was Merodach-Baladan's uncle, and thus Mukin-zeri's propaganda put Balassu in a dilemma: either to show hostility toward his own nephew or to stop collaborating with Assyria (ND 2603:13'–14'). Balassu suggested that Tiglath-pileser III intervene as soon as possible, hoping that the presence of the Assyrian royal army would cause Merodach-Baladan to change his mind.

Moreover, to keep his allies loyal, Mukin-zeri did not hesitate to use violence. In particular, he organized a punitive campaign against the city of Dilbat and felled its date-palms (ND 2717:50'-53').

4.1.7 Evaluation

According to these two case studies, the preferred tool of Assyrian PsW was diplomatic negotiation. Most of the missions described in the previous sections did not meet with success. The common denominator of these failures was the reluctance of the people to collaborate with the Assyrians—either because their army was still too far away or because the locals doubted that the Assyrians would intervene at all. It seems that Assyrian PsW became much more effective once the troops had pitched camp in the backyard of Babylon. The Babylonians first hesitated, but then welcomed the king and complied. The city of Larak (ND 2603:21') and PA.DAN's people also collaborated (ND 2632:42).

4.2 Psychological warfare in Babylonia during Sargon II's twelfth and thirteenth campaigns

The anti-Assyrian coalition in Babylonia consisted of several ethnic groups united under the leadership of Merodach-Baladan.[29] To disrupt this coalition, the Assyrians used, besides conventional warfare, a whole spectrum of political and psychological means tailored to ethnic and cultural circumstances.

---

[28] Brinkman, "Merodach-Baladan," 10.

[29] For a historical introduction, see section 3.3.1.

4.2.1 Case-studies

The following case studies will illustrate how the Assyrians employed these techniques in their diplomatic missions and negotiations with the local inhabitants. This series of case studies, together with other Neo-Assyrian documents, will form the basis for a model of Neo-Assyrian PsW as used during Sargon II's twelfth and thirteenth campaigns, and for an evaluation of the efficiency of Neo-Assyrian PsW.

4.2.1.1 Counterpropaganda

SAA XV 1; ABL 158; K 530
Sender: Issar-duri (governor of Arrapha)
Date: 710 B.C.E. (Pre-campaign phase)
Propaganda Agent: Nabû-zeru-ibni[30]
Object of the mission: Aramean tribe Ru'ua
Location of the mission: between the Tigris and the Uqnu Rivers

Of the diplomatic missions attested in the Neo-Assyrian archives, Nabû-zeru-ibni's mission was the first that the Assyrians conducted in Babylonia during Sargon II's twelfth and thirteenth campaigns. Nabû-zeru-ibni was an Assyrian eunuch of Ru'uean origin whom the king moved for this purpose from Damascus to Arrapha (XV 1:4–6). Nabû-zeru-ibni's origin and experience were probably what prompted the king to move him from one end of the empire to the other: he was a Ru'uean who spent several years as a eunuch in Syria and was brought to influence his Ru'uean kinsmen.

However, Issar-duri did not share the king's high opinion of Nabû-zeru-ibni. The tone of his letter, his characterization of Nabû-zeru-ibni as "p[laying] would-be-king" (XV 1:r.15'), and his evaluation of Nabû-zeru-ibni's stay as "totally unproductive" (XV 1:r.10'–13') indicate that he harbored certain doubts about the efficiency of Nabû-zeru-ibni's mission and the transparency of his intentions.

[30] Tablet XV 203 mentions Nabû-zeru-ibni in connection with Elam. However, the tablet is too fragmentary to permit any conclusions.

Nabû-zeru-ibni started his mission by addressing $^{md+}$E[N *x x x*] of Abdudu, a city located in Ru'uean territory (XV 1:7–9). The goal of his mission was expressed thus: *ma-a i–su-ri* KUR.*ru-'u-*[*a-a*] UN.MEŠ-*šu ina* UGU-*hi-šu il-l*[*a-ku-ni*], "perhaps the land of Ru'ua and its people would come to him (Nabû-zeru-ibni)" (XV 1:9–10).[31]

A more reluctant faction among the Abdudaeans entertained Nabû-zeru-ibni's offer:

> They have not been assembled yet. Delaying their messenger, they did not send their report to me (Issar-duri) [32] (thinking): "(If) we send (it) and the kin[g delivers] the defeat to Merodach-Baladan [and] these words … [*then*] …" (XV 1:19–23)

Trying to gain time by delaying the messenger who was to deliver their acceptance or rejection report, they pondered the repercussions which would follow, if Merodach-Baladan's coalition were to suffer defeat.

Since the tablet was written after Nabû-zeru-ibni's mission was finished, Issar-duri could also inform the king about its results. Merodach-Baladan, after finding out about Nabû-zeru-ibni's subversive activity, launched his counterattack forthwith. His challenge to the city rulers found great resonance within the anti-Assyrian faction and resulted in the overt rejection of Nabû-zeru-ibni's offer:

> Why should we run away? (This) brother of ours (Nabû-zeru-ibni) who has come is on the other side (of the river). He came, but he will go back again." (XV 1:16–19)

According to S II Ann 281–88, the Ru'ua tribe participated in the defense of Dur-Athara. After the conquest of Dur-Athara, Ru'ueans together with other Aramean tribes found shelter in the marshes of the Uqnu River. Even starvation brought only partial success: Sargon II was able to

---

[31] The generally negative tone of Issar-duri's report and the expression "to him" instead of "to the king, my lord" might indicate Nabû-zeru-ibni's intention to take advantage of his mission.

[32] This translation is based on parsing *la iš-pa-ru-niš-šú* (XV 1:21) as the G preterite of *šapāru* with ventive (translated "to me") and pronominal suffix 3rd p. sing. (referring to *ṭè-e*[*n-šú-nu*], "their report").

compel only one Ru'uean sheik to pay homage and high tribute. One year later, the Ru'ua tribe was again Merodach-Baladan's active ally in the defense of Dur-Yakin.[33] If we take these facts into consideration, it is possible to conclude that Nabû-zeru-ibni's mission failed or, in other words, that the counterpropaganda that Merodach-Baladan launched prior to Sargon II's invasion was strong enough to paralyze Nabû-zeru-ibni's mission.

4.2.1.2 Manipulation of the masses

SAA XV 157; ABL 1041; Sm 30
Sender: Il-yada' (Assyrian official operating north of the Tigris and the Nar-Šarri canal)
Date: 710 B.C.E. (Dur-Athara or Diyala phase)
Propaganda Agent(s): Ṣala-il and NN (NN was most likely Ṣala-il)
Object of the mission: an Aramean tribe Tu'manu
Location of the mission: the Tigris River[34]

This tablet contains two diplomatic missions: the mission reported on the obverse of the tablet was carried out by Ṣala-il but the tablet is too damaged to determine the object of his mission; the reverse of the tablet describes a mission aimed at the Tu'manu tribe living amidst the Hatalla tribe. Since both propaganda agents were of Aramean origin and held important offices, it is possible that the reverse and obverse of tablet XV 157 describe two different activities of Ṣala-il. However, the tablet is too damaged to decide for sure.

Ṣala-il, "being one of them" (XV 157:6'), was well suited for the mission within his own tribe. He not only spoke their language, but Il-yada' even called him EN *ša da-bu-bi-šu-nu*, "a master of litigation with them" (XV 157:7').[35] A direct quotation from Ṣala-il's speech yields a glimpse of

[33] After Sargon II's campaigns were completed, one of the main leaders of the Ru'uean resistance, Ilumma-taklak, was deported from Babylon at the command of Nabû-belu-ka''in (XV 40).

[34] The object of the mission was the Tu'manu tribe living in the midst of the Hatallu tribe. Therefore, the mission took place on the territory of the Hatalla tribe, located "in the steppe southwest of Assyria proper and west of the Wādī Tartār, in the Iraqi Ǧazira"; see Lipinski, *The Aramaeans: Their Ancient History, Culture, Religion*, 426.

[35] The governor of Mannea used a similar expression for the propaganda agent, Kubaba-ila'i. Kubaba-ila'i is called EN *li-šá-ni*, "master of language" (V 217:17). Comparing both

his persuasion technique: *ina* UGU ^{m}DINGIR–*ia-da-a' ni-*⌜*ik*$^{!}$⌝-[*mi-si*] *ni-il-lik*, "let us get together and go to Il-yada'" (XV 157:8'–9'). Employing cohortatives (the 1st p. pl.) and the verb *kamāsu* 'to gather in (animals, population, etc.)', Ṣala-il conveyed the following message: "let you and me act together" (XV 157:8'–9'). What he was using here is a very well known dynamic of mass persuasion, *verba movent, exempla trahunt,* and in this way he showed himself as a genuine leader who not only spoke but also acted.[36] According to the news brought to Merodach-Baladan (XV 157:11'–12'), Ṣala-il's mission succeeded and his kinsmen allied themselves with Assyria.

The second mission aimed to reach the Tu'manu tribe living amidst the Hatalla tribe. It was conducted by the messengers of an Aramean leader dwelling among his brothers along the Uqnu River, whose rank can be deduced from the fact that he was in charge of inspecting several cities in the region.

> He has se[nt] his messengers to the Tu'man[eans] who live in the Hatalla tribe, saying: "The king, my lord, is coming forth to my house. As for you, move on and [come] to me!" (XV 157:r.6'–9')

The prospect of the king's approach put psychological pressure on the Tu'maneans, who were thus compelled to take a stand before it was too late. The result of the mission was unknown at the time Il-yada' was filing his report for the king. According to S II Ann 20–21 and Zyl 18, the Tu'manu tribe was conquered in 721 B.C.E. during Sargon II's first campaign to Babylonia. Since the Tu'manu tribe is not reported among the tribes subjugated during Sargon II's twelfth and thirteenth campaigns, it is

---

expressions (V 217 and XV 157), it is possible to conclude that the expression EN + *xxx* describes the quality of the propaganda agent. In Ṣala-il's case it was his capacity to argue, whereas in Kababa-ila'i's case it was his capacity to use the language.

36 With the phrase *ni-*⌜*ik*$^{!}$⌝-[*mi-si*], "let us ge[t together]" (XV 157:8'), he appealed to the unity of his tribe, making clear that acting as a group capable of overcoming discord was the best way out of distress. Thus, he offered a solution to a confused mob aware that it was incaple of stopping Sargon II's army from marching down along the Tigris: abandon Merodach-Baladan and join Sargon II! Since the nature of his solution implied a betrayal of their ally, Merodach-Baladan, Ṣala-il's willingness to be the instigator of this action allowed the mob to transfer its responsibility to him: thus the mob was able to act in a way that an individual could not.

possible to conclude that the rest of the Tu'manu tribe allied itself with the Assyrians; in other words, PsW attained its goal.

4.2.1.3 Conditions

Some preserved tablets describe diplomatic negotiations in which the other party laid down the conditions of its collaboration (XV 162 and XVII 8).

XV 162; ABL 662; K 661
Sender: Il-yada' (Assyrian official operating in north of the Tigris and the Nar-Šarri canal)
Date: 710 B.C.E. (north Tigris phase)
Propaganda Agent(s): Kutayu, Yasamu, Il-yada'
Object of the mission: Isuqaeans living in Arranu (an Aramean clan[37])
Location of the mission: Diyala and Tigris Rivers (?)

> As for the brothers of Kutayu, son of Se'-*salam,* they are Isuqaeans. He (Kutayu), together with Yasamu, went from here (from Il-yada') to the town of Arranu.
> Now ten of them, (i.e.) from Arranu, came [to] my (Il-yada''s) presence [*x*] ⸢*i*⸣-*bi-is-su-ni* (obscure) and said as follows: "As for [the re]st of our brothers [who are th]ere, [s]ome are [se]rvants of the house of the palace herald. Swear to us by the name of god! If you give (them) to us,[38] we will come, gather our brothers, and go."

[37] Since the expression "our brothers" is used mostly to describe the Aramean tribes, and the diplomatic mission happened while Merodach-Baladan was still in Babylon—i.e., during the first phase when the main target of PsW was the Aramean clans along the Uqnu and the Tigris—it therefore stands to reason that the Isuaqaeans were an Aramean tribe.

[38] S. Parpola and A. Fuchs translate this line as follows: "[I]f you give us (to him), [w]e shall go, gather our brothers and go (away)"; see SAA XV, 111. The translations differ in taking the 1st person plural pronominal suffix -*nāšu* as dative (the translation proposed above) or accusative (S. Parpola's translation). J. Hämeen-Anttila suggests that -*nāšu* is a Neo-Babylonian variant of the accusative pronominal suffix; see SAAS XIII, 50. Since line r.6 reads Babylonian *kamāsu* instead of Neo-Assyrian *kannušu* 'to gather', the ending -*nāšu* could also be taken as a Neo-Babylonian variant of Neo-Assyrian -*nāši;* see SAA XV, 111. Line XV 162:r.3 MU DINGIR *še-la-an-na-šú*, which contains the same suffix -*nāšu*, helps us to decide whether -*nāšu* is the strictly accusative or the accusative/dative pronominal suffix. *CAD* E, 135 lists several examples of the pattern PN *ina* MU DINGIR/DN *ana* PN_2 *šālû* (various forms), "PN swear(s/swore...) to PN_2 by the name of

> If the king, my lord, so commands, I will swear to them by the name of god. Later on, the king, my lord, may do as he deems best.
> News of the son of Zerî: his army is in Kiš, he himself is staying in Babylon.

The letter presents the results of the diplomatic mission of Kutayu and Yasamu, the Isuqaeans, who were sent to stir up interest among their kinsmen in aligning themselves with the Assyrians. Their mission found positive resonance among their kinsmen and ten of them returned to Il-yada' with an offer to ally themselves with the Assyrians under the condition that Il-yada' would allow their brothers to return home.[39] The pact would have been guaranteed by Il-yada''s oath given in the name of god. Relating the core of the discussion to the king, Il-yada' suggested accepting the conditions of the pact: to swear in the name of god. However, he immediately added that the oath did not bind the king categorically. If the king deemed it necessary, he could simply change it. The fact that Neo-Assyrian archival documents do not mention any of these names indicates that the Isuqaean clan did not pose a threat serious enough to be reported in the archival documents. In other words, the mission of Kutayu and Yasamu accomplished its goal, and Il-yada' accepted their conditions.

---

god/DN." This indicates that the *-nāšu* suffix in the phrase MU DINGIR *še-la-an-na-šú* must be dative. Thus, the *-nāšu* suffix is not strictly accusative but, like most of the Neo-Assyrian pronominal suffixes, dative/accusative. Consequently, line XV 162:r.4, [*šúm-m*]*a ta-dan-an-na-šú*, can be translated as "if you give (them) to us" (dative) or "if you give us (to him)" (accusative). Investigation of the SAA volumes indicates that the first variant better reflects the Neo-Assyrian style. In all cases of the combination *tadānu/nadānu* + *nāši* with a clear context, the 1st person plural pronominal suffix stands for the dative ("to us"), thus I 1:9; 143:r.5.9; X 158:6. Moreover, in several cases the Neo-Assyrian scribes often omitted the direct object (accusative) and preferred to write the dative when two pronominal suffixes (dative and accusative) should be suffixed to the finite verb; e.g., XV 121:e.18 omits "them" and I 143:r.11 omits "it". Thus, in my translation, I take *-nāšu* as the dative ("to us") with an omitted accusative pronominal suffix ("them").

[39] The difficulty in serving far from their own people is expressed in XV 121. In this case the king allowed the Labdudaeans to return to their lords: "Let them give their people back to them, so they can be induced to work. (As long as) their attention is (directed) to their people, they cannot be induced to work, they being here, the(ir) people there." (XV 121:r.1–15)

SAA XVII 8; ABL 468; Rm 217
Sender: Nabû-ahhe-lumur (Assyrian commander of the troops operating in Sippar)
Date: 710 B.C.E. (Chaldean phase)

The princes, the leaders of the Aramean tribes, brought the tribes living around Sippar to the point of starvation (XV 8:r.6'). This starvation triggered a rebellion of at least four Aramean tribes (Hamaraneans, Lihuateans, Rabileans, and Hatalleans; XVII 7–8) who even plundered a temple in Sippar (XVII 8:r.1'–5'). The leading tribe in this rebellion was the Hamaraneans, who proposed the conditions of peace: "We shall not make peace until they make the town of Ganata ours!" (XVII 8:r.11'–13'). According to S II Ann 318, Sargon II, after entering Babylon, had to dispatch parts of his troops to quench the rebellion. Thus, the Assyrians probably did not accept the Aramean conditions of surrender and resorted to military intervention.

4.2.1.4 Military support of Assyrian allies

SAA XV 116; ABL 1044; Sm 117
Sender: Nabû-belu-ka''in (governor of Lubda)
Date: Post-campaign
Propaganda Agent: Nabû-belu-ka''in and Ahu-lê
Object of the mission: the inhabitants of Gabê
Location of the mission: along the piedmont of the Hamrin range between Meturna and Der

A peaceful trade exchange, uninterrupted information flow, and swift access to Gambulu territory required control over the cities lying on a strategically important road connecting Meturna and Der. The Gar[...eans]' attempt to block this access road by a raid on the city Gabê (location unknown) was carefully monitored and was countered without delay. The offer of immediate military support to an endangered ally is a well-known psychological technique and, in the case of the Gabeans, it bore fruit almost instantly. After the pacification of Gabê, the city delegation led by Ahu-lê visited the governor Nabû-belu-ka''in. The content of their discussion can be reconstructed from their answer to this governor (XV 116:r.4'–15'): the Gabeans recognized that their running away upon the arrival of the raiders was cowardly, and they made a resolution to seize the raiders, should they attack the city again. Thus, they learned an important lesson: Assyrian allies had nothing to fear as long as they remained loyal to Assyria. Having learned such a lesson in person, Ahu-lê and his companions could in turn spread the word about the Assyrians' willingness and ability to protect their allies. This part of the message was above all intended to encourage the local inhabitants to collaborate with the Assyrians more proactively. The second part of the message was addressed to the attackers: raids would not be tolerated and transgressors would not escape unpunished. However, tablets XV 30 and 118 indicate that the bands did not stop their attacks. They took full advantage of Elamite support, as well as of the incapacity of the Assyrian provincials to mobilize an army large enough to punish Elam for supporting the bands. In other words, while PsW was effective on the Assyrian adherents, it was ineffective on the Elamites and the raiders.

Tablets XVII 150–52 illustrate the other side of this psychological technique. During Sargon II's invasion of Babylonia, the sheiks of Tubliaš sent the Assyrian king a series of urgent messages urging him to intervene as soon as possible. The insurrection and unrest in the region threatened to undermine Sargon II's influence:

> The army should quickly get there! There is talk that people are rising up in great numbers. Persuade the magnates and come in five days' time! You must not lose the land! Come quickly! Come! XVII 150:r.2–11

Thus, supporting his allies played a crucial role not only during Sargon II's invasion but also after the campaigns were brought to a successful end. If Sargon II did not protect his allies, it might suggest that he was unwilling or unable to do so, which in turn might have had a strong psychological impact on the other tribes.

4.2.1.5 Incentives and promises

SAA XV 184; ABL 438; K 177
Sender: Marduk-šarru-uṣur (Assyrian prefect in Babylonia)
Date: 710 B.C.E. (Chaldean phase)
Propaganda Agent: a Babylonian
Object of the mission: Chaldean cavalrymen
Location of the mission: Chaldea

After the desertion of the commander of the cavalry (one of the *šandabakku*), other cavalrymen sent a message to Marduk-šarru-uṣur, the prefect of Babylonia, to negotiate the conditions of their own desertion. Marduk-šarru-uṣur, aware of the strategic importance of this offer, sent them *ithurāte* by means of a Babylonian, which were supposed to facilitate their desertion.

Even though the word *ithurāte* occurs very rarely in Akkadian, it is possible to interpret it as an incentive serving to motivate the soldiers' desertion. However, its nature remains obscure. The following interpretations are the most plausible. A. Fuchs interprets it as "a kind of passport to spare their users serious troubles. Such as, for example, being treated as prisoners of war and sold as slaves."[40] Such a pass[41] guaranteed the deserters human dignity, if they surrendered. In the case of Merodach-Baladan's coalition army, which suffered great losses on the east Tigris, and had little hope of stopping the advance of Sargon II's troops, such surrender passes were a well-aimed psychological ploy used at the right time.

Another interpretation stems from comparison of the word *ithuru* with *urigallu*, the royal standard or emblem,[42] similar to standards which accompanied military officials in the field, known from Ashurnaṣirpal II's reliefs.[43] Thus, *ithurāte* could mean an object representing a royal, in particular a military office. Consequently, to send cavalrymen the *ithurāte* would encourage their desertion by promising them that after desertion their military ranks would be preserved and their material gains assured, as was the case for a top Chaldean official in XV 216.

The Babylonian mediator was to report the result of his mission to Marduk-šarru-uṣur, who in turn was to send it to the king. There are two reasons to suppose that the employment of these incentives met with

---

[40] SAA XV, XVIII. To buttress his opinion, A. Fuchs quotes the example of three tailors of Merodach-Baladan who were sold for money (XV 214).

[41] The strategy of surrender passes was employed in several wars. Excellent examples are the surrender leaflets dropped by the US Air Force in Iraq in 2004, or by the coalition army over the German units at the end of World War II, as illustrated in Linebarger, *Psychological Warfare*, 70.

[42] *CAD* 7, 296.

[43] E. Weidner, "Hof- und Harems-Erlasse assyrischer Könige aus dem 2. Jahrtausend v. Chr.," *AfO* 17 (1954): 278.

success. First, the Neo-Assyrian archival texts do not describe any military encounter between Chaldean tribes and Assyrian troops. Second, there was an increasing number of deserters during the Chaldean phase.

Besides the above mentioned example of *ithurāte*, several other examples can be adduced to illustrate how the Assyrians used the promise-incentive strategy in Psyops. Thus, the king guaranteed safe conduct for the Urukians, if they opened the gate to the Assyrian army (XVII 3:r.4–14), and promised that one of his collaborators would become the successor to the Urukian throne (XVII 5:5'–13'). In another case, a high financial reward was offered for collaboration in capturing the Aramean rebel Haza'-il (XVII 148:5–9). Several tablets in the archives indicate that after the successful completion of the invasion, some people profited from the king's generosity: Sargon II generously forgave sinners (XVII 52:16–20; 53:14–20; 54:4'-r.3; 83:2'–8'), promoted his collaborators (XVII 16:3–5; 39:r.16–18), materially rewarded his faithful servants (XVII 48:6–9), and granted financial privileges to temples (XVII 145:9–16).

4.2.1.6 Good guy and bad guy, or the carrot-and-stick strategy

Letters XV 159, 210, 305, and XVII 111 indicate that one of the tools the Assyrians used to recruit their allies was "encouraging" them and "speaking kindly with" their tribal representatives. The best description of this technique is preserved in XV 159:7'–8': LUGAL *be-lí dib-bi ṭa-bu-u-ti i-se-e-šu lid-bu-bu,* "let the king, my lord, speak kindly with him." The recruiting speech was based on the alternating "bad guy/good guy" strategy. Alternation of severe psychological pressure (bad guy)[44] with a kind, considerate and forbearing speech full of promises (good guy) loosened enemy resistance and facilitated the alliance with the Assyrians. According to the Neo-Assyrian archives, such rhetoric was carried out on several levels: by local propagandists addressing their kinsmen; by Assyrian officials dealing with representatives of the tribes; and by the king himself, talking to tribal envoys during the audience that he generously granted them. At all three levels, the goal of the "good guy" strategy was to "make them trust" (XV 159:9') so that they, in their turn, would spread the word about Assyrian kindness (XV 159:10'–11').

---

[44] For an example of a threatening message sent to rebels, see Streck, *Asb.*, 142:53–144:71.

The "bad guy" strategy can be illustrated on tablet XVII 1, coming from the king, which describes how the king held a son of NN (unpreserved) as hostage to force his father to collaborate. Another example of this strategy is the terrorization of the Kibatki in order to make them comply with the Assyrian requirements (V 202:r.2'–16').

4.2.2 Reconstruction of Neo-Assyrian psychological warfare in Babylonia in 710–709 B.C.E.

Taking into consideration the case studies presented above, and also the rest of the Neo-Assyrian documents dealing with Sargon II's invasion, in the following paragraphs I will reconstruct the types of agents hired to spread Neo-Assyrian propaganda, their tools and strategies, the targets of their missions, and feedback on the efficiency of their propaganda during Sargon II's campaigns into Babylonia.

4.2.2.1 Agents

The Neo-Assyrian propaganda machinery operated at three administrative levels. In increasing order of importance, these were the field agents, the provincial officials, and the king.

The success or failure of PsW depended largely on the field agents. They walked from town to town and from village to village arguing with the residents, encouraging or intimidating the people to abandon Merodach-Baladan and to ally themselves with the Assyrians. The Neo-Assyrian archives record the activities of several field agents: Nabû-zeru-ibni (Ru'uaean); Ṣala-il (unknown ethnicity) and (his) messengers, Kutayu and Yasamu (Isuqaeans); and an unnamed Babylonian of Chaldean origin. Judging from the available data, the field agents were not chosen randomly but had to conform to at least one of the following criteria:

(a) The agent had to have sufficient experience in the diplomatic services to conduct the mission (Nabû-zeru-ibni acquired his experience in the diplomatic services in Damascus; Ṣala-il was called the "master of persuasion").

(b) The agent had to be "one of them." Propaganda was better received if presented by a kinsman who spoke the language of the people, shared their culture, and believed in the same gods. Thus, an Aramean addressed the Arameans; a Chaldean addressed the Chaldeans.

(c) The agent had to have Assyrian connections. The credibility of the message increased if it was presented by an official who not only gave promises but also had executive authority (Nabû-zeru-ibni was a eunuch in Damascus, Ṣala-il was on good terms with Il-yada', and the promoter of the second mission in XV 157 claimed that Sargon II was coming to his house).

Assyrian provincial officials such as delegates, governors, or prefects coordinated and backed up the threats and promises of their field agents. Before and during Sargon II's invasion into Aramean territory northeast of the Tigris, the coordinator of PsW in this region was Il-yada'. Several field agents, such as Ṣala-il, Kutayu, and Yasamu, answered directly to him. He also functioned as a mediator between Sargon II and the tribes during negotiations.[45] After the conquest of the region northeast of the Tigris and the surrender of Babylon, responsibility for PsW shifted into the hands of Marduk-šarru-uṣur, a Neo-Assyrian prefect in Babylonia, whose goal was to negotiate with the Chaldean tribes. The Assyrian king represented the acme of Neo-Assyrian propaganda. The provincial officials sent ambassadors and tribal representatives to the king (XVII 17) advising him to use the carrot or the stick according to circumstances.

4.2.2.2 Means

The religious and political validation of a campaign and the discrediting of enemy leadership were the primary nonviolent tools used by Neo-Assyrian propaganda. Thus, Sargon II presented his campaign not as an imperial invasion but rather as a mission of liberation. The letters coming from the dissatisfied priests of Babylon[46] and Nabû-šarru-iddina reported on the Lahireans, who were extremely glad to become Sargon II's servants (XV 136:8–11), and thus confirmed Sargon II's claim that his invasion had some liberating aspects. For the citizens of Sippar, Nippur, Babylon, and Borsippa imprisoned by Merodach-Baladan, who could again see "the light of the day" (S II Ann 373) when Sargon II broke their fetters, Sargon II's invasion was definitively the mission of liberation. Moreover, Sargon II claimed that his liberating mission, however destructive it might have

[45] Issar-duri, governor of Arrapha, sent his men to help Il-yada', but he was not directly responsible for waging PsW.
[46] Vera Chamaza, *Omnipotenz*, 21–70.

seemed, aimed at reestablishing order in the country of Babylonia. Correspondingly, he presented himself as the builder of irrigation canals (S II Ann 316) and roads in an inaccessible land full of thorns, thistles, dogs, and jackals (Prism D vii 47–56). Letter XV 2 confirms Sargon II's claim: Issar-duri's boatmen were reluctant to undergo a journey to the south because they had to sail through territory in which bandits harried travelers, and the boatmen preferred to wait until the king reached Uruk and brought stability to the region. Thus, if we are to give history its due, it is necessary to admit that imperial power indeed reined in the "slave-raiders and marauders who preyed upon travelers and caravans"[47] along the trade routes between Babylon-Nippur-Uruk and Nippur-Der.[48]

The success of Sargon II's PsW depended on his ability to discredit his adversaries. Neo-Assyrian propaganda gave Merodach-Baladan and his allies all kinds of derogative epithets such as "evil" and "treacherous" (S II Ann 260, 309) and maligned them as those who committed all kinds of evil deeds (S II Ann 260). Merodach-Baladan was a weakling, who cried and tore his garments in despair (S II Ann 309–10), and who, instead of facing his enemy face to face, escaped from Babylon as a "field mouse" under the cover of night (Prunk 125–26)—gestures unworthy of a great warrior. Contrasting Merodach-Baladan's negative epithets with a series of positive epithets attributed to Sargon II had psychological effects on domestic and foreign audiences. Merodach-Baladan's major supporter, the Elamite king Šutur-Nahundi, was also presented as an operator. At the sight of his collapsing kingdom, Merodach-Baladan asked Šutur-Nahundi for help. Šutur-Nahundi accepted his gift, but fearing the Assyrian army, refused to come to his aid (S II Ann 309). Furthermore, Šutur-Nahundi behaved like a coward who was afraid to face his enemy face to face and escaped into the mountains before the Assyrians arrived (S II Ann 304–5). One of Merodach-Baladan's major allies, the steppe-dwelling Suti, were called fugitives and a treacherous race. They were portrayed as letting thriving cities collapse into ruin, and building their tents over the ruins. Thanks to their barbarian life style, spiders wove their webs over the irrigation canals, the pride of Mesopotamian engineering. "Their rich meadows had become like a wilderness; their cultivated grounds were forlorn of the sweet harvest song; grain was quite cut off" (Prism D vii 65–68).

[47] SAAS IV, 17–29.

[48] See for example ibid., 81.

Another important element of nonviolent PsW was the religious validation of Sargon II's intervention. Merodach-Baladan was presented as a blasphemous king who did not fear the gods, preferring to rely on his geographical position and on human help (S II Ann 255–56; Prunk 121–23) instead of trusting in the gods. He broke the oath that he swore in the presence of the gods (S II Ann 256–58) and became a symbol of evil incarnate—the very image of a *gallû*-demon[49] (Prunk 121–22). His twelve-year reign in Babylon was derided as a reign against the will of the gods (S II Ann 260). On the other hand, it was Marduk himself who, seeing Merodach-Baladan's evil deeds, made Sargon II's weapon strong and ordered him to bring Merodach-Baladan's evil kingdom to an end (S II Ann 260–61). After Merodach-Baladan's expulsion, Sargon II presented himself as a pious king who offered pure offerings in Babylon. He rebuilt the cultic places and reinitiated religious life (Prunk 140–41).

To recruit allies from among the Aramean and Chaldean tribes, Neo-Assyrian propaganda relied heavily on incentives and promises. In negative terms, Neo-Assyrian propaganda agents threatened the local inhabitants with deportation, presenting a fearful image of life in an unknown land, if the tribes decided not to accept the Assyrian offer. This technique often succeeded: "they became extremely afraid" (XV 221:r.7) and surrendered.

While the Assyrians were employing nonviolent tools, Merodach-Baladan still had a chance to neutralize their propaganda and launch his counterarguments. First of all, he dealt directly with the tribes exposed to Assyrian propaganda (XV 1). Like the Assyrians, Merodach-Baladan threatened those tribes with punishment, if they were to side with the Assyrians (XV 208:4), or he humbly pleaded with them not to abandon him (XV 245:r.1–3). In his royal inscriptions Merodach-Baladan presented himself as a humble, prayerful, and pious king who feared the gods.[50] He claimed that his twelve-year reign in Babylon was part of Marduk's design: when Marduk generously became reconciled with Babylon, he strengthened Merodach-Baladan's hand and let him expel the evil enemies of Babylon—the Assyrians. Moreover, Merodach-Baladan renovated the dilapidated temples and sanctuaries and reintroduced the rituals that pleased the gods.[51]

---

[49] *CAD* 5, 18–19.
[50] RIMA 2, 137.
[51] Ibid., 136–42.

He was a solicitous king who built irrigation canals and bridges in his country.[52]

In several cases, the tribes remained faithful towards Merodach-Baladan despite all sorts of Neo-Assyrian propaganda. In such cases, the nonviolent tools of PsW were replaced with violence and force. The least costly path was simply to eliminate the anti-Assyrian faction in a given city. Nabû-šumu-idinna, the commander of Lahiru fortress situated at the Elamite border, reported on his negotiations with the city of Marpada (in the vicinity of Lahiru). While negotiations between the Assyrians and one of the city leaders (son of Halama) were going on, the pro-Assyrian faction suggested:

> There are two families in Ma[rpada], one of them inclined towards the (Assyrian) king, my lord, the other not. They sent me (Nabû-šumu-idinna) (this message): "We shall k[ill] this family who is not willing to go with us, and thereafter we shall g[o] and have audience with the king, our lord." (XV 136:21–e.28)

If the anti-Assyrian faction kept resisting, Sargon II did not hesitate to employ more violent tools. Starvation was the most effective and often the only certain means of bringing a city to surrender. Following this practice, Sargon II blocked the Tubliaš River, on which the Arameans depended for their food supply, and starved the Aramean tribes out of the territory that was inaccessible to the army (S II Ann 283–85).

The tribes that resisted starvation and still "listened to Merodach-Baladan and Šutur-Nahundi" (S II Ann 288–89) surrendered when Sargon II's soldiers started to cut down "date palms, their (Aramean) sustenance, and the tree gardens, the pride of their (Aramean) districts" (S II Ann 289–90). A slow and systematic destruction of the enemy's fruit trees, such as the date palms (S II Ann 357), whose cultivation required a human lifetime, was a powerful psychological tool of siegecraft that has been used over the centuries. S. W. Cole,[53] comparing the tactics employed by nomads during siege, quotes historian F. Donner:

---

[52] Ibid., 142.

[53] S. W. Cole, "The Destruction of Orchards in Assyrian Warfare," in *Assyria 1995: Proceedings of the 10th Anniversary Symposium of the Neo-Assyrian Text Corpus Project, Helsinki, September 7–11, 1995* (Helsinki: Helsinki University Press, 1997).

> It was normal procedure for nomads wishing to subject an oasis to resort to a process of psychological warfare; they invested the whole settlement, and then gradually cut down palm trees a few at a time until the residents, watching the destruction of the town's livelihood from the safety of their towers, finally agreed to pay tribute before too much damage was done.[54]

If none of the above mentioned means succeeded, Sargon II would resort to siege. Before the final attack was carried out against a settlement, the Assyrians talked to its inhabitants.[55] The best example of the combination of violence and psychological pressure mustered against the besieged is Nabû-šumu-idinna's dispatch (XV 136).

> *ina* UGU BÀD *ša* ^{m}*mu-še-zib* [*ša* L]UGAL *be-lí iš-pur-an-ni* [*a-na-ku*][56] ^{m}EN–MAN–PAB LÚ*.*qur-bu-tú* [*is-sa-he*]-*iš ina* ŠÀ-*bi ni-ta-lak* [*x x x*] *pu-ut* URU *ak-ta-la* [*ina* UGU *uš*]-*še*[57] ^{m}EN–MAN–PAB *iq-ṭi-ri-ib* [*is-si-šú-nu*] *i-du-bu-ub* [*ma-a* ^{m}][58]*mu-še-zib nu-še-ṣi-a* [*a-na* UGU LU]GAL *be-lí-i-*[*ni*] [*nu-še-bil* ERIM.MEŠ *nu*]-*še*$^{!}$-⌜*ri*⌝-*ib a-ki-i* [*x x x x*] *ina* UGU *i-si-ta-ti* [*x x x x*] *a-ki-i ha-mi-'i* [*x x x ba*]-*si ni-kit-ta-*⌜*ša*$^{!}$⌝ [*x x x*] *la-áš-šú*

> Concerning the city-wall of Mušezib [about which the k]ing, my lord, wrote to me, [I] and the bodyguard, Bel-šarru-uṣur, went there [togeth]er. I detained [...] opposite the city, (while) Bel-šarru-uṣur approached [the foun]dations. He spoke [to them] thus: "We wish to bring out Mušezib, [take him to the k]ing, [our] lord, and bring in [troops]." *When* [...] on the towers [...] *thus he is confident* [... s]o there is no fear [...]. (XV 131:r.1–14)

The letter may be dated to the Yadburu phase. Nabû-šumu-idinna, the commander of the Assyrian fort at Lahiru, reported on his siege of

---

[54] F. McGraw Donner, *The Early Islamic Conquests* (Princeton, N.J.: Princeton University Press, 1981), 30.

[55] It is important to notice that both of the tactics just discussed—starvation and cutting down fruit trees—often took place during siege.

[56] The reconstruction of the personal pronoun is based on the 1st p. pl. verb (*ni-ta-lak*).

[57] The reconstruction of [... *uš*]-*še* has a parallel in I 137:6.

[58] [*ma-a* ^{m}] *mu-še-zib*: the reconstruction of *ma-a* could be justified by the change from the 3rd p. sing. to the 1st p. pl.; thus *ma-a* would introduce the direct speech of Nabû-šumu-idinna and Bel-šarru-uṣur.

Mušezib's city (unknown location). While he stationed his troops opposite the city, the bodyguard Bel-šarru-uṣur approached the city walls and boastfully proclaimed the Assyrian intention to capture Mušezib.[59] Lines XV 131:r.11–14 are too fragmentary to show the result of Bel-šarru-uṣur's negotiations. However, if the sheik Mušezib mentioned in Sargon II's annals (S II Ann 298) is the same person as the Mušezib mentioned in XV 136,[60] then he together with three other sheiks from the land of Lahiru surrendered and brought tribute to Sargon II.

If all nonviolent and violent means of PsW failed, the Assyrians did not hesitate to employ extreme measures, such as the destruction of cities, the deportation of inhabitants, and public executions: displaying a flayed king in public was a brutal but eloquent statement of Assyrian power. The "messengers of terror,"[61] in the absence of mass media, spread the news about these atrocities from village to village and town to town in order to soften up enemy resistance.[62]

4.2.2.3 Efficiency of Sargon II's psychological warfare

Did the Assyrians receive feedback that enabled them to assess the efficiency of their PsW? The archives contain several letters useful for answering this question. First of all, the royal court received reports from local informers on whether Asssyrian propaganda was succeeding. From among three preserved letters that explicitly mention the results of PsW, only one report describes the failure of the diplomatic mission (XV 1),

[59] Bel-šarru-uṣur's threat was primarily directed against the city ruler Mušezib. There is no indication in his speech that he would have also threatened the people. Thus, it seems possible that his speech aimed to undermine the people's trust in their leader.

[60] The conclusion that both Sargon II's annals and XV 136 speak about the same person can be supported by two arguments. First, both personages operated in the same territory, i.e., in the land of Lahiru. The sender of letter XV 136 was the commander of Lahiru (see SAA XV, 255), and the Mušezib mentioned in Sargon II's annals was the sheik of Lahiru (S II Ann 298). Second, both letter XV 136 and S II Ann 298 are dated to the same period, i.e., the Yadburu phase. According to H. D. Baker's research (*Prosopography* 2/II, 781), there are only a few individuals bearing this name, and of those only two (XV 136 and S II Ann 298) are dated to Sargon II's reign. We can thus safely conclude that the Mušezib mentioned in S II Ann 298 was the same person as the Mušezib mentioned in XV 136.

[61] Saggs, "Assyrian Warfare in the Sargonid Period," 154.

[62] Šarru-emuranni's report, dated to the Chaldean phase, confirms that this strategy often succeeded: after the fall of Babylonia, the Puqudueans living in Bit-Amukani were terrified at the prospect of being deported (XV 221:r.7).

whereas the other two describe its success (XV 157 and 242). The royal court could also deduce the success of Neo-Assyrian PsW from Merodach-Baladan's despairing responses: "the whole country turned its face towards Assyria" (XV 150:8'; for similar statements see XV 208:3–4; 245:e.1'–r.3). The Assyrians could also assess the efficiency of their propaganda from the responses of tribal leaders, who were afraid of deportation (XV 221:r.3–9) and thus willing to comply with Assyrian demands, if the Assyrians promised to release their brothers (XV 162, see above), or to secure for them some material advantages (XV 216[63]). Another indicator of the efficiency of Neo-Assyrian PsW was the increasing number of deserters, especially during the Chaldean phase (XV 243:1'–r.3; 244:4–12; 255:r.3–5). Neo-Assyrian scribes compiled precise records of soldiers who with their horses deserted to the Assyrians (XVII 132), and the provincial officials passed these reports on to the royal court (XV 294:3–10). Of particular interest was the desertion of high military commanders–the Chaldean cavalry commander (XV 184:r.10–16) and three tailors of Zerî[64] (XV 214:r.1–13). Since these cases were reported separately, it is possible to conclude that provincial officials were required to report immediately on the desertion of high military officials. Finally, information coming from

---

[63] Such a claim is based on the following reconstruction of tablet XV 216:

> He (PN_1) has made Ahi[...]-naṣir his third man [... to ...] with him instead of me (of PN_2) and does not speak with me (with PN_2). Now he (Ahi[...]-naṣir) has been inciting the men, saying: "I (Ahi[...]-naṣir) will [...] and run away to the (Assyrian) king. Let the king swear to me in the name of god; if and when the king comes to Chaldea, the king should give me (to Ahi[...]-naṣir) all the people of mine whom I shall conquer." (XV 216:5'-12')

PN_1 replaced PN_2 with Ahi[...]-naṣir, his third man. PN_2 was set apart and the new leaders no longer spoke to him. The new opportunistic leadership became pro-Assyrian and incited the people to join the Assyrian side. PN_1's new orientation, of course, was not disinterested, and PN_1 hoped to reap some material advantages: "If the king comes to Chaldea, the king should give me all the people of mine whom I shall conquer" (XV 216:10'–12'). The fact that the Chaldean officials dared to ask the king himself to guarantee the pact by his own oath—in contrast with the situation described in XV 162, when Aramean clan leaders only dared to compel the provincial governor Il-yada' to swear in the name of a god—indicates that all three Chaldean officials were of sufficiently high importance to demand that the pact be guaranteed by the king himself.

[64] LÙ.*kāṣiru* was a low-ranking official in a household; see *CAD* 8,264–65. Because "Son of Zerî" is another name for Merodach-Baladan, these officials belonged to the household of Merodach-Baladan, and thus their desertion was significant enough to be reported by provincial officials.

temple personnel could also provide the Assyrian court with an idea of how efficient their PsW was. It was such personnel, for example, who informed the king about the Babylonians who joyfully expected the king's troops to enter the city of Babylon, (XVII 20–25).

4.2.2.4 General evaluation

Sargon II's campaign in 710–709 B.C.E. can be divided into four major phases: pre-campaign phases which included the period before the siege of Dur-Athara; the north Tigris phase (Dur-Athara, Uqnu, Yadburu phase), which was delimited by the destruction of the Dur-Athara and Yadburu fortresses; the Chaldean phase, which was delimited by the crossing of the Tigris and Sargon II's entrance into Babylon; and the Bit-Yakin phase, whose goal was the destruction of Dur-Yakin. Appendix 3 shows that Neo-Assyrian PsW completely failed during the pre-campaign and Bit-Yakin phases.[65]

On the contrary, Neo-Assyrian PsW was quite successful during the north Tigris and Chaldean phases (Appendix 3). Among the ethnic minorities, the Chaldean tribes were the most responsive to Assyrian pressure. The least successful PsW was among groups directly connected with Elam. The most frequently targeted group was the Aramean tribes. These two phases (north Tigris and Chaldean) differed not only in their conduct of conventional war, but also in their conduct of PsW. The Chaldean tribes were more urban and better organized, in contrast with the predominantly pastoral Aramean groups, which were less integrated into Babylonian politics.[66] Consequently, in the north Tigris phase the Assyrian field agents addressed the sheiks of a given Aramean tribe, and the "conversion" of one sheik did not entail the surrender of the rest of the sheiks of the same tribe (this was true for the Gambulu, Ru'ua, Puqudu, Hindaru, Yadburu, and Hamaranu tribes). In contrast, several sheiks remained allied with Merodach-Baladan until the very end of the war. Despite the heavy diplomatic pressure put upon the Aramean tribes, most of the negotiations failed. This reluctance of the Aramean tribes to collaborate

---

[65] It is necessary to be aware of the fact that the statistical results presented in Appendix 3 include only the data available in or reconstructed from the Neo-Assyrian letters and royal inscriptions. The discovery of new documents may bring to light new Psyops and thus significantly change the statistical results.

[66] See section 4.2.1.1 and SAAS IV, 18.

with the Assyrians during the pre-campaign phase can be explained by the difficulty that the Assyrians experience in obtaining an ally when the Assyrian army did not pose imminent pressure. Failure to acquire allies by diplomatic negotiations resulted in the employment of violent methods. The severe repercussions that the rebels captured from Dur-Athara had to bear gave a new weight to Assyrian PsW. As a result of such violent measures, several sheiks surrendered, and only the Yadburu tribe maintained its recalcitrant attitude. Once the possibilities of acquiring new allies among the Arameans were exhausted, the Assyrians concluded the second phase with the destruction of the fortresses controlled by the Elamites (Yadburu phase). Such a violent action compelled the Yadburu tribe to surrender. There is no evidence of any diplomatic mission attempting to negotiate with Elam or the steppe-dwellers of Suti.

A new ethnic and cultural environment and the heavy losses that Merodach-Baladan's allies suffered during the north Tigris phase triggered a new round of PsW. Four major Chaldean groups accepted the terms of the *Pax Assyriaca*. As noted by A. Fuchs, the Chaldean tribes did not consider Merodach-Baladan's war against Sargon II "as a business of theirs"[67] and surrendered peacefully en bloc during the Chaldean phase. No violent tools were needed to compel their surrender. Once the Assyrians exhausted the possibilities of acquiring new allies by diplomatic and violent means, they concluded this phase with the destruction of Dur-Yakin.

The last aspect of Sargon II's campaign in 710–709 B.C.E. to be evaluated is the short-term versus long-term effects of PsW used on Aramean tribes (Appendix 4). Of 38 Aramean groups subjugated by Tiglath-pileser III during his campaigns in Babylonia, 13 groups (34.2%) reappeared as problematic during Sargon II's reign. Of 19 Aramean groups subjugated by Sargon II,[68] 12 (63.2%) reappeared as problematic during Sennacherib's reign. In addition, 4 tribes subjugated by Tiglath-pileser III, and which were not problematic during Sargon II's reign, later joined the rebellion against Sennacherib. From these statistics, it is possible to conclude that the PsW waged by Sargon II and his officials was able to produce only short-term alliances with the Assyrians.

---

[67] SAA XV, XIX.

[68] Thirteen are known from Tiglath-pileser III's archives; the other six are not mentioned in Tiglath-pileser III's archives.

5

Contextualization of Hezekiah's story

The previous case studies in Neo-Assyrian intelligence provide the background to the final part of this study—the contextualization of Hezekiah's story as analyzed in chapter 2. In doing so, I will take into consideration the different meanings of intelligence (intelligence as information, intelligence as a structure, and intelligence as an activity) as well as the different sources used for the reconstruction of the Neo-Assyrian intelligence services (Neo-Assyrian royal inscriptions, Neo-Assyrian archives, and biblical documents).

5.1 Intelligence as a structure

Intelligence networks are the material structures without which intelligence remains only a theoretical enterprise. If there is no intelligence network, there is no intelligence. Consequently, if the Assyrians did not set up an intelligence network in Palestine, then they could not gather information they needed or use their intelligence structures for furthering their interests. The case studies on Neo-Assyrian intelligence services and operations have demonstrated that the information network had three branches: Assyrian, local, and temple (3.3.4.2). As for the temple branch, neither biblical nor Assyrian sources mention the collaboration of the Judahite clergy in passing information to the Assyrians.[410] In this section I will present textual and archaeological evidence for the existence of the

---

[410] However, a similarity between Sargon II's invasion of Babylonia and Sennacherib's campaign against Palestine invites speculation on the role of the Judahite clergy in information gathering. Sargon II's intelligence agents quickly established contacts with the discontented clergy of Babylon, and the Babylonian clergy became an important source of information for Sargon II. Similarly, it is possible to assume that Hezekiah's reform, which probably entailed the loss of social and material benefits connected with the services at the high places, marginalized a certain number of clergymen. The history of recruiting intelligence agents proves that the people harmed by a new regime are often easily recruited for collaboration. Consequently, it would not be surprising if the Judahite clergy estranged by Hezekiah's reform became a source of information for the Assyrians.

Assyrian and local branches of the Neo-Assyrian intelligence network in Palestine.

5.1.1 Assyrian branch

The basic presupposition of the reconstruction of the Assyrian branch of Neo-Assyrian intelligence services was studied in sections 3.1.5.2 and 3.3.4. This study demonstrated that Assyrian governors, provincial officials, garrison and fort commanders, tax-collectors, and postmasters were obliged to send reports to the royal court about everything they saw or heard. Therefore, in order to untangle the knots of the Assyrian branch of the intelligence network, it will be necessary to locate the seats of these officials.

5.1.1.1 Textual evidence

5.1.1.1.1 Intelligence centers

Intelligence hubs

Analysis of the role of provincial officials in Neo-Assyrian intelligence services has demonstrated that they were a sort of intelligence hubs. The governors were responsible for gathering information, evaluating its reliability and sending information to the royal court on regular basis. They gathered information by means of the Neo-Assyrian administrative structures or received it from the local sources. Keeping the royal court posted about the situation in a given province was not question of the good will of the provincial governors, but was a part of their job description. Thus, the bellow-listed cities of the Levant served as the intelligence centers to which intelligence was forwarded and from which it was forwarded to the royal court.

According to the Neo-Assyrian documents the Assyrian kings established several provinces in the Levant (see Table 21).[411] Since

[411] According to M. Cogan, this process had three stages: "(1) a vassal relationship was established, marked by the payment of the annual dues and tribute, and the enlistment of national troops for Assyrian campaigning; (2) upon the discovery of disloyalty, military action to remove the unreliable vassal was undertaken, followed by his deportation and that of his supporters; a new ruler over the reduced territory, bearing increased obligations, was

communication between the royal court and the Levantine provinces was carried out in Aramaic and on papyri or parchments, only a few reports coming from these Levantine intelligence hubs have been preserved.

Table 21. Assyrian provincial governors in the Levant

NAME	DATE	LOCATION	OFFICE
Qurdi-aššur-lamur (ND 2662; 2716; 2773; 2686; 2715)	TP III	Lebanon?	Probably a governor. Governed territory: Sidon, Tyre, the western side of the Lebanese range, Helbon (close to Damascus, but associated by trade with Tyre see Ez 27,18), and Moab.
Iddin-ahhe (VI 66:r.11'–12'; 67:r.2–3; 68:r.2-3; 69:r.4–5; SAAS II, 95)	Senn.	Ṣimirra	Governor of the province
Bel-liqbi (I 177–79; 181) Mannu-ki-Adad (VI 90:r.17–18; VI 108:r.2–3; 109:r.8'–9'; SAAS II, 98–99)	S II Senn.	Zobah (Ṣupat)	Governor of the province (PNA 1/II, 322) Governor of the province
Adda-hati (I 173, 174, 175, 176)	S II	Hamath	Governor of the province
Gihilu (VI 149:8'–9'; SAAS II, 94)	Senn.	Hatarikka	Governor of the province
Assyrian eunuch (Borger 1956, p. 49 line 13 – Nin. A III:13)	Esarh.	Sidon	Governor of the province
Bel-Harran-šadua (SAAS II, 89–90)	Ashur.	Tyre	Governor of the province
Bel-duri (I 171,172) Ilu-issiya (VI 37:r.16–17; 39:r.10–11; SAAS II, 95)	S II Senn.	Damascus	Governor of the province Governor of the province
Nabû-kenu-uṣur (VI 147:7'–8'; 148:4'–5'; SAAS II, 105) Nabû-šar-ahhešu (SAAS II, 106)	Senn. Esarh.	Samaria	Governor of the province Governor of the province
Issi-Adad-anenu (VI 223:r.9; SAAS II, 96)	Esarh.	Megiddo	Governor of the province

appointed; (3) in the end, and after further rebellion, even this vassal might be removed, his kingdom incorporated and provincialized after the Assyrian fashion." M. Cogan, "Judah under Assyrian Hegemony: A Reexamination of *Imperialism and Religion*," *JBL* 112 (1993), 406.

Three other cities–Haurina (XI 1:r.i 3'), Manṣuate (XI 1:r.i 10'; XI 2:ii 5), and Dor (XI 1:r.i 11'; XI 2:ii 3)–can be added to the above-presented list of the provinces. It is generally agreed that both geographical lists mentoning these three cities (XI 1 and 2) can be dated to Ashurbanipal's reign.[412] These cities are mentioned among other provinces and vassal states and, thus, it is impossible to determine whether these cities were the capital cities of their respective provinces. In each case, they played a role important enough in Assyrian administration to be mentioned in the Neo-Assyrian geographical lists. Consequently, it can be assumed that the Assyrian officials employed in these cities were involved in gathering information, processing it, and sending reports to the royal court.

Comparing the number of the intelligence hubs controlling Elippi—five (see 3.2)—with the number of intelligence hubs in the Levant—twelve, it is possible conclude that the Levantine states and Egypt were at least as carefully monitored as Elam and Elippi.

Neo-Assyrian provincial network

After the various part of the Levant were attached to Neo-Assyrian administrative orbit, these regions were reorganized according to Assyrian administrative rules. Besides their administrative and military duties, these officials were also involved in intelligence gathering. The Neo-Assyrian letters mention some Assyrian officials operating in the Levant: chief-eunuch, LÚ*.GAL–SAG; the commander-in-chief, LÚ*.*tur-ta-nu*, who discussed the problems of policing in the Rable region with Šamaš-aha-iddin (ND 2766:3,13); tax inspectors, LÚ*.*ma-ki-sa-ni*.MEŠ, stationed on the western flanks of the Lebanon range, in Zobah and Huzaza[413] (ND

[412] SAAS XI, XIV.

[413] The king was informed about the illegal trade in iron sold to the Arabs in Huzaza; the source of the information is unknown, but it was not Bel-liqbi, the governor of Zobah, under whose command was the city Huzaza. This information channel can be reconstructed from the apology of Bel-liqbi who felt obliged to respond to the royal letter accusing him of supporting the illegal trade (I 179:r.21-23). From the rhetorical question: "Am I less loyal to the king, my lord, than a toll-collector?" it is possible to conclude that the accusation of Bel-liqbi regarding the illegal trade came from the toll-collector at Huzaza. The verbs *i-sa-ka-nu* (I 179:r.8–9) are in the third person plural which indicates that it was not Bel-liqbi who stationed the toll-collectors in Zobah and Huzaza, but they were

2715:11–14; I 179:r.7–8) and probably in Gaza[414]; prefects and village managers, LÚ*.GAR-*nu*!!.MEŠ-*te*, LÚ*.GAL–URU.MEŠ-*te*, imposed upon the local population in the Hamath province (I 176:4); city-overseers and gate-guards, LÚ*.*šá*-UGU–URU, LÚ*.Ì.DU₈.MEŠ (I 176:r.32);[415] officials of the road stations in the vicinity of Damascus (I 172:30–36); Aia-nuri, a high-ranking official working in the city of Dabilu (biblical Dibon) in Moab (ND 2763:4);[416] and Assyrian officials visiting Samaria (ND 2417:5'–10').

Besides the above-mentioned officials the names of two other Assyrian officials active in the Levant have been preserved: Šamaš-aha-iddin, the sender of letter ND 2766, who was stationed in Rable during the reign of Tiglath-pileser III and Itti-Šamaš-balaṭu, an Assyrian official active in northern Phoenicia during the reign of Esarhaddon (XVI 126–28).

Though these officials represent the few examples of the Assyrian bureaucratic structure controlling the Levant, these data are sufficient to show that a full-fledged Assyrian administration machinery was imposed upon those Levantine states which were turned into Assyrian provinces. The Assyrian officials active in the Levant, like their colleagues in the other parts of the Empire, had to comply with the administrative norms as well, including the duty to report on everything they saw and heard.

Neo-Assyrian royal network

Besides various provincial officials, there were other Assyrian officials who answered directly to the king. Among these the best documented was the *qēpu* office. The Neo-Assyrian texts mention a *qēpu*

---

appointed by the king. This indicates that the king received information both from toll-collectors and from Bel-liqbi, the governor of Zobah.

[414] Besides imposing regular vassal obligations, Tiglath-pileser III turned Gaza into an Assyrian emporium (*bīt kāri*): "[The city of Ga]za (URU.*Ha-az-z*]*u-tú*), I turned into an Assyrian emporium," whose main task was to collect taxes from the harbor; see E. Frahm, "Rezensionen. H. Tadmor, the Inscriptions of Tiglath-Pileser III, King of Assyria," *AfO* 44–45 (1997/1998): 222–25, N. Na'aman, "The Brook of Egypt and Assyrian Policy on the Border of Egypt," *TA* 6 (1979): 83.

[415] Adda-hati complained that these officials were missing in Zobah. This indicates that the Assyrians used to station their overseers in the major cities in Syria-Palestine and at the gates of the cities.

[416] Fales, *Cento*, 132.

whom Tiglath-pileser III appointed over the Arabian Queen Samsi and who had at his disposal 10,000 soldiers to control the Arabian tribes (TP III Sum 7:r.2'; 9:r.22; 13–17').[417] Furthermore, there were *qēpu* officials in Birat (I 84:7), Ṣibtu (I 97:r.7'), Tyre (II 5:iii 6'–14'; VII 128:6), and Hamu, an unknown location in the Levant (XVII 155:r.14). Esarhaddon's and Ashurbanipal's annals mention the *qēpu* officials appointed in Egypt.[418] The exact position of the *qēpu* officials in the Neo-Assyrian administrative structure remains unclear. The *qēpu* officials are often listed among the top officials of a given region (VII 128:6; XVI 92:11-4). It seems that the *qēpu* officials were not one clearly-defined type of official, but rather under this name can be included the officials of different administrative ranks and responsibilities. The responsibility of the *qēpu* officials covered three major areas: civil (II 5:iii 6'-14'; VI 150:2; 188:r.7'), temple (X 364:4-8; XVII 43:r.1), and military (I 97:r.7'; XVII 120:9). The *qēpu* officials were required to report on everything they saw and heard (V 38:5-9). Because the *qēpu* officials were high-ranking Neo-Assyrian officials, who controlled several areas of the regions they were entrusted with, their reports had high value for monitoring a given region. The role of the *qēpu* officials in the Neo-Assyrian intelligence network can be illustrated from the reports coming from Aššur-reṣuwa, the *qēpu* official in Kumme (see 3.1.3 and 3.5.2). His reports demonstrate the quality of information he got hold of and the extent of the territory he covered.[419]

---

[417] Given the similarities between Gaza and Tyre, it may be assumed that a *qēpu* official similar to the one who controlled trade in Tyre was appointed in Gaza; see Na'aman, "The Brook of Egypt and Assyrian Policy on the Border of Egypt," 84.

[418] Borger *Asarh* 99:r.47; Streck *Asb* 6:i 58.

[419] The *qēpu* office played an important role in the administration of the Neo-Assyrian Empire; however, this office was known before the Neo-Assyrian Empire and also used after the fall of Assyria (*CAD* 8,264-8). The word *qēpu* comes from the verb *qiāpu* 'to trust, entrust' and its adjectival form *qīpu* 'trustworthy, trusted person'. In the Neo-Assyrian texts it is spelled most often as *qēpu*, sometimes also as *qīpu* or LÚ.TIL.(LA.AN).GÍD.DA. The importance of the *qēpu* officials for Neo-Assyrian administration can be demonstrated by the fact that they were appointed all over the Neo-Assyrian Empire. Besides the above-mentioned *qēpu* officials active in the Levant, these officials were also active in Mesopotamia, in particular, in Babylonia (X 352:r.9; 354:12; XIII 178:29), Uruk (X 349:28), Bit-Dakuri (XVII 22:8), Araši (XV 35:8; XVI 137:10; 138:8-9; XVII 152:r.16; 153:19), and Der (XV 142:5', XVII 120:9). In the northern and northeastern provinces the *qēpu* officials were in Kumme (V 106:22'-6'; 106:12'-6'), Kar-Šamaš (VI 188:r.7'), and Kitipata (XI 31:4).

The presence of six *qēpu* officials in the Levant indicates that the Assyrians in gathering information relied not only on the regular administrative structures but also on the officials who were under direct control of the king. As in the case of Aššur-reṣuwa, who provided high-quality intelligence from the northern border, it may be assumed that these six *qēpu* officials active in the Levant served as an important source of intelligence partly independent on the regular provincial administration.

5.1.1.1.2 Issues

The previous section demonstrated that the Assyrians established full administrative control over the Levant. Information provided by the Assyrian officials can be divided into three categories: military intelligence, economic intelligence, and various other matters.

Military issues

Monitoring local upheavals and wars constituted that part of intelligence which helped the Assyrians not only to control their vassal states but also to plan their invasions (see 3.5.2.5). The extant letters covering the Levant illustrate the Assyrian monitoring of the Arabian raids (see 3.4) and a military clash in Moab.

Qurdi-aššur-limur, probably governor in Lebanon, informed Tiglath-pileser III about a military clash in Moab: the Arabian tribe of Qederites invaded Moab and defeated it (ND 2773).[420] This information reached the royal court by means of two messengers. Messenger I carried the message itself; Messenger II brought the king information about Messenger I. Only the accompanying letter has been preserved (the tablet carried by Messenger II); the message itself (the sealed document carried by Messenger I) has not been preserved. In the accompanying letter Qurdi-aššur-limur provided two types of information: he defined the identity of Messenger I, who carried the letter (his name, his origin and his superior), and provided a concise summary of the content of the letter carried by Messenger I. Qurdi-aššur-limur in this accompanying letter also informed the king of when both

[420] M. Fales suggests that the purpose of the letter was to ask Tiglath-pileser III for help. Thus, the letter can be dated after 732 B.C.E., i. e. after Moabites had paid tribute to Tiglath-pileser III; see Fales, *Cento*, 132.

messengers had departed.[421] Thus, the king and his officials could easily check the identity of the messenger, who carried the letter (Messenger I), they could estimate and compare the time necessary for delivering the message, check the seal as well as the content of the sealed document brought by Messenger I and compare it with the tablet brought by Messenger II.

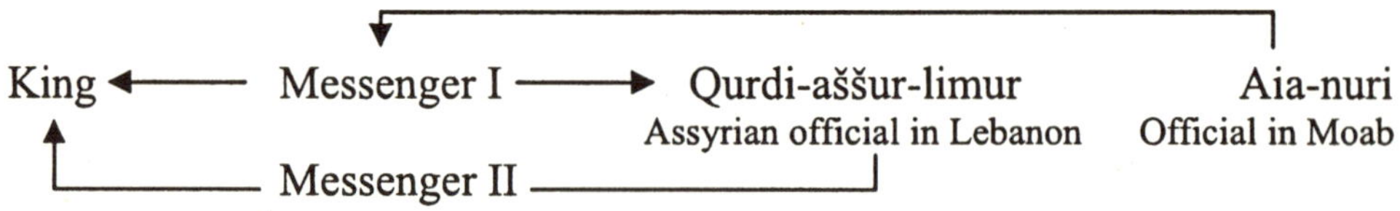

Figure 9. Information flow

Economic issues

Several studies have demonstrated that the Assyrian interest in the Levant was motivated by lucrative Mediterranean trade.[422] Consequently, the reports of provincial and local informers contained important pieces of intelligence regarding three kinds of commercial activities: trade in the Mediterranean harbors, trade in timber, and trade in iron.[423]

Monitoring the wealth passing through the Mediterranean harbors was one of the priorities of the Assyrian officials controlling the Levant.[424] Letters XVI 127 and 128 provided important information about illegal trade in Phoenicia during the reign of Esarhaddon. The Assyrians established a harbor in which the boats coming to Phoenicia should have been unloaded. The profit from this trade was to go to the Assyrian king. However, a local official Ikkilu forced the incoming boats to be unloaded in his port by "providing for anyone who came to him, killing anyone who docked at the Assyrian harbor, and stealing his boat" (XVI 127:18–21). Ikkilu justified

[421] This information is based on Saggs' reading of sign *ú* in line 23: *⸢ú⸣-ṣu-ni,* they departed.
[422] C. S. Ehrlich, *The Philistines in Transition: A History from ca. 1000–730 B.C.E.*, *Studies in the History and Culture of the Ancient near East 10* (Leiden and New York: E.J. Brill, 1996), 85–94.
[423] For compromising an illegal trade with iron see section 3.4.3.
[424] Some aspects of the control of this trade were also regulated by a treaty concluded with Baal, the king of Tyre (II 5:iii15'–26').

these actions by appealing to a written permission from the Assyrian king. Itti-Šamaš-balaṭu, the Assyrian official operating in this region, reported that even though he knew about Ikkilu's activities, he was unable to intervene because some high royal officials from the king's entourage profited from this illegal trade. Thus, this report informed the royal court about illegal trade which channeled a substantial part of wealth into the pockets of Ikkilu and some Assyrian officials. Furthermore, in this letter Itti-Šamaš-balaṭu denounced a spy operating in the royal court:

> There is a man called Ilu-ma'adi, from Ṣimirra. He goes back and forth to Assyria, finds out in detail whatever matter (and) news there is, and goes and tells it to him (Ikkilu). (XVI 127:24–r.2)

The Assyrians were also interested in controlling trade in timber in Lebanon.[425] Qurdi-aššur-limur, probably governor in Lebanon during the reign of Tiglath-pileser III, filed a detailed report about the trade in timber in Tyre and Sidon (ND 2715). The trade was completely in the hands of the ruler of Tyre. Tiglath-pileser III asked Qurdi-aššur-limur to "talk nicely to him" (ND 2715:4) that indicates that the Assyrian goal was not to take over the timber trade but to profit from this trade by taxing it. For this reason Qurdi-aššur-limur appointed several tax-collectors along the Lebanese range and at the city entrances. The appointment of the tax-collectors was not well received in Sidon. Qurdi-aššur-limur reported that the Sidonias revolted against the Assyrian tax-inspector appointed by Qurdi-aššur-limur. The rebels captured the Assyrian tax-inspector and hid him in the mountains. The revolt was pacified by a military intervention. Qurdi-aššur-limur sent his soldiers to the mountains to terrify the people and after this intervention the rebels brought the tax-inspector to Sidon (ND 2715:14–29).

Another priority of the Assyrian intelligence network in the Levant, especially during the *Pax Assyriaca*, was to control a continuous flow of wealth to Assyria. Thus, the Assyrians monitored the delivery of tributes, reported on the collection of taxes, and on the transfer of booty. These intelligence activities in the Levant can be reconstructed from the Neo-Assyrian letters and administrative documents. Even though the letters coming from the Levant are far less numerous and in a much worse state of

---

[425] For the significance of timber see section 3.1.1.3.

preservation than those coming from the north or the east of the Empire, it is still possible to compile a table illustrating the Assyrian monitoring of the "material" compliance of the Levantine states with the Assyrian requirements (see Table 22).

Table 22. Flow of wealth to Assyria

Place	Period	Type of delivery
Ekron	TP III	Silver (ND 2064:7–9)
	S II	The tablet is heavily damaged. An Ekronite is mentioned after the list of horses delivered from the Levant (I 110:r.12–13).
	?	Tribute? (XI 34:14').
Tyre	TP III	Silver (ND 2430:5'); the letter is very fragmentary. Reconstruction of the lines preserved suggests that Mitenna, king of Tyre, was responsible for collecting silver.[426]
	TP III	Taxes imposed upon the trade in lumber on the western side of the Lebanese mountains (ND 2715:5–29).
Sidon	TP III	Taxes imposed upon the trade in lumber on the western side of the Lebanese mountains (ND 2715:5–29).
Damascus	S II	The letter mentions the problems of transferring the booty to Assyria (I 175:11–23).
	S II	Precious items made out of silver listed in the inventory (VII 57:I 10).
	?	Deficit of textiles mentioned in the account of wool and madder (VII 116:5'–6').
	?	5 trays of fruit (XI 40:4'–5').
	?	A fragmentary account of sheep (XI 80:7').
Huzaza	S II	The letter mentions the problems of transferring the booty taken from Huzaza to Assyria (I 175:11–23).
Hamath	S II	Silver of local population collected by Adda-hati, governor of Hamath (I 176:4–7).
Egypt	S II	List of tributes recorded by Marduk-remanni, governor of Calhu. The emissaries with the tribute in horses came to Calah (I 110:r.4–13).
Gaza	S II	List of tributes recorded by Marduk-remanni, governor of Calhu. The emissaries with the tribute in horses came to Calah (I 110:r.4–13).
Judah	S II	List of tributes recorded by Marduk-remanni, governor of Calhu. The emissaries with the tribute in horses came to Calah (I 110:r.4–13).
	?	10 minas of silver (XI 33:5–6).
	?	[1] talent of silver (XI 57:1).

[426] Text in italics indicates that the entry is based on the reconstruction of a very fragmentary tablet.

Moab	S II	List of tributes recorded by Marduk-remanni, governor of Calhu. The emissaries with the tribute in horses came to Calah (I 110:r.4–13).
	S II	62 sil[ver b]owls from Moab listed in the inventory (VII 57:iii 4).
	?	1 mina of gold (XI 33:3–4).
	?	Tribute? (XI 34:11').
Amon	S II	List of tributes recorded by Marduk-remanni, governor of Calhu. The emissaries with the tribute in horses came to Calah (I 110:r.4–13).
	?	2 minas of gold (XI 33:1–2).
Edom	S II	The damaged part of the letter records the tributes of the Edomite, [Ashdo]dite, and Ekronite emissaries (I 110:r.12–13).
Ashdod	S II	The damaged part of the letter records the tributes of the Edomite, [Ashdo]dite, and Ekronite emissaries (I 110:r.12–13).
	S II	Sennacherib mentioned Ashdodite tribute brought to Calhu (I 29:r.22) at the end of his summary report.
Samaria	S II	Corn tax (I 220:4–7).
	?	Account of wool and madder delivered from [... Sam]aria (VII 116:1').
Megiddo	?	15 talents of textiles mentioned in the account of wool and madder (VII 116:6').
	?	Very fragmentary list of contributors (XI 6:10').
	?	A fragmentary account of sheep (XI 80:r.3').
Ṣimirra	?	[x] talents of textiles mentioned in the account of wool and madder (VII 116:8', r.12').
	S II	Sheep for the regular offering (XII 77:I 24').
Hatarikka	?	[x t]alents of textiles mentioned in the account of wool and madder (VII 116:9', r.10').
	?	Very fragmentary list of contributors (XI 6:9').
	S II	Sheep for the regular offering (XII 77:I 24').
Zobah	?	[x t]alents of textiles mentioned in the account of wool and madder (VII 116:10', r.11').
	?	Very fragmentary list of contributors (XI 6:7').
Manṣuate	?	Very fragmentary list of contributors (XI 6:8').
Haurina	?	Very fragmentary list of arrivals from the provinces (XI 10:13').

Various issues

Besides the above-listed groups of intelligence, the Assyrian network also provided information on agricultural activities in the Levant (ND 2430:r.1'–4'; ND 2686:r.24–25; I 176), climactic conditions (heavy rain I 178:8–9), infection of water in Kašpuna (ND 2715:46–49), epidemics in Damascus (I 171:14–15), situation in the courts in Tyre and Ušše (ND 2686:5–7), hostile feelings towards the Assyrians in Hamath (I 176:24–28), unwelcome religious activity in Tyre (ND 2686:9–12), fugitives and runaways (I 171:3–13; 179:r.13), and construction activities (V 291:15'–r.1; XI 19:r.1'–3'; 21:8').

An important part of intelligence gathering included mutual denunciations and reporting on colleagues. Thus, the king learned about the expenditure of some local Assyrian officials (I 172), illegal opening of the royal granaries (I 181), and about the unwillingness of Bel-duri's colleagues to raise provisions for Assyria (I 172).

These examples of intelligence activities of the Assyrian officials demonstrate that both the issues covered by the Neo-Assyrian intelligence services and the way of gathering intelligence in the Levant were similar to intelligence operations in the other parts of the Neo-Assyrian Empire.

5.1.1.2 Archaeological evidence

Besides textual sources, I shall also use archaeological evidence to identify the seats of the Assyrian officials. The study of archaeological evidence proves the existence of some Assyrian administrative centers reconstructed on the basis of the written documents and identifies some smaller Assyrian establishments which might have been involved in intelligence gathering as well.

Archaeological evidence for the Assyrian presence in the Levant can be divided into three categories: architecture, pottery, and special finds. Assyrian traces in the architecture of Palestine can be discerned on the basis of comparison with Assyrian architectural formulas employed at Khorsabad, Tell Halaf, Til Barsip, Arslan-Tash, and Zinjirli.[427] J. B. Bloom distinguished three types of buildings characteristic of Assyrian

[427] E. Heinrich, "Neuassyrische Paläste, Paläste in Spätbabylonischen Reich," in *Die Paläste in Alten Mesopotamien*, ed. E. Heinrich (Berlin: Denkmaler Antiken Architektur, 1984), G. Loud, "An Architectural Formula for Assyrian Planning Based on Results of Excavations at Khorsabad," *RA* 33 (1936), R. Reich, "Dur Sharrukin (Khorsabad)," *Qadmoniot* 12 (1979), and G. Turner, "The State Apartment of the Late Assyrian Palaces," *Iraq* 32 (1970).

architecture: open-court buildings, palaces, and military arsenals.[428] The hallmarks of these structures are elevated platforms, open courts, throne rooms, double-cell shrines, vaults laid in pitched brick technique, floors paved with square baked bricks, and shallow niches.[429] Assyrian traces in Palestinian pottery include characteristic shapes and some special features (Appendix 5).[430] Only a few vessels imported from Assyria have been preserved. Most of the Assyrian-influenced remains are local imitations of Assyrian ware. The last group of artifacts bespeaking the Assyrian presence in Palestine can be divided into the following subgroups: glyptic material (cylinder seals, stamp seals, sealings, and bullae), epigraphic material (cuneiform tablets, stellae), military material (arrowheads and spearheads, crescent-shaped standards), and burial material (bathtub coffins or *Hockersärge* or *Wannensarkophage*).

Appendix 6 lists the most important archaeological finds documenting Assyrian influence on the material culture of Israel and Judah.

---

[428] J. B. Bloom, "Material Remains of the Neo-Assyrian Presence in Palestine and Transjordan" (Ph.D., Bryn Mawr College, 1988), 83–148.

[429] V. Fritz, "Die Paläste während der Assyrischen, Babylonischen und Persischen Vorherrschaft in Palästina," *MDOG* 111 (1979) and R. Reich, "Palaces and Residences in the Iron Age," in *The Architecture of Ancient Israel: From the Prehistoric to the Persian Period*, ed. R. Reich (Jerusalem: 1992).

[430] I here follow the conclusions of major studies of Assyrian pottery such as those by R. B. K. Amiran, *Ancient Pottery of the Holy Land* (Jerusalem: Massada Press, 1969), 291-2, Bloom, "Material Remains", 149-89, L. C. Courtois, "Technologie de Céramique Levantines au Temps de la Domination Assyriennen (IX-VIIIe Siècles av. J.C.)," in *Comptes Rendus du 108e Congès National des Sociétés Savantes, Grenoble, 1983* (Paris: Comité des Travaux historiques et scientifiques, 1983), M. A. Gatti, "La Ceramica Neo Assira (X-VII sec.): Tipologie e Difusione" (Ph.D., Università degli Studi di Padova, 1987), A. Gilboa, "Assyrian-Type Pottery at Dor and the Status of the Town During the Assyrian Occupation Period," *EI* 25 (1996), R. Hestrin and E. Stern, "Two 'Assyrian' Bowls from Israel," *IEJ* 23 (1973), G. Lehmann, "Trends in the Local Pottery Development of the Late Iron Age and Persian Period in Syria and Lebanon, ca. 700 to 300 B.C.," *BASOR* 311 (1998), J. Lines, "Late Assyrian Pottery from Nimrud," *Iraq* 16 (1954), J. Oates, "Late Assyrian Pottery from Fort Shalmaneser," *Iraq* 21 (1959), B. J. Parker, "Archaeological Manifestation of Empire: Assyria's Imprint on Southeastern Anatolia," *AJA* 107 (2003), B. J. Parker, *The Mechanics of Empire: The Northern Frontier of Assyria as a Case Study in Imperial Dynamics* (Helsinki: Helsinki University Press, 2001), P. S. Rawson, "Palace Wares from Nimrud: Technical Observations on Selected Examples," *Iraq* 16 (1954), E. Stern, "The Assyrian Impact on the Material Culture of Palestine," *EI* 27 (2003). I also express my deep gratitude to P. Bikai, the director of ACOR, who allowed me to consult the not-yet-published late seventh c. B.C.E. Assyrian pottery from Nineveh excavated in 1990–1992, and to E. D. Oren, who showed me the pottery from Tel Sera'.

The Assyrian-style pottery found in apparently Judahite sites makes it clear that the presence of imported Assyrian-style pottery or its local imitation does not immediately prove that a given site was an Assyrian installation. It is rather a combination of various archaeological finds that indicates whether a site was or was not an Assyrian installation. If we combine these features with textual evidence and the case studies presented above (3.1.5.2.1; 3.3.3.4; 3.5.2.2; 4.2.2.1), it is possible to distinguish three levels of Assyrian intelligence centers corresponding to the three levels of the Assyrian administrative structure: Assyrian provincial centers (intelligence hubs), secondary centers, and fortified installations.

5.1.1.2.1 Assyrian intelligence hubs

During the campaigns of Tiglath-pileser III, Sargon II, Sennacherib, and Esarhaddon, the Levantine kingdoms were turned into vassal states and sometimes into full-fledged Assyrian provinces (see 5.1.1.1.1). After the conquest of the Aramean kingdoms, Tiglath-pileser III established the province of Damascus. During the reigns of his successors, the next two provinces—Samaria and Megiddo—were established on the territory of Israel.[431] Numerous pieces of textual and archaeological evidence corroborate the Assyrian presence in Megiddo (see Appendix 6).[432] R. Reich[433] listed several elements of Assyrian-style architecture in Megiddo Stratum III: narrow niches in room 490, a bathroom and drainage system in

---

[431] G. W. Ahlström, *The History of Ancient Palestine from the Palaeolithic Period to Alexander's Conquest* (Sheffield, England: Sheffield Academic Press, 1993), 665–740, E. Forrer, *Die Provinzeinteilung des Assyrischen Reiches* (Leipzig: Hinrich, 1920), B. E. Kelle, "What's in a Name? Neo-Assyrian Designations for the Northern Kingdom and Their Implications for Israelite History and Biblical Interpretation," *JBL* 121 (2002), N. Na'aman, "Province System and Settlement Pattern in Southern Syria and Palestine in the Neo-Assyrian Period," in *Neo-Assyrian Geography*, ed. M. Liverani, *Quaderni di Geografia Storica* (Roma: Studium Urbis, 1995), E. Stern, "Hazor, Dor and Megiddo in the Time of Ahab and under Assyrian Rule," *IEJ* 40 (1990), E. Stern and A. Mazar, *Archaeology of the Land of the Bible: The Assyrian, Babylonian, and Persian Periods, 732-332 BCE*, 1st ed. (New York: Doubleday, 2001), 3–13, K. L. Younger, "Assyrian Involvement in the Southern Levant at the End of the Eighth Century B.C.E.," in *Jerusalem in Bible and Archaeology: The First Temple Period*, ed. A. E. Killebrew (Atlanta: Society of Biblical Literature, 2003).

[432] Na'aman, "Province System and Settlement Pattern in Southern Syria and Palestine in the Neo-Assyrian Period.", Younger, "Assyrian Involvement in the Southern Levant at the End of the Eighth Century B.C.E."

[433] Reich, "Palaces," 218.

the room north of 493,[434] and doorpost sockets.[435] Thus, archaeological data as well as textual evidence confirm that Megiddo was the seat of an Assyrian governor. In Samaria, no remains of Assyrian-style architecture have been revealed.[436] However, the textual evidence and other finds such as pottery, Assyrian bullae, and a cuneiform tablet are sufficient to justify the assumption that Samaria became the provincial center of the province of Samerina.[437] Since provincial governors were required to report on a regular basis, the provincial governors of these three cities—Damascus, Megiddo, and Samaria—must have complied with these requirements. Thus, it is safe to conclude that these cities constituted three major intelligence hubs providing information about Israel and Judah.

5.1.1.2.2 Assyrian secondary administrative centers

Besides the provincial centers, other Assyrian administrative centers in the Levant, such as Dor[438] and Gezer,[439] were a further channel through which information flowed to the royal court.[440]

---

[434] *Megiddo I*, Fig. 85.

[435] *Megiddo I*, Fig. 84.

[436] A possible explanation for the lack of the Assyrian-style architecture in Samaria is to assume that the Assyrians reused the monumental palaces of the previous royal city of Samaria; see Reich, "Palaces," 219.

[437] N. Na'aman and R. Zadok, "Assyrian Deportations to the Province of Samerina in the Light of Two Cuneiform Tablets from Tel Hadid," *TA* 27 (2000).

[438] Gilboa, "Assyrian-Type Pottery at Dor and the Status of the Town During the Assyrian Occupation Period.", I. Sharon, "Phoenician and Greek Ashar Construction Techniques at Tel Dor, Israel," *BASOR* 267 (1987), E. Stern, *Dor, Ruler of the Seas: Twelve Years of Excavations at the Israelite-Phoenician Harbor Town on the Carmel Coast* (Jerusalem: Israel Exploration Society, 1994), Stern, "Hazor, Dor and Megiddo in the Time of Ahab and under Assyrian Rule.", E. Stern, "New Evidence from Dor for the First Appearance of the Phoenicians Along the Northern Coast of Israel," *BASOR* 279 (1990).

[439] R. Reich and B. Brandl, "Gezer under Assyrian Rule," *PEQ* 117 (1985).

[440] Two other centers could be added to this list: Ashod and Hazor. For evaluation of arguments that Ashdod was the seat of a Neo-Assyrian official see M. Dothan and D. N. Freedman, "Ashdod I: The First Season of Excavations 1962," *Atiqot* 7 (1967): 11–5. The question whether Hazor was the seat of an Assyrian official depends on whether the open-court building 3002 of Stratum III (*Hazor I*, Pl. CLXXVII) is dated to the Neo-Assyrian or to the Neo-Babylonian period. This discussion goes far beyond the limits of this study.

5.1.1.2.3 Assyrian fortified installations

Since the case studies presented above did not deal explicitly with the role of fortified installations in the Assyrian intelligence network, I shall offer a general introduction to them here. M. Liverani proposed that the Assyrians expanded their empire not by conquering entire areas and demarcating a clear borderline between Assyrian and non-Assyrian territory, but rather by planting Assyrian islands in the midst of peripheral zones.[441] These "islands," in fact, were various kinds of Assyrian fortified installations. The vocabulary commonly used by the Assyrian officials allows the following classification of the Assyrian fortified installations: fortified cities (URU.HAL.ṢU, URU.*bīrtu*),[442] citadels (URU.HAL.ṢU, URU.*bīrtu*), fortresses and forts (URU.HAL.ṢU, URU.*bīrtu*, HAL.ṢU, *bīrtu*),[443] and fortified places (É–BÀD, *bēt dūri*). The citadels were fortified sections of individual cities,[444] whereas the fortresses and forts were placed in strategic locations outside the cities. Fortified places were usually smaller installations such as walled villages and camps.[445] A network of these installations spread throughout the Assyrian empire. First of all, they were located along the Assyrian frontiers. Letters mention the citadels, fortresses, forts, and fortified places built at most of the nerve centers of the empire: along the roads and rivers, at road junctions and fords, in the midst of vassal states and in important agricultural regions, and close to harbors.[446] The

---

[441] M. Liverani, "The Growth of the Assyrian Empire in the Habur/Middle Euphrates Area: A New Paradigm," *SAAB* 2 (1988).

[442] The writing of the logogram URU.HAL.ṢU for *bīrtu* follows the transliteration proposed in SAA XVII, 170.

[443] Since Liphur-bel, the governor of Amidi, used in his greeting formula both URU.HAL.ṢU and HAL.ṢU, it seems that the expressions with and without the logogram URU are interchangeable (with logogram: V 2:4; 3:4; 14:5; 18:5; without logogram: V 1:5; 6:5; 15:5).

[444] URU.HAL.ṢU can refer both to the citadel within the city (the city Dur-Illil is called *bīrtu*, IV 30–32; the city Marhua is called a *bīrtu* on the Šubrian border V 53:21–2) and to the city which contains the citadel (V 15:r.5).

[445] I 176:r.37; 247:r.6; V 21:17; X 2:r.8; XV 16:7.

[446] Assyrian fortified installations were located in Syria (I 176:r.37), in Melid (IV 1–11), in Kumme (I 29:8), in Parsua (V 199:14; XV 54:r.11), in Mazamua (V 210:r.9), in Media (XVI 148:9–12), in Hubuškia (XVI 148:9–12), in Babylonia (XV 166:r.5; 222:r.1), at the frontier with Ellipi (IV 77:2–3), at the frontier with Mannea (IV 30:2–3; 31:2–4; 267:2–4; V 131:3'; XVI 148:9–12), at the frontier with Šubria (IV 18:9), at the frontier with Urartu (I 31:r.7, V 2:14; 21:17; 115:7; XVI 148:9–12), along the upper Tigris (V 5:4'6'), along the rivers (XV 294:r.12; ND 2666), along the canals (XV 166:r.5), and in the midst of agricultural regions (V 15:r.5; XV 166:r.5).

location of these installations determined their triple function: 1) military (surveillance of insecure zones, protection of borders, pacification of rebels, refuge centers before in time of invasions);[447] 2) economic/administrative (collection of the tribute, overseeing agricultural production and deportees, protection of trade and mail routes, storage facilities for military campaigns);[448] and 3) intelligence (spying on the local or distant population).[449] This triple function is commonly described by the expression *maṣṣartu ša* PN *naṣāru*, "to keep one's watch." The Neo-Assyrian archives show that the royal court demanded that reports about the "watch" be dispatched on a regular basis. Besides regular reports on the situation in the region,[450] reports on hostilities, raids, and any expansionistic tendencies shown by the enemies of Assyria were also dispatched to the royal court. Since the fortresses along the enemy borders (XV 54:r.11) were the most distant Assyrian outposts, they were often involved in espionage in the true sense of the word. They were asked to penetrate the enemy heartland and to collect special information, and they were sometimes entrusted with special tasks such as paying special attention to deserters, interrogating them, sending the news by express mail to the court, and bringing the deserters themselves to the court for further investigation (XVI 148).

Intelligence gathering in the fortified Assyrian installations was organized on two levels (Figure 10). The fort commanders reported on everything they had heard and seen (the ground level). This gathering of raw intelligence was coordinated by an intermediary Assyrian official, who was ordered by the royal court to gather certain types of information and

---

447 Fortresses could completely stop smaller troops of invaders. In the case of a larger invasion, the fortresses slowed down the advance of invaders and gave local kings time to organize a defense (see the case of the Urartian fortresses attacked by the Manneans; V 131).

448 F. Malbran-Labat, *L'armée et l'organisation militaire de l'Assyrie: D'après les lettres des Sargonides trouvées à Ninive* (Paris: Libraire Droz, 1982), 13-4.

449 Ibid., 19.

450 The primary function of the fortresses was to "keep their watch" (XVI 148). The Assyrian fortresses were regularly inspected (XV 341:r.3) and the royal court asked to be informed about the weaponry (XV 166:15–23; 220:r.3'–7'), the state of the fortifications and their repair or reconstruction (V 80:7–r.4'; 199:r,12'–5'; XV 113:s.1–4), provisions (XV 166:6–14), and the number and ethnic composition of the guards serving in the fortresses (V 152:12–17; XV 119:s.2–5; 166:20–23). The fortresses also provided information about administrative complaints (XV 74).

who sent regularly dispatches to the court. In some cases, the commanders of the fortresses also sent their dispatches directly to the royal court.

ROYAL COURT	INTELLIGENCE HUB	HUB FORTRESS	FORTRESSES
King ← Sennacherib ←	Aššur-reṣuwa ←	Nabû-le'i ← - - - →	Guards (I 31)
King ←	←	Aššur-ušallim ← - - →	Guards (XVI 148)
King ←	Bodyguard ←	Commander (XV 74)	
King ← Sennacherib ←	←	←	Guards (I 31)
King ←	←	Commanders (XVII 62–85)	

Figure 10. Information flow

From the eighth millennium B.C.E.[451] until the present time, fortresses, forts, and fortified places have been necessary installations for furthering the interests of the powers that control Palestine. The Assyrians were no exception. According to my research, there is no extant textual evidence corroborating the Assyrian construction or maintenance of such installations in Palestine, and therefore their existence can be established only on the basis of archaeological remains. A. Alt for the first time attempted to reconstruct the network of these installations.[452] Though most of his conclusions were later challenged, the project itself was taken up by several scholars.[453] The stumbling block in the identification of Assyrian fortified installations is the definition of those specific Neo-Assyrian features that distinguish an Assyrian from a non-Assyrian fortress. The Neo-Assyrian letters suggest some architectural elements of the Assyrian URU.HAL.ṢU, understood as a city with a citadel, to be looked for in the archaeological record: a citadel, a royal palace, an image of the king, walls (XV 15), and in some cases also a moat (I 19). Letter ND 2666 provides a description of a fortress located outside of the city. Additional elements to be looked for are Assyrian weaponry and signs of administration such as

[451] The oldest tower serving military purposes was excavated under the direction of K. M. Kenyon. Based on Carbon-14 dating, the fort must have been constructed around 8,000 B.C.E.; see *Jericho III*, 6.
[452] A. Alt, "Neue Assyrische Nachrichten über Palästina und Syrien, 3: Assyrische Königsstrassen in Palästina und Syrien," *ZDPV* 67 (1945).
[453] Bloom, "Material Remains", N. Na'aman, "An Assyrian Residence at Ramat Rahel?," *TA* 28 (2001), Na'aman, "The Brook of Egypt and Assyrian Policy on the Border of Egypt.", idem, "Province System and Settlement Pattern in Southern Syria and Palestine in the Neo-Assyrian Period."

seals and Assyrian pottery.[454] The problems of identifying such fortresses are obvious. First, this description fits most of the fortresses in the ancient Near East; second, several Neo-Assyrian letters mention that the same fortresses changed their lords several times within a short period of time (IV 18:10–11; 31:1–9; V 15); third, the fortresses were usually manned by non-Assyrian allies, as well as deportees, and it is reasonable to assume that the latter brought with them their own material culture (V 152:12–17; XV 74:7'–11'; 119:s.2–5; 166:6–23). For these reasons, attempts to identify Neo-Assyrian fortresses outside cities, given the present state of our knowledge, run into great difficulties; and therefore my investigation of Neo-Assyrian fortified installations as the basis of the Neo-Assyrian intelligence network in Palestine will be limited to possible examples of the URU.HAL.ṢU, understood as a citadel within a city.

Southern intelligence bases

A group of Assyrian installations of the seventh c. B.C.E. can, with various degrees of probability, be identified in five southern sites: Tell Jemmeh, Tell esh-Shari'a, Tell Abu Hureirah, Tell el-Heṣi, and Khirbet Hoga.[455] None of these sites have been fully published, and the following conclusions are based on preliminary reports, personal communications from the excavators, and the investigation of not-yet-published pottery assemblages.

Tell Jemmeh (Tel Gamma)[456]

---

[454] The fortress was surrounded by a wall and moat. It contained a courtyard and drainage and water systems. The area inside the fortress was divided into two parts: *bēt ubri* 'the residence of the garrison commander' and *bēt napṭarte* 'the residence of the garrison soldiers'. Additional elements mentioned in the letter are a special gate lock and bitumen used to seal doors and other wooden objects; see B. J. Parker, "Garrisoning the Empire: Aspects of the Construction and Maintenance of Forts on the Assyrian Frontier," *Iraq* 59 (1997).

[455] Stern, "Assyrian Impact." and Stern and Mazar, *Archaeology*, 3-57.

[456] Preliminary reports: D. Gazit, "Petrie in Tell Jemmeh: Excavation Methods and Scientific Discipline," *Archaeologya* 3 (1992), A. Mallon, "Tell Djemmeh," *Bib* 8 (1927), G. L. Mattingly, "Neo-Assyrian Influence at Tell Jemmeh," *NEASB* 15 (1980), B. Mazar, "Yurza: The Identification of Tell Jemmeh," *PEQ* 84 (1952), J. Naveh, "Aramaic Ostraca and Jar Inscriptions from Tell Jemmeh," *Atiqot* 21 (1992), J. Naveh, "Writing and Script in Seventh-Century B.C.E. Philistia: The New Evidence from Tell Jemmeh," *IEJ* 35 (1985), F. Petrie, *Gerar* (London: British School of Archaeology in Egypt, 1928), W. J. Phythian-

Archaeological evidence attesting to Assyrian presence on the tell during the seventh c. B.C.E.[457] can be divided into two groups: evidence from architecture (an open-court building, vaulted rooms, square bricks) and evidence from pottery (Assyrian Palace Ware). The first series of excavations was conducted by F. Petrie in 1927.[458] During the excavations, he unearthed an open-court building[459] and a significant amount of Assyrian Palace Ware.[460] R. B. K. Amiran and I. Dunayevsky, comparing Assyrian open-court buildings with their Levantine derivates, including Tell Jemmeh, concluded that this architectural feature is foreign to Palestine and was introduced by the Assyrians.[461] A new series of excavations in Tell Jemmeh was conducted under the direction of G. W. van Beek. During the excavations in field I (in the northern part of the mound) in 1972 his team unearthed a building with at least six vaulted rooms.[462] The rooms were built from square bricks. All rooms had brick floors with plaster on the inner walls. In the northern room was found a large quantity of Assyrian Palace Ware.[463] Excavations in 1975 brought to light further details about this structure. The structure functioned until the late seventh c. B.C.E. when it was destroyed in a conflagration. Under the collapsed vaulting seventh c. B.C.E. pottery was buried.[464] Moreover, the excavations revealed that field I contained two buildings that G. W. van Beek called the Assyrian

---

Adams, "Reports on Soundings at Tell Jemmeh," *PEF* 55 (1923), R. Reich, "A Note on the Relative Chronology of Buildings a and B at Tell Jemmeh," *EI* 25 (1996), W. G. van Beek, "Ancient Methods for Minimizing Earthquake at Tell Jemmeh," *EI* 25 (1996), idem, "Are There Beehive Granaries at Tell Jemmeh? A Rejoinder," *BA* 49 (1986), idem, "Assyrian Vaulted Building at Tell Jemmeh," *Qadmoniot* 6 (1973), idem, "The Rammed Earth Revetment at Tell Jemmeh," *EI* 23 (1992): 112, idem, "The Reexcavation of Sites: Tell Jemmeh," in *Biblical Archaeology Today: Proceedings of the Second International Congress on Biblical Archaeology*, ed. A. Biran (Jerusalem: Israel Exploration Society, 1990), W. G. Van Beek, "Tel Gamma," *IEJ* 20 (1970), idem, "Tel Gamma," *IEJ* 22 (1972), idem, "Tel Gamma," *IEJ* 24 (1974), idem, "Tel Gamma, 1975-1976," *IEJ* 27 (1977), idem, "Tel Jemmeh - 1984," *Excavations and Surveys in Israel* 5 (1984).

[457] Van Beek, "Tel Gamma, 1975-1976," 172.

[458] Petrie, *Gerar*.

[459] Ibid., pl. XI.

[460] Ibid., pl. LXV.

[461] R. B. K. Amiran and I. Dunayevsky, "The Assyrian Open-Court Building and Its Palestine Derivates," *BASOR* 149 (1958).

[462] This technique was mainly confined to the Iranian plateau. The best example of the vaulted rooms were unearthed in Nush-i Jan; see W. G. Van Beek, "Arches and Vaults in the Ancient near East," *Scientific American* 257 (1987).

[463] Van Beek, "Tel Gamma," 245.

[464] Van Beek, "Tel Gamma, 1975-1976," 172.

Monumental Building and the Assyrian Residence. The Assyrian Monumental Building, located west of the Assyrian residence, had a courtyard paved with cobblestones. Excavations in 1972 and 1973 in field II revealed a seventh c. B.C.E. fortification system containing outer and inner walls.[465]

Basing themselves on these preliminary reports, several scholars concluded that the structures in fields I and II were built and occupied by the Assyrians during the seventh c. B.C.E.[466] The examination of two monumental buildings containing several Assyrian features led G. W. van Beek to the conclusion that these buildings were used by an Assyrian official.[467] Thus, the site would qualify as an URU.HAL.ṢU—in other words, as the seat of the Assyrian military governor controlling Nahal Beṣor, which Na'aman identifies with the Brook of Egypt.[468] The proposed identification of Tell Jemmeh with Egyptian Yurtza,[469] whose Assyrian equivalent is Arza,[470] which became one of the Assyrian installations during Esarhaddon's reign, would further support the idea that Tell Jemmeh became an important Assyrian administrative center during the seventh c. B.C.E. Using the terminology proposed in section 3.3.4.2, I infer that such an Assyrian military governor would correspond to a medium- or low-ranking Assyrian intelligence official, such as a deputy-governor, legate, magnate, or commander of the troops (see 3.3.4.2).

Tell esh-Shari'a (Tel Sera')[471]

---

[465] Ibid.

[466] Na'aman, "Province System and Settlement Pattern in Southern Syria and Palestine in the Neo-Assyrian Period," 112, Stern and Mazar, *Archaeology,* 26, Van Beek, "Assyrian Vaulted Building at Tell Jemmeh.", idem, "Tel Gamma," 246.

[467] Van Beek, "Tel Gamma, 1975-1976," 245.

[468] Na'aman, "The Brook of Egypt and Assyrian Policy on the Border of Egypt," 74-80, Na'aman, "Province System and Settlement Pattern in Southern Syria and Palestine in the Neo-Assyrian Period," 112.

[469] Mazar, "Yurza: The Identification of Tell Jemmeh."

[470] Na'aman, "The Brook of Egypt and Assyrian Policy on the Border of Egypt," 77 and H. Tadmor, "Philistia under Assyrian Rule," *BA* 29 (1966).

[471] *NEAEHL* 4, 1329–36; E. D. Oren, "Ashlar Masonry in the Western Negev in the Iron Age," *EI* 23 (1992), idem, "A Cultic Building in the Excavation of Tel Sera`," *Qadmoniot* 6 (1973), idem, "Chronique Archéologique: Tel Sera' (Tell Esh-Shari'a)," *RB* 80 (1973), idem, "Tel Sera' (Tell Esh-Shari'a)," *IEJ* 22 (1972), idem, "Tel Sera' (Tell Esh-Shari'a)," *IEJ* 23 (1973), idem, "Tel Sera' (Tell Esh-Shari'a)," *IEJ* 24 (1974), idem, *Tell esh-Shari'a*

According to the preliminary reports, Tell esh-Shari'a seems to provide the best attestation of the Assyrian presence in the southern Levant. The excavations were conducted by E. D. Oren. Stratum VI contained ashlar masonry and eighth c. B.C.E. pottery.[472] This stratum was destroyed in a conflagration, most likely set by the Assyrians. Architectural features such as elevated platforms, paved courtyards, and long narrow halls indicate that the following stratum (Stratum V) served as an Assyrian fortress (URU.HAL.ṢU). In area A (the southwestern part of the mound) a citadel with long narrow magazine halls and small rooms were uncovered, all surrounded by 5-m-thick defensive walls. A rectangular building with a narrow hall about 14 m long surrounded by a 4-m-thick wall was unearthed in area D (the northern part of the mound).[473] This indicates that the structure had a defensive function. North of the hall was an elevated rectangular platform and east of the hall was a square courtyard paved with pebbles and gravel. The stratum was destroyed in a conflagration at the end of the seventh c. B.C.E.[474] Besides these architectural features, other remains attest to Assyrian presence. Together, Tell Jemmeh and Tell esh-Shari'a have more Assyrian Palace Ware sherds than all the cities of Philistia put together.[475] Moreover, in the northern hall of area D was found a bronze crescent-shaped standard (symbol of the god Sin), next to which was a bronze bell.[476] A bronze socketed spearhead and an iron chain at whose end was a long pitchfork-like prong (probably a grappling device

---

(Tell Sera'): A Biblical City on the Edge of the Negev (Beersheva: Archaeological division Ben-Gurion University of the Negev, 1972), idem, "Ziklag: A Biblical City on the Edge of the Negev," *BA* 45 (1982), and F. Volkmar, "Where Is David's Ziklag?," *BAR* 19 (1993).

[472] E. D. Oren's comparative studies on ashlar masonry from Tell esh-Sharia, Tell Abu Hureirah, Tell el-Heṣi, Tell er-Ruqeish, Ashdod, and Tel Miqne indicate that ashlar techniques in the western Negev and southern Philistia were modeled on the Phoenician pattern; at least in the case of Tell esh-Sharia and Tell Abu Hureirah, they can be dated to pre-Assyrian occupations. See Oren, "Ashlar Masonry in the Western Negev in the Iron Age."

[473] Following B. J. Parker's reconstruction of the Assyrian fortresses at the peripheries, this part could have been the soldiers' quarters, the *bēt napṭarte*; see Parker, *Mechanics*, 143.

[474] *NEAEHL* 4, 1329–36.

[475] D. Master, "Trade and Politics: Ashkelon's Balancing Act in the Seventh Century B.C.E.," *BASOR* 330 (2003): 51. I express my gratitude to E. D. Oren for allowing me to consult the collection of Neo-Assyrian pottery from Tell esh-Shari'a. According to E. D. Oren, only a few sherds of pottery can be safely assumed to come from Assyrian imports. The locally imitated Neo-Assyrian pottery amounts to some dozens of sherds.

[476] The bell was probably originally attached to the handle of the standard, which was used for ritual purposes; see *NEAEHL* 4, 1333.

used for climbing the walls of a besieged city) indicate that Tell esh-Shari‘a served as a military garrison.[477] The architecture of stratum V and the rest of the finds led E. D. Oren to the conclusion that during the seventh c. B.C.E., the site was occupied by an Assyrian military administration.[478] Using the terminology of the Neo-Assyrian intelligence network, I infer that the commander of this military garrison would have been a low-ranking Assyrian intelligence official, such as a commander of troops or of a fortress (see 3.3.4.2).

Tell el-Heṣi, Tell Abu Hureirah, and Khirbet Hoga

The Assyrian presence in Tell el-Heṣi, Tell Abu Hureirah, and Khirbet Hoga is discernable only from a relatively large amount of Assyrian Palace Ware, mostly local imitations.[479] In all three sites, Assyrian Palace Ware was found together with seventh c. B.C.E. pottery. In comparison with the total absence or scarcity of Assyrian Palace Ware in Tell Halif,[480] Tel Ira,[481] Lachish,[482] Ekron,[483] Tell er-Ruqeish,[484] Tell el-Far`ah (S),[485] and

---

[477] E. Stern mentions that the remains of an Assyrian chariot were found on the tell; see Stern and Mazar, *Archaeology*, 26.

[478] *NEAEHL* 4, 1334.

[479] The Neo-Assyrian pottery has not yet been published. I express my gratitude to J. A. Blakely who allowed me to consult these local imitations of Neo-Assyrian pottery. Among the collection was at least one piece of imported pottery. For other details about Tell el-Heṣi, see J. A. Blakely and J. W. Hardin, "Southwestern Judah in the Late Eighth Century B.C.E.," *BASOR* 326 (2002): 32.

The excavation at Tell Abu Hureirah (Tel Haror) revealed two towers and a fortification wall. The surface of the top of the mound is 4 acres, i.e., as large as the surface of Tell esh-Shari‘a. The distance between the two sites and the flat terrain suggests that both sites could communicate via smoke and fire signals. This indicates that both sites played similar roles in the Neo-Assyrian control of the surrounding territory. See also E. D. Oren, "Tel Haror," *Excavations and Surveys in Israel* 13 (1995), idem, "Tel Haror - 1988," *Excavations and Surveys in Israel* 9 (1989/90), E. D. Oren and M. A. Morrison, "Land of Gerar Expedition: Preliminary Report for the Seasons of 1982 and 1983," in *Preliminary Reports of ASOR-Sponsored Excavations 1980-84*, ed. W. E. Rast (Winona Lake: Eisenbrauns, 1986).

For Khirbet Hoga, see J. Porath, "Khirbet Hoga," *Had. Arch.* 59-60 (1976), D. Varga, "Horbat Hoga," *Had. Arch.* 110 (1999).

[480] *NEAEHL* 2, 553–60; *OEANE* 3, 325–26; O. Borowski, "The Iron Age Cemetery at Tel Halif," *EI* 23 (1992), J. D. Seger, "Investigations at Tell Halif," *BASOR* 252 (1983).

[481] Only a few sherds of Assyrian Palace Ware were found during the excavations; see *NEAEHL* 2, 645.

[482] O. Zimhoni, "Two Ceramic Assembledges from Lachish Level III and II," *TA* 17 (1990): 30–49.

Ashkelon,[486] the relatively higher concentration of Assyrian Palace Ware in these three sites indicates that they should also be identified as Assyrian fortresses and forts. According to the terminology of the Neo-Assyrian intelligence network, these sites would have been the seats of low- or medium-ranking intelligence officials (see 3.3.4.2).

Let us now consider all five of these eighth and seventh c. B.C.E. sites—Tell Jemmeh, Tell esh-Shari'a, Tell Abu Hureirah, Tell el-Heṣi, and Khirbet Hoga. Their locations in the southwestern corner of Judah determined their threefold function: 1) to control trade routes; 2) to watch Egypt; and 3) to monitor local vassal kings. As regards the first function, the fortified places were located on the important intersections of the trade routes accessing the coastal ports in Ashkelon and Gaza. The northern set of these Assyrian installations (Tell el-Heṣi and Khirbet Hoga) controlled the routes coming from Hebron to Ashkelon and Gaza.[487] The southern installations (Tell Jemmeh, Tell esh-Shari'a and Tell Abu Hureirah)[488] controlled the Arabian routes passing through Beer-sheba to Gaza.[489] Moreover, the fortified places controlled the way of the sea[490] connecting

---

[483] Four Neo-Assyrian vessels were uncovered among the seventh c. remains from Tel Miqhe-Ekron; see S. Gitin, "Tel Miqne-Ekron in the 7th Century B.C.E.: The Impact of Economic Innovation and Foreign Cultural Influences on a Neo-Assyrian Vassal City-State," in *Recent Excavations in Israel: A View to the West*, ed. S. Gitin (Dubuque, Iowa: Kendall/Hunt, 1995), 65, Fig. 4.5 no. 9–12.

[484] A. Biran, "Tell Er-Ruqeish to Tell Er-Ridan," *IEJ* 24 (1974), W. Culican, "The Graves at Tell Er-Ruqeish," *AJBA* 1 (1973), Master, "Trade and Politics," 51, E. D. Oren, "A Phoenician Emporium on the Border of Egypt," *Qadmoniot* 19 (1986).

[485] *NEAEHL* 2, 441–45

[486] Master, "Trade and Politics," 52.

[487] Blakely and Hardin, "Southwestern Judah in the Late Eighth Century B.C.E.," 13-4, A. D. Dorsey, *The Roads and Highways of Ancient Israel* (Baltimore, London: The Johns Hopkins University Press, 1991), 193-201, Master, "Trade and Politics."

[488] The strategic importance of the plain created along Nahal Beṣor and Nahal Gerar had been known since the Middle Bronze Age and is indicated by the relatively high concentration of mounds in this area (Tell el-Ajjul, Tell Jemmeh, Tell el-Far'ah South, Tell Abu Hureirah, Tell Nagila, and Tell Halif); see Oren, *Tell Esh-Shari'a (Tell Sera'): A Biblical City on the Edge of the Negev*, 2–3.

[489] L. Singer-Avitz, "Beersheba-a Gateway Community in Southern Arabian Long-Distance Trade in the Eighth Century B.C.E.," *TA* 26 (1999).

[490] There were two important international highways in the Levant: "The way of the see" and "The king's highway". The former and the most important of them ran the length of the country's coastland; the latter ran along the length of the Transjordanian range. Even though the individual stations of this coastal highway changed according to historical

Egypt with Phoenician ports, and thus this region served as the commercial gateway to Egypt.[491]

The role of the way of the sea as the fastest and most accessible route from Egypt to the Levant and vice versa determined the second function of the Assyrian installations in this region—to keep watch on the frontier with Egypt.[492] Also, these installations might have served as the starting point and supply bases for the Assyrian campaigns against Egypt. The third function of these fortified places was to oversee the vassal states. The Assyrian installations in the southern Levant could not have escaped the notice of the Judahite and Philistine vassals. Such a military presence ensured that the vassal kings realized that they were closely watched and needed to behave accordingly. Moreover, by creating a sort of buffer zone between Philistia and Judah, the fortified places also separated the rival vassal states and enforced the *Pax Assyriaca.*[493]

The threefold function of these Assyrian installations determined the nature of the intelligence provided by Assyrian officials serving in these military and administrative installations. First, insofar as they controlled the trade routes, the Assyrian officials could obtain economic intelligence that included information about compliance with trade regulations and tax rules.

---

circumstances, it remained in use during all historical periods. In the Egyptian sources it was known as “the ways of Horus”, in the biblical sources it was called “the way of the sea” (Is 9:1) and “the way to the land of the Philistines” (Ex 13:17), and in the Roman tradition it was known as the *Via Maris*; see Y. Aharoni, *The Land of the Bible: A Historical Geography* (Philadelphia: The Westminster Press, 1976), 43–63. Because the *Via Maris* is a later term, I will use the term “the way of the sea”, the name used by the Isaiah, which better reflects the Neo-Assyrian period.

491 S. Gitin, "Neo-Assyrian and Egyptian Hegemony over Ekron in the Seventh Century BCE: A Response to Lawrence E. Stager," *EI* 27 (2003): 57*.

492 Stern, "Assyrian Impact," 218. The Gerar wadi traditionally represented the southernmost part of the way of the sea. Thus, in the case of Asa’s war with the Egyptians, for example, he chased them as far as the Gerar Valley (2 Chr 14:12).

493 The excavations in Beth Shemesh revealed that the city was left abandoned after Sennacherib’s invasion. Only a small group returned and lived in huts. In contrast to the Philistine cities of Ashkelon and Ekron, which flourished during the first half of the seventh c. B.C.E., the Judean Shephelah was deliberately left unpopulated; see Gitin, "Neo-Assyrian and Egyptian Hegemony." Thus, the buffer zone separating Philistia from Judah was created in the south by establishing Assyrian garrisons and in the Judean Shephelah by maintaining an unpopulated area as an agricultural buffer zone; see S. Bunimowitz and Z. Lederman, "The Final Destruction of Beth Shemesh and the *Pax Assyriaca* in the Judean Shephelah," *TA* 30 (2003): 22.

The sources of this kind of information would have been merchants, caravan riders, and tax officials.[494] Second, by controlling in particular the way of the sea, these Assyrian installations, as the southernmost Assyrian outposts,[495] were the most promising Assyrian bases for gathering military and political intelligence regarding Egypt. Third, because of their location between Philistia and Judah, these installations could easily monitor the compliance of the vassal kings with Assyrian demands, such as tribute delivery and conscription. Moreover, they could easily monitor any suspicious international contacts, expansionist aspirations, and military or construction activities of the Philistine and Judahite vassal kings. They could similarly monitor the behavior of local semi-nomadic and semi-sedentary pastoralists.[496]

Besides these three types of intelligence, the very location of the fortified places allowed the officials to collect "encyclopedic data" such as information on rainfall, water resources, terrain, crop yields, and natural calamities such as famine.[497] Regular dispatches from these officials, thus,

---

[494] The network of tax-collectors who, besides taxing the access routes to the harbor of Gaza, also provided the Assyrians with intelligence is reconstructed on the basis of the similarity between Tyre and Gaza. Both of them were important harbors and the terminals of important trading routes. According to ND 2715, dated to Tiglath-pileser III, the Assyrian officials taxed everyone carrying goods to Tyre. Since the line of fortresses controlled the access route to Gaza, it is possible to conclude that a similar network of tax-collectors was established to tax the flow of goods to Gaza; see Na'aman, "The Brook of Egypt and Assyrian Policy on the Border of Egypt," 83–4, J. N. Postgate, *Taxation and Conscription in the Assyrian Empire* (Rome: Biblical Institute Press, 1974), 390–92.

[495] The southernmost known Assyrian outpost was Sheikh Zuweid (Tell Abu Salima). It served as one of the fortresses along the way of the sea close to the Egyptian frontier. The Assyrian features present in Tell Abu Salima include: square, fired bricks used to pave the floor of the temple cella; offset-inset city walls made out of sun-dried mud brick; and Assyrian Palace Ware dated to the seventh c. B.C.E. Thus, it is possible to conclude that this site also served as an Assyrian administrative center; see Na'aman, "Province System and Settlement Pattern in Southern Syria and Palestine in the Neo-Assyrian Period."

[496] This area has always been used by shepherds and goatherds. N. Na'aman suggested that Asuhili, the king of Arza, who rebelled against the Assyrians, was one of the local pastoral leaders. His rebellion was crushed in 679 B.C.E.; see Na'aman, "An Assyrian Residence at Ramat Rahel?" 265.

[497] This region has always been an important agricultural resource. One of the characteristics of Assyrian imperial expansion was the exploitation of local agricultural resources. The southern part of the region along the Nahal Beṣor and Gerar is located at the border with the Negev desert and receives only 300 mm of rainfall. Consequently, during a good rainy season this area can produce very high yields. However, if the rainfall is under

constituted one of the information channels through which political, military, and economic intelligence concerning the southern Levant flowed to the Assyrian court. By comparing this information with information coming from local vassal kings or the Arab tribe of the Idibi'ilu, the latter particularly useful for intelligence relating to Egypt, the court officials could evaluate the reliability of their sources and receive timely warnings of trouble even if one of their sources failed.

Northern intelligence bases

Tel Chinnereth

A candidate for an Assyrian military and administrative installation controlling the road along the western shore of the Sea of Galilee is Tel Chinnereth (Tell el-'Oreimeh). The site was excavated by V. Fritz.[498] The heavily fortified Israelite citadel (Stratum II) was destroyed in the second half of the eighth c. B.C.E. The city of Stratum II was less than 1ha large, and the inhabited area was limited to the top of the mound. V. Fritz attributed the violent destruction marking the end of the Israelite city to Tiglath-pileser III's invasion in 733 B.C.E.[499] The southern quarter of the mound was rebuilt after the destruction with only poor dwellings (Stratum I). However, building 928 of Stratum I indicates that some survivors of the destruction were able to construct not only a well-designed house but also to add a cistern for private use.[500] The finds (iron tools, including two points of a ploughshare)[501] suggest that the owner was a farmer.[502]

Outside of the limits of the former Stratum II (area E_1), there was a large open-court building (737).[503] The layout of this building is similar to that of open-court buildings 1052 and 1369 of Stratum III in Megiddo,

---

the average and there is no irrigation system, crop failure is frequent. The northern part of the region, around Tell el-Heṣi, is more reliable for producing crops.

[498] V. Fritz, *Kinneret: Ergebnisse der Ausgrabungen auf dem Tell el-'Oreme am See Gennesaret 1982-1985* (Wiesbaden: Otto Harrassowitz, 1990).

[499] V. Fritz, "The Decline of Chinnereth after the Campaign of Tiglath-Pileser III against Damascus in 733," *Jahrbuch des Deutschen Evangelischen Instituts für Altertumswisenschaft des Heiligen Landes* 5 (1997): 61.

[500] Ibid.: 62.

[501] Fritz, *Kinneret*, Pl. 116.

[502] Fritz, "The Decline of Chinnereth," 63.

[503] Fritz, *Kinneret*, 99–102.

which seem to have been inhabited by the governor of the province of Megiddo. This similarity led V. Fritz to conclude that the open-court building in Kinneret was occupied by an Assyrian high official.[504] Assyrian presence is further confirmed by the discovery of a lion bowl[505] and tripod bowls.[506]

V. Fritz's conclusion is consonant with the pattern of Neo-Assyrian psychological strategy. Assyrian collaborators were often rewarded by being entrusted with responsibilities for agricultural production which, of course, included financial advantages that were reflected in the quality of their houses.[507] At the same time, Assyrian supervision was guaranteed by the military and administrative installation. The open-court building was the seat of a middle- or low-ranking Assyrian official. Information available to such an official concerned the agriculture of the region, trade along the road passing through Northern Galilee, political developments in the nearby cities, and deportees settled in northern Israel. Since the owner of house 928 was under the close control of the Assyrian official living in building 737, he had to remain on good terms with the Assyrian official by sharing information with the Assyrians.

Ayyelet ha-Shahar[508]

---

504 V. Fritz, "Kinneret: Excavations at Tell el-'Oreimeh (Tel Kinrot) 1982-1985 Seasons," *TA* 20 (1993): 214. See also idem, "Die Paläste während der Assyrischen, Babylonischen und Persischen Vorherrshaft in Palästina," *MDOG* 111 (1979): 63–74. However, it is necessary to mention that only the western part of building 737 has been preserved; the eastern part of the building has been eroded away. Thus, the layout of the bulding and the conclusions drawn from it are based on Fritz's reconstruction. Moreover, while a few pieces of Persian pottery were unearthed in the open-court building, only one carinated sherd, possibly from a Neo-Assyrian bowl, was uncovered during the excavations; see Fritz, *Kinneret*, Pl. 99:1–3. Despite this counterevidence, V. Fritz's interpretation of building 737 in area E_1, that it was an open-court building that served as the residence of an Assyrian official and was reused after the fall of Assyria during the Persian period, seems to be the most plausible interpretation of the archaeological data. According to my bibliographical research, this interpretation has not been undermined by recent studies.

505 The lion bowl shows strong Assyrian influence that is probably a reflection of the rise of the Assyrian empire; see V. Fritz, "The Lion Bowl from Kinneret," *BA* 50 (1987): 239.

506 Fritz, *Kinneret*, Pl. 108:15, 17–18.

507 See for example Senn Ann III:31–35 and XVII 48:6–9.

508 O. Lipschitz, "The Date of the "Assyrian Residence" at Ayyelet Ha-Shahar," *TA* 17 (1990), R. Reich, "The Persian Building at Ayyelet Ha-Shahar: The Assyrian Palace of Hazor?" *IEJ* 25 (1975).

This site is located in the vicinity of Hazor, and several pieces of evidence indicate that the site was a secondary administrative center of the Megiddo province. A monumental brick structure in the area of Kibbutz Ayyelet ha-Shahar was excavated by P. L. O. Guy in 1950 and dated to the Persian period.[509] The building was re-examined in 1975 by R. Reich, who pointed out similarities between the monumental building of Ayyelet ha-Shahar and the Assyrian throne room in Arslan-Tash.[510] The proposal was later examined by O. Lipschitz, who narrowed down the date of the Assyrian-style palace. The different location of the bathroom in Arslan-Tash and Dur Šarrukin indicates that the building in Arslan-Tash was constructed before Dur Šarrukin. Since the building in Ayyelet ha-Shahar has the same layout as the Arslan-Tash building, O. Lipschitz concluded that the building in Ayyelet ha-Shahar had been constructed before the construction of Dur Šarrukin.[511] R. Reich studied other features of Ayyelet ha-Shahar architecture and concluded:

> Other features—such as the ante-room of the audience hall (and especially the pair of door sockets which held the heavy double doors), the use of shallow niches, the thick plaster floor, the drainage system consisting of sections of terra-cotta pipes, and the thick walls of terre pisee—are unmistakable characteristics of royal Assyrian architecture.[512]

These architectural features led N. Na'aman to the conclusion that the Assyrians built a secondary administrative center in the province of Megiddo at Ayyelet ha-Shahar.[513] The presence of the Assyrian throne room-like structure indicates that Ayyelet ha-Shahar was the seat of a medium- or high-ranking Assyrian intelligence official.

5.1.1.3 Conclusion

The examination of the textual and archaeological evidence allows us to draw some conclusions regarding the Assyrian branch of the Neo-

---

[509] B. Maisler, "Archaeology in the State of Israel," *BA* 15 (1952): 22.
[510] Reich, "The Persian Building at Ayyelet Ha-Shahar: The Assyrian Palace of Hazor?"
[511] Lipschitz, "The Date of the "Assyrian Residence" at Ayyelet Ha-Shahar."
[512] Reich, "Palaces," 215.
[513] Na'aman, "Province System and Settlement Pattern in Southern Syria and Palestine in the Neo-Assyrian Period," 110.

Assyrian intelligence network in Palestine. If the intelligence hubs of this branch can be located in the capitals of the Neo-Assyrian provinces, then the intelligence activities of the Levant were coordinated from nine centers: Ṣimirra, Zobah, Hamath, Hatarikka, Sidon, Tyre, Damascus, Samaria, and Megiddo. A lower level of coordination of Neo-Assyrian intelligence activities was conducted in four secondary administrative centers: Haurina, Manṣuate, Dor, and Gezer. The ground level of collecting information was done by numerous officials listed in 5.1.1.1.1 and the Assyrian officials working in the Assyrian fortified installations such as Tell Jemmeh, Tell esh-Shari'a, Tell Chinnereth, and Ayyelet ha-Shahar.

The intelligence activities followed the rules similar to those drawn up in the other parts of the Empire. The Assyrians double-checked the gathering and the transmission of information and collected information on similar issues (5.1.1.1.2) as the officials in the rest of the Empire. Thus, comparing the results of the Neo-Assyrian intelligence networks operating in the other parts of the Empire with the Assyrian branch in the Levant, we can conclude that the Assyrians established a full-fledged Assyrian branch of intelligence network able to collect information they needed.

5.1.2 Local branch

The obligation of the local kings and officials to report depended on their relations with Assyria. The more tenuous their relations with Assyria were, the less pressure the Assyrians could put on them to report (see 3.1.3 and 3.1.5.2.1). By examining the Assyrian royal inscriptions it is possible to discern three types of local intelligence sources in the Levant: vassals bound by *adê*, treaty,[514] vassals-tributaries bound by *maddattu*, tribute,[515] and *biltu*, tax,[516] and local tribes entrusted with a special task. In section 3.6 I demonstrated that vassals bound by *adê* had to report on everything they had seen or heard. Falling short of the obligation to report, they violated a treaty sworn in the presence of the gods, and this offence was punished accordingly. Consequently, it is possible to assume that the Levantine vassals bound by *adê* reported to the Assyrians on a regular basis, though this does not imply that they were the most reliable of sources. The Assyrian royal inscriptions mention following vassals bound by *adê*:

---

[514] *CAD* 1/1, 131.
[515] *CAD* 10, 13–16.
[516] *CAD* 2, 229.

Table 23. List of vassals in the Levant

NAME	DATE	LOCATION	OFFICE
Samsi, the Arab queen	TP III	East of Jordan	She broke the treaty with the Assyrians (TP III Ann 23:18').
Mitinti, king of Ashkelon	TP III	Ashkelon	He broke his treaty with TP III and revolted against the Assyrians (TP III Ann 18:8'; 24:12'–3').
Padi, king of Ekron	Senn.	Ekron	He remained faithful to the Assyrians and paid for his loyalty to Assyria by being taken in fetters to Jerusalem (Senn Ann II:74; F1:23)
Iauta', king of Qederites	Esarh.	Arab tribe	He violated the treaty and incited a revolt against Assyria (Piepkorn, pp. 80–81, vii:93–99, viii:1).
Baal, king of Tyre	Esarh.	Tyre	He was bound by the oath with Esarhaddon (II 5).

The second type of local intelligence source took the form of vassal-tributaries bound by the obligation to pay *maddattu* and *biltu*, who were less closely tied to Assyria. By investigating the reports dispatched by and about the vassal kings of Šubria, Kumme, and Ukku (section 3.1.3), I have shown that even the vassals whose relations with Assyria were quite tenuous were nonetheless providing important information about their neighbors. Even though the Assyrian annals show that most kings took advantage of every occasion to throw off the Assyrian yoke, they still had to maneuver to keep their Assyrian overlords sufficiently satisfied so as not to be deposed or even executed. Besides payment of tribute, reporting was another way to comply with Assyrian demands. Consequently, we may safely presume that the Levantine vassal-tributaries were another source of information. Of course, this information had to be carefully scrutinized.

During the period after the first invasions of Tiglath-pileser III until the end of Ashurbanipal's reign all the Levantine states paid tributes or taxes to the Assyrians.[517] Thus, all the Levantine kings could be considered potential informers especially on their neighbors with whom they were at

[517] See I. Ephal, "The Assyrian Domination of Palestine," *WHJP* (1979), B. E. Kelle, "What's in a Name? Neo-Assyrian Designations for the Northern Kingdom and Their Implications for Israelite History and Biblical Interpretation," *JBL* 121 (2002) and K. L. Younger, "Assyrian Involvement in the Southern Levant at the End of the Eighth Century B.C.E.," in *Jerusalem in Bible and Archaeology: The First Temple Period*, ed. A. G. Vaughn and A. E. Killebrew (Atlanta: Society of Biblical Literature, 2003), 235–63.

odds. For the purposes of reporting about the situation in the region, the most important were the local kings who fully complied with Assyrian demands. In this group can be included Moab, Amon, Edom, and Judah. For example, Kamašalta, the king of Moab, during the reign of Ashurbanipal, collaborated with the Assyrians in defeating the rebellious troops[518] and was called an obedient servant, ARAD.*da-gil pa-ni-ia*.[519] This level of collaboration with the Assyrians probably included reporting and sharing intelligence. The pro-Assyrian kings of Judah and Israel, especially those who willingly assumed Assyrian yoke or remained at power for a long time, were also potential informers (see Table 24 and 25).

Table 24. Anti-Assyrian and pro-Assyrian kings in Israel

INDEPENDENT		ANTI-ASSYRIAN		PRO-ASSYRIAN	
Uzziah	785-33				
Jotham	759-43				
				Ahaz	743-27
				Hezekiah	727-20?
		Hezekiah	720?-697		
				Manasseh	
		Manasseh			697-42
				Manasseh	
				Amon	642-640
		Joshiah			

Table 25. Anti-Assyrian and pro-Assyrian kings in Judah

INDEPENDENT		ANTI-ASSYRIAN		PRO-ASSYRIAN	
Jeroboam	785-45				
Zechariah	745				
		Shallum	745		
				Menahem	745-36
				Pekahiah	736-735
		Pekah	735-32		
				Hoshea	732-27
		Hoshea	727-23		
		No king	723-21		

518 Piepkorn, p. 84, viii:43–50.
519 Piepkorn, p. 84, viii:44.

The third type of intelligence source in Palestine was provided by local tribes who had concluded special agreements with the Assyrians. Tiglath-pileser III entrusted the Arab tribe Idibi'ilu with the office of "gate-keepership", which included reporting on the status of the border with Egypt.[520] Moreover, Sargon II put the sheikh of the city of Laban in charge of deportees whom he settled in the region of the Brook of Egypt. According to I. Ephal, Sargon II gave him status in the Assyrian governmental system.[521]

5.1.3 Conclusion

Investigation of the written sources and archaeological material allow me to answer the question posed at the beginning of this section: Did the Assyrians set up an intelligence network in Palestine by means of which they collected the information they needed? The answer is affirmative. At the end of the eighth and during most of the seventh century B.C.E., the Assyrians had at their disposal an intelligence network that consisted of both local and Assyrian branches and was large enough to gather the information they needed for governing the Levant.

5.2 Intelligence as information

Having reconstructed the framework of the Assyrian intelligence network in Palestine, I can now approach the contextualization itself of Hezekiah's story. In chapters 2 and 3, I presented the type of information the Assyrians were interested in. The main goal of this section will be to evaluate whether the Assyrians were interested in gathering the same kinds of information according to both biblical and Assyrian sources. Thus, I will examine the biblical account of 2 Kgs 18–19 in the immediate context of Senancherib's annals as well as in the larger context of the Neo-Assyrian archives.

5.2.1 Context of Neo-Assyrian royal inscriptions

Placing the biblical account within the context of the Neo-Assyrian royal inscriptions requires a consideration of the celebratory literary style of

[520] I. Eph'al, *The Ancient Arabs: Nomads on the Borders of the Fertile Crescent, 9th-5th Centuries B.C.* (Jerusalem: Magnes Press Hebrew University, 1982), 93.
[521] Ibid., 94.

the royal inscriptions, which, according to several scholars, was geared to promote the glory of the gods and kings of Assyria.[522] The literary style in which the events of Assyrian campaigns are presented to the reader requires that we not take the royal inscriptions as factual reports but rather as literary compositions and that we approach them with the tools of literary criticism.[523] For the purpose of reconstructing the intelligence categories of the royal inscription, I will have to investigate one literary technique in detail.

The description of the campaigns in the royal annals often contains four parts: an introduction, the 3rd person part (he/they-part), the 1st person part (I-part), and a description of results.[524] The he/they-parts elaborate the reasons for the king's intervention and the I-parts describe the king's response to the challenges raised in the he/they-part (see Table 26). Examples collected from the royal inscriptions of major Neo-Assyrian kings (Aššur-naṣirpal II, Shalmaneser III, Šamši-Adad V, Tiglath-pileser III, Sargon II, Esarhaddon, and Ashurbanipal) demonstrate that the scribes used this literary structure regularly over several centuries. Obviously, the celebratory character of the royal inscriptions required that scribes dedicate more space to the I-part than to the he/they-part. Moreover, the importance of a given enemy and of a given campaign determined whether all four

---

[522] F. M. Fales, "Narrative and Ideological Variations in the Account of Sargon's Eighth Campaign," in *Ah, Assyria...: Studies in Assyrian History and Ancient near Eastern Historiography Presented to Hayim Tadmor*, ed. M Cogan and I. Ephal (Jerusalem: The Magnes Press, 1991), M. Liverani, *Guerra e Diplomazia nell'antico Oriente 1600-1100 a.C.* (Rome: Laterza, 1994), idem, "The Ideology of the Assyrian Empire," in *Power and Propaganda: A Symposium on Ancient Empires*, ed. M. T Larsen (Copenhagen: Akademisk Forlag, 1979), and C. Zaccagnini, *I Trattati nel Mondo Antico: Forma, Ideologia, Funzione* (Rome: "L'Erma" di Bretschneider, 1990).

[523] The general structure of the Neo-Assyrian royal inscriptions was investigated by W. Schramm, *Einleitung in die Assyrischen Königsinschriften,* vol. 2 (Leiden and Köln: E.J. Brill, 1973), 13–7. The purpose of the following section is not to question Schramm's proposal, but rather to investigate a specific literary structure used by the Neo-Assyrian scribes. This analysis can be helpful for determining the content of pre-campaign intelligence.

[524] F. M. Fales, analyzing a literary code in Ashurbanipal's inscriptions, concluded that the basic structure of these royal inscriptions contains seven elements which are, with some variations, repeated in all of Ashurbanipal's inscriptions mentioning his invasion of Egypt; see F. M. Fales, "A Literary Code in Assyrian Royal Inscriptions: The Case of Ashurbanipal's Egyptian Campaigns," in *Assyrian Royal Inscriptions: New Horizons in Literary, Ideological, and Historical Analysis*, ed. F. M. Fales (Rome: Instituto per l'Oriente, 1981), 198–200.

sections were included or whether some of them were omitted, expanded, or repeated.

Table 26. Literary structure of the Neo-Assyrian royal inscriptions

Literary structure	**Example**	**ARAB references**
Introduction a) *palû*	If the campaigns took place at the beginning of a new *palû*, then the first line mentions the *palû*: "In my ninth *palû* ..." (S II Ann 165)	I:440, 558, 564; II:770
b) campaign	The list of the kingdoms against which the campaign was led: "I marched against the lands of Ellipi, Media, and Karalla." (S II Ann 165–66)	I:558, 564; II:770
He/they-part a) trespasses	Description of the transgressions that compelled the Assyrian king to intervene: "Azuru, the king of Ashdod, plotted in his heart to withhold the tribute and sent (messages) of hostility to the kings around him." (S II Ann 241–43)	I:561, 583, 715, 726, 734; II:12, 501, 770, 773
b) information source	"To me, Sennacherib, they reported these evil deeds." (Senn A1:16)	I:443; II 775
I-part a) gods' mission	The transition to the I-part opens with a reference to the gods, which makes clear that the following campaign should be understood as the king's fulfillment of the gods' mission. There are several ways in which this transitional part was expressed: 1) "Marduk, the great lord, saw the evil works of the (people of) Chaldea, which he hated, and decreed that his (Merodach-baladan's) royal scepter and throne should be taken away (from him). Me, Sargon, the humble king, he singled out from among all the princes and raised my head. That I might turn back the feet of the hostile and evil Chaldean people from the land of Sumer and Akkad, he made mighty my weapons. At the command of the great lord Marduk ..." (S II Ann 260–64); 2) "I raised my hands to Aššur" (S II Ann 102); 3) "with the help of god Adad I mobilized..." (ARAB I:443)	II:12; II:504, 770
b) intervention	The description of the destruction of the enemies. If the campaigns had several stages, the description was divided in several subsections. (S II Ann 264–321)	I:440, 442, 443, 583, 724; II:20
Aftermaths	The list of booty, a description of the punishment of the leaders, and accounts of deportations and the reorganization of the region, etc. (S II Ann 174–94)	I:741; II:13, 25, 774

In the he/they-parts, Assyrian scribes summarized their understanding of the pre-campaign *status quo* and their assessment of the situations in rebellious regions that compelled Assyria to intervene. There are several reasons to believe that the he/they-parts also contain information reflecting pre-campaign intelligence. First, the three occurrences listed above mention information sources, i.e., some kind of information channel through which the king learned about the rebellion. Second, the case studies of Ellipi, the northern provinces, and Babylonia examined earlier in this study allow us to match the events described in the royal inscriptions with the intelligence reports of the Neo-Assyrian archives (sections 3.1.5; 3.2; 3.3). The result shows that the concise description of the situation in the he/they-parts of the royal archives is only the tip of the iceberg in comparison with how much the Assyrians really knew about the situation in these regions. Third, to achieve its goal, a good portion of propaganda must rely on true information.[525] Propaganda efficiency comes not from inventing data and spreading lies but rather from the "right" selection of data and from the "right" interpretation of information according to propaganda goals. Therefore, it can be assumed that the he/they-parts are not totally or even largely a product of the literary imagination of scribes but present their interpretation of events. Finally, from the logistical point of view it makes sense to presuppose that the Assyrian campaigns were not random invasions but carefully planned military operations each responding to a given

---

[525] Several scholars have demonstrated that the Neo-Assyrian royal inscriptions betray many signs of royal propaganda; see for example M. Liverani, "The Ideology of the Assyrian Empire," in *Power and Propaganda: A Symposium on Ancient Empires*, ed. M. T Larsen (Copenhagen: Akademisk Forlag, 1979), 297–318. Thus, the Neo-Assyrian inscriptions containing royal propaganda had to comply with the common-sense rules of propaganda. If propaganda officers resort to false data, their propaganda can easily be turned into counter-propaganda by internal or external hostile forces. For illustration, US propaganda officers after World War II were instructed "not make promises to persons in occupied territory, to friendly guerillas, to underground movements, or to enemy troops when those promises [were] not backed up by word-for-word quotations from the head of his government or someone of Cabinet rank"; see Linebarger, *Psychological Warfare*, 52. On the other hand, however honest propaganda officers would like to be, historical reality has often voided their promises. The post-World War I analysts of the British propaganda office could only admit: "Germans did overthrow their leaders, chase the Hoehnzollerns into Holland and set up a republic with a blacksmith as President: only to find that the propaganda promises were entirely empty.... Useless for us to argue that our intention had been honorable and that we have implemented the promises implicit in our propaganda.... The German public cannot but have concluded that they had been deceived and that our propaganda had merely been a means of persuading them to end their resistance"; Rogerson, *Propaganda in the Next War*, 40.

rebellion.[526] Planning military campaigns, of course, presupposed a certain amount of intelligence data, such as where and when the rebellion had taken place, who its leader was, what sort of enemy troops the Assyrians were to face and in what kind of terrain. For these reasons, I assume that the he/they-parts of royal inscriptions contain some elements of pre-campaign intelligence that has subsequently been shaped in accord with the literary form of royal propaganda justifying the king's intervention.

If we apply this concept to the he/they-parts of Sennacherib's annals describing his campaign against Palestine (Senn Ann II:61, 68–72, 73–III:1, 18–9, 37–41), knowledge of the following details can be attributed to the Assyrians:

1. Information about the persons who constituted the backbone of the rebellion: Sidka (Senn Ann II:60–61) and Hezekiah and his ethnic identity—a Judahite (III:18-9).
2. Information about the cities in which the rebellion evolved: Jerusalem (III:40), Eltekeh and Timnah (III:6), Ashkelon (II:61) and its satellite cities Beth-Dagon, Joppa, Banaibarka, and Asuru (II:69–70).
3. Information about the Philistine negotiations with Egypt (II:79–80).
4. Information about the whereabouts of the Egyptians (II:80–82).
5. Information about the composition of the Egyptian support troops: bowmen, chariots, horses (II:79–80).
6. Information about the atmosphere in the enemy camp: they were afraid (II:78).
7. Information about the terrain: Sennacherib conducted his campaign along the way of the sea.[527]
8. Information about the ethnic groups participating in the defense of Jerusalem: Arabs (III:39).

---

[526] See for example Mayer, *Politik und Kriegskunst der Assyrer*, 419–82 and P. Dubovský, "Tiglath-pileser III's Campaigns in 734-732 B.C.: Historical Background of Isa 7, 2 Kgs 15-16 and 2 Chr 27-28." *Bib* 87 (2006): 153-70.

[527] The campaign was divided into three parts: Phoenicia, Philistia, and Judah; see F. J. Gonçalves, *L'Expédition de Sennachérib en Palestine dans la littérature Hébraïque Ancienne* (Paris: Libraire Lecoffre, 1986), 109–10. Sennacherib's troops followed the most accessible road from the north, and thus it can be assumed that the organizers of these campaigns were aware that the terrain along the coast was more suitable for the rapid movement of troops than an advance through the Judean hills.

9. Information about the desertion of the Arab mercenaries brought in to defend the city (III:41).

Except for the account of the composition of the Egyptian troops (no. 5), which might reflect the post-war determination of booty, there is no reason to doubt that the rest of the points reflect pre-campaign intelligence. Comparing the intelligence data attributed to the Assyrians by the royal inscriptions with those attributed to the Assyrians by the biblical writers, it is possible to conclude that both pictures agree in points 1–7. The differences are: the biblical writers do not attribute to the Assyrians knowledge of the groups participating on the defense of Jerusalem; the negotiations with Egypt that, according to the royal inscriptions, were conducted by the Philistines were according to the Bible conducted by the Judahites (2 Kgs 18:19–25); the Bible does not mention the leading role of Ashkelon, the revolt in Ekron, or the incarceration of Padi, all of which are in the inscriptions; and finally, the royal inscriptions do not mention Hezekiah's religious reform, which is so prominent in the biblical accounts (2 Kgs 18:22).

5.2.2 Context of the Neo-Assyrian archives

Now we can place the data recovered from the Neo-Assyrian royal inscriptions and the biblical sources regarding the intelligence aspects of Sennacherib's invasion within the larger context of the Neo-Assyrian intelligence services as reconstructed mainly from the Neo-Assyrian letters. The following table organizes this comparison according to intelligence topics (Table 27).

Table 27. Comparison of Neo-Assyrian intelligence interests as attested in the literary sources

Topics	**Intelligence attributed to the Assyrians during Sennacherib's third campaign by**		**Neo-Assyrian intelligence services reconstructed from the case studies**
	Biblical sources	**Sennacherib's annals**	
Ethnographic information about vassal countries	Rab-shaqeh not only knew that the Jerusalemites spoke Hebrew but also was able to speak it himself (2.1.2.7).	Assyrians distinguished ethnic minorities such as Judahites and Arabs	The systematic collection and storing of reports allowed Assyrians to build up "ethnographic encyclopedias" of their subordinates (3.4.2). The reports contained data about the ethnic composition of the troops in fortresses (5.1.2.3) and determined the choice of

		(no. 1, 8).	propaganda agents according to the ethnicity of the targeted group (4.2.2.1).
Terrain reconnaissance data	Assyrian knowledge of terrain, in particular of routes and fortresses, is implied (2.2.1).	The Assyrian knowledge of terrain, in particular, routes (the way of the sea) and Phoenician, Philistine, and Judahite fortresses and fortified cities is implied (no. 7).	One of the priorities of the Neo-Assyrian intelligence network was gathering intelligence on terrain (3.2.4). The Assyrians collected hydrological data; information about mountain passes, roads, bridges, and fords; and intelligence on natural resources and fertility of the soil, as well as information on epidemics and earthquakes (3.1.1; 3.1.5.3).
Morale	There was a strong attempt to undermine the morale of the Jerusalemites, but there is no direct statement that the Assyrians knew about the morale within Jerusalem (2.1.2.2).	Information about the atmosphere within enemy camp (no. 6 and 9).	Information on the morale within enemy camps was carefully gathered and used for planning campaigns and for psychological warfare (3.5.2.5).
Military capabilities of vassals	Implied from the wager (number of horses and horsemen; 2.1.2.4).	Account of the composition of support troops; however, it could be post-campaign information (no. 5).	There is only one report mentioning the number and type of animals mustered for military purposes (V 88). The frequent references to the composition of the enemy troops in the royal annals may be the result of post-campaign booty reviews.
Shifting loyalty of vassals	Signs of declining loyalty (2.2.2).	Description of the act of rebellion of Sidka and Hezekiah (no. 1).	The loyalty of the vassals was carefully monitored by means of the indicators set up in the treaties (3.1.2; 3.1.3; 3.1.4; 3.2; 3.4).
Religious affairs	<u>Details on Hezekiah's reform</u>: centralization of the cult, abolishment of the high places, the role of the altar in Jerusalem; <u>Religious vocabulary and theological themes:</u>	No int. on religious affairs is mentioned or can be inferred.	Besides information on sacrifices (3.1.4.1; 3.1.5.2.2; 3.5.1.1), the royal court was informed about other cultic activities such as excursions of the gods from their temples (XIII 6; 58; 147; 152; 153; 189) and sacred marriage rituals (XIII 56; 70; 78). Moreover, the Assyrians monitored the clergy, in particular, when participating in or supporting the anti-Assyrian resistance (XIII 138;

	Exodus, Promised Land, curses and blessings, prophetic warnings against alliance with Egypt and relying on human forces, prediction of punishment for their sins (2.1.2.4).		143; XVI 21; 63). Thus, they learned about blasphemy against Ištar (XVI 63), changes in old rituals (XIII 135), illegal training in extispicy and divination (XVI 21), and received word-for-word reports of anti-Assyrian prophecies (XIII 37; 144).
Contacts of vassals with major powers	Negotiation with Egypt (2.2.2; 2.1.2.2; 2.1.2.4).	Negotiation with Egypt (no. 3).	The Assyrians carefully monitored vassals' international relationships (3.1.2, 3.1.3, 3.1.4, 3.1.5, 3.2.5, 3.3.2.2).
Information about the major powers	Egypt: symbol, political organization, whereabouts of the Pharaoh and his army, its military strengths, and its reliability (2.2.1, 2.2.2, 2.1.2.4).	Egypt: whereabouts of their troops and military forces (no. 4, 5).	Numerous details about events in Elam, Urartu, Phrygia (3.5); whereabouts of the kings and their troops (3.2.3, 3.3.2.1, and 3.5.1.3).

In this table I have compared eight intelligence topics of interest to the Neo-Assyrian intelligence services. Five intelligence topics, which according to the biblical sources the Assyrians monitored, match the main intelligence topics of interest to the Assyrians as reconstructed from the Neo-Assyrian archives. Three topics, which can only be inferred from the biblical sources (terrain reconnaissance, morale, and military capabilities), also find a match in the Neo-Assyrian archives. On the basis of this comparison, I conclude that the interests of Neo-Assyrian military and political intelligence as reconstructed from 2 Kgs 18–20 match the interests of Neo-Assyrian intelligence as reconstructed from the Neo-Assyrian documents.

5.3 Intelligence as an activity

According to both biblical and Assyrian sources, Neo-Assyrian intelligence services were also actively involved in furthering royal interests. Assyrian sources mention two types of intelligence: covert action and psychological warfare. Analysis of the biblical account of

Sennacherib's invasion also demonstrates that the Assyrians used PsW to compell the Jerusalemites to surrender.

5.3.1 Covert action

While there is no indication of any covert action in chapters 2 Kgs 18–20, the I-part of Sennacherib's annals describes the means by which the Assyrians captured Judahite cities:

> Forty-six of his (Hezekiah's) strong, walled cities, as well as the small cities in their neighborhood, which were without number—by leveling with battering-rams and by bringing up siege-engines, by attacking and storming on foot, by mines, tunnels and breaches I besieged and took. (Senn Ann III:19–23)

Analysis of the conquest of the city of Darati (section 3.3.2.4.2) showed that for digging the tunnels (*niksu*) it was necessary to establish contacts with the inhabitants of the city and that the whole action had to be carried out in complete secrecy. Thus, it is possible to assume that if some of the Judahite cities were conquered by digging tunnels, the Assyrians must have been helped by the local people. This way of conquering the city can be rightly considered a covert action.

5.3.2 Psychological warfare

To contextualize the presentation of Neo-Assyrian PsW in the biblical sources, it is necessary to examine both the immediate context of Sennacherib's annals and the larger context of the Neo-Assyrian archives. According to the royal inscriptions, Sennacherib's campaign in 701 B.C.E. had three parts: Phoenician, Philistine, and Judean.[528] The vocabulary of PsW can be traced in all three phases. Two expressions in Sennacherib's annals describing the Phoenician phase (Senn Ann II:37–59) reveal that the Assyrians employed PsW to help the Phoenicians to make the "right" choice:

> *pul-hi me-lam-me be-lu-ti-ia is-hu-pu-šú-ma*, the terrifying splendor of my sovereignty overcame him (Senn Ann II:38–39)

[528] Ibid.

ra-šub-bat ^{w}*kakki* ^{d}*Aššur bêli-ia is-hu-pu-šu-nu-ti-ma,* the terrors of the weapon of Assur, my lord, overcame them (Senn Ann II:45–46)

The former (Senn Ann II:38–39) is employed in connection with Lule, the rebellious king of Sidon, who was overcome by fear of the approaching Assyrian troops and escaped "into the midst of the sea where he died" (Senn Ann II:40). The latter (Senn Ann II:45–46) describes the effect of the Assyrian military and psychological operations on the rest of the vassals after the conquest of Sidon: they became terrified and "bowed in submission at my (Sennacherib's) feet" (Senn Ann II:46). Similar expressions are often used in the royal inscriptions to describe the fear that the Assyrians instilled into their enemies during military campaigns, referring in particular to the violent means employed by the Assyrian military after diplomatic measures had failed.[529]

---

[529] Expressions used to describe the fear instilled by the Assyrians:
na-mur-rat [*Aššur bēliya ishupūšuma...*], "the terrifying radiance of Aššur overwhelmed them" (TP III Ann 16:12; see also TP III Ann 8:4; RR:38; Sum 9:r.24).
na-mur-rat ^{giš}*kakkē*^{meš}*-ia ip-làh-ma*, "he became frightened of my terrible weapons" (TP III Sum 1:22).
^{giš}*kakkē*^{meš}*-ia dannūti*^{meš} *taš-hu-ut-ma,* "she became startled by my mighty weapons" (TP III Sum 4:25').
^{giš}*kakkē*^{meš}*-ia dannūti*^{meš} *ip-làh-ma,* "he feared my powerful weapons" (TP III Sum 8:14').
ra-šub-bat ^{w}*kakki* ^{d}*Aššur bêli-ia is-hu-pu-šu-nu-ti-ma,* "the terrors of the weapon of Assur, my lord, overpowered them" (Senn Ann II:45–46).
pul-hi me-lam-me ša Aš-šur bēli-ia is-hu-pu-šú-ma, "he was overwhelmed by the terrifying radiance of Ashur" (TP III Sum 7:27).
pul-hi me-lam-me be-lu-ti-ia is-hu-pu-šú-ma, "the terrifying splendor of my sovereignty overcame him"(Senn Ann II:38–39; see also III:38).
[*pu*]*-luh-ti me-*[*lam-me-ia is-hup*]*-šú-ma*, "my terrifying splendor overcame him" (Senn F1:18).
ta-nit-ti be-lu-ti-ia, "(they heard about) the fame of my majesty" (TP III Sum 7:r.4'; 13:12').
har-ba-šu tahâzi-ia eli-šu im-qut-ma, "the terror of my battle fell upon him" (Senn Ann III:54).
har-ba-šu tahâzi-ia ki-ma li-e zu-mur-šu-un is-hu-up, "the terror of my battle overturned them like a bull" (Senn Ann VI:26–27).
har-ba-šu tahâzi-ia dan-ni i-hup-šu-nu-ti-ma, "the dread of my terrible onslaught overcame them" (Senn H3:38–39).
har-ba-šu tahâzi-ia i-hup-šu-nu-ti, "the chilling terror of my battle overcame them" (Senn H4:53).
la-pa-an tahâzi-ia ip-la-hu, "he became afraid at my onslaught" (Senn Ann VI:17).

Since the conquest of Sidon and the surrender of several vassals did not compel Ashkelon, Ekron, and Jerusalem to follow their example, Sennacherib's troops headed southwards against Philistia (Philistine phase). They conquered Ashkelon and substituted Šarru-lu-dari for Sidka. The "heart of the Ekronites" became afraid (Senn Ann II:78), but instead of surrendering, they sent to Egypt for help. After the defeat of the Egyptian troops at Eltekeh, the Assyrians conquered Ekron. The rebels were severely punished and the bodies of the Ekronite leaders were publicly exposed on stakes (Senn Ann III:10). Using the terminology of PsW as proposed in 4.2.2, we may conclude that the Assyrians resorted to extreme measures agains the Philistine cities.

The Judean phase described in Sennacherib's annals can be divided into two parts: Senn Ann III:18–36 and III:37–49. The description starts with a list of the severe measures, such as the destruction of cities and the siege of Jerusalem, employed by Sennacherib to compel the recalcitrant Hezekiah to surrender. These measures produced positive results: first, overcome by fear,[530] Hezekiah's mercenaries (Arab troops brought to Jerusalem to fight against the Assyrians) deserted him; then, Hezekiah and his people surrendered and paid tribute to Assyria (Senn Ann III:38–49).[531]

The annals presented Sennacherib's PsW during his campaign against Phoenicia and Palestine as quite successful. Most of the members of the anti-Assyrian coalition surrendered as soon as the Assyrian army entered the region. Assyrian PsW failed only in the cases of Ashkelon, Ekron, and Jerusalem. The description of Sennacherib's PsW is limited to the Psyops employed during the campaign itself; no pre-war negotiations are mentioned. In the case of Hezekiah, the annals present only the very last

---

na-mur-ra-tum at-bu-uk, "I poured out terror" (Senn Ann III:71).
hat-tu pu-luh-tu eli [l]*Elamti*[ki] *ka-li-šu-un it-ta-bi-ik-ma*, "fear and terror were poured over all of Elam" (Senn H3:41).
ri-gim [w]*kakkê*[pl]*-ia dan-nu-ti* [pl] *e-dúr-ma*, "he became afraid at the tumult of my mighty arms" (Senn F1:35).
ti-ib ta-ha-zi-ia e-du-ru-ma, "he feared the onset of my battle" (Senn F2:26).

[530] "*pul-hi me-lam-me be-lu-ti-ia is-hu-pu-šú-ma*, "the terrifying splendor of my sovereignty overcame him (Hezekiah)" (Senn Ann III:38).

[531] According to modern PsW studies, enemy propaganda initially affects the conventional soldiers, conscripts, or hired soldiers who, thanks to well-aimed propaganda, soon consider the war as someone else's problem and abandon the battlefield; see M. Lloyd, *The Art of Military Deception* (London: L. Cooper, 1997), 138–39.

phase of Sennacherib's PsW, when Hezekiah's recalcitrance forced Sennacherib to employ the most extreme measures.

If we analyze the PsW during all three phases of the campaign, the following techniques emerge:

1. Military support of the Assyrian allies: the loyal kings, such as Padi, were saved and protected by the Assyrian army (Senn Ann III:14–15).
2. Reward of the collaborators: the vassals who surrendered quickly were reappointed on their thrones (Senn Ann II:50–58); the leaders who were not directly responsible for the rebellion were graciously forgiven (Senn Ann III:12–14); and some of the faithful vassals were even rewarded by the annexation to their kingdoms of new territories taken from the rebels (Hezekiah's western territories were given to the kings of Ashdod, Gaza, and Ekron; Senn Ann III:31–35).
3. Extreme measures: destruction of cities, deportation of rebels and their families, and siege.
4. Spreading news about Assyrian punishments and victories.

To place the Neo-Assyrian PsW reconstructed on the basis of the biblical narratives and Sennacherib's annals into the larger context of Neo-Assyrian PsW as it can be reconstructed from the Neo-Assyrian archives, I will investigate the types, agents, targets, techniques, and effects of the Neo-Assyrian PsW (Tables 28–37).

Table 28. Spreading news about the extreme measures

BIBLICAL SOURCES	SENN.'S ANN.	LARGER CONTEXT
Extreme measures: The destructions of all fortified cities of Judah (18:13); Transmission of the news about destruction: No explicit notice but it can be inferred from the sequence of verses 18:13 and 18:14 (literary ellipsis).	II:18-III:49 Extreme measures: destruction of 46 cities, siege of Jerusalem; Transmission: the term "heard" is not mentioned.	Spreading the news about the defeat of enemies, exemplary punishments, deportations, and destructions was one of the most efficient methods of Neo-Assyrian PsW; see 4.2.2.2 and TP III Sum 7:r.4'; 13:12'; Senn F2:26.

EVALUATION
According to both the biblical text and Sennacherib's annals, the Assyrians employed extreme measures during the Judean phase. From the sequence of 2 Kgs 18:13–14, it is clear that king Hezekiah had to have heard about the destruction of his fortified cities, which compelled him to pay tribute (source A). Thus, source A witnesses the most efficient means of Neo-Assyrian PsW—spreading news about Assyrian victories.

Table 29. Negotiations

BIBLICAL SOURCES	LARGER CONTEXT
18:17–25: • Targets: Judahite representatives. • Place: outside Jerusalem. • Procedure: communication of the king's message followed by a discussion. • The army was in Hezekiah's immediate environs when the negotiations took place.	Tiglath-pileser III and Sargon II: • Targets: high-ranking Babylonian representatives. • Place: outside Babylon. • Procedure: discussion between both parties (4.1.2.1). • Negotiations before and during the campaign (if done before the campaign, then less efficient; see 4.2.2.4).
EVALUATION 2 Kgs 18:17–25 reflects the Assyrian style of negotiations with representatives of the city.[532] The letters of Tiglath-pileser III and Sargon II demonstrate that such negotiations were a common way of influencing local people. Negotiations could take place before the campaign, with the aim of the peaceful resolution of the problems; or during the campaign, with the aim of avoiding the troubles connected with military conquest. The letters illustrate that whereas the negotiations often failed when the Assyrian army was far away, they became much more successful when Assyrian troops were operating in the enemy's backyard. Consequently, the first speech of Rab-shaqeh can be considered in the context of these diplomatic negotiations. It took place during the campaign. Some further similarities between the biblical texts and the Nimrud letters (4.1.2) can be pointed out: both the Jerusalem and Babylon negotiations took place outside the city, the high officials of the cities participated in both negotiations, and in both cases the Assyrians tried to bolster their arguments and the local representatives presented their counterarguments. Sennacherib's annals do not mention any negotiations.	

Table 30. Letters

BIBLICAL SOURCES	LARGER CONTEXT
19:9b–13: • The letter was addressed to the king. • The letter was accompanied by messengers.	Sending letters to local kings accompanied by a royal messenger was a normal practice in Neo-Assyrian diplomacy (XVII 3).
EVALUATION Another way of influencing the local leaders was to send them letters, often	

[532] Gallagher, "Assyrian Deportation Propaganda."

accompanied by a royal messenger who was frequently interrogated and thus further explained the interests of the sender,[533] and who later reported the answer to the Assyrian king. Seen in this context, 2 Kgs 19:9b–13 reflects a common style of Neo-Assyrian diplomatic pressure—attempting to manipulate Hezekiah by means of written media.

Table 31. Speeches

BIBLICAL SOURCES	LARGER CONTEXT
18:28-35: • The speech was delivered at the city wall. • It was delivered by a top Assyrian official, Rab-shaqeh, • It was addressed to the people under siege.	XV 136 (see 4.2.2.2): • Delivered at the foundation of the city wall. • Delivered by one of the military commanders. • Addressed to a general public.
EVALUATION Rab-shaqeh's speech in 2 Kgs 18:28–35 has generated an ongoing discussion among scholars about whether such a speech would have been delivered or was only a literary fiction. The first objection raised was the physical possibility of delivering a speech under the city walls so that it could be understood by the people sitting on the walls. Acoustic calculations by M. Kumorovitz, the former director of the Department of Acoustics of the Slovak Academy of Science, have demonstrated that under the worst acoustic conditions a well-trained speaker can be understood at a distance of 50 m (49 dB over the hearing threshold).[534] Moreover, the experience of missionaries in Africa confirms that preachers on special occasions could address crowds of up to 2,000 people without any amplifying device and still be understood.[535] The second objection raised regards the lack of Near Eastern documents corroborating such a practice. There are, however, two pieces of evidence that attest to the existence of this practice in the ancient Near East: first, a Neo-Assyrian relief from Nineveh depicts an official reading a scroll under the city walls;[536] and second, letter XV 136 even reports a part of such a speech (4.2.2.2). In conclusion, these arguments indicate that a speech delivered under the city walls was both physically possible and used by the Assyrians to compel besieged citizens to surrender.	

[533] S. A. Meier, *The Messenger in the Ancient Semitic World* (Atlanta, Ga.: Scholars Press, 1988), 163–79.

[534] The personal communication of M. Kumorovitz in February 2003.

[535] The personal testimony of Š. Hirjak, a missionary in Zambia since 1950, as communicated to me in December 2003.

[536] *Monument de Ninive*, pl. 145. This relief was brought to modern scholarly attention by Y. Yadin, *The Art of Warfare in Biblical Lands in the Light of Archaeological Study*, vol. 1 (New York: McGraw-Hill, 1963), 320 ; and H. Tadmor, "On the role of Aramaic in the Assyrian Empire," in *Near Eastern Studies dedicated H. I. H. Prince Takahito Mikasa on the Occasion of his Seventy-fifth Birthday*, eds. M. Mori, H. Ogawa, and M. Yoshikawa (Wiesbaden: Otto Harrassowitz, 1991), 419–26.

Table 32. Promises and incentives

BIBLICAL SOURCES	SENN.'S ANNALS	LARGER CONTEXT
18:28-35: • Food and peaceful life in a new promised land (2.1.2.2). • Material advantages (2.1.2.6). • No punishment if they surrender (2.1.2.6).	Incentives and promises can be inferred from military support of the Assyrian allies (no. 1) and the reward of the collaborators (no. 2).	Both Tiglath-pileser III's and Sargon II's PsW successfully used promises and incentives to recruit new allies and to disrupt enemy coalitions (4.1.2.1 and 4.2.1.5). The policy of the promises was confirmed by military support of the allies and rewards for their collaborators (4.2.1.4).
EVALUATION Rab-shaqeh's promises as presented in the biblical narrative fit the general picture of Neo-Assyrian PsW. Letter V 210 uses language similar to that of the Promised Land.[537] The Assyrians alternated the "bad guy" policy (threats) with the "good guy" policy (promises, incentive, and support). This alternation can also be traced in the biblical story (bad guy: 18:19–25.27; good guy: 18:30–32). In both cases, promises and incentives are an integral part of the "speaking kindly" technique (4.2.1.6).[538]		

Table 33. Repetition

BIBLICAL SOURCES	LARGER CONTEXT
• The Assyrians employed several types of propaganda agents in order to compel the Jerusalemites to surrender. • The Assyrians repeated the same argument in two different Psyops (the list of the cities destroyed by the Assyrians; sources B^1 and B^2).	• In order to compel the Aramean tribes to participate on the campaign against Mukin-zeri, the Assyrians sent several propaganda officials who repeated the same messages with slight changes (ND 2717). • The same threat (to write a letter to Tiglath-pileser III about the Babylonian unwillingness to collaborate) was repeated twice in the same letter ND 2632:27–28,38).
EVALUATION The repetition of the same argument and the employment of different types of propaganda agents seem to have been standard strategies of Assyrian PsW. Thus, the repetition of the same argument with slight changes attributed to the Assyrians (list of the destroyed cities) fits the patterns of Neo-Assyrian PsW against the Babylonians and Aramean tribes during Tiglath-pileser III's reign.	

Table 34. Undermining the authority of the leaders

BIBLICAL SOURCES	SENN.'S ANNALS	LARGER CONT.
18-19: Rab-shaqeh accused Hezekiah • for failing in his	The post-campaign description presented the Philistines as poor strategists who relied on an	The case studies showed that religious validation of the

[537] Gallagher, "Assyrian Deportation Propaganda."
[538] Gallagher, *Sennacherib's Campaign*, 171.

domestic and international policy (2.1.2.3 and 2.1.2.5) and • for religious failure (acting against the will of God).	Egyptian army that was quickly defeated (in contrast to Senn. who relied on Aššur), and as obstinate rebels. The annals also present Hezekiah as a recalcitrant rebel who arrested faithful Padi.	campaign, including diminishing the enemy by attributing to them all kinds of negative epithets, was part of Assyrian propaganda (4.1.2.1, 4.2.2.2).
EVALUATION Several features are common to the biblical and Assyrian sources: Assyrian propaganda was well disposed towards people ready to collaborate; Sennacherib is presented as truly interested in the well-being of the people in distress; and the people were not responsibly for the disastrous situation; rather, the fault belonged to their leaders.[539] In conclusion, the technique of "undermining the authority of the leaders" as reconstructed from the biblical texts was an integral part of Neo-Assyrian PsW.		

Table 35. Targets of Neo-Assyrian PsW

BIBLICAL SOURCES	SENNACHERIB'S ANNALS	LARGER CONTEXT
18-19: • King Hezekiah. • The Judahite representatives. • Jerusalemites on the city walls.	The annals present • A list of local kings who, overcome by fear, submitted to Assyria. The following groups might also have been targeted by Neo-Assyrian Psyops: • *A group of local leaders under the jurisdiction of Ashkelon who did not submit quickly enough to be forgiven;* • *Local potentates in Ekron who were found not guilty;* • *An ethnic group—Arabs—who deserted Hezekiah.*	Assyrians covered a wide range of targets (4.2.2.2; 4.2.2.3): • Vassal kings, who received letters and special envoys; • Local representatives, dealt with by the Assyrian representatives; • High- and middle-ranking military officials; • Ethnic minorities; • The larger public.
EVALUATION Three biblical targets are included among the multiple targets of Assyrian propaganda.		

Table 36. Propaganda agents

BIBLICAL SOURCES	LARGER CONTEXT
Types (2.1.2.5, 2.1.2.7): • Messengers delivering letters; • High-ranking officials. Profiles (2.1.2.4, 2.1.2.7):	Types (4.2.2.1): • Messengers delivering letters; • Local officials; • Royal envoys;

539 Ibid., 171–87.

• Fluent in local dialects; • Masters of rhetoric; • Well-informed about their targets; • Invested with executive and military authority.	• Special agents. Profiles of the special agents (4.2.2.1): • Belonging to the same ethnic group as the target; • Experienced in propaganda; • Possessed of strong Assyrian connections.
EVALUATION Both the types and profiles of propaganda agents described in the Bible are among the types and profiles typical of Neo-Assyrian propaganda agents.	

Table 37. Effects of Neo-Assyrian PsW

BIBLICAL SOURCES	SENN.'S ANNALS	LARGER CONTEXT
Submission (18:13–16): • Account of the destruction of the fortified cities of Judah. • Hezekiah recognized his sin and asked the Assyrian king for terms of peace. • The Assyrian king imposed upon him a tribute of 300 shekels of silver and 30 shekels of gold. • Hezekiah paid. Persistence in resistance (18:16–19:37): • Hezekiah relied on his God and did not surrender.	Phoenician phase: • Lule escaped. • List of the kings who paid tribute and kissed Sennacherib's feet. Philistine phase: • Sidka, who continued in his resistance, was deported; his cities were destroyed. • Ekronites called upon Egypt to come to their aid. • After the defeat of the Egyptian troops Ekronite rebels were executed. Judean phase: • Hezekiah persisted in his resistance. • Siege of Jerusalem. • Hezekiah sent to Nineveh to pay tribute.	Submission: • Rebels heard about/saw the destruction caused by the advancing Assyrian army (ARAB II:504, 505, 524, 543). • Recognition of sin (ARAB II:593). • Assyrian conditions of peace (ARAB II:31). • After the tribute was paid, the Assyrians did not destroy the cities and often reappointed the repentant kings. Flight: • Frightened vassals escaped and were either pursued and captured or lived in exile (ARAB II:20, 66, 6234, 241). Persistence in resistance: • Relying on their own forces (ARAB II:31, 502). • Relying on their allies and asking them for help (ARAB II:6). • Relying on their gods.
EVALUATION According to the reconstruction of Neo-Assyrian PsW (4.2.2), Neo-Assyrian psychological pressure caused by the presence of the Neo-Assyrian Assyrian troops, their successful advance, and the impossibility of resisting the Assyrian war machine generated three types of attitudes among the frightened rebels: 1) they surrendered; 2) they left the city and escaped; or 3) they continued in their resistance. The biblical narrative reflects the effects of Neo-Assyrian PsW. However, the biblical redactors do not present the normal Assyrian pattern of submission (recognition of sin → imposed		

payment → end of military and psychological pressure). After Hezekiah paid tribute (source A), the Assyrians started a new round of PsW, as described in account B.

5.4 Implications

In the previous sections I have demonstrated that the types of information that the Assyrians were interested in according to the biblical sources correspond to the types of information the Assyrians gathered on a regular basis. The same is also true of Neo-Assyrian PsW. Furthermore, the Assyrians had at their disposal a sufficient network by means of which this information was gathered and intelligence activities performed. One can rightly ask, what are the implications of these investigations for the historicity and meaning of 2 Kgs 18–19?

5.4.1 Historicity

As I mentioned in the introduction, there are several reasons to doubt the historicity of 2 Kgs 18–19. Two of those reasons are important for the purposes of this study.[540] First, chapters 2 Kgs 18–19 contain at least three sources (A, B^1, and B^2). Because these sources cannot be dated to the same period—A and B^1 can be dated to the pre-exilic period, whereas B^2 may be dated to the post-exilic period—chapters 2 Kgs 18–19 reflect the ideas of biblical redactors writing some one hundred years after Sennacherib's invasion. Second, for most scholars the similarity between 2 Kgs 18–19 and other biblical passages is a clear sign that 2 Kgs 18–19 cannot be taken at face value, but rather that these passages place a biblical apology in the mouth of the Assyrian representatives.

The ongoing discussion about the historicity of 2 Kgs 18–19 and its parallel in Is 36–39 has been revived once again in the most recent publications by W. R. Gallagher, who introduced an original argument.[541] Since the Assyrians had a highly developed espionage network, close similarities between 2 Kgs 18–19 and other parts of the Bible demonstrate

[540] For bibliographical references, see chapter 1.

[541] Gallagher, "Assyrian Deportation Propaganda"; idem, *Sennacherib's Campaign*.

the quality of the intelligence that Neo-Assyrian agents could procure. Scholars have both praised and criticized R. W. Gallagher's proposal.[542]

The conclusions drawn in sections 5.1, 5.2, and 5.3 cast new light on this problem. In those sections, I tried to demonstrate that Neo-Assyrian intelligence as described in the biblical texts corresponds to the Neo-Assyrian intelligence services and operations reconstructed on the basis of Sennacherib's annals and the Neo-Assyrian archives. Thus, these conclusions prove the value of W. R. Gallagher's argument. However, these similarities can be explained in two ways.

First, because Neo-Assyrian intelligence as reconstructed on the basis of both biblical and Neo-Assyrian sources is alike, it is possible to conclude that the biblical redactors, even those responsible for the redaction of sources B^1 and B^2, were still aware of how the Neo-Assyrian intelligence services operated and used this knowledge while writing and redacting 2 Kgs 18–19. Thus, 2 Kgs 18–19 still reflects Neo-Assyrian intelligence.

Second, the similarities in Neo-Assyrian intelligence as it can be reconstructed from the biblical and Neo-Assyrian sources do not mean that the biblical sources reflect the historical reality exclusive to the Neo-Assyrian empire. Rather, the similarities can be explained by the fact that Neo-Assyrian intelligence as reconstructed from both sources represents standard modes of intelligence gathering that were in use over a long period of time. Thus, the biblical redactors, while writing and redacting 2 Kgs 18–19, drew on their knowledge of intelligence operations as practiced by the imperial powers of the first millennium B.C.E. Consequently, the features of the intelligence services as reconstructed from both biblical and Neo-Assyrian sources are not exclusive to the Neo-Assyrian intelligence services, but are features shared by the Neo-Assyrian, Babylonian, Persian, and Greek intelligence services.

To prove that the features of the intelligence services common to both biblical and Neo-Assyrian sources are the exclusive characteristics of the Neo-Assyrian period, we would need the intelligence archives, at least, of Babylonian and Persian kings. Such archives would allow us to compare

[542] For positive reviews of W. R. Gallagher's work, see J. J. M. Roberts, *JBL* 120 (2001): 539–41 ; K. A. Kitchen, *JSS* 47 (2002): 133–36 and M. Köckert, *ZAW* 115 (2003): 304–5; for the critique, see Grabbe, *Updating the Messages*, 34.

which features of intelligence were commonly shared by the imperial powers of the first millennium and which were exclusive to the Neo-Assyrian period. Unfortunately, such documents have not been excavated.

Because it is impossible to conduct such a comparative study, the conclusions drawn in sections 5.1, 5.2, and 5.3 will be tested from two other angles. First, I will consider the results of linguistic, historical, and archaeological research on 2 Kgs 18–19. Second, I will consider the possibility that redactional activity has distorted an originally accurate picture of Neo-Assyrian PsW.

Three independent lines of research have addressed the historicity of 2 Kgs 18–19: linguistic, historical, and archaeological. C. Cohen reviewed the vocabulary of these passages in light of the Neo-Assyrian texts and demonstrated that 2 Kgs 18–19 contains a number of Neo-Assyrian elements such as titles, expressions, and specific vocabulary.[543] Second, N. Na'aman and S. Holloway argued from the archaeological data that while sources A and B^1 were written in the pre-exilic period, source B^2 is a duplicate of B^1 and was written after the exile.[544] Third, analyzing the passages from the historico-critical point of view, E. Vogt pointed to several elements within the passages whose historicity can be confirmed from other sources, such as the siege of Lachish, the sending of Assyrian troops to Jerusalem, the use of Aramaic as a lingua franca, the role of the scribes in Judahite administration, the deportation policy of Assyria, and the exchange of letters.[545] To these results can be added the following: the features of the intelligence services that the biblical redactors attributed to the Neo-Assyrian intelligence services correspond quite accurately to the features of the Neo-Assyrian intelligence services as they can be reconstructed from the Neo-Assyrian sources. If we view all four arguments together, it is possible to conclude that these passages still reflect the Neo-Assyrian world.

The biblical assertion that a new round of PsW (negotiations, letters, and speeches) followed Hezekiah's submission to Assyria contradicts the traditional way the Assyrians waged their PsW. The Neo-Assyrian documents contain no example of the Assyrians continuing their

---

543 Cohen, "Neo-Assyrian Elements."

544 Holloway, "Harran"; and Na'aman, "Updating the Messages."

545 E. Vogt, *Der Aufstand Hiskias und die Belagerung Jerusalems 701 v. Chr.* (Rome: Biblical Institute Press, 1986), 39–48.

propaganda after they had already achieved their goal (Table 37). This fact must be assessed in light of what source criticism and literary analysis reveal about 2 Kgs 18–19. A number of scholars demonstrated that the primary goal of 2 Kgs 18–19 was to convey a theological interpretation of the history of Judah and Israel, and that these chapters were composed according to the pattern of other biblical passages.[546] Moreover, after comparing the Deuteronomistic orations, including 2 Kgs 18–19, M. Weinfeld came to the conclusion that these orations were literary compositions used by the biblical redactors to convey their own ideas. Similarly, the Greek historians, such as Thucydides and Herodotus, habitually put into the mouths of national heroes speeches that conformed with their own ideas.[547] In light of these literary considerations, it is not suprising that the final version of the Masoretic text of 2 Kgs 18–19 combines sources A and B to create an account that does not reflect the typical Neo-Assyrian way of waging PsW. Thus, the final version of 2 Kgs 18–19 should not be read as a word-for-word re-creation of Assyrian propaganda techniques; rather, the Masoretic text telescopes several PsW techniques and media into one account, and in a chronological order that does not correspond to the typical sequence of Neo-Assyrian Psyops.

Thus, it can be concluded that 2 Kgs 18–19 reflects many features typical of the intelligence services of the first millennium B.C.E. Insofar as several of these features were originated in the Neo-Assyrian Empire, 2 Kgs 18–19 reflects the standard operating methods of the Neo-Assyrian intelligence services.

5.4.2 Meaning

If the main goal of these biblical passages was not to present a factual account of a sequence of historical events, then the next question arises: What is the meaning of these passages? Several scholars have already investigated the significance of the controversy between Hezekiah

---

[546] L. Camp, *Hiskija und Hiskijabild: Analyse und Interpretation von 2 Kön 18-20* (Altenberge: Telos Verlag, 1990), C. Hardmeier, *Prophetie im Streit vor dem Untergang Judas: Erzählkommunikative Studien zur Enstehungssituation der Jesaja- und Jeremiaerzählungen in II Reg 18–20 und Jer 37–40* (Berlin and New York: de Gruyter, 1990), Smelik, *Converting the Past: Studies in Ancient Israelite and Moabite Historiography*, idem, "Distortion", and Ben-Zvi, "Who Wrote the Speech."

[547] M. Weinfeld, *Deuteronomy and the Deuteronomic School* (Oxford: Clarendon Press, 1972), 52.

and Sennacherib from various points of view.[548] In the following section I will investigate the significance of 2 Kgs 18–20 as a representation of the dramatic encounter between Judahites accustomed to managing ad hoc intelligence operations and the qualitatively superior Neo-Assyrian intelligence system. This new way of controlling and monitoring vassals challenged the political, social, and religious traditions of Israel and Judah and generated a whole spectrum of reactions. First, I will describe how the Israelites and Judahites understood and practiced intelligence according to the biblical sources. Then, I will discuss the challenges posed by Neo-Assyrian intelligence operations to Israelite and Judahite religious traditions, and finally I will investigate how the biblical writers reacted to those challenges.

5.4.2.1 Categories of intelligence in the Bible

A careful reading of all biblical texts indicates that the Israelites and Judahites practiced two main kinds of intelligence activities: surveillance and reconnaissance.

Surveillance is defined as the continuous, stationary observation of a single location, such as a critical road junction or rail hub.[549] Surveillance in ancient Israel and Judah was performed by צֹפִים 'observers, members of Israelite administrative and armed forces', who watched and reported from observation posts.[550] Observation posts were situated on elevated places (1 Sam 14:16), on the top of the city tower (2 Kgs 9:17), or on the top of the city gate (2 Sam 18:24). The main task of observers was to keep a watchful eye on the surroundings and report any unusual activity. Thus, during the military campaign against the Philistines, Saul set up observers to watch the Philistine camps. They immediately noticed that "the enemy camp had scattered and they were running about in all directions" (1 Sam 14:16;

---

[548] It is beyond the possibilities of this study to offer an exhaustive bibliography of studies on the meaning of these passages. Here are some original studies: W. Brueggemann, *Interpretation and Obedience: From Faithful Reading to Faithful Living* (Minneapolis: Fortress Press, 1991), 41–99 and Machinist, "The *Rab Šāqēh.*"

[549] J. M. House, *Military Intelligence, 1870–1991: A Research Guide* (Westport, Conn.: Greenwood Press, 1993), 6.

[550] Placing observers on observation posts is not only an ancient practice. In several areas of the modern Middle East, observation and check points are still the most helpful safeguards against enemies, especially in mountainous regions (e.g., eastern Turkey and Israel).

NAB). The observers situated on the top of the gate and city towers kept watch over the surroundings of the city and its access roads. When an observer saw danger, he blew a trumpet (Ez 33:1–6; Jer 6:17) or simply shouted what he saw (2 Sam 18:25). The observers were well-trained people, able to recognize a runner simply from his running style (2 Sam 18:27) and a horseman simply from his riding style (2 Kgs 9:20).[551] In most cases, the observers situated at the observation posts were the only source that warned citizens about an imminent attack. The system of observation posts, which were often in visual contact and could communicate via fire and smoke signals, became an important part of the defensive network designed to protect the king, the city, or the military camps against surprise attacks.[552] Thus, Ezekiel constructed a powerful parable around the concept that the observer is responsible for the lives of the people who have chosen him to protect them (Ez 33:1–9).

Reconnaissance is defined as the process of collecting intelligence by visual or other observation of the area of operations.[553] Thus, whereas surveillance is performed by a stationary observer, reconnaissance implies that a mobile observer is searching through an area. Reconnaissance operations in ancient Israel and Judah were conducted by scouts. Some of the most famous biblical stories describe scouts and their actions: scouts explore Canaan (Nm 13–14; Dt 1:19–46; Josh 14:7–8), the desert (Nm 10:29–36), Jazer (Nm 21:32), Jericho (Josh 2; 6:19–25), Ai (Josh 7–8), Bethel (Judg 1:22–26), Laish (Judg 18), and the Amalekite and Midianite camp (Judg 7:9–18); scouts also report on Saul's whereabouts (1 Sam 26:1–5). In addition, the Bible contains several incidents where people are accused of being scouts or of aiding enemy scouts or spies: Joseph accuses his brothers of spying on Egypt (Gn 42), the Ammonites treat David's ambassadors as spies (2 Sam 10), and Isaiah charges Hezekiah with inadvertently giving information to Merodach-Baladan (2 Kgs 20:12–19).

---

[551] A similar ability to recognize types of enemy airplanes was still required of the military sentinels observing the border between Czechoslovakia and Western Germany in the late eighties of the twentieth c. C.E.

[552] In Judah, this defensive system was formed by a double line of fortresses on its southern and western border and by a circle of fortresses around Jerusalem; for a description and references, see Stern, *Archaeology*, 143–68.

[553] House, *Military Intelligence*, 5.

M. Rose's and W. von Siegfried's investigations[554] of the literary structure of the three most elaborate spy accounts (Canaan, Jericho, and Laish) demonstrated that the common denominator of these accounts is a simple plot: certain men are entrusted with the task of collecting information about a completely or partially unknown territory. Then the men return from the reconnaissance expedition and inform their sender about what they have observed, and the sender makes a decision. This simple story line, transposed into the terminology of intelligence, connects the individual links of the general intelligence cycle. The consumer specifies the kind of intelligence he needs and the producer decides how to obtain it and whom to contact. The collector, the actual field agent, gathers raw intelligence and feeds it back to the producer. The producer turns raw intelligence into finished intelligence and presents it to the consumer who uses it during his decision- making process (Figure 11).[555]

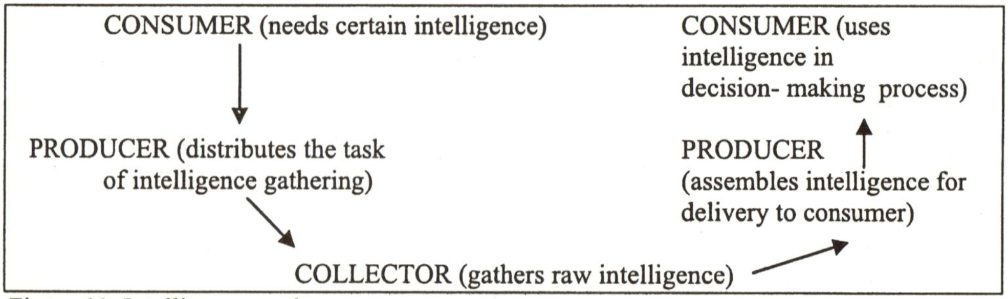

Figure 11. Intelligence cycle

The commissioners of reconnaissance missions (i.e., the consumers) varied: God,[556] Moses (Nm 21:32), Joshua (Josh 2:1; 7:2), David (1 Sam 26:4), and the people of the tribe of Dan (Judg 18:5). The scouts (the collectors of information) also belonged to different social groups. Some scouts are identified on the basis of their tribal origin. Thus, God/Moses sent out tribal leaders to reconnoiter the land of Canaan (Nm 13:2).[557]

[554] M. Rose, *Deuteronomist und Jahwist: Untersuchungen zu den Berührungspunkten Beider Literaturwerke* (Zürich: Theologischer Verlag, 1981), 264–94 and W. von Siegfried, "Die Kundschaftergeschichten im Alten Testament," *ZATW* 76 (1964).

[555] Laqueur, *A World of Secrets: The Uses and Limits of Intelligence*, 19–21.

[556] In the case of the reconnaissance of Canaan, according to the P source the mission was commanded by God (Nm 13:1–2), whereas according to the D source, the mission was requested by the people and approved by Moses (Dt 1:22).

[557] Further identification of the spies in the P source of Nm 13–14: chieftains, important personages (אֲנָשִׁים), the heads of the sons of Israel; the P writer even provides the names of

Similarly the spies reconnoitering Laish[558] and Bethel[559] were members of the tribe of Dan and Joseph, respectively. Another category of scouts consisted of army men and other types of people selected to reconnoiter the city of Jericho,[560] Ai,[561] and to discover Saul's whereabouts (1 Sam 26:4). During the military campaign against the Amalekites and Midianiates, the commander Gideon and his servant Purah (Judg 7:11) went to eavesdrop on the enemy camp. In this category can also be included Hobab, son of Reuel, Moses' father-in-law, who being a Midianite had a thorough knowledge of the desert and was able to guide the Israelites through the desert and indicate to them suitable places for camping (Nm 10:29–31). The third category of scouts was composed of royal envoys who, under various pretenses, investigated enemy country. Thus, the Ammonite princes accused David's servants of spying under the pretense of expressing the king's sympathy for the death of the Ammonite king Nahash (2 Sam 10:1–4), and Isaiah accused Hezekiah of revealing the treasures of his kingdom to the envoys of Merodach-Baladan (2 Kgs 20:12–19). The last category of spies

---

twelve tribal representatives (Nm 13:2–16; 14:36). The D source also employs the term אֲנָשִׁים '(important) personages' (Dt 1:22) and tribal leaders (Dt 1:23). In both sources the collective and individual identifications of the men sent out to investigate the land of Israel indicates that they were not professional scouts but rather tribal representatives. Analyzing Nm 13–14, J. A. Beck concludes that by both collective and individual designations, from the narrative point of view the reader is led to view the men sent to Canaan as esteemed and honored leaders of the community; see J. A. Beck, "Geography and the Narrative Shape of Numbers 13," *BS* 157 (2000): 273.

558 Five valiant spies were chosen from among the Danite clans (Judg 18:2). The narrator also used general expression הָאֲנָשִׁים (18:7, 14, 17)

559 The spies belonged to the tribe of Joseph and are called הַשֹּׁמְרִים (Judg 1:24)

560 Joshua sent out שְׁנַיִם־אֲנָשִׁים מְרַגְּלִים 'two men, spies' (Josh 2:1; 6:22). The people of Jericho and the narrator called them simply הָאֲנָשִׁים 'people' (Josh 2:3, 4, 5, 9, 14, 17, 24), הַנְּעָרִים (6:23) or הַמַּלְאָכִים (6:25). The use of the term הַנְּעָרִים for the description of the spies led Y. Zakovitch to conclude that Joshua selected the spies in a careless manner, taking two inexperienced men from the ranks of the common people. F. M. Cross in response to Y. Zakovitch's paper demonstrated that such a claim is baseless. The text does not allow the interpretation that the scouts selected by Joshua were incompetent, naïve, or of low birth. For the discussion see F. M. Cross, "A Response to Zakovitch," in *Text and Tradition: The Hebrew Bible and Folklore*, ed. S. Niditch (Atlanta, Ga.: Scholars Press, 1990); and Y. Zakovitch, "Humor and Theology or the Successful Failure of Isrelite Intelligence: A Literary-Folkloric Approach to Joshua 2," in *Text and Tradition: The Hebrew Bible and Folklore*, ed. S. Niditch (Atlanta, Ga.: Scholar Press, 1990). To bolster F. M. Cross's argument, it is worth mentioning that Rab-Shaqeh and his companions are also called נַעֲרֵי מֶלֶךְ־אַשּׁוּר (2 Kgs 19:6).

561 The DtrH source uses the term אֲנָשִׁים (Josh 7:2).

was composed of those who, in the guise of merchants, entered a foreign land in order to spy on it. Thus, Joseph accused his brothers of spying when they came to purchase grain from Egypt (Gn 42).

The goals of the missions also varied according to context and according to the interests of the commissioners (the consumers of intelligence). The geographical area to be reconnoitered was generally designated by the term "the land." In practice, this meant collecting of information on either larger territories (Canaan,[562] Egypt, Judah, Ammon, and the territory of Laish) or a concrete city and its immediate surroundings (Jazer, Jericho,[563] Ai, Bethel). In times of war, scouts were employed to reconnoiter enemy military camps (the Amalekite and Midianite camp and Saul's camp). The nature of the mission depended on the goal of the commissioners. In all cases but one, the commissioners either made no specific request or defined the information they wanted very broadly: "Go and explore the land!" (Josh 2:1; 7:2; Judg 18:2). Only in the case of the reconnaissance of Canaan did Moses spell out the goals of the mission more clearly:

P source: to investigate the land of Canaan (Nm 13:2).

JE source: Moses gave the scouts a command to bring back: 1) information about the people: "whether the people who live in it are strong or weak, whether they are few or many" (Nm 13:18); 2) information about the land: "what kind of country it is" (Nm 13:18), "whether the land they live in is good or bad" (Nm 13:19), and "whether the land is rich or poor, and whether there are trees in it or not" (Nm 13:20); 3) information about the cities: "whether the towns that they live in are unwalled settlements or fortified cities" (Nm 13:19); 4) samples of the fruit (Nm 13:20).

D source: to investigate the access road to the Promised Land and bring back information about the cities of the land (Dt 1:22).

DtrH source: no specific request mentioned (Josh 14:7-8).

[562] The object of the investigation of Canaan varies according to the sources. The P source: the land of Canaan (Nm 13:2), i.e., the land from the wilderness of Zin to Rehob at Lebo-ramath (Nm 13:21); the JE source: Negev and the mountains (Nm 13:17, 22), Hebron and Nahal Eshkol (Nm 13:22–23); the D source: the mountains and Nahal Eshkol (Dt 1:24); the DtrH source: only a general term "the land" (Josh 14:7).

[563] Joshua sent out spies to reconnoiter the city of Jericho (Josh 2:1); the king of Jericho claimed that they came to investigate "the (whole) land" (Josh 2:2.3). The MT reads in 2:3 אֶת־כָּל־הָאָרֶץ 'the whole land'.

The process of reconnaissance can be further illuminated by studying the specific vocabulary used to describe various reconnaissance missions (Table 38).

Table 38. Verbs used to describe reconnaissance activities in the Bible

SPYING ON	VERBS USED FOR DESCRIPTION OF RECONNOITERING
Ai	The DtrH source uses the verbs עלה and רגל (Josh 7:2).
Ammon	The DtrH source uses the verbs בוא (2 Sam 10:2), רִגֵּל and חקר (10:3).
Bethel	The DtrH source uses the verbs תור (Judg 1:23) and ראה (1:24).
Canaan	The P source uses the verbs תור (Nm 13:2, 16, 17, 21, 25, 32; 14:6, 7, 34, 36, 38), עלה (13:21), and ראה (13:32); the JE source employs the verbs בוא (13:22, 23, 27), עלה (13:17, 22, 31) and ראה (13:18); the D source uses the verbs עלה and בוא (Dt 1:24), חפר (1:22), and רגל (1:24) for reconnoitering performed by the people whereas תור and הלך are used for reconnoitering performed by the Lord as he leads his people through the desert (1:32.33); the DtrH source employs the verbs עלה (Josh 14:8) and רגל (14:7).
Desert	The JE source uses ידע in the expression חֲנֹתֵנוּ בַּמִּדְבָּר וְהָיִיתָ לָּנוּ לְעֵינָיִם יָדַעְתָּ (Nm 10:31) and the verb תור (Nm 10:33); the D source uses the verb תור (Dt 1:33).
Egypt	The J source uses the verbs בוא (Gn 42:9, 10, 12), רגל (42:9, 11, 14, 16, 30, 31, 34)[564] and ראה (42:9, 12).
Jazer	The DtrH source uses the verbs רגל (Nm 21:32).
Jericho	The DtrH source uses the verbs הלך (Josh 2:1), בוא (2:2.3), ראה (2:1), חפר (2:2.3), and רגל (2:1; 6:22, 23, 25).[565]
Midianite and Amalekite camp	The DtrH source uses the verbs ירד (Judg 7:10, 11) and שמע (7:11, 15).

[564] According to some scholars, verses Gn 42:11, 14, 16 belong to the E source; see N. K. Gottwald, *The Hebrew Bible: A Socio-Literary Introduction* (Philadelphia: Fortress Press, 1985), 153.

[565] The attribution of Josh 2 to the DtrH source follows G. M. Tucker, "The Rahab Saga," in *The Use of the Old Testament in the New and Other Essays: Studies in Honor of William Franklin Stinespring*, ed. J. M. Efird (Durham, N.C.: Duke University Press, 1972). For a discussion and critique of the presence of J, E, and D sources in Josh 2, see S. Mowinckel, *Erwägungen zur Pentateuch Quellenfrage* (Oslo: Universitetsforlaget, 1964), 107–11; L. M. Newman, "Rahab and the Conquest," in *Understanding the Word: Essays in Honor of Bernhard W. Anderson*, ed. J. T. Butler, E. W. Conrad, and B. C. Ollenburger (Sheffield, England: JSOT Press, 1985); and M. Noth, *A History of Pentateuchal Traditions* (Chico, Calif.: Scholars Press, 1981).

Judah	The DtrH source uses the verb ראה (2 Kgs 20:13, 15).
Laish	The DtrH source uses the verbs הלך (Judg 18:2, 7, 17), בוא (18:2, 7, 17), רגל (18:2, 14, 17), חקר (18:2), and ראה (18:7.9).
Saul's camp	The DtrH source uses the verb רגל (1 Sam 26:4).

The technical term for scouts is מְרַגְּלִים, a piel active participle formed from a denominative verb whose root is the noun רֶגֶל meaning 'foot'.[566] This suggests that the very activity of scouting was related to movement.[567] Table 38 demonstrates that all of the sources (D, DtrH, J, JE, and P) and most of the stories connect scouting activity with verbs of movement such as הלך, בוא, ירד, and עלה. Thus, reconnaissance meant to move from one place to another in order to obtain information otherwise unavailable to the consumers. The actual investigation of the target specified by the consumers is described by several different verbs (see Table 38). The least specialized verb used to describe the activity of scouts, ראה emphasizes simple visual observation and the perception of usual and unusual things that might help further the consumers' interests.

The nuance given to intelligence activity by the use of the piel form of רגל can be determined from Ps 15:3 and 2 Sam 19:28. The verb means to "go around as a slanderer."[568] The etymological connection between "to slander" (qal and piel) and to "spy out" (only piel) suggested by E. Jenni[569] can be discerned in Josh 2. The scouts were dispatched to spy on Jericho. One would expect that they would collect combat intelligence, such as the number of soldiers in Jericho and the types of their weaponry and fortification. In reality, they reported on the rumors circulating in the city. This episode demonstrates the nature of the etymological connection suggested by E. Jenni: the piel form of רגל means both to walk around spreading rumors (to go around as a slanderer) as well as to walk around

---

[566] The piel stem, especially its participle, is used to designate professional activity (Judg 9:25); see Waltke and O'Connor, *An Introduction to Biblical Hebrew Syntax*, 416.

[567] This idea is verbalized in the expression וַיַּעֲלוּ חֲמֵשֶׁת הָאֲנָשִׁים הַהֹלְכִים לְרַגֵּל אֶת־הָאָרֶץ, "Meanwhile the five men who had gone to reconnoiter the land went up" (Judg 18:17; NAB).

[568] *HALOT*, 1184.

[569] E. Jenni, *Das hebräische Pi'el: Syntaktisch-semasiologische Untersuchung einer Verbalform im Alten Testament* (Zürich: EVZ-Verlag, 1968), 220.

listening to rumors (to go around as a spy). The verb שמע likewise indicates the role that listening played in intelligence gathering. This verb and the verbs רגל and ראה define scouts as the extended eyes and ears of their commissioners (Nm 10:31).

The nuance conveyed by employing the verb חפר has been investigated by M. Rose, who suggests that both meanings of the verb are relevant—"to dig" and "to be ashamed." The goal of scouts is to dig up information[570] that will reveal the shameful "nakedness of the land" (Gn 42:9.12) and that can be used, for example, to undermine the morale of the country in question.[571] While the verb חפר indicates that the scouts should get hold of information about enemy vulnerabilities that may be useful for combat, the verb תור has a neutral meaning and indicates that the scouts should not limit themselves to gathering intelligence about the weaknesses of the enemy but should also collect information about the strengths of enemy.[572] The verb חקר includes not only the activity of diligently searching for hidden things[573] but also the aspect of cross-examination and the careful posing of questions (1 Sam 20:12). This verb is often used in the context of juridical investigations (Dt 13:15; Job 13:9; 29:16; Ps 18:17) or investigations of ritual purity (Ez 39:14). In both cases, the investigation is conducted by posing questions.

In sum, from this linguistic analysis it is clear that the act of scouting comprised moving into an unexplored territory in order to observe (listen and watch) and obtain knowledge of the enemy's strengths and weaknesses by listening to rumors and asking questions.

In only three cases (Jericho, Bethel, and Laish) has a short description of the very process of collecting information been preserved. The Jericho mission took place in secret. The scouts entered the city during the night (Josh 2:2). The requisite information was acquired with the help of a local collaborator (the prostitute Rahab). The MT lists two reasons for her

[570] Viewed in the context of Jb 3:21, the scout is similar to a treasure hunter who digs for hidden treasures.
[571] Rose, *Deuteronomist*, 272–74.
[572] Ibid., 274–75.
[573] The verb חקר is often used to describe penetration into the most secret and thus normally inaccessible spheres, such as the human heart (Ps 139:1; Jer 17:10).

collaboration: first, religious motivations—she had heard about the mighty deeds of the Lord and recognized the supremacy of the God of Israel; second, personal benefit—if the Israelites conquered the city of Jericho, they had to guarantee her safe conduct. Like the Jericho mission, the Bethel mission was accomplished with the help of a local collaborator. The goal of the scouts was to discover a (secret) passage into the city in order to facilitate its capture. A man questioned by the scouts revealed, in exchange for the promise of safe conduct, the (secret) entrance into the city (Judg 1:22–26). During the Laish mission, the scouts concentrated their efforts on investigating the road to the city through the mountains of Ephraim and gathering information about the inhabitants of Laish (Judg 18).

The intelligence cycle was closed when the scouts returned and made their report, and the commissioners made a decision on the basis of the new intelligence.[574] According to the biblical stories, this was the weakest link in the intelligence cycle. On the one hand, the information collected about Laish and its correct assessment encouraged the Israelites to undertake a campaign (Judg 18:9–10) and conquer the city (Judg 18:28).[575] On the other hand, a few military and religious failures can be ascribed to faulty assessment of the intelligence as well as wrong decisions based on such faulty assessments. In the case of the Canaan mission, the combination of the P and JE sources in Nm 13–14 casts negative light on the quality of the investigation and the report of the tribal representatives. According to Nm 13:17, Moses asked them to investigate Negev and the mountains. However, the spies went much further north than they were told to go by Moses (Nm 13:21), and they reported on territories they were not asked to report on (Nm 13:29).[576] Moreover, the spies added important conclusions to their report: a minority of the scouts, Caleb and Joshua, concluded that

---

574 The technical term for bringing a report to the commissioners is וַיָּשִׁיבוּ אוֹתָם דָּבָר (Nm 13:26; Dt 1:22.25; 13:26; Josh 14:7); see B. A. Levine, *Numbers 1–20: A New Translation with Introduction and Commentary*, 1st ed. (New York: Doubleday, 1993), 356.

575 The task of the scouts sent to spy on Laish consisted of two parts: to scout the road through the mountains of Ephraim, and to gather information on Laish. As for the latter, the information that the scouts gathered on the inhabitants of Laish (Judg 18:7) pertained to their customs (Phoenician), their style of life (quiet and unsuspecting people), their wealth (the residents were wealthy and lacking nothing), their political organization (no hereditary ruler), their international relations (they were connected with Sidon and living in good relations with the neighbors), and the possibility that they might receive military help (Sidon was far from Laish).

576 Beck, "Numbers 13," 277–78.

the Israelites would be able to conquer the land (Nm 13:30; 14:6–10), whereas the majority, ten spies, concluded that since the land was devouring its inhabitants and that the size of the current inhabitants of the land made the scouts feel like grasshoppers, the Israelites would not be able to mount a successful conquest (Nm 13:31–33).[577] The decision was made in public as the people were debating these two conflicting reports. In the case of the Ai mission, the scouts also misled the troops by underestimating the enemy. Instead of presenting a factual report, they rather presented their own assessment and recommendation, which turned out to be wrong (Josh 7:3).

Besides the two most common intelligence operations, reconnaissance and surveillance, the Bible also alludes to some special operations. The first can be grouped under the heading of *loyal collaborators informing on somebody's whereabouts*:

- Joshua learned that the five kings were hidden in a cave (Josh 10:17).
- Saul's collaborators informed him about David's whereabouts (1 Sam 19:19; 23:7, 13; 26:1; 27:4).
- Solomon's collaborators informed the king about the whereabouts of Joab (1 Kgs 2:29) and Shimei (1 Kgs 2:41).
- Ahab's collaborators informed the king about the whereabouts of Elijah (2 Kgs 6:13).
- The collaborators of the king of Damascus informed the king about the arrival of Elijah into the city (2 Kgs 8:7).

The second group of special intelligence operations consists of *warnings* received to prevent a military attack:[578]

- Abimelech learned about the ambush and revolt (Judg 9:25, 47).
- David learned about the mobilization of the Arameans and the Ammonites (2 Sam 10:17).

---

[577] Likewise, discouraging additions by the scouts that cause the people to rebel appear in the D (Dt 1:26, 28) and DtrH (Josh 14:8) versions.

[578] In one case, there is no verb to indicate the activity of intelligence gathering or communication, such as the hophal of נגד, but from the context it can be assumed that the king learned about the rebellion since he intervened: king Joram learned that Edom had rebelled against Judahite suzerainty and appointed a king. The rebellion was punished by an invasion (2 Kgs 8:20–11).

- Ahaz learned about the conspiracy of Pekah and Rezin against Judah (Is 7:2).
- Elisha learned from God about the Aramean plans and thus saved Israel many times (2 Kgs 6:8–12).

The last group of intelligence operations includes the story of the honey trap (Samson and Delilah; Judg 16) and David's clever infiltration of Absalom's council of advisors (2 Sam 15).

In conclusion, the biblical writers operated with two main intelligence categories in mind: surveillance and reconnaissance. The former was concerned primarily with domestic security and was carried out by observers; the latter was concerned with enemies and foreign lands and was carried out by scouts. The intelligence operations collecting data on an enemy were always ad hoc reconnaissance operations. When a specific need arose, the commissioners sent out scouts to gather the required data. With the exception of David's shrewd infiltration of Absalom's high command, the process of collecting and transmitting intelligence was very simple: the scouts departed, gathered data, returned, and presented their report. There is no evidence that there was any systematic gathering, processing, and archiving of intelligence data, as in Assyria. The scouts' reports were never double-checked against an independent source. The collectors of intelligence never presented raw intelligence but always added their own evaluations, impressions, and conclusions. It was often the case that such enhancements included an exaggeration or underestimation of reality that led to confusion among the decision-makers and bad decisions.[579] As for the type of intelligence gathered during these ad hoc operations, it can be classified as military intelligence focused on the enemy's capabilities, and terrain reconnaissance necessary for leading troops through an unknown territory and conquering a foreign land.[580]

---

[579] The Deuteronomist distinguished between the factual report commissioned by Moses (Dt 1:25) and the scouts' additions, which caused confusion among the people (Dt 1:28).

[580] Y. Yadin was the first biblical scholar who distinguished between the nature of the intelligence obtained by the spies sent out by Moses (Nm 13) and the spies sent out by Joshua (Josh 2). He called the former strategic intelligence, whereas the latter was tactical intelligence. This distinction was further elaborated by A. Malamat, who defined the Canaan episode as strategic intelligence interested in demographic, political, and economic data, whereas the Rahab episode was a story describing tactical intelligence aimed at gathering data of a strictly military nature; see A. Malamat, *History of Biblical Israel:*

5.4.2.2 The challenge of Neo-Assyrian intelligence and the biblical response

In contrast to the biblical categories of intelligence, which were limited to reconnaissance and surveillance, Assyrian intelligence represented a qualitative advance over such ad hoc methods. Innovative intelligence structures enabled the Assyrians to learn numerous details about their vassals, to monitor their fidelity, and to intervene against rebels in a timely fashion. Since the Assyrians used their detailed knowledge against their vassals and enemies in psychological warfare, the psychological impact of these innovative intelligence structures can hardly be overestimated; it may be compared to the psychological impact of modern intelligence agencies such as the CIA, KGB, or Mossad on their satellites and enemies. By systematically gathering, processing, and storing data, the Assyrians created an impression of omniscience. By pretending to be omniscient, the Assyrians challenged the sovereignty of the Lord. Thus, the controversy between Sennacherib and Hezekiah became a controversy over the Lord's sovereignty. The triumph of the Lord is dramatized on three levels in 2 Kgs 18–19. On the practical level, the faithful king Hezekiah was able to neutralize Assyrian propaganda by preparing the people to face the Assyrian threat beforehand. On the literary level, the final redactors of 2 Kgs 18–20 demythologized Assyrian omniscience by pointing out the flaws and lacunae of the Neo-Assyrian intelligence services. Finally, on the theological level the biblical writers proved the sovereignty of the God of Israel over Assyrian intelligence operations and military might.

5.4.2.2.1 Practical level

Silence, the reaction of the people to Rab-shaqeh's second speech (2 Kgs 18:36), is generally interpreted as marking the failure of Rab-shaqeh's

---

Major Problems and Minor Issues (Leiden and Boston: Brill, 2001), 173; and Y. Yadin, *The Art of Warfare in Biblical Lands in the Light of Archaeological Study*, vol. 1 (New York: McGraw-Hill, 1963), 110. Following J. M. House's classification of military intelligence, I propose to categorize biblical reconnaissance as "military intelligence." This term includes several types of intelligence grouped according to the level of detail required, and the purpose to which the information would be put: strategic, operational, and tactical intelligence, and combat information. According to this distinction, the object of the Canaan expedition would have been operational intelligence, and the information gathered in the Rahab episode would have qualified as tactical intelligence; see House, *Military Intelligence*, 2–6.

propaganda to undermine Hezekiah's authority.[581] The people remained faithful to Hezekiah and followed his orders despite Rab-shaqeh's eloquence in pointing out Hezekiah's unreliability.[582] There was more than one reason to remain silent. First, a religious reason: religious people should not engage in discussion with a blasphemer and should ignore his speech.[583] Second, a military reason: in difficult moments, the simplest and most efficient way to keep troops under control has always been to order them to keep silent and thus prevent discussions which could undermine their morale. Indeed, such an order is attested in verse 18:36: "But the people remained silent and did not answer him one word, for the king had ordered them not to answer him" (NAB). Naturally, this verse raises the question:

---

[581] K. D. Fricke, *Das zweite Buch von den Königen*, 2. Aufl. (Stuttgart: Calwer, 1972), 268; G. Hentschel, *2 Könige* (Würzburg: Echter, 1985), 91 and G. H. Jones, *1 and 2 Kings: Based on the Revised Standard Version* (Grand Rapids, Mich.: W.B. Eerdmans; London: Marshall Morgan & Scott, 1984), 573.

[582] The MT of 2 Kgs 18:36 reads: וְהֶחֱרִישׁוּ הָעָם, "but the people remained silent." This means that the *wᵊqātal* form indicates a contrast: "but (in spite of what has been said by Rab-shaqeh) the people remained silent." The text of Is 36:21 (וַיַּחֲרִישׁוּ) and all the Greek variants of 2 Kgs 18:36 (καὶ ἐσιώπησαν) omit the object הָעָם and also have a *wayyiqtol* form instead of a *wᵊqātal* form. Thus, Isaiah and the Greek versions syntactically connect this verse with the return of the representatives (2 Kgs 18:37–19:7; Is 36:22–37:4). Only the Latin version S (Syro-hexaplar) follows the MT and adds *populus*; see Brook, 364. Most scholars recognize the word הָעָם 'the people' as a marginal note added to the main text; see Hentschel, *2 Könige*, 91; and R. F. Person, *The Kings-Isaiah and Kings-Jeremiah Recensions* (Berlin and New York: Walter de Gruyter, 1997), 63. The addition of הָעָם in the MT specifies the object of the king's command. Without הָעָם, the text is ambiguous: the object of the command might have been either the Judahite representatives or the people on the walls. W. Brueggemann prefers the Greek versions over the MT and suggests that the object of the king's command was the Judahite representatives: "The last verses (18:37) may suggest that the Assyrian argument has hit its target, that the officials of Jerusalem were persuaded by the argument that diminished Yahweh. The narrative withholds judgment and the king's agents, good diplomats as they are, give no clue to their reaction"; see W. Brueggemann, *1 & 2 Kings* (Macon, Ga.: Smyth & Helwys, 2000). For a similar opinion, see V. Fritz, *Das zweite Buch der Könige* (Zürich: Theologischer Verlag, 1998), 115. The addition in the MT indicates the final redactor's difficulty in assuming that the object of the king's order was the Judahite representatives. The addition of הָעָם in the MT and the *wᵊqātal* form in v. 18:36 present the logical conclusion: since the Judahite representatives had already broken the king's order in 2 Kgs 18:26, verse 18:37 should be connected with what precedes, and thus the object of the king's command should be "the people sitting on the wall."

[583] D. J. Wiseman, *1 and 2 Kings: An Introduction and Commentary* (Leicester, England and Downers Grove, Ill.: InterVarsity Press, 1993), 278.

> How could the king have given an order to the people to remain silent before the confrontation with Rab-shakeh, when only during the negotiations did it become known to Jerusalem's defenders that they were the object of the Assyrian's speech?[584]

P. R. House has outlined the answer: "The people remained silent because Hezekiah has anticipated such tactics and commanded them to do so."[585] If Rab-shaqeh's speech was indeed anticipated and the people of Jerusalem had been prepared for it, then its delivery would cause just the opposite effect: instead of becoming frightened, the people became even more convinced that they were fighting against a blasphemer of their God.[586]

5.4.2.2.2 Literary level

The literary critique of Assyrian omniscience was accomplished through a skillful redaction of sources by the Deuteronomistic editors.[587] In the present form of the Masoretic text, the annalistic sources (18:1–16) present an introduction to the encounter between Rab-shaqeh and Hezekiah. The writer provides the reader with hermeneutical clues that the writer wants the reader to use in assessing the polemic between Hezekiah and Sennacherib. The reader finds in this introduction several details about Hezekiah's life and reign. The reader learns that Hezekiah's religious reform and his military campaigns were approved by the Lord, that the real reason for the fall of Samaria was the Israelites' disobedience, and finally that Hezekiah had already paid a heavy tribute to Assyria in order to save his kingdom. The fact that Hezekiah and his courtiers as well as Rab-shaqeh and his envoys knew only some of these things created a great potential for the use of literary irony. The reader can judge the arguments of Sennacherib and Hezekiah. Sennacherib and his envoys acted as if they knew everything; they boasted of their detailed knowledge of the Judahite domestic politics and religious affairs, and they even felt authorized to announce God's plans

---

[584] Cogan and Tadmor, *II Kings: A New Translation*, 233.
[585] P. R. House, *1, 2 Kings* (Nashville, Tenn.: Broadman & Holman, 1995), 364.
[586] According to M. Lloyd's study of military deception, "the impact of an anticipated propaganda coup may be limited by frank and early admission of error or by introduction of a new theme of greater potential interest or impact to the target audience"; Lloyd, *The Art of Military Deception*, 142.
[587] The following discussion relies on the detailed narrative analysis of 2 Kgs 18–20 by Hardmeier, *Prophetie im Streit*, 87–160.

for Israel. The reader, to whom the writer has told details that none of the characters knew, can smile on the arrogance and naïveté of "the great king, the king of Assyria" (18:19) and sympathize with Hezekiah.[588] Indeed, the reader possesses better knowledge than the supposedly "omniscient" Assyrians.

A good example of this dramatic irony is the seemingly illogical combination of sources A and B^1.[589] Whereas, from a historical point of view, such a combination raises a difficult question—why did Sennacherib send his envoys when he had already received the tribute?—from the narrative point of view the shift from annalistic description to disputation is a nice example of literary irony. Sennacherib accepted Hezekiah's heavy tribute. After reading 18:13–6, the reader would expect Sennacherib to depart from Judah. Instead, Sennacherib dispatches his diplomatic envoys to compel the Jerusalemites to surrender. All three Assyrian speeches aimed at convincing the people not to trust in Egypt, their king, and their God but to believe the promises offered by the Assyrians. What irony! The Assyrians, who had just violated the terms of their negotiations with Hezekiah, were now denouncing others as unreliable and asking the Jerusalemites to trust their new promises.

Moreover, the writer allows the reader to compare the information provided in the introduction with Rab-shaqeh's boastful knowledge of Judah. The reader quickly discovers that the Assyrians were omitting, intentionally or unintentionally, some crucial information, and that other information was incomplete or completely wrong (Table 39).

Table 39. Flaws in Neo-Assyrian intelligence

Assyrian intelligence	**Intelligence viewed through the interpretative lenses of the introduction/*other passages***
Hezekiah's reliance on Egypt (18:21)	Faulty intelligence. According to the introduction, Hezekiah relied only on God (18:5); no negotiations with Egypt are mentioned.
Intelligence about the	Wrong attribution. The high places destroyed by

[588] However, the writer quickly puts the reader in a similar position: after letting the reader hear the words of God, the reader understands that even his or her own knowledge has only been partial.

[589] For definitions of different types of irony see J. L. Ska, *"Our Fathers Have Told Us": Introduction to the Analysis of Hebrew Narratives* (Rome: Potifical Biblical Institute, 1990), 57–61.

high places that were destroyed by Hezekiah (18:22)	Hezekiah did not belong to the God of Judah (18:4–5).
Denunciation of Hezekiah's self-confidence and the misplaced trust that led him to rebel against Assyria (18:19–20)	Wrong evaluation of Hezekiah's trust. According to the introduction, it was Hezekiah's trust in the Lord that caused the Lord to be with him in everything he undertook (including his rebellion against Assyria; 18:6–7) and that put him on the top of the list of "the just kings" (there was no king like him before him; 18:5).
Evaluation of Hezekiah's valor: too many words, and no deeds (18:20)	Wrong. In 18:8, Hezekiah is described as a warrior who expanded the borders of Judah at the expense of the Israelites' traditional enemy, the Philistines.
Reference to the command of the God of Israel who entrusted Assyria with the task of inflicting punishment on Judah (18:25)	Wrong. According to the introduction, the God of Judah was with Hezekiah and not against him (18:7). *Isaiah in his prophecies rejected as blasphemy Rab-shaqeh's claim to act in the name of the God of Judah (19:6–7, 20–34).*
Evaluation of insufficient water resources in Jerusalem (18:27)	*Wrong. According to the DtrH summary of Hezekiah's reign, Hezekiah built an impressive water system (20:20–21). Thus, the Assyrian threat "You will drink your urine!" was quite unrealistic since Hezekiah brought water into the city. He not only fortified the Gihon source to protect it against the Assyrians but also, by bringing water into the Siloam pool.*
Assessment of Egypt as an unreliable ally (18:21)	*Wrong assessment. the Egyptian king did come to help his allies (19:9).*
Reference to Hezekiah's prophecy that God will save Jerusalem (18:30, 32)	Partially wrong. The introduction does not mention any such prophecy. *This prophecy was delivered by Isaiah only after Rab-shaqeh's second speech (19:7).*
Promise of safe conduct and peaceful life in a new land, if they surrender (18:31–32)	Partially correct. In the description of the fall of Samaria, the Samarians were deported (a different word is used) and settled in new land (18:11).
Intelligence on Hezekiah's reform (18:22)	Partially correct. Hezekiah did destroy the high places, but the introduction does not mention that he destroyed any altars or centralized the cult in Jerusalem (18:4–5).
Assessment of Hezekiah's military capability (18:23)	Correct. Hezekiah's military resources, decimated by the Assyrian army and by the payment of heavy tribute (18:13–16), were incomparably smaller than those of Assyria.
Evaluation of Hezekiah as a king weaker than the least of the Assyrian governors (18:24)	Correct. Israelite and Judahite armies were unable to withstand the Assyrian invasion (18:9–16).
Fall of Samaria (18:34)	Correct. Samaria fell after a three-year siege (18:10).

In sum, when viewed through the interpretative lenses of the introduction (18:1–16), the Assyrians' shockingly good knowledge of Judahite domestic and religious affairs turns out to be partial and in some cases even wrong. Such pinpointing of the flaws of the "omniscient" intelligence services placed the Neo-Assyrian intelligence network in a broader context and demonstrated that the Assyrians were not as omniscient as they seemed to be. Stories of an enemy's ridiculous mistakes, comic caricatures of opposition leaders, and subtle irony were not original inventions of the DtrH writers. Rather, they are part of a recurring pattern in narratives that describe a weaker party's dealings with an opposition that is militarily, politically, and economically superior. The story of the midwives' deception of Pharaoh (Ex 1), as well as the stories in the book of Esther, are biblical examples of such a demythologizing of arrogant powers. For modern examples, it is sufficient to mention stories that circulated in Eastern Europe about the naïveté and blunders of the KGB and its satellite secret services, or stories circulating in the Middle East nowadays that ridicule American, British, and Israeli high-tech intelligence services for committing elementary mistakes. Thus, I propose that in its present form, the story of the controversy between Hezekiah and Sennacherib successfully uses irony to demythologize the innovative and technologically advanced intelligence services of Assyria.

5.4.2.2.3 Theological level

Arriving at a correct evaluation of religious movements is often a stumbling block for intelligence agencies.[590] The DtrH redactors demonstrated how the Assyrians also misunderstood Judahite religious movements and motivations. The Assyrians' first stumbling block was their incorrect evaluation of the nature of Hezekiah's reform. Rab-shaqeh's arguments in his first speech dealt with Hezekiah's centralization of the cult. If Hezekiah had removed the Lord's high places, then Rab-shaqeh might have been right: Assyria was the rod with which the Lord punished Israelite and Judahite infidelity. However, if the removal of the high places was required by the Lord, then Rab-shaqeh's argument "turned out to be a formidable declaration of Hezekiah's piety."[591]

[590] For a modern example of a similar failure, see, for example, the CIA's underestimation of the role of religious reform in Iran and its contribution to the shah's fall.
[591] Ben-Zvi, "Who Wrote the Speech," 86.

Another fallacy in Rab-shaqeh's argument was his interpretation of the campaign of Jerusalem as a punishment willed by the God of Israel. According to the DtrH redactors, the main sins of Jerusalem were committed in its high places. Once there were no more high places in Jerusalem, then there was no longer reason for punishment. On the contrary, since Hezekiah's reform purified Jerusalem, the attack against Jerusalem was an attack against a holy city, and the Lord himself had to defend it for the sake of David and his holy name (2 Kgs 19:34).

The next flaw in the Assyrian argument concerned the destroyed cities, Samaria in particular. It was true that these cities, including Samaria, did not withstand the Assyrian attacks. However, Samaria was destroyed because of its sins (18:12).[592] Therefore, the argument that the Lord had failed to protect his own kingdom was invalid because it was the Lord who decided to use Assyria as a punishing rod against sinful Israelites.[593] While presenting this argument, Rab-shaqeh made his last and fatal mistake: he put the God of Israel on the same level as the gods of the Syrian and Babylonian cities, who were unable to protect their peoples. This argument, presented in the context of Hezekiah's prayer and Isaiah's responses, disclosed Rab-shaqeh's true nature: he was a blasphemer who dared to manipulate religion to serve his own purposes. Thus, the biblical writers depict Sennacherib and his propaganda agents not only as incorrectly interpreting religious matters, but as blasphemers *par excellence.*

The identification of Assyrian propaganda agents as blasphemers *par excellence* may be interpreted in terms of "enimification" process.[594] Enimification process consists of two parts. First, it is necessary to create an evil enemy. Second, the villainy of the enemy is put in contrast with the piety and goodness of the friendly leader. During the first part of the enimification process, a human being is stripped of human features. As the

---

[592] That Hezekiah's story should be read in relation to the story of the fall of Samaria is supported by two linguistic indicators: first, the mention of Moses and the occurrence in 18:6 and 18:12 of the verb צוה, which only rarely occurs in the DtrH evaluation of the kings (2 Kgs 14:6; 21:8); second, the similar annalistic openings that describe the campaign of Shalmaneser against Samaria (18:9–10) and Sennacherib's campaign against Judah (18:13–4).

[593] See the theological interpretation of the fall of Samaria in 2 Kgs 17.

[594] R. W. Rieber and R. J. Kelly, "Substance and Shadow: Images of the Enemy," in *The Psychology of War and Peace: The Image of the Enemy*, ed. R. W. Rieber (New York: Plenum Press, 1991).

result of this process, a human being is no longer human and therefore can be enslaved, tortured, and even killed. From a theological point of view, during the enimification process the Assyrians are demonized[595] and presented as blasphemers who deserve appropriate punishment for offending God (see 4.2.2.2). Thus, misinterpretation of Judahite religion was not only a simple failure in the processing of raw intelligence on the part of the Assyrians; it turned out to be an act of blasphemy. From this point of view, the death of the 185,000 Assyrian soldiers, who were struck down by the angel of the Lord, and the murder of Sennacherib were appropriate punishments for their blasphemy (19:35–37).

[595] Machinist, "The *Rab Šāqēh*," 164.

6

Conclusion

In this study, I have sought to investigate the Neo-Assyrian intelligence network and to draw some conclusions for the historicity and meaning of 2 Kgs 18–20. Keeping in mind the complexity of modern scholarly discussions of 2 Kgs 18–20, I dedicated the second chapter to investigating Neo-Assyrian intelligence as presented in 2 Kgs 18–20. The main goal of chapter 2 was to show what kind of information and intelligence activities the biblical writers attributed to the Assyrians. In chapters 3 and 4, I turned to Neo-Assyrian sources and collected a series of representative case studies illustrating the activities, interests, and agents of the Neo-Assyrian intelligence network, as well as its process of collecting and verifying information.

In chapter 5, I compared the biblical and Neo-Assyrian pictures of Neo-Assyrian intelligence operations. First, I asked whether there was an intelligence network in Palestine by means of which information might have been gathered. If there had not been an intelligence network in Palestine, then no information could have been gathered. My reconstruction of intelligence networks in other parts of the Neo-Assyrian empire indicated a way to answer that question. There were three branches in the Neo-Assyrian intelligence network: Assyrian, local, and temple. Certain Assyrian and local officials were obligated to report on various matters of interest to the intelligence hubs and the royal court, where their information was double-checked against other sources. Once I was able to establish which Assyrian and local officials had to perform such reporting as part of their "job description", I was able to reconstruct the Neo-Assyrian intelligence network in Palestine by identifying the seats of those officials. Thus, I demonstrated that the Assyrians had at their disposal an intelligence network in Palestine by means of which the desired information could have been gathered and transmitted to Assyria.

After reconstructing the Neo-Assyrian intelligence network in Palestine, I began comparing Neo-Assyrian intelligence operations as they can be reconstructed from biblical and Neo-Assyrian sources. First, I investigated what sort of information the Assyrians were interested in according to biblical and Neo-Assyrian sources. The results of this comparison indicated that the interests of Neo-Assyrian intelligence as reconstructed from the biblical passages matched the interests as reconstructed from the Neo-Assyrian sources. Biblical and Neo-Assyrian sources also concurred on the use of agents and psychological warfare.

Once these comparisons were made, I investigated their implications for the historicity and meaning of 2 Kgs 18–20. First, I suggested that these conclusions do not necessarily prove that chapters 2 Kgs 18–20 contain a word-for-word transcription of Assyrian speeches. Rather, I suggested reading these conclusions in the context of other studies. On the basis of several arguments, I concluded that these passages can neither be simply discarded as a literary fiction nor taken at face value. Chapters 2 Kgs 18–19 reflect many features typical of the intelligence services of the first millennium B.C.E. Insofar as several of these features were originated in the Neo-Assyrian Empire, 2 Kgs 18–19 reflects the standard operating methods of the Neo-Assyrian intelligence services. This conclusion raised another important question: why did the biblical writers felt compelled to devote so much attention to the Neo-Assyrian intelligence services? I argued that the Israelites and Judahites—who were used to two types of intelligence, reconnaissance and surveillance—encountered for the first time in the form of the Neo-Assyrian intelligence services a qualitatively new way of gathering, transmitting, and processing intelligence. The innovative Neo-Assyrian intelligence services, especially when combined with the Assyrians' overpowering military, administration, engineering, and cultural might, posed a sharp challenge to Israelite religious traditions. Therefore, I suggested that, besides performing other theological and literary functions, these passages present the reaction of the biblical writers to this new intelligence system. The biblical writers and redactors responded to the challenge raised by the Assyrians' qualitatively superior intelligence on three levels. On the practical level, the biblical writers presented Hezekiah as a skillful king capable of redirecting the attacks of Neo-Assyrian propaganda. On the literary level, by demonstrating that the speeches of the Assyrian propaganda agents contained false and incomplete information, the biblical writers undermined the impression of Assyrian omniscience. Finally, on the theological level, they demonstrated how the Assyrians misunderstood Judahite religion and at the same time underlined the blasphemous nature of Assyrian propaganda. The biblical writers let the God of Judah combat and triumph over the Assyrian blasphemers, thus demonstrating his superiority over the kings of the world, including their intelligence services.

Appendixes

Appendix 1. Information flow in the Assyrian eastern provinces

	Informat. hub ←	Source ←	Territory	Tablet
King ←	Šarru-emuranni Governor of Mazamua Ep. 712 B.C.E.	Kumesean	Kumesi (Unknown location)	V 202
		Šarru-emuranni's soldiers returning from terrorizing of Kibatki	Kibatki (Unknown location)	V 202
		Kubaba-satar (Envoy sent to Šarru-emuranni)	Unknown	V 203
		Šamaš-ukin (Šarru-emuranni's envoy sent to Izirtu)	Izirtu (Mannea)	V 204
		Unknown	Parsua Detailed knowledge of the terrain	V 199
		Unknown	Allabria Information about Bel-iddina	V 199, 200
		Unknown	Bit-Hamban	V 200
		Unknown	Hirite (Unknown location)	V 200
		Unknown	Sumbi (Unknown location)	V 200
		Unknown	Arzuhina (Assyria)	V 201
		Unknown	Arrapha (Assyria) Knowledge about the movements of the governor of Arrapha	V 199

	Informat. hub ←	Source ←	Territory	Tablet
King ←	Šamaš-belu-uṣur Governor of Arzuhina, ep. 710	First-hand (Review)	Broken away	V 230
		Unknown	Mannea	V 236
		Unknown	Mazamua	V 227, 229, 234
		Unknown	Arrapha	V 227, 228

	Inform. hub ←	Source ←	Territory	Tablet
King ←	Adad-issiya Governor of Mazamua before Šarru-emuranni	Kubaba-le'i (Adad-issiya's envoy to Tikriš)	Tikriš (Unknown location)	V 217
		Adad-issiya's cohort commanders	Sanha and Ulušia (Unknown location)	V 217
		Adad-issiya's third man	Mannea (Ullusunu)	V 217
		Nabû-hamatua	Karalla (Aššur-le'i)	V 218
		Nabû-hamatua	Mannea (Ullusunu)	V 218
		Aššur-le'i's eunuch	Prob. Karalla	V 218
		Bel-ahhe (merchant)	Unknown	V 218
		Unknown	Urartu	V 222, 223
		Unknown	Mannea (kings Aza and Ullusunu)	V 216, 220, 222
		Unknown	Karalla (Aššur-le'i)	V 219

	Information hub ←	Source ←	Territory	Tablet
King ←	Nabû-remanni Governor of Parsua	Messenger from Parsua	Zalipa	XV 53
		Unknown	Mannea	XV 53
		Unknown	Mannea (runaways)	XV 54
		Unknown	Mazamua (runaways)	XV 54
		Unknown	Nikkur, Tizu, Kiguhtu, Kizahasi (border fortresses)	XV 54
		Unknown	Bit-Hamban (runaways)	XV 54
		First hand (Nabû-remanni's visit in Media)	Media	XV 54
		Chief of trade	Bit-Kapsi	XV 58

	Crown Prince	Informat. hub ←	Source ←	Territory	Tablet
King←	Sennacherib	Aššur-reṣuwa Royal delegate in Kumme	Unknown	Urartians campaigning in Mannea and Zikirtu	I 29
			Mannean messengers and emissaries	Mannea (tribute brought to Sennacherib)	I 29, 32
			[Zikir]tean messengers	[Zikir]tu (tribute brought to Sennacherib)	I 39

	Information hub ←	Source ←	Territory	Tablet
King←	Hu-Tešub Šubrian king	Unknown	Urartians campaigning in Mannea and Zikirtu	V 45
	Bel-iddina Allabrian king	Unknown	Urartu on the campaign to east	V 165, 167
		Informers	Zikirtu and Andia sent messengers to Urartu	V 164
	Issar-šumu-iqiša Prob. a vassal king	Unknown	Urartian messengers visited Zikirtu	V 169
	Unattributed letter	Unknown	Karalla	XV 74
	Unattributed letter	Unknown	Karalla	XV 75
	Unattributed letter	Unknown	Andia	V 176, 177
	Unattributed letter	Unknown	Zikirtu	V 188, 189

	Informat. hub ←	Source ←	Territory	Tablet
King ←	Nabû-hamatua Delegate in Mazamua	Governor (messenger: a Mede)	Prob. governor of Mazamua	V 210
		Kuškayu	Unknown	V 213, 214
		Unknown	Allabria (Bel-iddina is a traitor)	V 210
		Govern. of Mazamua?	Mazamua	V 211

Appendix 2. Information hubs in the Assyrian eastern provinces

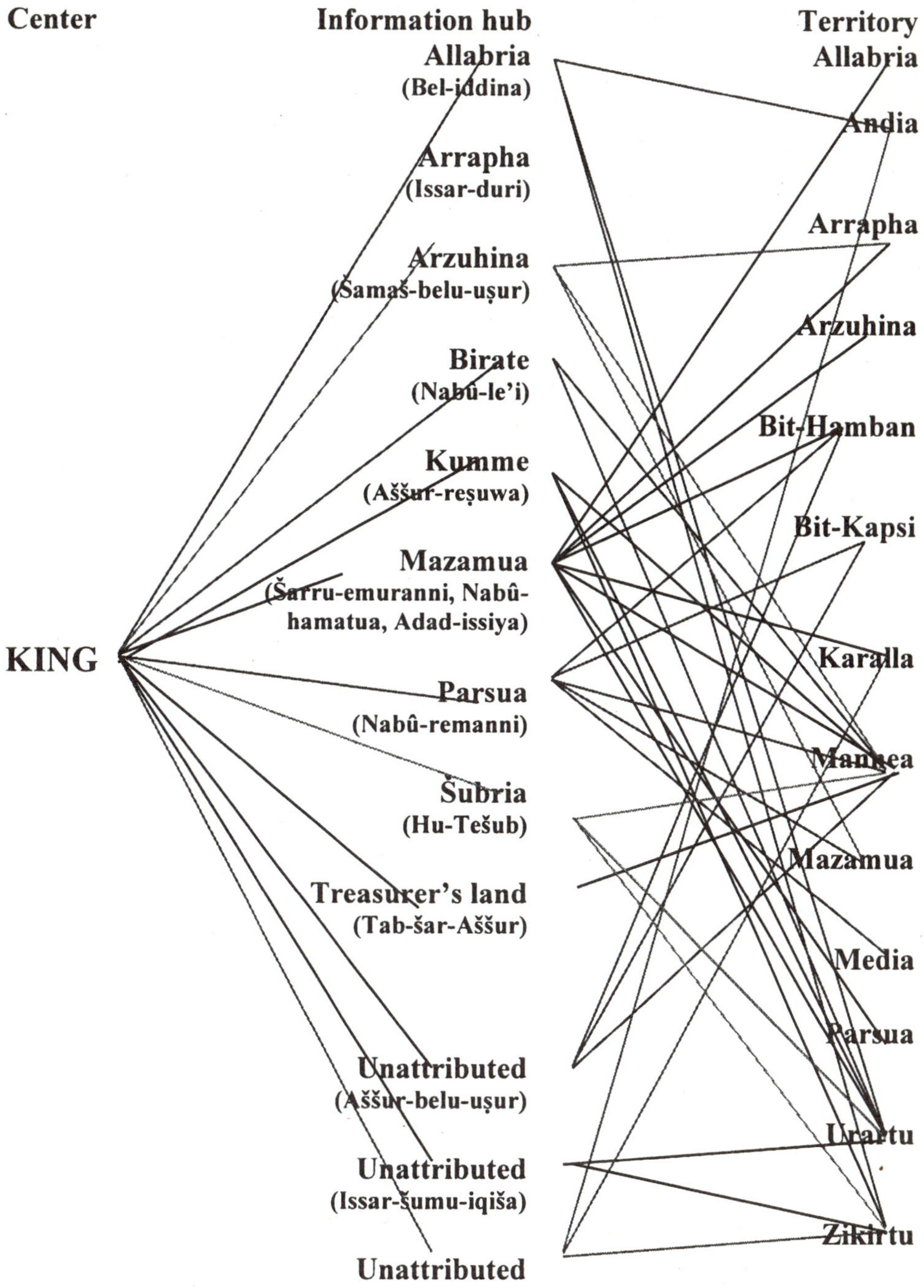

Appendix 3. Phases of Sargon II's twelfth and thirteenth campaigns

F – failed; S – succeeded; PS – partly succeeded

Pre-campaign phase

Tribe	**Psychological warfare**	**Results**
Ru'ua (Aramean)	See section 4.2.1.1; no violent means used. RESULT: **Failed**	Assyrian influence was limited to the territory around Der, Dur-Šarrukku, and Dur-Kurigalzu. F:1 (100%)

Dur-Athara phase

<table>
<tr><th>Tribe</th><th>Psychological warfare</th><th>Results</th></tr>
<tr><td>Gambulu in Dur-Athara (Aramean)</td><td>The city was destroyed and 18,430 people were deported.
RESULT: Failed.</td><td rowspan="8">8 sheiks surrendered;

18,430 deportees from Dur-Athara;

Strongholds: Dur-Athara

Conquered territory: Gambulu land (6 districts with 44 cities)

F: 5 (56%)
S: 3 (34%)
PS: 1 (10%)</td></tr>
<tr><td>Gambulu along Uqnu river (Aramean)</td><td>1. Merodach-Baladan gathered the Gambulu tribe into Dur-Athara.
2. After the conquest of the city, part of the Gambulu tribe was deported (S II Ann 266–71).
3. Eight Gambulu sheiks living along Diyala river were panic stricken after hearing of the fall of Dur-Athara and surrendered; Sargon forgave them and did not deport them.
RESULT: Partly succeeded.</td></tr>
<tr><td>Hindaru (Aramean)</td><td rowspan="4">1. The Ru'ua, Hindaru, Puqudu, and Yadburu tribes participated in the defense of Dur-Athara.
2. After the conquest of Dur-Athara, all four tribes did not surrender but fled to the Uqnu swamps (S II Ann 281–91; Prunk 19–21).
RESULT: Failed, since the tribes refused to collaborate in this phase.</td></tr>
<tr><td>Puqudu (Aramean)</td></tr>
<tr><td>Ru'ua (Aramean)</td></tr>
<tr><td>Yadburu (Aramean)</td></tr>
<tr><td>Itu'u (Aramean)</td><td rowspan="2">All three tribes crossed the Tigris with Merodach-Baladan to harass Assyrian establishments (XV 186). Since they are not listed among the opposing tribes in S II Ann</td></tr>
<tr><td>Lita'u (Aramean)</td></tr>
</table>

Rubu'u (Aramean)	but in the general list of the subjugated tribes (Prunk 18–19; S4 70–74; Tang I-Var 31–32), it is possible to assume that at a certain point the tribes preferred to ally themselves with the Assyrians rather than fighting against them. Since the Assyrians did not hesitate to boast when they used violent means to subdue an enemy, it is possible that the tribes surrendered during diplomatic negotiations. RESULT: **Succeeded** .	

Uqnu phase

	Psychological warfare	Results
Yadburu (Aramean)	Yadburu, together with the Ru'ua, Hindaru, and Puqudu tribes, participated in the defense of Dur-Athara, but none of the Yadburu sheiks surrendered during the Tubliaš operation (S II Ann 281–91; Prunk 19–21). Since Yadburu was still active in the Uqnu phase, the logical conclusion is that Yadburu did not surrender (S II Ann 298). RESULT: **Failed.**	10 sheiks surrendered; 14 cities along Diyala and their surrounding villages surrendered
Hindaru (Aramean)	1. After the conquest of Dur-Athara, the Ru'ua, Hindaru, and Puqudu tribes tribes fled to Diyala region.	Conquered territory: surroundings of Diyala and Tubliaš river
Puqudu (Aramean)	2. After being starved out, one sheik of the Ru'ua tribe, five sheiks of the Puqudu, and four sheiks of the Hindaru surrendered.	F: 1 (25%) PS: 3 (75%)
Ru'ua (Aramean)	4. The rest found shelter in the marshes of Diyala. After Sargon destroyed some villages and orchards and deported some citizens, 14 cities surrendered (S II Ann 281–91; Prunk 19–21). 5. A year after the fall of Dur-Athara (709 B.C.E.), the Ru'ua, Hindaru, and Puqudu participated in the defense of Dur-Yakin (Prunk 126); RESULT: **Partly succeeded.**	

Additional tribes in the Dur-Athara and Uqnu phases

Tribe	Psychological warfare	
Labdudu (Aramean) **Hatalla** (Aramean) **Ubulu** (Aramean)	No violent means were necessary. The Hatalla, Labdudu, and Ubulu tribes are mentioned among the subjugated tribes on the Tigris (Prunk 18; S4 70–74; Tang I-Var 31–32). Since no violent encounter between the Assyrian and these tribes is mentioned, it is possible to assume that these tribes surrendered when faced with non-violent PsW tools. XV 157 mentioned Hatalla in connection with Tu'manu but not as the object of a diplomatic mission. The sheiks of Tubliaš (XVII 150–52) invited Sargon II to come quickly. RESULT: **Succeeded**	
Hamaranu (Aramean)	Listed among the conquered tribes (Prunk 18; S4 70–74; Tang I-Var 31–32). Some of them took refuge in Sippar. Sargon II sent his eunuch to massacre them during the Chaldean phase (S II Ann 318–20). RESULT: **Partly succeeded**	
Tu'manu (Aramean)	AGENTS: NN and Ṣala-il (XV 157). RESULT: **Succeeded.**	No violent means were necessary. Since Sargon II conquered Tu'manu in 721 B.C.E. (S II Ann 20–21; Zyl 18) and the tribe is not listed among subjugated tribes in Prunk 18; S4 70–74; Tang I-Var 31–32, it stands to reason to assume that the tribe, living in its own territory, did not resist during the campaign in 710 B.C.E. Only those Tu'manu living among the Hatalla tribe were exposed to Assyrian psychological pressure.
Isuqu (Aramean)	AGENTS: Kutayu, Yasamu, Il-yada' (XV 162). RESULT: **Succeeded.**	No violent means. Part of the clan had already allied with the Assyrians before the mission started.
Gibriye **Haggarunu** **Nabatu** **Ubudu** (Aramean)	These four Aramean tribes are mentioned among the Aramean tribes pacified by Tiglath-pileser III (Sum 7:5-9), not mentioned in Sargon II's archives, but again mentioned among not-submissive tribes to be subjugated by Sennacherib (Senn Ann I:43-9; A1 12-14.55-6; B1 14). RESULT: **Succeeded.**	
Rahihu (Aramean?)	Involved in Merodach-Baladan's military raids (XV 186), but not mentioned among fighters. RESULT: **Succeeded.**	

Yadburu phase and return through Raši region

<table>
<tr><th>Tribe</th><th>Psychological warfare</th><th>Results</th></tr>
<tr><td>Gurumu
(Aramean)</td><td rowspan="2">After the destruction of two major strongholds, Sam'una and Bab-duri, the Gurumu tribe and the Elamites serving in the Yadburu strongholds were deported (S II Ann 295–97).
RESULT: Failed.</td><td rowspan="7">6 sheiks of Yadburu surrendered;
Deportation: 7,520 Elamites, 12,062 Gurumaeans;
Conquered territory: Yadburu land + Elamite territory around Naditu river + Rāši land;
Conquered strongholds: Sam'una, Bāb-dūri, Lahiru, Sulaja, Gurmuk, Ahilimmu, and Pilattu, Dur-Telīte, Bubē, Til-Humba, Dunni-Šamaš (S II Ann 298–300, 378–80; Prunk 20)

F: 4 (66%)
S: 1 (17%)
PS: 1 (17%)</td></tr>
<tr><td>Elam
(other)</td></tr>
<tr><td>Yadburu
(Aramean)</td><td>Six sheiks of Yadburu surrendered (S II Ann 298).
RESULT: Partly succeeded.</td></tr>
<tr><td>Lahiru of Yadibiru</td><td>Lahiru, a city of the Yadibiru region (not too far from Yadburu), was attached to Assyria (S II Ann 300);[596] the Lahireans were considered "good guys" and thus not to be reported (XV 40).
RESULT: Succeeded.</td></tr>
<tr><td>Suti
(other)</td><td>The tribe was mentioned in the context of Yadburu invasion; Sargon II had to employ extreme measures (Prism D vi:71); one year later the tribe participated in the defense of Dur-Yadin.
RESULT: Failed.</td></tr>
<tr><td>Raši
(other)</td><td>Šutur-Nahundi evacuated Elamites from 4 fortresses of Raši and retired to the mountains (S II Ann 302–3); the Assyrians established a royal delegate over the region (XV 35).
RESULT: Failed.</td></tr>
</table>

Chaldean phase

<table>
<tr><th>Tribe</th><th>Psychological warfare</th><th>Results</th></tr>
<tr><td>Hamaranu
(Aramean)</td><td>Some of them took refuge in Sippar. Sargon II sent his eunuch to massacre them (S II Ann 318–20). One of them was reported as a deserter (XV 244; XVII 8).
RESULT: Partly succeeded.</td><td rowspan="2">Conquered territory: All Chaldea;
Major strongholds: Dur-Ladinni, Babylon,</td></tr>
<tr><td>Uruk</td><td>Negotiation to open the city gates (XVII 3). RESULT: Succeeded.</td></tr>
</table>

[596] Following the distinction between Yadburu and Yadibiru proposed by M. W. Waters in SAAS XII, 20.

Bit-Amukani (Chaldean) **Bit-Dakkuri** (Chaldean) **Bit-Šilani** (Chaldean) **Bit-Sa'alli** (Chaldean)	Sargon II set up his stronghold in Dur-Ladinna (S II Ann 304–5); Merodach-Baladan, frightened of Sargon II, escaped from Babylon (S II Ann 305–7); all the Chaldean tribes surrendered (S II Ann 314–16; Prunk 21–22). Neo-Assyrian archives record several offers coming from Chaldean leaders (XV 184; 216) and the number of deserters increased (XV 243). After the invasion, Bit-Dakkuri wanted to be directly under the king, not under the rule of Nabû-taklak (XV 230). The inhabitants of Sadiri (Bit-Amukani) made peace with the king (reconstructed) XV 269. The king offered an incentive to the ruler of the city (XVII 5). RESULT: **Succeeded.**	Sippar; S: 5 (83%) PS: 1 (17%)

Bit-Yakin phase

Tribe	**Psychological warfare**	**Results**
Damunu (Aramean)	Participated at the defense of Dur-Yakin (Prunk 126; Stier 29-30; Prism 10). RESULT: **Failed.**	Deportation: 90,580 people from Bit-Yakin (S II Ann 354); 20,000 of them were moved to Kummuhi (Prunk 116-7); Conquered territory: Bit-Yakin; Conquered cities: Dur-Yakin, + 15 strongholds (Prism D vi 50-60) F: 8 (100%)
Maršanu (Aramean) **Sūti** (other)	Two major support troops were defeated during the defense of Dur-Yakin (S II Ann 348–50; Prunk 130). Suti is listed among the subjugated tribes (Prunk 18; S4 70–74; Tang I-Var 31–32). RESULT: **Failed.**	
Bit-Yakin (Chaldean)	Sargon II burned down Dur-Yakin (S II Ann 372) and deported its citizens (S II Ann 352–53). RESULT: **Failed**	
Gambulu (Aramean) **Hindaru** (Aramean) **Puqudu** (Aramean) **Ru'ua** (Aramean)	Those members of the Gambulu, Ru'ua, Hindaru, and Puqudu tribes who remained faithful to Merodach-Baladan participated in the defense of Dur-Yakin (Prunk 126). RESULT: **Failed**	

Appendix 4. Subjugated Aramean tribes mentioned in the royal inscriptions

	Tiglath-pileser III	Sargon II	Sennacherib
‘Adiliye	Yes		
‘Ammatu	Yes		
‘Ubayanat			
Abdudaeans		Yes	
Amlatu	Yes		
Dahha			
Damunu	Yes	Yes	Yes NS; EH
Dunanu	Yes	No	No
Gambulu	No	Yes	Yes NS; EH
Gibriye	Yes		Yes NS
Guluš	Yes		
Gurasimmu	No	No	No (earliest in Esarhadon)
Gurru			
Gurumu	Yes	Yes	Yes NS
Haggarunu	Yes		Yes NS
Hallatu	Yes	Yes	Yes
Hamaranu	Yes	Yes	Yes NS
Hatalla	Yes	Yes	Yes EH (Rapiqu)
Hindaru	Yes	Yes	Yes NS; EH
Hiranu	Yes		
Hudadu	Yes		
Isuqu		Yes	
Itu’u	Yes	Yes	No
Kapiri	Yes		
Karma’	Yes		
Labdudu	Yes	Yes	No (?)
Lita’u	Yes	Yes	Yes NS
Luhu’atu	Yes		No
Malhu			Yes NS; EH
Maršanu		Yes	
Marusu	Yes		
Nabatu/ Nabayatu	Yes	No	Yes NS
Naqri	Yes		
Naṣir	Yes		
Nilqu	Yes		
Puqudu	Yes	Yes	Yes NS; EH
Qabi	Yes		
Rabbi-ʾIl	Yes		

Rade	Yes		
Rahihu		Yes	Yes NS
Rahiqu	Yes		
Rapiqu	Yes		
Ru'ua	Yes	Yes	Yes NS; EH
Rubu'u	Yes	Yes	No
Rummulutu	Yes	No	No
Taniye	Yes		
Tu'manu		No (conquered in 721, not in 710)	Yes NS
Ubudu	Yes		Yes NS
Ubulu	Yes	Yes	Yes NS; EH
Udda			
Ya'ša-'il			
Yadaqqu			Yes NS
Yadburu		Yes	
Yakimanu			

NS (not submissive) from Senn Ann I:43–49; A1 12–14.55–56; B1 14.
EH (enemy host) from Senn Ann V:49–52

Appendix 5. Neo-Assyrian pottery shapes and special features

DESCRIPTION		ASSYRIA	PALESTINE
Bottle	Elongated bottle with wide neck, tapering base, everted rim, narrow shoulders	*Iraq* 21:Pl. XXXVII:60–67	*Qedem 42*, Pl. 37:12
Bottle	"Balloon-shaped" bottle, small and squat shape, narrow neck with sharp ridge, straight rim	*Iraq* 21:Pl. XXXVIII:85	*Qedem 42*, Pl. 59:10
Bottle	"Balloon-shaped" bottle, small and squat shape, narrow neck without ridge, everted rim	*Iraq* 21:Pl. XXXVIII:81–84	*TA* 26:Fig. 10:32
Bottle	"Carrot-shaped" bottle, tall, short narrow neck, triangular everted rim	*BASOR* 311:Fig. 7:13	*Megiddo I*, Pl. 9:7
Jar	Ring Collared jar, folded rim, ridge under the rim, flat base	*Iraq* 16:Pl. XXXIX:1–3	*Hazor II*, Pl. XCVII:11
Goblet	Plain goblet with wide flaring neck	*Iraq* 21:Pl. XXXVII:78	*Ramat Rahel*, Fig. 18:21–3
Goblet	Decorated goblet with wide flaring neck	*Iraq* 21:Pl. XXXVII:60–67	*Gerar*, Pl. LXV:4–8
Istacan	Relatively small vessel with heavy walls and flat base	*Iraq* 21:Pl. XXXVII:43–48	*TA* 26:Fig. 10:35–36
Rhyton	Ram-headed vessel	Mallowan, *Nimrud 1*, Fig. 124	*Tell el-Far'ah 1*, Pl. 64:4
Bowl	*Zungenphialen*, straight slightly thickened rim, flat bottom	*IEJ* 23:Fig. 2	*IEJ* 23:Fig. 1
Bowl	Wide, flared rim	*Iraq* 21:Pl. XXXVII:59	*Gerar*, Pl. LXV:1–3
Bowl	Tripod bowl with heavy walls	*Iraq* 21:Pl. XXXV:15–16	Kinneret, Pl. 108:15, 17–18
Bowl	Sharp carination, hammered rim	P. Bikai's excavation in Nineveh (not yet published)	*EI* 25:Fig. 1:14–15

DESCRIPTION	ASSYRIA	PALESTINE
Nipple base: the base of goblets and bottles forms a button	*Iraq* 21:Pl. XXXIV	*Gerar*, Pl. LXV:4
Pushed-in walls	*Iraq* 21:Pl. XXXIV	*Ramat Rahel*, Fig. 18:21–23
Brown or red horizontal lines painted on the rim, neck, shoulder, mid and/or lower body	*BASOR* 311:Fig. 7:13	*Qedem 42*, Pl. 49:10
Ribbed walls on goblets and bowls	*Iraq* 21:Pl. XXXVII:59	*Gerar*, Pl. LXV:1–3
Sharp carination	*Iraq* 16:Pl. XXXVII:8	*Qedem 42*, Pl. 26:20–22
Well-levigated clay, eggshell	Bikai's exc. in Nineveh	*EI* 25:Fig. 2:3–5

Appendix 6. Neo-Assyrian archaeological remains

SITE	ASSYRIAN-STYLE POTTERY	ARCHITECTURE	OTHER ARTIFACTS
ʻEn Gev	APW: *IEJ* 14:30		
Arad	Bowl: *TA* 29:134, Fig. 10:B 15 Bottle: *TA* 29:154, Fig. 21:JD 7		
Ashdod	Bowl: *Ashdod I*, Fig. 37:1–4; 40:1–3; *Ashdod II–III*, Fig. 5:7; 39:2; 93:1–9,11; Pl. 52:7–8		Stella: Stern, 15
Ayyelet ha-Shaḥar		Throne room arrangement;[597] Square bricks;	
Beer-sheba	Bowl: *TA* 26:Fig. 9:10 Bottle: *TA* 26:Fig.10:28–32 Istacan: *TA* 26:Fig.10:35–36		
Beth-Schemen			Stella: *TA* 27:181
Beth-Shean	Bowl: *BIES* 30: 88–95, Pl. 5, 6.		Seal: *JANES* 12:45–48
Dan	APW: *EI* 23:230–40		
Dor	Bowl: *EI* 25, Fig. 2:1–10 Goblet: *EI* 25, Fig. 2:11–12		Assyrian seals; Emblem of moon god Sin; Bathtub coffin: *Dor IB*, Fig. 1.7:9
Dothan			Bathtub coffin: *BASOR* 156: Fig. 3
En-Gedi	Bowl: *En-Gedi*, Pl. XXV:7		
Gezer	Bowl: *Gezer III*, Pl. 22:7; 27:19–22	Horseshoe-shaped doorway stone with molded profile; Excavation of *Gezer I*, Fig. 73, 74	Two cuneiform tablets (7th c.): *Gezer I*, 22–29; Lance heads and arrowheads: Stern, 6; Four seals: *PEQ*

[597] Lipschitz, "The Date of the 'Assyrian Residence' at Ayyelet Ha-Shahar"; and Reich, "The Persian Building at Ayyelet Ha-Shahar: The Assyrian Palace of Hazor?"

			117: Fig. 6; Two stamp seals: *PEQ* 117: Fig. 7; Armour scale: Excavation of *Gezer III*, Pl. CXCVII:9
Hazor	Bowl: *Hazor II*, Pl. XCVIII:44; Bottle: *Hazor II*, Pl. XCVII:11	Open-court building: *Hazor I*, Pl. CLXXVII	Bathtub coffin: *Hazor II*, Pl. C:28
Khirbet Hoga	APW: not yet published	Large building (?): *Had. Arch.* 59–60:41–42	
Horvat Qitmit	Bowl: *Horvat Qitmit*, Fig. 4.1:37–40; 4.5:2; 4.6:1; 4.12:3; 4.18:3		
Jokneam	APW		
Khirbet Kusyi			Cuneiform tablet (not yet published): *TA* 27:181
Lachish	Bottle: *Lachish III*, Pl. 90:383–84		Lamashtu tablet: Stern, 17; Cylinder seal: *Lachish III*, Pl. 44A:154, 45:154
Megiddo	Goblet: *Megiddo I*, Pl. 9:12 Bottle: *Megiddo I*, Pl. 9:7, 16	Elevated platform: *Megiddo I*, Fig. 89; Open-court building: *Megiddo I*, Fig. 71, 89	Emblem of moon god; Cylinder seal: *Megiddo I*, Pl. 66:2, 11, 72:15; Bathtub coffin: *Megiddo Tombs*, Fig. 87
Qaqun			Fragment of a stela: *TA* 27:181
Ramat Rahel	Goblet: *Ramat Rahel*, Fig. 18:21–23	Assyrian double-cell shrine: *TA* 30:124–29; Open-court building: Aharoni, Fig. 6	Assyrian style painted sherd: *Ramat Rahel*, Pl. 28
Rishon le-Zion			Open-court building: Stern, 27
Samaria	Bowl: *Samaria III*, Fig. 10:8–10, 11:22, 32:3,4 Bottle: *Samaria III*, Fig. 11:26		Bulla: Stern, 15; Tablet mentioning the Assyrian official: Stern, 16;

			Seal: *Samaria III*, Pl. 1:5
Shechem	Bowl: *BASOR* 169: Fig. 22:2		
Shiqmona	APW: Na'aman, "Provinces," 111		
Tel 'Ira	Bottle: *Tel 'Ira*, Fig. 6.86:18; 6.103:5 Bowl: *Tel 'Ira*, Fig. 6:80:3		
Tel Dothan	Bowl: *BASOR* 135: Fig. 2; *NEAEHL 1*, 373		
Tel Hadid			Two tablets: *TA* 27:159–88
Tel Haror	APW: not yet published		
Tel Malhata	Bowl: *Qadmoniot* 3, 24		
Tel Miqne-Ekron	Bowl: Gitin: 65, Fig. 4.5:9–12 Bottle: Gitin: 65, Fig. 4.5:13, 17		
Tel Qiri	Bottle: *Qiri*, Fig.8:9, 44:7, 66		
Tel Rekhesh	Bowl: *IEJ* 23:Fig. 2		
Tel Sera'	APW: not yet published	Elevated platform: *NEAEHL 4*, 1329–36	Bronze crescent-shaped standard: *NEAEHL 4*, 1333; Bronze socketed spear-head: *NEAEHL 4*, 1333
Tell Abu Hawan			Bathtub coffin: *QDAP IV*: Pl. XXXVI:100
Tell el-'Oreimeh	Bowl: unpublished *Qedem* 42, 44 Lion bowl: *Kinneret*, Pl. 49 Tripod bowl: *Kinneret*, Pl. 108:15, 17–8 Bottle (?): *Kinneret*, Pl. 65:15	Open-court building: *Kinneret*, Plan 17; Fritz, 203–4; *TA* 20:203–4	
Tell el-Far`ah (N)	Bowl: *RB* 58, Fig. 12:1–4, 6 Bottle: *Tell el-Far'ah I*, Pl. 61:13, 16 (?)		Bathtub coffin: *Tell el-Farah I*, Pl. 47:10–12
Tell el-Heṣi	Bowl: not yet published		

Tell el-Kheleifah	Bowl: *APHL*, 301, 328, 329; *Tell el-Kheleifeh*, Pl. 36:1–3; Bottle 1: *Tell el-Kheleifeh*, Pl. 27:13–14		
Tell el-Qitaf	APW		
Tell en-Naṣbeh,	Bowl: *TN II*, Pl. 53:1164; 54:1196; Bottle: *TN II*, Pl. 27:444, 446–47		
Tell Jemmeh	Bowl: *Gerar*, Pl. LXV:1–3, 10–23, LI: 26f, 26l, 26w; Goblet: *Gerar*, Pl. LXV:4–9	Open-court building; Vaulted rooms; Square bricks; *IEJ* 20: 245–46; *IEJ* 27: 171–76.	
Tell Keisan	Bottle: *Keisan*, Pl. 37:10a–c, 11, 13 Bowl: *Keisan*, Pl. 37:11a–e		Administrative tablet: *IEJ* 32:32–35 Sin seal-stamp: *RB* 80:384–95 Assyrian style figure: *Keisan*, Pl. 102:10
Tell Qasile	Bowl: *Qasile II*, Fig. 55:28		
Timnah (Tel Batash)	Bottle: *Qedem 42*, Pl. 37:8–13, 14(?); 49:8–10; 59:10; 69:1–3; 75:1 Bowl: *Qedem 42*, Pl. 14:5; 24:4(?); 26:20–22; 57:16; 96:4		Bronze bell: *Qedem 42*, Pl. 39:9

Bibliography

Ackroyd, P. R. "Isaiah 36–39: Structure and Function." In *Von Kanaan bis Kerala: Festschrift für Prof. Mag. Dr. Dr. J. P. M. Van der Ploeg O.P. zur Vollendung des siebzigsten Lebensjahres am 4. Juli 1979*, edited by W. C. Delsman and J. P. M. van der Ploeg, 3–21. Kevelaer, Neukirchen-Vluyn: Verlag Butzon & Bercker, Neukirchener Verlag, 1982.

Aharoni, M. "Excavations at Ramat Rahel." *BA* 24 (1961): 96–118.

———. *Excavations at Ramat Rahel: Seasons 1959 and 1960*. Vol. 1. Rome: Centro di Studi Semitici, 1962.

———. *Excavations at Ramat Rahel: Seasons 1961 and 1962*. Vol. 2. Rome: Centro di Studi Semitici, 1964.

Ahlström, G. W. *The History of Ancient Palestine from the Palaeolithic Period to Alexander's Conquest*. Sheffield, England: Sheffield Academic Press, 1993.

Alt, A. "Neue Assyrische Nachrichten über Palästina und Syrien, 3: Assyrische Königsstrassen in Palästina und Syrien." *ZDPV* 67 (1945): 147–59.

Amiran, R. B. K. *Ancient Pottery of the Holy Land*. Jerusalem: Massada Press, 1969.

Amiran, R. B. K. and I. Dunayevsky. "The Assyrian Open-Court Building and Its Palestine Derivates." *BASOR* 149 (1958): 25–32.

Arutjunjan, N. V. *Korpus Urartskich klinopisnych nadpisej*. Jerevan: Gitutjun, 2000.

Bahat, D. "The Fuller's Field and the 'Conduit of the Upper Pool'." *EI* 20 (1989): 253–55.

Bakan, D. "Some Philosophical Propadeutics toward a Psychology of War." In *The Psychology of War and Peace: The Image of the Enemy*, edited by R. W. Rieber, 41–58. New York: Plenum Press, 1991.

Barnett, F. R. and C. Lord. *Political Warfare and Psychological Operations: Rethinking the US Approach*. Washington, D.C.: National Defense University Press in cooperation with National Strategy Information Center, 1989.

Barnett, R. D. "Urartu." In *The Cambridge Ancient History*, edited by J. Boardman and Edwards I. E. S., 314–71. Cambridge: Cambridge University Press, 1982.

Baroni, P. *La Guerra Psicologica*. Rome: Ciarrapico Editore, 1986.

Beck, J. A. "Geography and the Narrative Shape of Numbers 13." *BS* 157 (2000): 271–80.

Ben-Zvi, E. "Who Wrote the Speech of Rabshakeh and When?" *JBL* 109 (1990): 79–92.

Biran, A. "Tell er-Ruqeish to Tell er-Ridan." *IEJ* 24 (1974): 141–42.

Blakely, J. A. and J. W. Hardin. "Southwestern Judah in the Late Eighth Century B.C.E." *BASOR* 326 (2002): 11–64.

Blenkinsopp, J. *Isaiah 1–39: A New Translation with Introduction and Commentary*. 1st ed. New York: Doubleday, 2000.

Bloom, J. B. "Material Remains of the Neo-Assyrian Presence in Palestine and Transjordan." Ph.D. diss., Bryn Mawr College, 1988.

Boehmer, R. M. "Forschungen in und um Mudjesir (Irakisch-Kurdistan)." *AA* 4 (1973): 479–98.

———. "Zur Lage von Musasir." *BagM* 6 (1973): 39.

Borger, R. *Die Inschriften Asarhaddons, Königs von Assyrien, Archiv für Orientforschung*. Graz: Selbstverlage des Herausgebers, 1956.

Borowski, O. "The Iron Age Cemetery at Tel Halif." *EI* 23 (1992): 13*–20*.

Botta, P. E. and E. Flandin. *Monument de Ninive II*. Paris: Imprimerie nationale, 1849.

Brinkman, J. A. "Bel-Ibni's Letters in the Time of Sargon and Sennacherib." *RA* 77 (1983): 175–76.

———. "Merodach-Baladan II." In *Studies Presented to A. Leo Oppenheim: June 7, 1964*, 6–53. Chicago, 1964.

———. *A Political History of Post-Kassite Babylonia, 1158–722 B.C.* Rome: Pontifical Biblical Institute , 1968.

———. "Sennacherib's Babylonian Problem: An Interpretation." *JCS* 25 (1973): 89–95.

Brueggemann, W. *1 & 2 Kings*. Macon, Ga.: Smyth & Helwys, 2000.

———. *Interpretation and Obedience: From Faithful Reading to Faithful Living*. Minneapolis: Fortress Press, 1991.

Bunimowitz, S. and Z. Lederman. "The Final Destruction of Beth Shemesh and the *Pax Assyriaca* in the Judean Shephelah." *TA* 30 (2003): 3–26.

Byrne, R. "Early Assyrian Contacts with Arabs and the Impact on Levantine Vassal Tribute." *BASOR* 331 (2003): 11–25.

Callot, J. P. *L'Espionnage à travers les âges*. Paris: Stock, 1977.

Camp, L. *Hiskija und Hiskijabild: Analyse und Interpretation von 2 Kön 18–20*. Altenberge: Telos Verlag, 1990.

Caroz, Y. *The Arab Secret Services*. London: Corgi, 1978.

Cavigneaux, A. and B. K. Ismail. "Die Statthalter von Suhu und Mari im 8. Jh. v. Chr." *BagM* 21 (1990): 321–410.

Chamaza, G. W. V. "Der VIII. Feldzug Sargons II. Eine Untersuchung zu Politik und historischer Geographie des späten 8. Jhs. v. Chr. (I)." *Archäologishe Mitteilungen aus Iran* 27 (1994): 91–118.

Chatty, D. *From Camel to Truck: The Bedouin in the Modern World.* 1st ed. New York: Vantage Press, 1986.

Clarridge, D. R. and D. Diehl. *A Spy for All Seasons: My Life in the CIA*. New York: Scribner, 1997.

Codevilla, A. *Informing Statecraft: Intelligence for a New Century*. New York: Free Press, 1992.

Cogan, M. and H. Tadmor. *II Kings: A New Translation*. 1st ed. Garden City, N.Y.: Doubleday, 1988.

Cogan, M. "Judah under Assyrian Hegemony: A Reexamination of *Imperialism and Religion,*" *JBL* 112 (1993), 403–14.

Cohen, C. "Neo-Assyrian Elements in the First Speech of the Biblical Rab-šaqe." *IOS* 9 (1979): 32–47.

Cole, S. W. "The Destruction of Orchards in Assyrian Warfare." In *Assyria 1995: Proceedings of the 10th Anniversary Symposium of the Neo-Assyrian Text Corpus Project, Helsinki, September 7–11, 1995*, 29–40. Helsinki: Helsinki University Press, 1997.

Courtois, L. C. "Technologie de céramique Levantines au temps de la domination Assyriennen (IX–VIIIe siècles av. J.C.)." In *Comptes rendus du 108e Congès National des Sociétés Savantes, Grenoble, 1983,* Section des Sciences, Fasc. 4, 125–36. Paris: Comité des Travaux historiques et scientifiques, 1983.

Cribb, R. *Nomads in Archaeology*. Cambridge, England and New York: Cambridge University Press, 1991.

Cross, F. M. "A Response to Zakovitch." In *Text and Tradition: The Hebrew Bible and Folklore*, edited by S. Niditch, 99–106. Atlanta, Gerg.: Scholar Press, 1990.

Culican, W. "The Graves at Tell er-Ruqeish." *AJBA* 1 (1973): 66–106.

Daugherty, W. E. *A Psychological Warfare Casebook*. Baltimore: Johns Hopkins University Press, 1958.

Deguise, V. *Attaque et défense des forteresses: Tactique de la guerre de siège*. Brussells: Polleunis et Ceuterick, 1898.

Deller, K. "Ausgewählte neuassyriche Briefe betreffend Urartu zur Zeit Sargons II." In *Tra lo Zagros e l'Urmia: Ricerche Storiche ed Archeologiche nell'Azerbaigian Iraniano*, edited by P. E. Pecorella and M. Salvini, 97–122. Rome: Edizioni dell'Ateneo, 1984.

Donner, F. McGraw. *The Early Islamic Conquests*. Princeton, N.J.: Princeton University Press, 1981.

Dorsey, A. D. *The Roads and Highways of Ancient Israel*. Baltimore and London: Johns Hopkins University Press, 1991.

Dothan, M. and D. N. Freedman. "Ashdod I: The First Season of Excavations 1962." *Atiqot* 7 (1967): 1–171.

Dubovský, P. "Tiglath-Pileser III's Campaigns in 734-732 B.C.: Historical Background of Isa 7, 2 Kgs 15-16 and 2 Chr 27-28." *Bib* 87 (2006): 153-70.

Duru, R. *Keban Projesi Degirmentepe Kazisi 1973: Keban Project Degirmentepe Excavations 1973*. Ankara: Türk Tarih Kurumu Basimevi, 1979.

Dvornik, F. *Origins of Intelligence Services: The Ancient Near East, Persia, Greece, Rome, Byzantium, the Arab Muslim Empires, the Mongol Empire, China, Muscovy*. New Brunswick, N.J.: Rutgers University Press, 1974.

Emerton, J. A. "The Historical Background of Isaiah 1:4–9." *EI* 24 (1993): 34*–40*.

Eph'al, I. *The Ancient Arabs: Nomads on the Borders of the Fertile Crescent, 9th–5th Centuries B.C.* Jerusalem: Magnes Press Hebrew University, 1982.

———. "On Warfare and Military Control in the Ancient Near Eastern Empires: A Research Outline." In *History, Historiography, and Interpretation: Studies in Biblical and Cuneiform Literatures*, edited by H. Tadmor and M. Weinfeld, 88–106. Jerusalem: Magnes Press Hebrew University, 1984.

Fales, F. M. "Narrative and Ideological Variations in the Account of Sargon's Eighth Campaign." In *Ah, Assyria...; Studies in Assyrian History and Ancient near Eastern Historiography Presented to Hayim Tadmor*, edited by M Cogan and I. Ephal, 129–47. Jerusalem: The Magnes Press, 1991.

———. "A Literary Code in Assyrian Royal Inscriptions: The Case of Ashurbanipal's Egyptian Campaigns." In *Assyrian Royal Inscriptions: New Horizons in Literary, Ideological, and Historical Analysis*, edited by F. M. Fales (Rome: Instituto per l'Oriente, 1981), 169–202.

Follet, R. ""Deuxième Bureau" et information diplomatique dans l'Assyrie des Sargonides: Quelqe notes." *Rivista degli Studi Orientali* 32 (1957): 61–81.

———. "Une Nouvelle Inscription de Merodach-Baladan II." *Biblica* 35 (1954): 413–28.

Forrer, E. *Die Provinzeinteilung des Assyrischen Reiches*. Leipzig: Hinrich, 1920.

Frahm, E. "Rezensionen. H. Tadmor, the Inscriptions of Tiglath-Pileser III, King of Assyria." *AfO* 44–45 (1997/1998): 399–404.

Frame, G. *Babylonia 689–627 B.C.: A Political History*. Istanbul: Nederlands Historisch-Archaeologisch Instituut te Istanbul, 1992.

———. "The Inscription of Sargon II at Tang-I Var." *Or* 68/1 (1999): 31–60.

Fricke, K. D. *Das zweite Buch von den Königen*. 2. Aufl. Stuttgart: Calwer, 1972.

Fritz, V. *Das zweite Buch der Könige*. Zürich: Theologischer Verlag, 1998.

———. "The Decline of Chinnereth after the Campaign of Tiglath-Pileser III against Damascus in 733." *Jahrbuch des Deutschen Evangelischen Instituts für Altertumswissenschaft des Heiligen Landes* 5 (1997): 59–66.

———. "Die Paläste während der Assyrischen, Babylonischen und Persischen Vorherrschaft in Palästina." *MDOG* 111 (1979): 63–74.

———. *Kinneret: Ergebnisse der Ausgrabungen auf dem Tell el-'Oreme am See Gennesaret 1982–1985*. Wiesbaden: Otto Harrassowitz, 1990.

———. "Kinneret: Excavations at Tell el-'Oreimeh (Tel Kinrot) 1982–1985 Seasons." *TA* 20 (1993): 187–224.

———. "The Lion Bowl from Kinneret." *BA* 50 (1987): 232–40.

———. "Where Is David's Ziklag?" *BAR* 19 (1993): 58–61, 76.

Frolík, J. *Špión vypovídá*. 1. vyd. Köln: Index, 1979.

Fuchs, A. *Die Inschriften Sargons II. aus Khorsabad*. 1. Aufl. Göttingen: Cuvillier, 1994.

Gallagher, W. R. "Assyrian Deportation Propaganda." *SAAB* 8 (1994): 57–65.

———. *Sennacherib's Campaign to Judah: New Studies*. Leiden and Boston: Brill, 1999.

Garavelli, M. B. *Manuale di Retorica*. Milano: Bompiani, 1989.

Garelli, P. "Le Dynamisme Assyrien." In *Assyria 1995: Proceedings of the 10th Anniversary Symposium of the Neo-Assyrian Text Corpus Project Helsinki, September 7–11, 1995*, edited by S. Parpola and R. M. Whiting, 65–68. Helsinki: The Neo-Assyrian Text Corpus Project, 1997.

Gatti, M. A. "La Ceramica Neo-Assira (X–VII Sec.): Tipologie e Difusione." Ph.D. diss., Università degli Studi di Padova, 1987.

Gazit, D. "Petrie in Tell Jemmeh: Excavation Methods and Scientific Discipline." *Archaeologya* 3 (1992): 34–40.

Gelb, I. J. "Rezension: D. J. Wiseman, the Vassal-Treaties of Esarhadon." *BiOr* 19 (1962): 159–62.

Géré, F. *La Guerre Psychologique*, Bibliothèque Stratégique. Paris: Economica, 1997.

Gilboa, A. "Assyrian-Type Pottery at Dor and the Status of the Town During the Assyrian Occupation Period." *EI* 25 (1996): 122–35.

Gitin, S. "Neo-Assyrian and Egyptian Hegemony over Ekron in the Seventh Century BCE: A Response to Lawrence E. Stager." *EI* 27 (2003): 55*–61*.

———. "Tel Miqne-Ekron in the 7th Century B.C.E.: The Impact of Economic Innovation and Foreign Cultural Influences on a Neo-Assyrian Vassal City-State." In *Recent Excavations in Israel: A View to the West*, edited by S. Gitin, 61–79. Dubuque, Iowa: Kendall/Hunt, 1995.

Glad, B. *Psychological Dimensions of War*. Newbury Park, Calif.: Sage Publications, 1990.

Godson, R. "Covert Action in 1990s: Neither Exceptional Tool nor Magic Bullet." In *Covert Action in the 1990s*, edited by R. Godson, R. J. Kerr and E. R. May, 1–58. Washington, D.C: Consortium for the Study of Intelligence, 1993.

Gonçalves, F. J. *L'expédition de Sennachérib en Palestine dans la littérature Hébraïque ancienne*. Paris: Libraire Lecoffre, 1986.

Gottwald, N. K. *The Hebrew Bible: A Socio-Literary Introduction*. Philadelphia: Fortress Press, 1985.

Grabbe, L. L. *"Like a Bird in a Cage": The Invasion of Sennacherib in 701 BCE*. London and New York: Sheffield Academic Press, 2003.

Grayson, A. K. "Akkadian Treaties of the Seventh Century B.C." *JCS* 39 (1987): 127–60.

———. *Assyrian and Babylonian Chronicles*. Texts from Cuneiform Sources, no. 5. Locust Valley, N.Y.: J. J. Augustin, 1975.

Günay, D. A. *Keban Baraj Gölü Yöresi Halkbilim Arastirmalari*. 1. baski. Ankara: Türk Tarih Kurumu Basimevi, 1980.

Handel, M. I. "Intelligence and the Problem of Strategic Surprise." In *Paradoxes of Strategic Intelligence: Essays in Honor of Michael I. Handel*, edited by R. K. Betts and T. G. Mahnken, 1–58. London: Frank Cass, 2003.

Hardmeier, C. *Prophetie im Streit vor dem Untergang Judas: Erzählkommunikative Studien zur Enstehungssituation der Jesaja- und Jeremiaerzählungen in II Reg 18–20 und Jer 37–40*. Berlin and New York: de Gruyter, 1990.

Heinrich, E. "Neuassyrische Paläste, Paläste in Spätbabylonischen Reich." In *Die Paläste in Alten Mesopotamien*, edited by E. Heinrich, 98–231. Berlin: Denkmaler Antiken Architektur, 1984.

Hentschel, G. *2 Könige*. Würzburg: Echter, 1985.

Hestrin, R. and E. Stern. "Two 'Assyrian' Bowls from Israel." *IEJ* 23 (1973): 152–55.

Hillers, D. R. *Treaty-Curses and the Old Testament Prophets*. Rome: Pontifical Biblical Institute, 1964.

Hobbs, T. R. *2 Kings*. Waco, Texas: Word Books, 1985.

Hodgson, M. A. Y. *The Siege of Kumassi*. New York: Longmans, 1901.

Holloway, S. W. "Harran: Cultic Geography in the Neo-Assyrian Empire and Its Implications for Sennacherib's 'Letter to Hezekiah' in 2 Kings." In *The Pitcher Is Broken: Memorial Essays for Gösta W. Ahlström*, edited by S. W. Holloway and L. K. Handy, 276–314. Sheffield, England: Sheffield Academic Press, 1995.

Hopkins, D. C. "Pastoralists in Late Bronze Age Palestine: Which Way Did They Go?" *BA* 56 (1993): 200–11.

House, J. M. *Military Intelligence, 1870–1991: A Research Guide*. Westport, Conn.: Greenwood Press, 1993.

House, P. R. *1, 2 Kings*. Nashville, Tenn.: Broadman & Holman, 1995.

Ivantchik, A. I. "Kimmerijci i Urartu na kanune vosmogo pochoda Sargona II." *Vestnik Drevnej Istorii* 194 (1990): 2–19.

———. *Les Cimmériens au Proche-Orient*, Orbis Biblicus et Orientalis, no. 127. Fribourg, Suisse Göttingen: Editions Universitaires, Vandenhoeck & Ruprecht, 1993.

Jabbur, J. S. *The Bedouins and the Desert: Aspects of Nomadic Life in the Arab East*. Albany: State University of New York Press, 1995.

Jenni, E. *Das hebräische Pi'el: Syntaktisch-semasiologische Untersuchung einer Verbalform im Alten Testament*. Zürich: EVZ-Verlag, 1968.

Jones, G. H. *1 and 2 Kings: Based on the Revised Standard Version*. Grand Rapids, Mich.; London: W.B. Eerdmans; Marshall Morgan & Scott, 1984.

Kaplan, K. *Nebezpečná bezpečnost: Státní bezpečnost 1948–1956*. 1. vyd. Edice Knihy, Dokumenty. Brno: Doplnek, 1999.

Kelle, B. E. "What's in a Name? Neo-Assyrian Designations for the Northern Kingdom and Their Implications for Israelite History and Biblical Interpretation." *JBL* 121 (2002): 639–66.

Kent, S. *Strategic Intelligence for American World Policy*. Princeton: Princeton University Press, 1949.

Kessler, K. *Untersuchungen zur historischen Topographie Nordmesopotamiens: Nach Keilschriftlichen Quellen d. 1. Jahrtausends v. Chr.;* Beihefte zum Tübinger Atlas des vorderen Orients. Reihe B, Geisteswissenschaften, No. 26. Wiesbaden: Reichert, 1980.

Khazanov, A. M. *Nomads and the Outside World*. Cambridge: Cambridge University Press, 1984.

Kim, Y. J. "The Role of Communication in the near Eastern Empires of the First Millenium BC." Ph.D.diss., Hebrew University, 1999.

Kleiss, W. and H. Hauptmann. *Topographische Karte von Urartu: Verzeichnis der Fundorte und Bibliographie*, Archaeologische Mitteilungen aus Iran, no. 3. Berlin: Reimer, 1976.

Köhler-Rollefson, I. "Camels and Camel Pastoralism in Arabia." *BA* 56 (1993): 180–88.

Krysko, V. *Sekrety psikhologicheskoj vojny: Celi, zadachi, metody, formy, opyt, kommandos*. Minsk: Kharvest, 1999.

Kuhrt, A. *The Ancient near East, c. 3000–330 BC*. Vol. 2, Routledge History of the Ancient World. London; New York: Routledge, 1995.

Lanfranchi, G. B. "Some New Texts About a Revolt against the Urartian King Rusa I." *OrA* 22 (1983): 123–36.

Laqueur, W. *A World of Secrets: The Uses and Limits of Intelligence*. New York: Basic Books, 1985.

Lehmann, G. "Trends in the Local Pottery Development of the Late Iron Age and Persian Period in Syria and Lebanon, Ca. 700 to 300 B.C." *BASOR* 311 (1998): 7–37.

Levine, B. A. *Numbers 1–20: A New Translation with Introduction and Commentary*. 1st ed. Anchor Bible, Vol. 4A. New York: Doubleday, 1993.

Levine, L. D. "Sennacherib's Southern Front." *JCS* 34 (1982): 28–58.

Linebarger, P. M. A. *Psychological Warfare*. 1st ed. Washington, D.C.: Infantry Journal Press, 1948.

Lines, J. "Late Assyrian Pottery from Nimrud." *Iraq* 16 (1954): 164–67.

Lipinski, E. *The Aramaeans: Their Ancient History, Culture, Religion*, Orientalia Lovaniensia Analecta, no. 100. Leuven and Sterling, Va.: Peeters, 2000.

Lipschitz, O. "The Date of the "Assyrian Residence" at Ayyelet Ha-Shahar." *TA* 17 (1990): 96–99.

Liverani, M. "The Growth of the Assyrian Empire in the Habur/Middle Euphrates Area: A New Paradigm." *SAAB* 2 (1988): 81–98.

———. *Guerra e Diplomazia nell'antico Oriente 1600–1100 A.C.* Rome: Laterza, 1994.

———. "The Ideology of the Assyrian Empire." In *Power and Propaganda: A Symposium on Ancient Empires*, edited by M. T Larsen, 297–318. Copenhagen: Akademisk Forlag, 1979.

Lloyd, M. *The Art of Military Deception*. London: L. Cooper, 1997.

———. *The Guinness Book of Espionage*. New York: Da Capo Press, 1994.

Long, B. O. *2 Kings*. Grand Rapids, Mich.: Eerdmans, 1991.

Loon, van. "The Inscription of Ispuini and Meinea at Qalatgah, Iran." *JNES* 34 (1975).

Loud, G. "An Architectural Formula for Assyrian Planning Based on Results of Excavations at Khorsabad." *RA* 33 (1936): 153–60.

Lowenthal, M. M. *Intelligence: From Secrets to Policy*. 2nd ed. Washington, D.C.: CQ Press, 2003.

Machinist, P. "The *Rab šāqēh* at the Wall of Jerusalem: Israelite Identity in the Face of the Assyrian 'Other.' " *Hebrew Studies* 41 (2000): 151–68.

Maisler, B. "Archaeology in the State of Israel." *BA* 15 (1952): 18–24.

Malamat, A. *History of Biblical Israel: Major Problems and Minor Issues,* Culture and History of thę Ancient near East, vol. 7 Leiden and Boston: Brill, 2001.

Malbran-Labat, F. *L'armée et l'organisation militaire de l'Assyrie: D'après les lettres des Sargonides trouvées à Ninive*. Paris: Libraire Droz, 1982.

Mallon, A. "Tell Djemmeh." *Biblica* 8 (1927): 381–83.

Master, D. "Trade and Politics: Ashkelon's Balancing Act in the Seventh Century B.C.E." *BASOR* 330 (2003): 47–64.

Mattingly, G. L. "Neo-Assyrian Influence at Tell Jemmeh." *NEASB* 15 (1980): 33–49.

May, E. R. *Strange Victory: Hitler's Conquest of France*. 1st ed. New York: Hill and Wang, 2000.

Mayer, W. *Politik und Kriegskunst der Assyrer*. Münster: Ugarit-Verlag, 1995.

Mayerson, P. "The First Muslim Attacks on Southern Palestine (A.D. 633–634)." In *Transactions and Proceedings of the American*

Philological Association, edited by D. W. Prakken, 155–99. Ithaca, NY: Cornell University Press, 1964.

Mazar, B. "Yurza: The Identification of Tell Jemmeh." *PEQ* 84 (1952): 48–51.

McNicoll, A. and R. Fletcher. *Taskun Kale: Keban Rescue Excavations, Eastern Anatolia*. Oxford, England: B.A.R., 1983.

Meier, S. A. *The Messenger in the Ancient Semitic World*. Atlanta, Ga.: Scholars Press, 1988.

Mikovic, M. *Samoubistva u okruzenom Sarajevu: Prilozi Socijalnoj Patologiji, Univerzitetska Knjiga*. Sarajevo: Studentska stamparija univerziteta, 1998.

Mitchell, S. *Asvan Kale: Keban Rescue Excavations, Eastern Anatolia*. Oxford, England: B.A.R., 1980.

Mowinckel, S. *Erwägungen zur Pentateuch Quellenfrage*. Oslo: Universitetsforlaget, 1964.

Na'aman, N. "An Assyrian Residence at Ramat Rahel?" *TA* 28 (2001): 260–80.

———. "The Brook of Egypt and Assyrian Policy on the Border of Egypt." *TA* 6 (1979): 68–90.

———. "New Light on Hezekiah's Second Prophetic Story (2 Kgs 19,9b–35)." *Biblica* 81 (2000): 393–402.

———. "Province System and Settlement Pattern in Southern Syria and Palestine in the Neo-Assyrian Period." In *Neo-Assyrian Geography*, edited by M. Liverani, 103–15. Rome: Studium Urbis, 1995.

———. "Updating the Messages: Hezekiah's Second Prophetic Story (2 Kings 19.9b–35) and the Community of Babylonian Deportees." In *"Like a Bird in a Cage": The Invasion of Sennacherib in 701 BCE*, edited by L. L. Grabbe, 201–20. London ; New York, NY: Sheffield Academic Press, 2003.

Na'aman, N. and R. Zadok. "Assyrian Deportations to the Province of Samerina in the Light of Two Cuneiform Tablets from Tel Hadid." *TA* 27 (2000): 159–88.

Naveh, J. "Aramaic Ostraca and Jar Inscriptions from Tell Jemmeh." *Atiqot* 21 (1992): 49–53.

———. "Writing and Script in Seventh-Century B.C.E. Philistia: The New Evidence from Tell Jemmeh." *IEJ* 35 (1985): 8–21.

Nelson, C. *The Desert and the Sown: Nomads in the Wider Society*. Berkeley,: Institute of International Studies University of California, 1973.

Nelson, R. D. *Deuteronomy: A Commentary*. 1st ed. Louisville, Ky.: Westminster John Knox Press, 2002.

Newman, L. M. "Rahab and the Conquest." In *Understanding the Word: Essays in Honor of Bernhard W. Anderson*, edited by J. T. Butler, E. W. Conrad and B. C. Ollenburger, 167–81. Sheffield, England: JSOT Press, 1985.

Noth, M. *A History of Pentateuchal Traditions*. Chico, Calif.: Scholars Press, 1981.

Oates, J. "Late Assyrian Pottery from Fort Shalmaneser." *Iraq* 21 (1959): 130–51.

Oded, B. "Observations on Methods of Assyrian Rule in Transjordania after the Palestinian Campaign of Tiglath-Pileser III." *JNES* 29 (1970): 182.

Odom, W. E. "Psychological Operations and Political Warfare in Long-Term Strategic Planning." In *Psychological Operations and Political Warfare in Long-Term Strategic Planning*, edited by J. Radványi, 8–18. New York: Praeger, 1990.

Olmstead, A. T. *History of Assyria*, Midway Reprint. Chicago: University of Chicago Press, 1975.

Oppenheim, A. L. ""The Eyes of the Lord"." *JAOS* 88 (1968): 173–80.

Oren, E. D. "Ashlar Masonry in the Western Negev in the Iron Age." *EI* 23 (1992): 94–105.

———. "Chronique Archéologique: Tel Sera' (Tell esh-Shari'a)." *RB* 80 (1973): 401–5.

———. "A Cultic Building in the Excavation of Tel Sera`." *Qadmoniot* 6 (1973): 53–56.

———. "A Phoenician Emporium on the Border of Egypt." *Qadmoniot* 19 (1986): 1–4.

———. "Tel Haror." *Excavations and Surveys in Israel* 13 (1995): 113–16.

———. "Tel Haror - 1988." *Excavations and Surveys in Israel* 9 (1989/90): 69–73.

———. "Tel Sera' (Tell esh-Shari'a)." *IEJ* 22 (1972): 167–69.

———. "Tel Sera' (Tell esh-Shari'a)." *IEJ* 23 (1973): 251–54.

———. "Tel Sera' (Tell esh-Shari'a)." *IEJ* 24 (1974): 264–66.

———. *Tell esh-Shari'a (Tell Sera'): A Biblical City on the Edge of the Negev*. Beersheva: Archaeological division Ben-Gurion University of the Negev, 1972.

———. "Ziklag: A Biblical City on the Edge of the Negev." *BA* 45 (1982): 155–66.

Oren, E. D. and M. A. Morrison. "Land of Gerar Expedition: Preliminary Report for the Seasons of 1982 and 1983." In *Preliminary Reports of ASOR-Sponzored Excavations 1980–84*, edited by W. E. Rast, 57–87. Winona Lake: Eisenbrauns, 1986.

Özgüç, T. *Altintepe II, Türk Tarih Kurumu Yayinlarindan.* Ankara: Türk Tarihi Kurumu Basimevi, 1969.

Pacner, K. *Československo ve zvláštních službách: Pohledy do historie Československých výzvedných služeb 1914 – 1989.* 3 Vols. Praha: Themis, 2002.

Paddock, A. H. "U.S. Military Psychological Operations: Past, Present, and Future." In *Psychological Operations and Political Warfare in Long-Term Strategic Planning*, edited by J. Radványi, 19–35. New York: Praeger, 1990.

Parker, B. J. "Archaeological Manifestation of Empire: Assyria's Imprint on Southeastern Anatolia." *AJA* 107 (2003): 525–57.

———. "Garrisoning the Empire: Aspects of the Construction and Maintenance of Forts on the Assyrian Frontier." *Iraq* 59 (1997): 77–87.

———. *The Mechanics of Empire: The Northern Frontier of Assyria as a Case Study in Imperial Dynamics.* Helsinki: Helsinki University Press, 2001.

Parpola, S. "Assyria's Expansion in the 8th and 7th Centuries and Its Long-Term Repercussion in the West." In *Symbiosis, Symbolism, and the Power of the Past*, edited by W. G. Dever and S. Gitin, 99–111. Winona Lake, Ind.: Eisenbrauns, 2003.

———. "A Letter from Šamaš-šumu-ukin to Esarhaddon." *Iraq* 34 (1972): 21–34.

———. "Neo-Assyrian Treaties from the Royal Archives of Nineveh." *JCS* 39 (1987): 161–87.

Parpola, S. and M. Porter. *The Helsinki Atlas of the near East in the Neo-Assyrian Period.* Helsinki: Casco Bay Assyriological Institute and Neo-Assyrian Text Corpus Project, 2001.

Person, R. F. *The Kings-Isaiah and Kings-Jeremiah Recensions*. Berlin and New York: Walter de Gruyter, 1997.

Petrie, F. *Gerar*. London: British School of Archaeology in Egypt, 1928.

Phythian-Adams, W. J. "Reports on Soundings at Tell Jemmeh." *PEF* 55 (1923): 140–46.

Piekalkiewicz, J. *World History of Espionage: Agents, Systems, Operations*. Washington, D.C.: National Intelligence Book Center, 1998.

Piepkorn, A. C. *Historical Prism Inscriptions of Ashurbanipal.* Chicago: University of Chicago Press, 1933.

Porath, J. "Khirbet Hoga." *Had. Arch.* 59–60 (1976): 41–42.

Portugali, J. "The Theoretical Speculations on the Transition from Nomadism to Monarchy." In *From Nomadism to Monarchy: Archaeological and Historical Aspects of Early Israel*, edited by I. Finkelstein and N. Na'aman, 203–17. Jerusalem: Yad Izhak Ben-Zvi Israel Exploration Society; Washington: Biblical Archaeology Society, 1994.

Postgate, J. N. *Taxation and Conscription in the Assyrian Empire.* Rome: Biblical Institute Press, 1974.

Potts, D. T. *The Archaeology of Elam: Formation and Transformation of an Ancient Iranian State*, Cambridge World Archaeology. New York: Cambridge University Press, 1999.

Powell, M. A. "Merodach-Baladan at Dur-Jakin: A Note on the Defense of Babylonina Cities." *JCS* 34 (1982): 59–61.

Rawson, P. S. "Palace Wares from Nimrud: Technical Observations on Selected Examples." *Iraq* 16 (1954): 164–67.

Reich, R. "Dur Sharrukin (Khorsabad)." *Qadmoniot* 12 (1979): 2–11.

———. "A Note on the Relative Chronology of Buildings A and B at Tell Jemmeh." *EI* 25 (1996): 264–67.

———. "On the Assyrian Presence at Ramat Rahel." *TA* 30 (2003): 124–29.

———. "Palaces and Residences in the Iron Age." In *The Architecture of Ancient Israel: From the Prehistoric to the Persian Period*, edited by A. Kempinski and R. Reich, 202–23. Jerusalem, 1992.

———. "The Persian Building at Ayyelet ha-Shahar: The Assyrian Palace of Hazor?" *IEJ* 25 (1975): 233–37.

Reich, R. and B. Brandl. "Gezer under Assyrian Rule." *PEQ* 117 (1985): 41–54.

Rieber, R. W. *The Psychology of War and Peace: The Image of the Enemy*. New York: Plenum Press, 1991.

Rieber, R. W. and R. J. Kelly. "Substance and Shadow: Images of the Enemy." In *The Psychology of War and Peace: The Image of the Enemy*, edited by R. W. Rieber, 3–39. New York: Plenum Press, 1991.

Rogerson, S. *Propaganda in the Next War,* The Next War Series. London: Geffrey Bles, 1939.

Rose, M. *Deuteronomist und Jahwist: Untersuchungen zu den Berührungspunkten beider Literaturwerke*. Zürich: Theologischer Verlag, 1981.

Rosen, S. A. "Nomads in Archaeology: A Response to Finkelstein and Perevolotsky." *BASOR* 287 (1992): 75–85.

Rosen, S. A. and G. Avni. "The Edge of the Empire: The Archaeology of Pastoral Nomads in the Southern Negev Highlands in Late Antiquity." *BA* 56 (1993): 189–99.

Roux, G. *Ancient Iraq*. 2nd ed., Pelican Books. Harmondsworth, Middlesex; New York: Penguin, 1980.

Rowton, M. B. "The Woodlands of Ancient Western Asia." *JNES* 26 (1967): 261–77.

Saggs, H. W. F. "Assyrian Warfare in the Sargonid Period." *Iraq* 25 (1963): 145–54.

———. *Cuneiform Texts from Nimrud*. Vol. 5. London: British School of Archaeology in Iraq, 2001.

———. "The Nimrud Letters, 1952–Part III." *Iraq* 18/1 (1956): 40–56.

———. "The Nimrud Letters, 1952–Part I." *Iraq* 17/1 (1955): 21–50.

———. "The Nimrud Letters, 1952–Part II." *Iraq* 17/2 (1952): 126–54.

Salvini, M. *Geschichte und Kultur der Urartäer*. Darmstadt: Wissenschaftliche Buchgesellschaft, 1995.

———. "La Bilingue Urarteo-Assira di Rusa I." In *Tra lo Zagros e l'Urmia: Ricerche Storiche ed Archeologiche nell'Azerbaigian Iraniano*, edited by P. E. Pecorella and M. Salvini, 79–96. Rome: Edizioni dell'Ateneo, 1984.

———. "La Storia della Regione in Epoca Urartea." In *Tra lo Zagros e l'Urmia: Ricerche Storiche ed Archeologiche nell'Azerbaigian Iraniano*, edited by P. E. Pecorella and M. Salvini, 9–52. Rome: Edizioni dell'Ateneo, 1984.

Schramm, W. *Einleitung in die Assyrischen Königsinschriften*. vol. 2 (Leiden and Köln: E.J.Brill, 1973)

Scurlock, J. "Neo-Assyrian Battle Tactics." In *Crossing Boundaries and Linking Horizons: Studies in Honor of Michael C. Astour on His 80th Birthday*, edited by G. D. Young and R. E. Averbeck, 491–517. Bethesda, Md.: CDL Press, 1997.

Seger, J. D. "Investigations at Tell Halif." *BASOR* 252 (1983): 1–23.

Sevin, V. "The Oldest Highway: Between the Regions of Van Elazig in Eastern Anatolia." *Antiquity* 62 (1988): 547–51.

Shafer, A. T. "The Carving of an Empire: Neo-Assyrian Monuments on the Periphery." Ph.D. diss., Harvard University, 1998.

Sharon, I. "Phoenician and Greek Ashar Construction Techniques at Tel Dor, Israel." *BASOR* 267 (1987): 21–42.

Shibl, Y. A. *The Aswan High Dam*. Beirut: Arab Institute for Research and Publishing, 1971.

Shulsky, A. N. and G. J. Schmitt. *Silent Warfare: Understanding the World of Intelligence*. 3rd ed. Washington: Brassey's, 2002.

Singer-Avitz, L. "Beersheba-a Gateway Community in Southern Arabian Long-Distance Trade in the Eighth Century B.C.E." *TA* 26 (1999): 3–74.

Ska, J. L. *"Our Fathers Have Told Us": Introduction to the Analysis of Hebrew Narratives*. Rome: Pontifical Biblical Institute, 1990.

Smelik, K. A. D. *Converting the Past: Studies in Ancient Israelite and Moabite Historiography*. Leiden and New York: Brill, 1992.

———. "Distortion of Old Testament Prophecy: The Purpose of Isaiah XXXVI and XXXVII." In *Crises and Perspectives; Studies in Ancient Near Eastern Polytheism, Biblical Theology, Palestinian Archaeology and Intertestamental Literature: Papers Read at the Joint British-Dutch Old Testament Conference Held at Cambridge, U.K., 1985*, 70–93. Leiden: Brill, 1986.

Stern, E. "The Assyrian Impact on the Material Culture of Palestine." *EI* 27 (2003): 218–29.

———. *Dor, Ruler of the Seas: Twelve Years of Excavations at the Israelite-Phoenician Harbor Town on the Carmel Coast*. Jerusalem: Israel Exploration Society, 1994.

———. "Hazor, Dor and Megiddo in the Time of Ahab and under Assyrian Rule." *IEJ* 40 (1990): 12–30.

———. "New Evidence from Dor for the First Appearance of the Phoenicians Along the Northern Coast of Israel." *BASOR* 279 (1990): 27–33.

Stern, E. and A. Mazar. *Archaeology of the Land of the Bible: The Assyrian, Babylonian, and Persian Periods, 732–332 BCE*. 1st ed., Anchor Bible Reference Library. New York: Doubleday, 2001.

Streck, M. *Assurbanipal und die letzten Assyrischen Könige bis zum Untergange Niniveh's*. Leipzig: J. C. Hinrichs, 1916.

Tadmor, H. *The Inscriptions of Tiglath-Pileser III, King of Assyria: Critical Edition, with Introductions, Translations and Commentary*. Jerusalem: The Israel Academy of Sciences and Humanities, 1994.

———. "On the role of Aramaic in the Assyrian Empire." In *Near Eastern Studies dedicated H. I. H. Prince Takahito Mikasa on the Occasion of his Seventy-fifth Birthday*, edited by. M. Mori, H. Ogawa, and M. Yoshikawa (Wiesbaden: Otto Harrassowitz, 1991), 419–26.

———. "Philistia under Assyrian Rule." *BA* 29 (1966): 86–102.

Tappy, R. E. *The Archaeology of Israelite Samaria*. Vol. 2. Atlanta, Ga.: Scholars Press, 1992.

Thureau-Dangin, F. *Une relation de la Huitième Campagne de Sargon (714 Av. J.- C.)*. Paris: Paul Geuthner, 1912.

Tsvetkov, A. J. "Turtsija; J-37-X, XI, XVI, XVII, XXI, XXIII." Moscow: Generalnij Shtab, 1942.

Tucker, G. M. "The Rahab Saga." In *The Use of the Old Testament in the New and Other Essays: Studies in Honor of William Franklin Stinespring*, edited by J. M. Efird, 66–86. Durham, N.C.,: Duke University Press, 1972.

Turner, G. "The State Apartment of the Late Assyrian Palaces." *Iraq* 32 (1970): 177–213.

van Beek, W. G. "Ancient Methods for Minimizing Earthquake at Tell Jemmeh." *EI* 25 (1996): 1*–8*.

———. "Arches and Vaults in the Ancient near East." *Scientific American* 257 (1987): 78–85.

———. "Are There Beehive Granaries at Tell Jemmeh? A Rejoinder." *BA* 49 (1986): 245–47.

———. "Assyrian Vaulted Building at Tell Jemmeh." *Qadmoniot* 6 (1973): 23–27.

———. "The Rammed Earth Revetment at Tell Jemmeh." *EI* 23 (1992): 4*–9*.

———. "The Reexcavation of Sites: Tell Jemmeh." In *Biblical Archaeology Today: Proceedings of the Second International Congress on Biblical Archaeology*, edited by A. Biran, 575–80. Jerusalem: Israel Exploration Society, 1990.

———. "Tel Gamma." *IEJ* 20 (1970): 245–46.

———. "Tel Gamma." *IEJ* 22 (1972): 245–46.

———. "Tel Gamma." *IEJ* 24 (1974): 138–39.

———. "Tel Gamma." *IEJ* 24 (1974): 274–75.

———. "Tel Gamma, 1975–1976." *IEJ* 27 (1977): 171–76.

———. "Tel Jemmeh – 1984." *Excavations and Surveys in Israel* 5 (1984): 54–55.

van Zeist, W., R. W. Timmers, and S. Bottema. "Studies of Modern and Holocene Pollen Precipitation in Southern Turkey." *Palaeohistoria* 14 (1968): 19–37.

Varga, D. "Horbat Hoga." *Had. Arch.* 110 (1999): 69*–70*.

Vaughn, A. G. *Theology, History, and Archaeology in the Chronicler's Account of Hezekiah*. Atlanta, Ga.: Scholars Press, 1999.

Vera Chamaza, G. W. "Der VIII. Feldzug Sargons II. Eine Untersuchung zur Politik und historischer Geographie des späten 8. Jhs. v. Chr. (I)." *Archäologische Mitteilungen aus Iran* 27 (1994): 91–118.

———. "Der VIII. Feldzug Sargons II. Eine Untersuchung zur Politik und historischer Geographie des späten 8. Jhs. v. Chr. (II)." *Archäologische Mitteilungen aus Iran* 28 (1996): 235–67.

———. *Die Omnipotenz Assurs: Entwicklungen in der Assur-Theologie unter den Sargoniden Sargon II., Sanherib und Asarhaddon*. Münster: Ugarit-Verlag, 2002.

Vogt, E. *Der Aufstand Hiskias und die Belagerung Jerusalems 701 v. Chr.* Rome: Pontifical Biblical Institute, 1986.

von Siegfried, W. "Die Kundschaftergeschichten im Alten Testament." *ZATW* 76 (1964): 255–69.

Wäfler, M. "Die Auseinandersetzungen zwischen Urartu und Assyrien." In *Das Reich Urartu: Ein altorientalischer Staat im 1. Jahrtausend v. Chr*, edited by V. Haas, 138. Konstanz: Universitätsverlag Konstanz, 1986.

Waltke, B. K. and M. P. O'Connor. *An Introduction to Biblical Hebrew Syntax*. Winona Lake, Ind.: Eisenbrauns, 1990.

Wartke, R. B. *Urartu, das Reich am Ararat*, Kulturgeschichte der Antiken Welt, no. 59. Mainz am Rhein: P. von Zabern, 1993.

Watanabe, K. *Die Adê-Vereidigung anlässlich der Thronfolgeregelung Asarhaddons*. Berlin: Gebr. Mann Verlag, 1987.

Weidner, V. E. "Hof- und Harems-Erlasse Assyrischer Könige aus dem 2. Jahrtausend v. Chr." *AfO* 17 (1954): 257–79.

Weinfeld, M. *Deuteronomy 1–11: A New Translation with Introduction and Commentary*. 1st ed. New York: Doubleday, 1991.

Willcox, G. H. "A History of Deforestation as Indicated by Charcoal Analysis of Four Sites in Eastern Anatolia." *AS* 24 (1974): 117–33.

Wiseman, D. J. *1 and 2 Kings: An Introduction and Commentary*. Leicester, England and Downers Grove, Il.: InterVarsity Press, 1993.

Yadin, Y. *The Art of Warfare in Biblical Lands in the Light of Archaeological Study*. 2 vols. New York: McGraw-Hill, 1963.

Younger, K. L. "Assyrian Involvement in the Southern Levant at the End of the Eighth Century B.C.E." In *Jerusalem in Bible and Archaeology: The First Temple Period*, edited by A. G. Vaughn and A. E. Killebrew, 235–63. Atlanta: Society of Biblical Literature, 2003.

Zaccagnini, C. *I Trattati nel Mondo Antico: Forma, Ideologia, Funzione*. Edited by L. Canfora and M. Liverani, Saggi di Storia Antica, no. 2. Rome: "L'Erma" di Bretschneider, 1990.

Zakovitch, Y. "Humor and Theology or the Successful Failure of Isrelite Intelligence: A Literary-Folkloric Approach to Joshua 2." In *Text and Tradition: The Hebrew Bible and Folklore*, edited by S. Niditch, 75–98. Atlanta: Scholar Press, 1990.

Zimansky, P. E. *Ecology and Empire-the Structure of the Urartian State*, Studies in Ancient Oriental Civilization, 41. Chicago: Oriental Institute of the University of Chicago, 1985.

Zimhoni, O. "Two Ceramic Assembledges from Lachish Level III and II." *TA* 17 (1990): 3–52.

Index of authors

Stampa: Dicembre 2006

presso la tipografia
"Giovanni Olivieri" di E. Montefoschi
Roma • info@tipografiaolivieri.it